Derrida and Husserl

CW00553162

LEONARD LAWLOR

Derrida and Husserl

The Basic Problem of Phenomenology

INDIANA
University Press

Bloomington & Indianapolis

This book is a publication of

Indiana University Press
601 North Morton Street
Bloomington, IN 47404-3797 USA

http://iupress.indiana.edu

Telephone orders   800-842-6796
Fax orders   812-855-7931
Orders by e-mail   iuporder@indiana.edu

Manufactured in the United States of America

Library of Congress Cataloging-in-Publication Data

Lawlor, Leonard, date
    Derrida and Husserl : the basic problem of phenomenology / Leonard Lawlor.
        p.   cm. — (Studies in Continental thought)
Includes bibliographical references and index.
    ISBN 0-253-34049-7 (cloth : alk. paper) — ISBN 0-253-21508-0 (pbk. : alk. paper)
    1. Phenomenology. 2. Derrida, Jacques. 3. Husserl, Edmund, 1859–1938.   I. Title. II. Series.
    B829.5 .L35 2002
    194—dc21

                            2001004035

1 2 3 4 5   07 06 05 04 03 02

For my daughter, Mary Casey

Contents

Acknowledgments

My thanks to the following friends for their generosity and inspiration: Renaud Barbaras, Mauro Carbone, Edward S. Casey, Pierre Cassou-Noguès, Olivia Custer, Natalie Depraz, Martin C. Dillon, Zeynep Direk, John Drabinski, Fred Evans, Linda Fisher, James Hanas, David K. Henderson, Jay Julian, Dragan Kujundzic, Philip Maloney, Valentine Moulard, Paul Naylor, Thomas Nenon, John Protevi, John Sallis, Dennis Schmidt, Amit Sen, Hugh J. Silverman, Nancy Simco, Theodore Toadvine, Kevin Thompson, and Donn Welton. I owe special thanks to Burt Hopkins, Rodolphe Gasché, Stephen Watson, and François-David Sebbah for their comments on an earlier draft of this book. Also, I owe special thanks to Ann V. Murphy who proofread and indexed the manuscript. It is hard for me to imagine having written this book without the constant friendship of Robert Bernasconi. My deepest thanks to Jennifer Wagner-Lawlor for her generosity, inspiration, and patience. The writing of this book was supported by two Professional Development Assignments from the University of Memphis (Fall 1992–Spring 1993; Spring 2000), and a Faculty Research Grant from the University of Memphis (Summer 1997).

Abbreviations

The following is a list of abbreviations of the books discussed. When reference is made to any of these texts, the first page number refers to the French or German edition, the second to the English translation. The English translations of *L'Origine de la géométrie*, traduction et introduction par Jacques Derrida, the essays from *L'Ecriture et la différence* ("'Genèse et structure' et la phénoménologie," and "Violence et métaphysique"), and especially *La Voix et le phénomène* have been frequently modified and sometimes entirely re-translated. All translations of *Le Problème de la genèse* are my own.

Books by Jacques Derrida

AEL   *Adieu à Emmanuel Levinas.* Paris: Galilée, 1997. English translation by Michael Naas and Pascale-Anne Brault as *Adieu to Emmanuel Levinas.* Stanford: Stanford University Press, 1999.

ED   *L'Ecriture et la différence.* Paris: Seuil, 1967. English translation by Alan Bass as *Writing and Difference.* Chicago: University of Chicago, 1978.

GT   *Donner le temps: 1. La fausse monnaie.* Paris: Galilée, 1991. English translation by Peggy Kamuf as *Given Time: 1. Counterfeit Money.* Chicago: University of Chicago, 1992.

LOG   Edmund Husserl, *L'Origine de la géométrie,* traduction et introduction par Jacques Derrida. Paris: Presses Universitaires de France, 1974 [1962]. English translation by John P. Leavey as *Edmund Husserl's "Origin of Geometry": An Introduction.* Lincoln: University of Nebraska Press, 1989 [1978].

MP   *Marges de la philosophie.* Paris: Minuit, 1972. English translation by Alan Bass as *Margins of Philosophy.* Chicago: University of Chicago Press, 1982.

PGH   *Le Problème de la genèse dans la philosophie de Husserl.* Paris: Presses Universitaires de France, 1990.

POS   *Positions.* Paris: Minuit, 1972. English translation by Alan Bass as *Positions.* Chicago: University of Chicago Press, 1981.

OS   *De l'esprit.* Paris: Galilée, 1987. English translation by Geoff Ben-
      nington and Rachel Bowlby as *Of Spirit.* Chicago: University of
      Chicago Press, 1989.
SM   *Spectres de Marx.* Paris: Galilée, 1993. English translation by Peggy
      Kamuf as *Specters of Marx.* New York: Routledge, 1994.
VP   *La Voix et le phénomène.* Paris: Presses Universitaires de France, 1983
      [1967]. English translation by David B. Allison as *Speech and Phe-
      nomena.* Evanston, IL: Northwestern University Press, 1973. Below
      I have rendered the title of this book as *Voice and Phenomenon.*

Other Books

LTS   Jean Cavaillès, *Sur la logique et la théorie de la science.* Paris: Presses
      Universitaires de France, 1947. English translation by Theodore J.
      Kisiel as "On Logic and the Theory of Science," in *Phenomenology
      and the Natural Sciences,* ed. Joseph J. Kockelman and Theodore J.
      Kisiel, 353–412. Evanston: Northwestern University Press, 1970.
PP   Eugen Fink, "Die Phänomenologische Philosophie E. Husserl in
      der Gegenwärtigen Kritik," originally published in *Kantstudien* 38,
      no. 3/4 (Berlin, 1933). Collected in Eugen Fink, *Studien zur Phänome-
      nologie.* Den Haag: Martinus Nijhoff, 1966. English translation as
      "The Phenomenological Philosophy of Edmund Husserl and Con-
      temporary Criticism," in *The Phenomenology of Husserl,* ed. R. O.
      Elveton, 73–147. Chicago: Quadrangle Books, 1970. For the French
      translation see Eugen Fink, *De la Phénoménologie,* translation by
      Didier Franck. Paris: Minuit, 1974.
LE   Jean Hyppolite, *Logique et existence.* Paris: Presses Universitaires de
      France, 1952. English translation by Leonard Lawlor and Amit Sen
      as *Logic and Existence.* Albany: State University of New York Press,
      1997.
PMD   Tran-Duc-Thao, *Phénoménologie et matérialisme dialectique.* Paris:
      Editions Minh-Tân, 1951. English translation by Daniel J. Herman
      and Donald V. Morano as *Phenomenology and Dialectical Material-
      ism.* Boston: D. Reidel, 1985.

Derrida and Husserl

The Original Motivation:
Defend the Derridean Faith

This book, I hope, will at least be the keystone of a genuine work of philosophy that I shall produce some day. Over the time that I wrote this book,[1] I slowly realized that Heidegger's attempt in *Being and Time* to re-open the question of being is the defining event of twentieth-century philosophy.[2] What I finally realized is that, when Heidegger re-opens the question of being, he defines being itself as a question: the question of being is the being of the question.[3] In the Introduction to *Being and Time*, Heidegger of course did not have in mind the kind of question that is posed in school, where the teacher, knowing the answer to the question in advance, relinquishes the students of all responsibility for thinking. A genuine question has two characteristics. On the one hand, a genuine question demands to be left open, even left without a response; a genuine question must be a quest. This openness is why the question can account for the universality of being. On the other hand, a genuine question demands to be closed off, even answered once and for all; a genuine question must be able to be finished. This closure is why the question can account for the determination of being. A question therefore is fundamentally differentiated between openness and closure, between irresponsibility and responsibility. Difference therefore defines the being of the question.

The idea that difference defines the being of the question allowed me to think about, in a new way, what I would call the great French philosophers of the sixties. It seems to me that Heidegger's being of the question comes into Merleau-Ponty as the ontology of interrogation found in *The Visible and the Invisible*. Yet because Merleau-Ponty left this book unfinished when he died in 1961, there is an ambiguity in his thought that derives from the experience of language, or, more precisely, from the experience of sense. This ambiguity, this point of divergence, opens up what I would call the two major strains of French thought. On the one hand, it seems to me that the being of the question comes through Merleau-Ponty, either directly or indirectly, into Levinas and then Derrida.[4] Due to a priority of the experience of the other (transcendence), Levinas and then Derrida transform the question into the *promise* and thereby transform what Heidegger called ontology into "religion" (the relation of alterity and faith). But, on the other hand, it seems to me that the being of the question comes through Merleau-Ponty, again either directly or indirectly, into Deleuze and Foucault. Due to a priority of the experience of force (immanence), Deleuze and Foucault transform the question into the *problem* and thereby transform what Heidegger called ontology into "epistemology" (the relation of power and knowledge). If we return to Merleau-Ponty, we can see that, within his own appropriation of Heideggerian ontology, he is divided between the probable sources of the difference between the promise and the problem: Husserl's concept of intentionality and Bergson's concept of duration. But it is just as probable that Merleau-Ponty unifies them in the concept of life: Husserl's *Erlebnis* and Bergson's *élan vital*. Coining a word, we might call this whole field of philosophy "lifeism." But we might just as well call it "mnemonics"; life and memory are inseparable. In "Indirect Language and the Voices of Silence," Merleau-Ponty, echoing Heidegger, speaks of "the power to forget origins and to give to the past not a survival, which is the hypocritical form of forgetfulness, but a new *life*, which is the noble form of *memory*."[5]

In its widest scope, this book attempts to reconstruct and reflect upon the Derridean transformation of Heideggerian ontology. Thus it concerns itself with the new form of thinking that Derrida calls deconstruction.[6] The newness of this thinking consists in its difference from what Derrida calls "the metaphysics of presence." We must start with precise definitions. Presence, for Derrida, consists in (a) the distance of what is over and against (object and form, what is iterable), what we could call "objective presence," (b) the proximity of the self to itself in its acts (subject and intuition or content), what we could call "subjective presence," and then (c) the unification of these two species of presence, that is, presence and self-presence, in the present (in the "form of the living present," which, Derrida will explain, mediates itself through the voice). "The metaphysics of presence" then, for Derrida, consists in the valorization of presence (as defined in this way, which can account for both ancient and modern philosophy as well as Husserl's phenomenology), that is, it consists in the validation of presence as a foundation. It is important to point out immediately that Derrida never contests the founding validity of presence; there can be no foundation without presence. Yet, for Derrida, there is a nonfoundation below it, what we could call, following what Derrida says in

"Violence and Metaphysics," the "non-Greek" non-foundation. The metaphysics of presence, however, has decided that the meaning of being is presence either as subject or object or as their unity. Thus it does not re-open the question of being; it remains above in the security of the foundation. It remains Greek.

In this investigation, we are going to insist on calling deconstruction a critique (cf. MP 162/134, SM 145/88). Deconstruction consists in limiting claims made by metaphysics (but also ethical and political claims) with experience; deconstruction is always enlightening: "the violence of light," as Derrida says in "Violence and Metaphysics." Yet Derrida's critique of metaphysics, and therefore his critique of phenomenology as metaphysics, contains two aspects. On the one hand, deconstruction engages in a classical phenomenological critique in which claims are limited with evidence, with presence; in this aspect, deconstruction relies on what Husserl of course called "the principle of all principles." In fact, as we shall see, Derrida turns "the principle of all principles" against any lapses in phenomenological vigilance; he turns it against any dogmatism that might remain in Husserl's philosophy. On the other hand, deconstruction engages in what we are going to call a "super-phenomenological critique," in which deconstruction limits metaphysical claims (or ethico-political claims) with the very *experience of the non-Greek non-foundation*,[7] with the very experience that in fact *Husserl himself* points us toward when he describes time and alterity: the experience of non-presence. The experience that functions as this undeconstructible measure is the test (*l'épreuve*) of the sign. It seems to me that it is impossible to dissociate deconstruction, Derrida's thought itself as a whole, from the experience or test of language. As we shall see, this test of language is an *aporia*.

But this test also defines Derrida's most familiar concepts from the sixties, in particular, différance. Derrida's concept of différance derives from the Husserlian concept of *intentionality*. Like intentionality, différance consists in an intending *to;* it is defined by the dative relation. This connection of différance back to Husserlian intentionality is why the Husserlian concept of the noema, what Derrida in "'Genesis and Structure' and Phenomenology," as we shall see, calls "the anarchy of the noema" (ED 242–243/163), is at its root. For Husserl, the noema (or meaning) consists in an ontological difference. It is at once *irreell,* that is, it is not a *reell* part of consciousness (as are the noetic acts and the hyle); thus it is different from, outside of, and other than consciousness. But it is also a non-real thing since it is ideal, which in turn means that the noema is identical to consciousness, inside of, and the same as consciousness. Thus it is at once *in* consciousness *without* it belonging to consciousness; it is at once inside and outside consciousness, immanent and transcendent, mundane and extra-mundane. It is at once related to acts of consciousness and iterable beyond them; it is in the passage between these poles. Because the noema is transcendent, outside, extra-mundane, iterable beyond, it always implies a relation to others; it always implies transcendental intersubjectivity. This relation to others means that whenever I intend something, it includes the possibility of absence or non-presence. The other, for Husserl—this phenomenological necessity is the center of Derrida's thought—can never be given to me in the same way as I have a presentation of myself; the other is only given in a re-presentation (never *Gegenwärtigung* but only ever *Vergegenwärtigung*). *I lack knowledge of the interior life of others.* Because however consciousness itself, transcendental life, consists for Husserl in intending, that is, in iterating a unity, we must conclude that even when I do not intend alterity, when I intend that the unity stay within, when I fulfill the form of sense with an intuition, alterity is always already there as a necessary possibility; the indefinite iterability of any sense structure necessarily implies the possibility of alterity, of non-presence, of non-intuition. But—and this phenomenological necessity is the other center of Derrida's thought—because consciousness is a consciousness *to*, the intending of a sense necessarily *ends* in (as well as necessarily *opens* up) some sort of fulfillment, in some sort of presence; the sense returns to me. What Husserl shows in the Fifth Cartesian Meditation is that I understand the other even though I cannot live his or her interior life. This description of the noema is the Derridean concept of différance reconstructed entirely in Husserlian terms.[8]

But we can also present différance in Derridean terms. In *La Voix et le phénomène,* différance is defined by what Derrida calls "the ultra-transcendental concept of life," that is, with auto-affection. When I have a thought or sense in the most minimal sense, I am affecting myself; I am having an interior monologue. I hear myself speak at the very moment that I speak. This is the *first* essential necessity in which différance consists: the sense of my words *must* be present to me, the same as me, immanent to me, in the world, as close to me as possible, subjectively present. How else could I say that I have the sense, that it functions, unless it was present, unless I was present to myself, unless I was alive? I am powerless to exit my living present (which, conversely, means that I have the power to remain in my living present). But, since auto-affection is temporal, the sense of the words lacks persisting presence. This lack or negativity implies that I am finite and mortal; there is non-sense. Just as I am powerless to exit my living present, I am as well powerless to remain in my living present. Subjective presence is always already passing away; something of me, some intuition or content such as an action that is singular, has always already passed away. I am always already *late* for subjective presence. Thus we have the *first* sense of différance: delay. In order for me, however, to endow the sense (or something singular of me, some intuition or content such as an action) with persisting or objective presence, I must bring my self back over and over again; this "over and over again" is the possibility, the power, of re-presentation in its most general form. The return of the form of the sense is a memory, or more precisely, a trace. Here we have the *second* necessity in which différance consists: since the form of the sense lacks objective or persisting presence, the sense *must* be indefinitely iterated; the second necessity is the necessity of survival. The sense must survive beyond my present; it demands a medium or mediation, which can be the voice but which *also* must include writing as a possibility. The sense must survive and that means that it must be no longer finite but infinite, no longer immanent but transcendent, no longer inside but outside, no longer mundane but extra-mundane; only the graphic possibility can make the sense be *different* from me, from my singularity. Thus we have the *second* sense of différance: difference. *But*, and this aspect of différance is crucial, since the form of sense (or something of me, some intuition or content such as an action) survives only in writing or in the trace or in memory, it is really *dead*; it is merely a body within a *subjectless* transcendental field. Here we return to différance's first necessity: the trace *must* be made present, must be immanent, must be made mundane, must be made close once more, must be made the same as me; it must be made to live again. When this return happens, presence that is both objective and subjective is constituted. This constitution of presence cannot, however, close off the second necessity; the trace still, always, demands to survive, which necessitates that it be sent out again *to* another fulfillment. Thus we could say—with a word we have invented by playing on the French word "fin"—that différance is "re-finition" (as opposed to "re-commencement").[9] In this very moment of refinition, I am at the threshold between the two necessities—I *must* keep the sense close by and I *must* make the sense distant—I am at the limit between life and death. Thus I am in the experience of the *aporia* of language. At the very moment in which I undergo the *aporia*, I cannot ask what language is (the phenomenological question) or why language is (the ontological question), since these questions ask for an essence, for presence, for being, all of which, according to Derrida, are themselves made possible by language. Since this *aporia* consists in how language constitutes essence (*ens*), we are no longer confronted by the question of the meaning of being. The *aporia* of language forces us deeper, more subterranean than being. Deconstruction consists, therefore, in bringing us to the experience of this precise *non-ontological aporia,* to the moment before a decision could be made about how to respond to it. It brings us to the experience of what Derrida in *La Voix et le phénomène* calls "the unheard-of question." Already, we can see, however, that, if Derrida defines deconstruction in *La Voix et le phénomène* as the experience of a non-ontological question, then he is already turning away from the question of being to the promise of justice. But this turn is still far away for us.

As I said, I hope that this book, at least, will contribute to a genuine work of philosophy that I have not yet written; this hope arose unexpectedly during the writing of *Derrida and Husserl: The Basic Problem of Phenomenology.* The original motivation for writing it came, as is obvious, from the controversy that has continued to swirl, in particular in the English-speaking world, for the last twenty-five years, around Derrida's interpretation of Husserl. It is easy to see now what contributed to the controversy. It is unfortunate that Derrida did not publish until 1990 his *Mémoire* from the academic year 1953–54, *Le Problème de la genèse dans la philosophie de Husserl.* This book alone does away with the question of Derrida's Husserl scholarship. It is also unfortunate that Derrida did not write the "systematic reading of Husserl's thought" that he announced in *La Voix et le phénomène* (VP 1n2/4n2). Such a systematic reading would have provided the elaboration that this little essay, about the same length as "Violence and Metaphysics," called *La Voix et le phénomène* really needs. The French title, *La Voix et le phénomène,* clearly announced the purpose of this essay. What *medium* can assure the iterability to infinity that defines the Husserlian concept of *phenomenon*? The answer to this question is, of course, the *voice*. Phenomen-ology itself is at stake here: voice (the *logos*) and phenomenon. Yet the title to the English translation (*Speech and Phenomena*) obscured this purpose, and this is why throughout *Derrida and Husserl* we will use the title *Voice and Phenomenon.* Critics paid insufficient attention to the conceptual context in which the ideas in *Voice and Phenomenon* were developed: Fink, Tran-Duc-Thao, Cavaillès, Hyppolite, Levinas, and, of course, Heidegger.[10] Critics as well paid insufficient attention to Derrida's other essays in which he discusses Husserl, in particular, " 'Genesis and Structure' and Phenomenology" and "Violence and Metaphysics." Although I do not here[11] engage any particular critic of Derrida's interpretation of Husserl, many of the chapters (for better or worse) have the tone of "setting the record straight." Indeed, the idea that I was going to "defend the Derridean faith" generated the very structure of the book. The result is that I have written a sort of narrative of Derrida's formative period from approximately 1954 to 1967, in which Derrida devoted himself to developing an interpretation of Husserl. This "narrative," like all narratives, has a beginning, a middle, and an end. It begins with the problem of genesis being resolved through an "originary dialectic of phenomenology and ontology." In the middle, there is the transformation of the problem of genesis into the problem of the sign, and phenomenology and ontology come to an end. The narrative then comes to its climax of course in 1967 with *Voice and Phenomenon:* Derrida deconstructs the metaphysics of presence to expose the experience of différance, which gives rise to the unheard-of question. The epilogue is the "turn" to the promise. The prologue, however, takes us back to the source of Derrida's interpretation of Husserl. Thus we begin with an investigation of Eugen Fink's famous *Kantstudien* essay, "The Phenomenological Philosophy of Edmund Husserl and Contemporary Criticism."

Part One.
Phenomenology and Ontology

1 Genesis as the Basic Problem of Phenomenology

It is well known that Eugen Fink's 1933 *Kantstudien* essay, "The Phenomenological Philosophy of Edmund Husserl and Contemporary Criticism," finally expanded the French understanding of Husserl's phenomenology;[1] in particular, Fink introduced terms such as "act-intentionality,"
"radical reflection," and "archeology," terms which Merleau-Ponty would
adopt in his discussions of Husserl.[2] Indeed, Fink's "The Phenomenological Philosophy of Edmund Husserl" provided "a fundamental interpretation of phenomenology in the unity of its development";[3] it provided the
basic principles, in other words, of all of Husserl's phenomenology. This
is why, in a 1966 review of Fink's *Studien zur Phänomenologie* (the volume
in which "The Phenomenological Philosophy of Edmund Husserl" was
collected), Derrida himself claims that this book is one of the most remarkable monuments in the history of the interpretation of Husserl's
thought.[4] In fact, Fink is the only Husserl commentator that Derrida either
cites or explicitly mentions in all three of his books on Husserl.[5] If we want
to understand Derrida's interpretation of Husserl, then we must begin
with Fink.[6] In fact, only an examination of Fink's 1933 essay shows that
Derrida's philosophy—his deconstruction—is continuous with Husserl's
phenomenology.

1

As is well known, in "The Phenomenological Philosophy of Edmund
Husserl and Contemporary Criticism," Fink responds to Husserl's con-
temporaneous neo-Kantian critics. He demonstrates that the then-current
criticisms of Husserl's phenomenology—which focused primarily on the
Logical Investigations and *Ideas I*—were based on one presupposition: that
Husserl's phenomenology wanted the same thing as critical philosophy.
Critical philosophy believed, in other words, that phenomenology held
the same idea of philosophy as it held (PP 96/90). What is needed, there-

fore, according to Fink, is a "destruction" (*Zerstörung*) of critical philosophy's basic presupposition (PP 99/93). A destruction can be achieved only by illuminating the "radical difference" (PP 106/100) that separates phenomenology from critical philosophy. As Fink says, "If it is true that every philosophy reveals its innermost essence less in its theoretical accomplishments . . . than in the basic question which is its motivating force, the difference between phenomenology and critical philosophy is principally defined as a difference in their basic problems" (PP 100/94).

According to Fink, critical philosophy wants to provide an account of the conditions for the possibility of human knowledge, in particular, human theoretical knowledge. This desire means that critical philosophy wants to go beyond the naive attitude of positivism, in which knowledge is restricted to knowledge of particular beings or things. Superseding the epistemological attitude restricted to facts, critical philosophy ascends to the ideal validities (*Geltungen*) which give sense (*Sinn*) to beings.[7] These validities are the presuppositions of every experience of beings as theoretical objects. In Fink's words, what critical philosophy wants then is to answer "the question concerning that realm of sense [*Sinnsphäre*] which forms the presupposition of all beings" (PP 100/94). In its greatest generality, this presupposition amounts to the "*a priori* form of the world" (PP 100/95). The *a priori* form of the world is "the relationship of theoretical validities, which are prior to all experience, to the pure form of consciousness . . . " (PP 100/95; cf. also 85/80). For critical philosophy, the pure form of consciousness is an epistemological ego (the transcendental apperception), and, as such, it must be determined as non-ontological and as unknowable. Being the condition for all beings, the pure form of consciousness cannot be said to be; it is not a being or a thing. Being the condition for all experience, it cannot be said to be given in experience; rather, the pure form of consciousness must be constructed.

On the basis of this analysis, Fink interprets the critical idea of philosophy as mundane and world-immanent (PP 102–03/97). Its transition from the naive, positivistic attitude to the critical, transcendental attitude merely abstracts from beings within the world; the presuppositional validities or ideal meanings are meanings of this world. Finally, the pure form of consciousness that it constructs is a pure form of the consciousness of a being which resides within the world: man (PP 151/141). In other words, critical philosophy constructs the relation between the theoretical validities and the pure form of consciousness on the basis of beings (PP 100/95). In contrast, Fink interprets Husserl's phenomenology as world-transcendent. It wants to uncover, in Fink's famous formulation, "the origin of the world" (PP 101/95). Phenomenology's idea of philosophy springs from the traditional metaphysical or speculative question of the origin of the world; yet phenomenology and speculative metaphysics are not identical, according to Fink.

Speculative metaphysics had tried to pursue its idea in terms of a cause or principle that transcends the world. What speculative metaphysics wanted and claimed to discover is another world or another being which explained this world and these beings.[8] Speculative metaphysics, moreover, conceived the relation between cause or principle and the world as a relation between two beings: separate or away from, outside of, next to, one another. In short, speculative metaphysics used beings to clarify beings. It conceived transcendence as a relationship "along the lines of the intramundane relations of one being to another (for example, reason and consequence, creation and product, the appearance of something hidden, etc.)" (PP 101/95–96). In phenomenology, however, according to Fink, transcendence has an "in principle different direction" (PP 105/99). Through the "phenomenological reduction"—and Fink says in a note that all phenomenology goes through the reduction; a phenomenology that would reject it would be mundane and dogmatic (PP 105n1/99n11, 152/141–142)—phenomenology overcomes the ontic conception of the relation. The phenomenological reduction "is a transcending passage" from the world to what is absolute, to what is, in other words, non-relative or non-human. As absolute, it cannot be conceived as a being of any sort; it cannot be found *within* the world. Yet, not being separated from the world like one thing separated from another, it also cannot be found *outside* of the world. This very specific sort of transition means, therefore, that, with the phenomenological reduction, one neither passes outside of the world nor remains within the world; one neither remains in the sense of being as an existent thing nor passes to non-being. Rather, this passage means both that one passes out of the world to what is absolute (non-being) and that one remains within the world (being) because the world is rediscovered as lying *within* the absolute. Rather than try to discover the absolute immanent to the world as critical philosophy attempts to do, phenomenology discovers the world, as Fink says, "immanent to the absolute" (PP 106/99). Rather than try to transcend the limits of the world to another world as speculative metaphysics does, phenomenology transcends the limits of the "natural attitude," the attitude from which speculative metaphysics arises. The phenomenological reduction, therefore, "remains in principle within the unity of the absolute" (PP 106/99); the reduction returns "to a transcendence which once again *contains* the world within it" (PP 106/100). In other words, as Fink says, "Phenomenology explicitly and knowingly wins back the world from within the depths of the absolute in which—*before* the phenomenological reduction—the world itself lies concealed" (PP 106/100, Fink's emphasis).

2

For Fink, clarifying phenomenology's world-transcendence in opposition to critical philosophy's world-immanence destroys the presupposition of identity that animates critical philosophy's criticisms (PP 105/99). Phenomenology does not begin with the critical project from which it could deteriorate and, while taking up the speculative project, phenomenology abandons its naive, ontic formulations. The clarification then allows Fink to eliminate the confusion surrounding other basic phenomenological doctrines, the first of which is the reduction. At the outset, mundane problems like the critical problem of human knowledge or the speculative problem of the world's origin always seem to motivate the phenomenological reduction; it always seems to present itself as a human possibility of knowledge.[9] In fact, according to Fink, this sort of motivation does not hold for the phenomenological reduction; the reduction does not present a possibility for, as Fink says, "our human *Dasein* (PP 110/104).[10] Thus, the phenomenological reduction is radically unfamiliar—both as a fact and as a possibility—for us. In relation to all mundane motivation, the phenomenological reduction is radically unmotivated. The mundane interpretations of the reduction are false. Yet such an association is unavoidable, for the reduction always starts from the worldly point of view, the natural attitude.

According to Fink, the natural attitude consists in the belief in the world; the world presents itself as having certain characteristics which have turned out to be valid for it. For instance, there is the belief that when something is dropped, it will fall to the ground. This belief has been validated by man in his life of meanings, in the projects and activities that he has carried out standing within the world (PP 114/108). At first, then, the natural attitude appears to be merely a human or psychological attitude; it seems that we must posit man as the subject in relation to the world. Under analysis—this is intentional analysis, as we shall see in a moment—however, as Fink explains, the validations show themselves to be in constant flux. Not only must we take into account our own experiences but also those of others. Our life of endowing things with valid meanings (or senses) not only is directed toward transcendent things but also to our own psychical or immanent being. Lastly, the horizon of beings—the past and future—which lead to the universal horizon which encompasses all horizons must be investigated (PP 114/108). Thus, the natural attitude consists not just in the one individual positing of being to which others are added; rather, it consists in the positing of a system. As Fink says, it consists in "the universal, constant, self-modifying consciousness of the world whose contents are in flux" (PP 114/108).

If this is the natural attitude, then *man's* universal believing in the world cannot clarify it (PP 115/109). Man, too, is found within this belief; man, too, is endowed with sense like any other particular, worldly being. As Fink says, "To call myself or someone else 'man' already implies being certain of myself as one man among others and hence a knowing of myself as existing within the world as a being related to the world in a conscious manner" (PP 115/109). The world does not present itself as an object over and against a human subject, because the human subject finds himself within the world. The interpretation, therefore, which posits man as the subject of this universal, constant, and ever-changing belief must be merely intramundane and false.

Instead of being a *human* attitude, as Fink stresses, the natural attitude turns out to be *transcendental* (PP 113/107). Being transcendental does not mean that the natural attitude completely leaves man behind. Rather, the natural attitude includes all human attitudes within itself and refers them back to transcendental subjectivity. For Fink, the natural attitude makes constant reference back to the "absolute and concrete life which carries the sense of the world's being totally and concretely within itself" (PP 118/112). Only such a transcendental life, which is not strictly human but within which humans can be found as ontic phenomena, can clarify how the valid meanings of the world, its being, can be universal, constant, and ever-changing. Thus, looking back to the reduction's starting point, we can see that the human subjectivity which seemed to possess the world as a universal, constant, and ever-changing system of validities actually sits upon layers of hidden transcendental productions (*Leistungen*) and processes. The phenomenological reduction regresses or questions back (*rückfragen*), therefore, to the transcendental subjectivity which originally achieved the possession of the world (PP 140/131; see also 134/126).[11]

Clearly, for Fink, the reduction cannot be conceived as a method for clarifying the *a priori* form of the world correlated to the pure form of consciousness. If it were, it would be equivalent to a method of abstraction and construction that results in something non-existent and unknowable through experience. Moreover, the phenomenological reduction cannot be conceived as a method for purifying human consciousness of transcendent objects (PP 124/118). In other words, it is not a method for delimiting the region known as psychological immanence. Although opposed—the first, exemplified by critical philosophy, results in a non-existent and unknowable form; the second, exemplified by psychology, results in an existent region given in inner experience—both of these interpretative poles remain mundane. Instead, according to Fink, given phenomenology's now recognized different direction (*Sinn*), the reduction transcends the world in such a way—through a radical reflection upon human subjectivity—that the transcendental subjectivity it discovers is both knowable and yet not a region of being. In opposition to critical philosophy, the origin of the world gives itself in a new type of transcendental experience (PP 119/112); the phenomenological *epoché* leads to the "absolute" which flows in transcendental experience and thinking. As Fink says, "This knowledge is intuitive (*intuitive*) if we understand by this *true self-givenness* and not 'intuition' (*Anschauung*) as a human capacity for knowledge opposed to discursive thought" (PP 134/126; cf. also PP 88/83).[12] In opposition to psychology, the reduction is not a disconnecting of one region of being (transcendence) in order to stake out another (immanence). Rather, it is a leading back to something that cannot be conceived at all as a being. Transcendental subjectivity exists, according to Fink, but exists in a way or mode different from things (PP 138/129–130). This difference is why Fink, following Husserl, calls absolute life *irreal* (PP 135/127), and why in the *Sixth Cartesian Meditation*, a text intimately connected to the 1933 essay that we are now analyzing, Fink defines the project of a transcendental theory of method in terms of meontics and appropriates the scholastic notion of the analogy of being.[13]

Only the doctrine of transcendental constitution (the doctrine, in other words, of intentionality) can, however, determine the precise way absolute life exists in contradistinction to ontic or psychological life. In the performance of the reduction—briefly described above and more thoroughly in Fink's essay—we see that one follows the clue called the "world." At first, this guiding thread leads back to what Fink calls "a provisional description of intentionality's elementary structure" (PP 140/131–132). Intentionality consists in "subjective" *acts* (as the noesis) in which the "world" (as the noema) comes to be valid and habitualities in which the validity gained holds sway (PP 141/132). Being indeterminately described here (as in *Ideas I*), "act-intentionality" seems to be psychological intentionality, especially, insofar as Husserl uses terms like *belief in the world, the meaning of the world, having the world in validity.* It seems to be human, and therefore, intramundane, intentionality. Thus, act-intentionality seems to describe the noesis as the mere recipient of meanings and sensations from the outside; in other words, it seems to be, as Fink stresses, passive (PP 140/131). This confusion between mere psychological intentionality and act-intentionality arises because, according to Fink, the level of act-intentionality is, in fact, one that is constituted and not constituting (PP 142/133). Thus, as Fink says, the level of act-intentionality is an intermediate, although necessary, level that has to be surpassed (PP 142–143/133).

Still guided by the *world,* one then penetrates to a deeper level of intentionality. Again, a worldly, human subjectivity cannot clarify how the world came to be as it is, its being as a system. Seeking, therefore, the world's origin, one inquires, according to Fink, "back beyond the worldly and objectivized intentional stream of life (as the intramundane *psyché*)" (PP 142/133). One makes the transition from the world-imprisoning psychological interpretation of the self to the level within which this interpretation is constructed. As Fink says, "the reduction deobjectifies transcendental life, deworlds it" (PP 142/133). The most important question becomes then: how to determine transcendental life, how to differentiate it from the other levels, and how to disclose its inner implications.

To do this, one must, according to Fink, certify "transcendental intentionality's *productive (produktiven)* character" (PP 143/133–134). Stressing the opposition to the *receptive,* intramundane intentionality, Fink also describes transcendental life in terms of "creation" (*Kreation*) (PP 143/134). Although Fink parenthetically adds the qualification that creation cannot be understood along the lines of an ontic relation, he says, "No matter how harsh and doctrinaire this determination of the essence of constitution as a productive creation may sound, it at least indicates the opposite character, a required being-in-itself character, to the receptive character of the ontic and mundane (psychical) life of experience" (PP 143/134).[14] Certifying transcendental life's opposition to psychical life, one then proceeds to the most basic level, transcendental temporalization. Here, it is not only the case that passively received, yet amorphous, sensations show themselves as constituted but also that the acts themselves, which impose form on the sensations, show themselves to be constituted. Within primordial temporalization, there is only pure becoming without opposition. Thus, as Fink says, "The true theme of phenomenology is neither the world, on the one hand, nor a transcendental subjectivity which is set over and against the world on the other, but *the world's becoming in the constitution of transcendental subjectivity* (PP 139/130).[15]

On the basis of the clarifications of the doctrines of the reduction and of constitution, Fink returns to the question of phenomenology's idea of philosophy. Phenomenological idealism is not, as Fink has already shown, the sort of idealism that critical philosophy espouses nor that espoused by psychology (which deteriorates into psychologism, if it makes objects of outer experience dependent on inner experience).[16] These two types of idealisms are mundane; concerned only with the priority over the world of a thing, man, which stands within the world, they are subjective idealisms. In contrast, as Fink says, phenomenology concerns itself with "the question of the priority over the world of a subjectivity, first discovered by the reduction, which is 'transcendental' in a new sense" (PP 137–138).[17] Phenomenology, in other words, concerns itself with the priority over the world of a subjectivity that is non-human and absolute, yet existing and knowable. As we have seen, in phenomenology, the world is never really left behind; rather, its dependence on absolute subjectivity is brought to light (PP 148/138; cf. also 137/128).

3

In this essay, Fink is not content with destroying critical philosophy's false presupposition that phenomenological philosophy has the same basic problem as it has. He also explains why critical philosophy could come to believe this. According to Fink, all confusions concerning the interpretation of Husserl's philosophy result from phenomenology's "transcendental *Schein*" (PP 153/142; see also 155/145, 80/75, 107/101).[18] After withdrawing from the world, phenomenology must appear in the world in order to share its knowledge of the world's origin. When phenomenology appears—enworlds itself[19]—it then seems to lose its character of being extramundane. The problem of its appearance is particularly troubling, as Fink points out, in the area of constitutive phenomenology, where one attempts to determine the nature of absolute subjectivity, the transcendental ego or transcendental life, in contradistinction from relative subjectivity (man), the psychological ego or psychological life (PP 153/142). The transcendental ego is not ontically separate from the psychological ego in the way that one thing stands outside of another; phenomenology's direction of transcendence, we recall, is not like that of speculative or dogmatic metaphysics. Yet, despite being ontically identical, the transcendental ego is somehow different from the psychological one; it *exists* in a different way. Thus, stressing the difference, one can make transcendental life appear to be another being standing next to psychological life; transcendental life then becomes a transcendent being. Or, stressing the identity, one can make transcendental life seem to be the intramundane region of being called psychological immanence; identifying the two, as Fink says in a slightly different context, "reduces (*abstellt*) the reduction" (PP 108/102).[20] This singular type of relation, which can be described neither as one of identity nor as one of difference, within the ego or life or intentionality makes the *Schein*, as Fink says, "ineradicable" and "undeniable." No matter how extramundane the phenomenologist becomes, there is no final exit from the world. Consequently, three paradoxes plague phenomenological research.

First, "there is the paradox of the situation of outward expression" (*die Paradoxie der Situation der Äußerung*).[21] Within the world, the natural attitude functions as the condition for the possibility of communication; it is our common or shared basis for communication. By means of the reduction, however, the phenomenological investigator surpasses the limits of the mundane attitude and proceeds to the transcendental level. Fink says that, as long as he remains in "this theoretical context, no additional problem presents itself" (PP 153/143); in fact, Fink even claims that the phenomenological expression is "transparent" for the phenomenologist himself in this context (PP 153/143). When, however, the investigator tries to communicate what he has discovered to others, then he is confronted with being reinserted into the world. His "depsychologized and deworlded" knowledge becomes "psychologized and enworlded"; the phenomenological spectator "appears" and is "localized" in the world. Yet, having transcended the natural attitude, the phenomenologist now lacks the common ground for communication; or better, he understands it differently. Anyone still residing in the natural attitude knows nothing of the absolute which supports his belief in the world; he knows the natural situation only as a natural situation. In contrast, after performing the reduction, the phenomenologist returns to the world and is able to see through the natural attitude; the phenomenologist knows the natural situation as a transcendental situation (PP 154/143). When the phenomenologist and someone still trapped in the natural attitude enter into communication, they do not, therefore, share the same situation and therefore cannot be talking about the same thing. The common ground needed for communication can be achieved only after *both* the speaker and the listener have traversed the reduction. The phenomenological outward expression must be seen then as an attempt to lead the one still trapped in the natural attitude into performing the reduction himself (PP 154/143). As Fink concludes, the impossibility of immediate communication explains why the reduction cannot be introduced into the natural attitude in a perfect way, but rather must be introduced in "false" or mundane terms (PP 154/143).

The second paradox—the paradox of the phenomenological statement—is closely connected to the first. As Fink says, "the phenomenologist who desires to communicate has only worldly concepts at his disposal" (PP 154/143).[22] In regard to mundane languages, the phenomenologist can take two tacks. On the one hand, he can try to reduce the mundane meanings of the words he must use. But in order to do this, he has to use other mundane expressions; thus he cannot eliminate the mundane meanings entirely. On the other hand, the phenomenologist can try to develop a technical language, a, so to speak, "nonworldly language." Yet, being entirely different from worldly languages, such a technical language would be entirely opaque to someone still residing in the natural attitude. In order then to explicate the technical meanings for the natural attitude person, one would have to resort to mundane expressions. Therefore mundane meanings would attach themselves to the technical terms. As Fink says, "Phenomenological statements necessarily contain an internal conflict between a word's mundane meaning and the transcendental meaning which it serves to indicate" (PP 154/144).[23] The expression of transcendental knowledge, therefore, is in constant danger; those still in the natural attitude can always misunderstand what the phenomenologist wants to say. This danger is why Fink in a later essay laments that Husserl never reflected on the possibility of a transcendental language.[24]

The third paradox returns to the question of the transcendental *Schein;* this is "the logical paradox of transcendental determinations" (PP 155/144). The very peculiar relation that constitutes life, the ego, or reflection demands, according to Fink, an equally peculiar logic. The logics developed so far, no matter how formal they may be, are worldly and thus incapable of resolving the logical *aporia* produced by the strange nature of the relation (PP 155/144).[25] One cannot, according to Fink, determine the relation by means of "the determinate relations of identity which persist throughout a variation of content (perhaps as identity in becoming, analogous to the identity of an organism, etc.)" (PP 155/144). In fact, one cannot determine it at all along the lines of determinate identity which hold among ontic beings. One cannot even determine the relation as analogous to such mundane determinate relations (PP 155/144).[26] Being a relation between an ontic being, man, and transcendental "being," absolute subjectivity, this relation is totally unlike any found in the world between two things. As Fink says, "Separating and distinguishing [the transcendental ego from the psychological ego] is as false as their direct equation" (PP 155/144). The relation, as Fink says, consists in a "unique identity" (PP 121/115), a "singular identity in difference, . . . [a] sameness in being-other" (PP 155/144). The ego's identity consists in a "tension" (PP 123/116); the egos, in other words, overlap or coincide.[27] No matter what, for Fink, the relation must be posited as "transcendental," and this means that man's worldly finitude is conceived as a constituted sense and thereby "taken back into the infinite essence of spirit" (PP 155/145).[28]

4

Despite the clearly Hegelian and Heideggerian language, Husserl unqualifiedly authorized Fink's interpretation of his philosophy (PP vii/73).[29] Due to the influence Fink's essay exerted on French interpretations of Husserl in the forties, fifties, and sixties,[30] anyone interested in criticizing Derrida's interpretation of Husserl cannot ignore this authorization. Fink's influence places Derrida firmly in the center of an incontestable tradition of Husserl interpretation. More importantly, Fink's 1933 "The Phenomenological Philosophy of Edmund Husserl" shows us that the basic problem of phenomenology is the basic problem with which Derrida starts: the origin of the world. The basic problem of Derrida's philosophy is the problem of genesis, as Derrida's very first book, *Le Problème de la genèse dans la philosophie de Husserl*, indicates. Yet, due to Fink, the word "problem" (or "question") in Derrida comes to mean paradox or *aporia*. Derrida radicalizes the "ineradicable" paradoxes of the transcendental *Schein*; indeed, everything for Derrida comes down to what Fink calls "the logical paradox of transcendental determinations." As Fink claims, the origin of the world is and must be non-mundane and non-existent; otherwise, it would not be transcendental, it would not be an origin. For Derrida, however, as we shall see, a reflection on the concept of evidence in his *Introduction to Husserl's "The Origin of Geometry,"* which he will extend to the concept of intuition in *Voice and Phenomenon*, shows, on the one hand, that such an origin must not only be determined as non-mundane and non-existence, but must also be determined as non-present and non-sense. An intuition, Derrida realizes, is always a finite intuition; evidence is always given in person. Thus intuition is always mundane, with the result being that an origin cannot be determined by presence and sense. To use language Derrida will adopt from Levinas, the origin is wholly other. On the other hand, the non-presence of the wholly other does not mean that it can never appear. The origin can and must be given *as* something. It can never and must never appear as such and yet it must appear as something in the world. It is this "must" which unites transcendental and mundane, other and same, essence and fact, non-presence and presence; it is this necessity that constitutes the paradox of genesis. This necessity of never appearing as such and yet appearing as something, in a specific experience, defines what Derrida in *Voice and Phenomenon* calls "différance" (or contamination). It is what Derrida implies when he says in the *Introduction to Husserl's "The Origin of Geometry,"* "the Absolute is Passage" (LOG 165/149). This absolute passage between transcendental and mundane, etc., means that the origin is not really an origin in the sense of an absolute beginning—it is not an *arche*—and that the end, *la fin,* is never an absolute end—it is not a *telos.* The paradox of genesis, for Derrida, is in-finite. As we are going to see, Derrida is going to transform this basic phenomenological problem of genesis into the problem of the sign (or the problem of language). But here too Derrida seems to follow (perhaps distantly) a Finkian inspiration. As Fink recognized, the phenomenological spectator must communicate his knowledge of the world's origin; the origin must appear—*Schein*—in the world. The word "Schein" implies both that the knowledge of the world's origin shines forth in its expression and that the expression falsifies the knowledge. For Derrida, the Finkian question of a "transcendental language" will be deepened in *The Origin of Geometry,* where Husserl will make language, indeed writing, fundamental in the constitution of ideal objects.[31] That writing is necessary in the constitution (or institution) of ideal objects means that language precedes all the distinctions that Husserl makes on the basis of the reduction. Insofar as the extra-mundane must be ideal for Husserl, it would have to be generated by language; and yet, insofar as language is the means of generating idealities, the differences—"the essential distinction"—that Husserl wants to make *within the domain of language* are themselves based in language. The very difference between mundane and extra-mundane, in other words, between fact and essence, ideality and reality, allows us to differentiate *within language* between indication and expression, equivocity and univocity, but language itself is a transcendental condition for these differences. Or, as Derrida is going to say in the Introduction to *Voice and Phenomenon,* "Language guards the difference that guards language" (VP 13/14). This complex relation of conditioning and conditioned, of generator and generated—in which language constitutes the very differences by means of which language is determined—is, for Derrida, the paradox or problem of the sign. But before we can chart Derrida's transformation of the problem of genesis into the problem of the sign, we are going to have investigate Derrida's critiques of both phenomenology and ontology.

The Critique of Phenomenology: An Investigation of " 'Genesis and Structure' and Phenomenology"

Although the examination of Fink's 1933 *Kantstudien* essay places Derrida firmly in the center of an incontestable tradition of Husserl's interpretation, Derrida's interpretation of Husserl must be seen as a critique of Husserlian phenomenology. The critique can be seen most easily in Derrida's " 'Genesis and Structure' and Phenomenology." Derrida originally presented this essay at a conference on the notions of genesis and structure in 1959. The proceedings of this conference were not, however, published until 1965 in *Entretiens sur les notions de genèse et de structure*. When it was published, " 'Genesis and Structure' and Phenomenology" appeared with this editor's note: "M. Derrida, qui a revu et complété son texte, a ajouté un certain nombre de notes explicatives et de références."[1] Derrida would not only revise the essay for its 1965 publication, but he would also revise it for its inclusion in the 1967 *Writing and Difference*. Because of its own peculiar genesis, this essay has an unrivaled privilege in regard to Derrida's interpretation of Husserl. That Derrida would continue to revise an essay written in 1959 indicates that it contains the most basic critique of phenomenology running from his 1954 *Le Problème de la genèse*, through his 1962 *Introduction to Husserl's "The Origin of Geometry"*, to his 1967 *Voice and Phenomenon*. Derrida always criticizes Husserlian phenomenology for deciding to close off genesis with a structure; Derrida's critique of phenomenology is always a critique of its teleology and therefore of its archeology. But as we shall see in " 'Genesis and Structure'," Derrida's critique takes two interrelated forms. On the one hand, Husserl closes off genesis with a structure for which he lacks intuitive evidence; on the other, he closes off genesis by supposing that the structure will be fully intuitable as such in the future: absolute presence. The first form of the critique depends on Husserl's intuitionism, in fact, on the "principle of all principles"; this critique is a phenomenological critique. Without eliminating the first critique, the second criticizes that very intuitionism; this second critique, which includes the first within itself, defines the deconstruction of the metaphysics of presence, and it anticipates what we are going to see in *Voice and Phenomenon*. This double critique (at once phenomenological and super-phenomenological) is based on the necessity of the problem of genesis.

1

In " 'Genesis and Structure' and Phenomenology," Derrida presents his "hypothesis" as a "confession"; he confesses it because it seems to go against the grain of what is most clear in Husserl. Derrida warns that Husserl had always tried to resist any type of thinking that is speculative or "dialectical," at least, Derrida says, "in the sense that Husserl always sought to ascribe to it" (ED 229/154). Husserl had always tried to resist a type of dogmatic thinking which would decide between two competing modes of description—in this case, genetic and structural—and thereby close off the debate (ED 229/155). In phenomenological description, there is no choice, option, or decision, according to Derrida. Instead, the thing itself determines whether a genetic or a structural description is appropriate; the thing itself keeps itself open to continuous interpretation.

Despite this warning, Derrida argues that Husserl succumbs to the speculative attitude: "a debate [between genesis and structure] regulates and gives its rhythm to the speed of [Husserl's] descriptions." Remaining "incomplete," the debate "leaves every major stage of phenomenology unbalanced" (ED 232/156–157). In order to respond to the debate, Husserl "appears," as Derrida says—and by this word he indicates that his "hypothesis" might not be confirmed—"to transgress the purely descriptive space and transcendental pretension of his investigation towards a metaphysics of history in which the solid structure of a *Telos* would permit him to reappropriate . . . a wild genesis" (ED 232/157). Being essentially internal to history and yet, somehow, prescribed to it from the outside, this *telos* would allow Husserl to reappropriate a genesis which "seemed to accommodate itself less and less to phenomenological apriorism and to transcendental idealism" (ED 232/157). Husserl, therefore, seems to respond to the debate's incompleteness with a decision, a decision through which phenomenology would relapse into dogmatic metaphysics, into "dialectic," at least in the sense that Husserl always sought to ascribe to it.

Derrida tries to confirm his hypothesis by examining briefly Husserl's writings on genetic phenomenology, which culminate in his last writings on history (ED 247/165). According to Derrida, what forces Husserl to consider history is the fundamental role given to passive synthesis, at least as formulated in *Cartesian Meditations* (ED 247/165).[2] Passive synthesis implies that consciousness does not constitute or create its object, but rather receives and unveils it. Unveiling an "already constituted" object, however, implies that a prior genetic process must have given rise to the object. But this genetic process, in turn, too would have to have a passive layer and an "already constituted" object, and so on. For Husserl, according to Derrida, a universal reason animates this infinite historic regression and, in turn, produces an infinite historic progression; teleological Reason animates all history with the Idea of an infinite task of knowledge. Pre-active and pre-predicative, the *Logos* intends an Idea in the Kantian sense, which itself is post-historical or post-temporal. Yet, as Derrida stresses, phenomenological consciousness functions now, in the present, in the living present. If one says that the Idea emerges into present consciousness as an advent, then one has to ask whether there can be phenomenological evidence for what seems to come from the outside. If one claims that the transformations through which Reason strives to complete the Idea are "always already indicated . . . 'in confusion and in the dark,' that is, not only in the most elementary forms of life and human history, but closer and closer in animality and nature in general" (ED 248/165), then one must ask, "[how] can such an assertion, made necessary *through* and *in* phenomenology itself, be totally assured there" (ED 248/165)? It seems that the assertion cannot be phenomenologically certain, for, as Derrida says, the assertion "no longer concerns only phenomena that are experienced and self evident" (ED 248/165). Lacking complete evidence for the Idea, Husserl, therefore according to Derrida, decides. On the basis of this decision for the *Logos* and its Idea, all genesis, even passive genesis, for Husserl, has a beginning and an end.

Derrida is content, he says, only to raise "these questions" and here, at the essay's end, he returns to the possibility that his hypothesis may not be confirmed. Derrida provides a succinct description of what Husserl is saying about Reason and history, about the *Logos* and being (or empiricity): "Reason unveils itself. Reason, Husserl says, is the *logos* that produces itself in history. It traverses being in view of itself, in view of appearing to itself, that is, as *Logos*, saying and hearing itself. . . . It goes out of itself in order to take itself up in itself, within the living present of its self-presence" (ED 248/166). Derrida comments on this description by saying that this language is not "immediately" speculative and metaphysical (ED 249/166). This language is not immediately speculative because, as Derrida always recognizes, there is no actual infinity in Husserl. The *logos* is *sens,* and, for Derrida, *sens* means "discourse, infinite discursivity" (ED 249/166).[3] As Derrida says, "this *logos* which calls itself and calls to itself as *telos,* and whose *dynamis* tends towards its energia or *entelechia*—this *logos* does not occur *in* history and does not traverse being as a foreign empiricity into which both its metaphysical transcendence and the actuality of its infinite essence would descend and condescend" (ED 249/166). Inversely however, while the *logos* depends on being, Derrida stresses, being depends on the *logos* for its sense (ED 249/166). Without this *irreal* difference between sense and being, existence would be without any order; it would be merely chaos, merely wild. Phenomenology, therefore, does not abdicate itself for the benefit of a classical metaphysical speculation, "which on the contrary," Derrida says, "would have to recognize in phenomenology the clarified energy of its own intentions" (ED 249/166). But it is still the case, for Derrida, that genesis overflows phenomenological evidence. This overflowing occurs with the "presence," as Derrida says, of "*Telos* or *Vorhaben*" (ED 250/167). According to Derrida, *Telos* "is indicated every time that Husserl speaks of an *Idea in the Kantian sense*" (ED 250/167, Derrida's emphasis). *Telos,* or the Idea in the Kantian sense is "totally open, is opening itself, ... the most powerful structural *a priori* of historicity ... the very birth of history and the sense of becoming in general ... structurally genesis itself" (ED 250/167). As we shall see, this discussion, in particular the contrast to Hegel in terms of infinity, the role of the Idea in the Kantian sense, and the difference between the *logos* and being, anticipates *Voice and Phenomenon.*

2

While Derrida admits that his hypothesis may not be confirmed, he also says in "'Genesis and Structure'" that at least the hypothesis allows him to accentuate the original characteristics of Husserl's attempt (ED 232/157). For Derrida, in this essay, there are four such characteristics, all of which focus on a certain kind of difference. First, there is the difference between wisdom and knowledge that Husserl develops in his criticisms of Dilthey's thought. As is well known and as Derrida recounts here, Dilthey attempts to use finite or factual totalities in order to account for all cultural productions, including philosophy (ED 237/160). Yet, as Husserl stresses, such structures miss truth or knowledge in its very meaning. Knowledge requires "an absolute, infinite omni-temporality and universality, without limits of any kind" (ED 237/160); in contrast, something like mere wisdom is finite and closed, relative to factual structures or *Zusammenhangen*. While finite ideas (*Weltanschauungen*) animate wisdom, an Idea in the Kantian sense animates knowledge. Only an Idea in the Kantian sense, therefore, can account for philosophy or truth in this strict sense. Being inadequate to this difference, *Weltanschauung* philosophy is a relativism; as Husserl recognizes, although Dilthey's thought appears at first to be a structuralism, it is actually a historicism.

Second, turning to the structuralism within Husserl's thought, Derrida focuses on Husserl's difference between exact and "anexact" essences (as Derrida prefers to call them) (ED 240–242/162). Dealing with the essences of consciousness, phenomenology is an anexact science, while mathematics, for example, dealing with essences of numbers, is exact. What defines exactitude, for Husserl, according to Derrida, is the possibility of closure. Closure means that an exact structure consists of an investigative domain that can be exhaustively determined. Even though it is possible to develop this domain infinitely—Derrida says that all exact essences arise on the basis of a process or idealization or infinitization, a passage to the limit (ED 241/162)[4]—these developments are not "creative" (cf. LOG 140/130); they are merely modifications of the object already outlined. In contrast, no such finite totality exists in phenomenology, according to Derrida, because of "the irruption of the infinite into consciousness" (ED 241/162). Although it permits the unification of consciousness's temporal flux as well as the unification of the object and world, an Idea in the Kantian sense produces an inexhaustibility that is not reducible to the infinite modification of an object; it produces an opening or a rupture.[5] On the basis of this discontinuity, an Idea in the Kantian sense renders every structural phenomenology incomplete; as Derrida says, "what we must retain here is the principled, essential, and structural impossibility of closing a structural phenomenology" (ED 242/162).

Third, Derrida turns to the differences within Husserl's well-known *Ideas I* formulation of intentionality (ED 242–244/162–164). Intentionality is a complex structure, as Derrida says, consisting of four poles and two correlations (noesis-noema, morphe-*hyle*). Organizing both correlations, a series of differences distinguishes the four poles. The noema, as Derrida says, "is distinguished in that [it] does not *réellement* belong to consciousness. *Within* (*dans*) consciousness in general, there is an agency (*une instance*) which *does not réellement* belong to it" (ED 242/162–163).[6] Consciousness, for Husserl, includes the noema within itself because the noema is not *real*. The noema is not a worldly fact, but an ideal sense intended by consciousness. Nevertheless, even though consciousness includes the noema, it is not a *reell* property of consciousness. As Derrida says, "[the noema] is neither of the world nor of consciousness, but it is the world or something of the world *for* consciousness" (ED 242/163). The noema does not really—in either sense of the word "real"—belong either to the world or to consciousness, even though it participates in both; it is therefore "the root and very possibility of objectivity and sense" (ED 243/163). That the noema does not originate in any region implies, as Derrida says, "an anarchy of the noema" (ED 243/163).[7] Just as the noema is an opening within the structure of consciousness, so is, according to Derrida, the hyletic pole. For Husserl, while the noema is non-*reell* but intentional, the *hyle* is non-intentional but *reell*.[8] As *reell*, the *hyle* is ideal not real; it participates in consciousness. Nevertheless, as non-intentional, it is not the same as consciousness and does not belong to consciousness. It comes from the outside, and precedes conscious constitution; it is something which consciousness receives passively. In *Ideas I,* Husserl himself admits that he cannot develop the issue, temporal constitution, which would be able to resolve the mysterious status of the *hyle.* Derrida therefore concludes by saying, "if [Husserl] renounces the examination of the possibilities entitled *formless materials and immaterial forms,* if he keeps to the constituted *hyle-morphic* correlation, it is that his analyses are still developed (and will they not always be so, in a certain way) from within a constituted temporality" (ED 243–244/163).[9]

Fourth, there is the difference between phenomenological psychology and transcendental phenomenology. As Derrida notes, Husserl conceives a phenomenological psychology that would exactly "parallel" transcendental phenomenology. The structures described on one level would be the same as on the other. Yet there must be a difference here, which, following Husserl's characterization of the relation as one of parallelism, Derrida characterizes as "the nothing" and as "distance"; strictly, there is nothing but space between parallel lines (ED 245–246/164). As Derrida notes, it is this very "nothing" which permits the transcendental reduction. Made possible by the transcendental reduction, transcendental phenomenology is then able to describe structures that are no longer mundane. Through the transcendental reduction, the phenomenologist proceeds to a level that is non-worldly, through which alone one can account for "the totality of

The Critique of Phenomenology 29

sense and the sense of totality," as Derrida says (ED 245/164). One proceeds, as Derrida explicitly quotes Fink, to "the origin of the world" (ED 246/164).[10] Therefore, an attempt by any type of psychology to account for the world would result in psychologism. Psychology would attempt to account for the world with something—the psychological ego—that is itself part of the world. Psychology's attempt would amount to "the crossing-over (*franchissement*) of the invisible difference which separates parallel things" (ED 245/164).

Revolving around a certain kind of difference, all four discussions reveal, as Derrida calls them, "the original characteristics of Husserl's attempt" (ED 232/157). Both the difference between wisdom and knowledge and the difference between exact and anexact essences refer to the notion of idealization or infinitization; the differences within the structure of intentionality refer to the notions of objectivity (noema) and temporalization (*hyle*); the difference between phenomenological psychology and transcendental phenomenology refers to the notion of parallelism. All of these original Husserlian concepts will be taken up again by Derrida and developed in *Voice and Phenomenon*. What most, however, permits us to see the development of Derrida's thought from the *Le Problème de la genèse* and the Introduction to *Voice and Phenomenon* are the revisions he made in the 1965 version of "'Genesis and Structure' and Phenomenology" for its 1967 re-publication in *Writing and Difference*.[11]

3

In both versions, Derrida's hypothesis is that Husserl's phenomenology relapses into dogmatic metaphysics, into "dialectic," in the sense that Husserl always sought to ascribe to the word. The basis for this claim, as we have seen, is that Husserl's philosophy of history, including texts such as the *Origin of Geometry*, describes a primitive teleological reason intending a future Idea in the Kantian sense, a correlation the poles of which lack adequate self-evidence. In the 1965 version, at the essay's conclusion, Derrida says that

> [The Idea in the Kantian sense] would signify the emergence of the
> metaphysical in the phenomenological. We see, however, that to desig-
> nate this incessant emergence *in phenomenology* rigorously is not to be
> left inundated by metaphysical dogmatism. [To want to designate it
> rigorously] is to want to respond from the consciousness where the

metaphysical announces itself, and from the discourse in which this anticipation is said. It is to want to stand watch upon the borders of phenomenology and metaphysics.

In the 1954 *Le Problème de la genèse* and in the 1962 *Introduction to Husserl's "The Origin of Geometry"*, what Derrida here calls "the emergence of the metaphysical in the phenomenological" is the emergence of the ontological in a non-Husserlian sense (that is, in a Heideggerian sense) out of phenomenology. Indeed, as we are going to see, both of these books respond to the basic phenomenological problem of genesis with a dialectic between Husserlian phenomenology and Heideggerian ontology. Yet by 1967, Derrida's positive utilization of Heidegger's term "ontology" has ended, primarily because of Derrida's investigation of Levinas, as we shall see in our investigation of "Violence and Metaphysics." Thus, in the 1967 version, without substituting any other sentence, Derrida entirely eliminates the "standing watch upon the borders of phenomenology and metaphysics" sentence (*Entretiens* 259; cf. ED 250/167).

This is not the only place in the essay, however, where Derrida speaks of the relation of phenomenology and metaphysics. In both versions, in the paragraph immediately prior to the deletion just mentioned, Derrida writes (and we quoted this passage above): "Despite all these classical notions, phenomenology does not *abdicate* itself for the benefit of a classical metaphysical speculation which on the contrary, according to Husserl, would have to recognize in phenomenology the clarified energies of its own intention" (ED 249/166; *Entretiens* 258). But then in 1967, Derrida interprets this claim with the following addition:

[To say that classical metaphysical speculation would have to see in phenomenology the clarified energies of its own intention] amounts to saying that in criticizing classical metaphysics, phenomenology accomplishes the most profound project of metaphysics. Husserl acknowledges or rather claims this himself, particularly in the *Cartesian Meditations*. The results of phenomenology are "metaphysical, if it be true that ultimate cognitions of being should be called metaphysical. On the other hand, what we have here is anything but metaphysics, in the customary sense; this metaphysics, degenerated during the course of history, does not at all conform to the spirit in which it was instituted as 'first philosophy.'" "Phenomenology eliminates only naive metaphysics . . . but it does not exclude metaphysics as such." (ED 249/166)[12]

The Critique of Phenomenology 31

Derrida will refer again to these passages from *Cartesian Meditations* in the Introduction to *Voice and Phenomenon*. While in the 1965 version Derrida sees metaphysics (or ontology) emerging from phenomenology and therefore in a dialectic with phenomenology, in the 1967 version he sees an identity between phenomenology and metaphysics as such.[13] As is well known, metaphysics as such, for Derrida, is the metaphysics of presence.[14] Thus, Derrida also inserts the following sentence in 1967, after discussing the problem of *hyle* in Husserl: "The constitution of the other and of time refer phenomenology to a zone in which its 'principle of all principles' (as we see it, its *metaphysical* principle: the original *self-evidence* and *presence* of the thing itself in person) is radically put into question" (ED 244/164).[15] This type of revision, which we shall see again in "Violence and Metaphysics,"[16] indicates a tension *within* Husserl's demand for evidential intuition or presence that Derrida will exploit in two ways as his thought develops. On the one hand, Derrida will criticize Husserl (and Levinas) for positing an end and origin of genesis for which he lacks intuitive evidence; on the other, Derrida will criticize Husserl for supposing that the end of genesis will be fully intuitable as such in the future. The first form of the critique depends on Husserl's intuitionism and his "principle of all principles"; it is a phenomenological critique turned against a lapse in Husserl's phenomenological vigilance. The second criticizes that very intuitionism and that very "principle of all principles." This second critique is a deconstruction of the metaphysics of presence. Because of the tension in Husserl's "principle of all principles," Derrida says, "[the Idea in the Kantian sense] is offered within phenomenological self-evidence as evidence of an essential overflowing of actual and adequate evidence. One would have to examine quite closely the intervention of the Idea in the Kantian sense at various points along Husserl's itinerary." This tension is also why, in 1967, Derrida adds one word to a sentence discussing the Idea; he now qualifies the Idea's presence with the adjective "strange." The strangeness of this presence will eventually lead Derrida to turn away from the epistemological concept of evidence as presence to the concept of experience that the closing pages of *Voice and Phenomenon* suggest, a concept of experience that comes from the Husserl who describes the constitution of time and the other. This concept of experience is why we are going to call the second critique a "super-phenomenological critique." The deconstruction of the metaphysics of presence is based in an experience of language.

For Derrida, the strangeness of the presence of an Idea in the Kantian sense is due to the fact that an Idea can be constituted only by means of a passage through signification. The internal necessity of language, of what is most generally called a sign, to every experience or thought is why Derrida adds, in 1967, the following:[17]

> In emerging from itself, hearing oneself speak constitutes itself as the history of reason through the detour of *writing*. *Thus it differs from itself in order to reappropriate itself*. The Origin of Geometry describes the necessity of this exposition of reason in a worldly inscription. An exposition indispensable to the constitution of truth and the ideality of objects, but which is also the danger to meaning from what is outside the sign. In the moment of writing, the sign can always "empty" itself, take flight from awakening, from "reactivation," and may remain forever closed and mute. As for Cournot, writing here is the "critical epoch."[18]

In order to be infinite, in order to be itself, in order to be, a sense must pass through a transition of writing, which, being bound to passivity, is dangerous.[19] As we shall see in the *Introduction,* writing produces a passage that is, simultaneously, discontinuous from and continuous with what went before, equivocal and univocal. Within this passage, there is at once (*à la fois* [cf. ED 235/158]) difference and identity; and the identity is such that, being indefinitely repeatable, it defers completion. This undecidability between genesis and structure, finitude and infinitude, between identity and difference, is why Derrida, in the 1967 version changed the word *différence,* as in the phrase *the différence between wisdom and knowledge,* into *différance* (ED 239/161; cf. *Entretiens* 251).[20] This revision indicates that on the basis of his investigation of *The Origin of Geometry,* Derrida is going to change the problem of genesis into the problem of the sign.

Within " 'Genesis and Structure' and Phenomenology," Derrida also describes the passage to infinity as "the structurality of the opening" (ED 230/155).[21] This phrase must be understood on the basis of the genitive. What is *in general,* as Derrida says at the end of " 'Genesis and Structure' and Phenomenology," precedes all the distinctions that Husserl dissociates in his analyses (ED 251/167): wisdom vs. knowledge, exact vs. anexact, *reell* vs. non-*reell, reell* vs. real, transcendental vs. psychological, etc.[22] It is the "nothing" which divides parallels or the "great opening" (*la béance* [ED 161/257]). The genus, therefore, is that on the basis of which "the transcendental reduction is possible" (ED 251/167). And thus, what the genitive in the "structurality of the opening" points to is "the common root" of the world and its origin (ED 235/158).[23] It constitutes what Derrida is going to call in *Voice and Phenomenon* "the ultra-transcendental concept of life."

3   The Critique of Ontology:
An Investigation of
"The Ends of Man"

The revisions Derrida made to "'Genesis and Structure'" for its inclusion in the 1967 *Writing and Difference* show that Derrida was in the process of rethinking the relation of phenomenology to metaphysics. In Derrida's 1968 "The Ends of Man," his "critique of phenomenology" is a critique of it as the metaphysics of presence. Here, in a "super-phenomenological critique," Derrida criticizes phenomenology because, while it recognizes the overflowing of evidence in an Idea in the Kantian sense, it still posits intuition, presence, absolute or perfect self-presence, as the origin and end of genesis. Derrida's critique of phenomenology really only takes one form: if we conceive archeology and teleology, *arche* and *telos,* as pure presence, as pure self-presentation as such, then archeology and teleology cannot define genesis, or, more precisely, do not respond to the problem of genesis. Husserlian phenomenology, however, does not hold center stage in "The Ends of Man." By 1968, everything turns on Heidegger—the discussion of Husserl in "The Ends of Man," in fact, occupies less than one page—especially insofar as Derrida attempts to conceive the outside or other of onto-theology, onto-theology being synonymous with the metaphysics of presence. Nevertheless, Derrida's "sketch" of "the hold [*la prise*] which the humanity of man keeps on the thought of being" amounts to a critique of "the thought of the truth of being." Derrida's critique of phenomenology simultaneously criticizes Heidegger's ontology.[1] Both phenomenology and ontology fall prey to the "profound necessity" (MP 158/ 131), which is at the bottom of Derrida's critique of teleology and archeology: although the *transcendens* pure and simple, being must be expressed in beings; being never appears as such, neither at the origin nor at the end. Similarly, as Fink's essay already implied, the transcendental in Husserl, although extra-mundane, must be expressed in the mundane; the transcendental never appears as such, neither at the origin nor at the end. Not taking account of this necessity, one falls prey to a naiveté, a naiveté so profound that one does not have the slightest chance of escaping from the "hold" of humanism and onto-theology. Because even Heidegger falls prey to this naiveté, because, in short, Heidegger's thought is teleological (like that of Husserl *and* Hegel), Derrida resorts to Nietzsche. Only Nietzsche in the doctrine of eternal recurrence conceives an end of man not organized "by a dialectics of truth and negativity" (cf. MP 144/121).[2] As we shall see, before "The Ends of Man," Derrida had already in the 1964 "Violence and Metaphysics" resorted to Levinas in order to criticize Heideggerian ontology. As a result of the investigation of Levinas, it seems that Derrida's thought eventually evolves into what we will call an "amalgamation" of Levinas and Nietzsche. Levinas of course is not the philosopher of the overman, but the philosopher of the other man.

1

The organizers of the conference for which Derrida wrote "The Ends of Man" asked him to address this question: "Where is France, as concerns man?" (MP 135/114). In order to answer this question, Derrida summarizes approximately thirty years of French philosophy. It is well known that immediately before World War II and up to the late sixties, two movements dominated French thought: existentialism and structuralism. Both movements tried to exit from the tradition of Western metaphysics; both movements based themselves in a certain reading of phenomenology, that is, of Hegel, Husserl, and Heidegger. Existentialism tried to exit metaphysics by defining human reality in a non-substantial manner; no essence (or structure) determines man's existence. Existentialism therefore was a humanism; and what the existentialists saw in phenomenology was a non-metaphysical humanism (MP 136/115). In contrast, structuralism tried to exit metaphysics by defining language as a structure; the system of language determines man's existence. Structuralism therefore was an anti-humanism; and what the structuralists saw in phenomenology was "the old metaphysical humanism" (MP 141/119). For Derrida, although the anthropologistic reading of phenomenology found in existentialism (MP 139/117) as well as the structuralist "amalgamation"[3] of phenomenology with the old metaphysical humanism (MP 141/119) were mistakes—they were mistakes insofar as they both missed phenomenology's critique of humanism—they were nevertheless justified. They were justified not because of the obvious and perhaps accidental humanistic comments that can be found in all three phenomenologists, but because of a structural necessity. Derrida in fact calls this necessity "subterranean"; a subterranean necessity "makes the Hegelian, Husserlian, and Heideggerian critiques or *de-limitations* of metaphysical humanism appear to belong to the very sphere of that which they criticize or delimit" (MP 142/119, Derrida's emphasis). The topic of "The Ends of Man," therefore, is this necessity that lies below any attempt to change terrains from metaphysics (MP 163/135), this necessity which "holds" (*prend*) one on the "same shore" as metaphysics even as one attempts to depart from it (MP 141/119).[4] Derrida's question is: "What is the re-elevation [*relève*] of man in the thought of Hegel, Husserl, and Heidegger" (MP 142/119)?

As we claimed above, in "The Ends of Man," Heidegger's ontology holds center stage. Nevertheless, Derrida devotes one section to Hegel and Husserl (with, as we just mentioned, Husserl receiving about a page of discussion). Derrida examines Hegel and Husserl together because the topic of this section—called "La Fin—Proche de l'Homme"—is phenomenology, "the thought of the *phainesthai*" (MP 112/145, my emphasis). Nevertheless, as Derrida will show in his discussion of Heidegger, the thought of being depends on the thought of the phenomenon. Thus the discussions of Hegel and Husserl's phenomenology set up the basic structural necessity that Derrida finds in Heidegger. It sets up "the hold" (*la prise*), which is also the same basic structural unity or schema that defines *the* metaphysics, that is, the metaphysics of presence, for Derrida. For both Hegel and Husserl, the thought of man, anthropology, is teleologically directed to the thought of the phenomenon (phenomeno-logy): "Man is that which is in relation to his end" (MP 147/123). While Husserl defines the teleological relation between anthropology and phenomenology in terms of an Idea in the Kantian sense, Hegel defines it with the term "aufheben," which Derrida translates with the French term "relever" (and which I have roughly translated above as "re-elevation"): "*Aufheben* is *relever*, in the sense in which *relever* can combine to relieve, to displace, to elevate, to replace and to promote, in one and the same movement" (MP 143/121). What is most important here, for Derrida, is that this *relève* implies that the relation between phenomenology and anthropology cannot be external (MP 142/120); since the relation is not external, the relation must be equivocal (MP 144/121). This "equivocal relation," according to Derrida, "marks the end of man, man past, but by the same token it also marks the completion of man, the appropriation of his essence. It is the end of finite man" (MP 144/121;

MP 147/123); in other words, the end of man, in the sense of mortality, is the end of man, in the sense of perfection. For Hegel, but one could make similar claims for Husserl based on his concept of transcendental intersubjectivity, these two senses of "end" are unified in the "we" which narrates *The Phenomenology of Spirit*: "The *we* is the unity of absolute knowledge and anthropology, of God and man, of onto-theo-teleology and humanism. '*Being*' and language—the groups of languages—that the *we* govern or opens: such is the name of what assures the passage between metaphysics and humanism through the *we*" (MP 144/121). Being here for Derrida is presence, or, more precisely, proximity; hence the title that Derrida gives to this section. Being as proximity implies a "value" (MP 161/134)—a dogmatism (as we saw in "'Genesis and Structure' and Phenomenology")—interfering with the subterranean necessity. This interference or preference for presence and proximity transforms the necessity, which was equivocal, into a unified sense: "the *unity* of absolute knowledge and anthropology." This unified sense, univocity instead of equivocity, defines metaphysics or onto-theology, for Derrida, "since always" (MP 147/123). Metaphysics for Derrida is always Greek: "The unity of these two *ends* of man, the unity of his death, his completion, his accomplishment, is enveloped in the Greek thought of *telos*, in the discourse on *telos*, which is also a discourse on *eidos*, on *ousia*, and on *aletheia*" (MP 144/121, Derrida's emphasis).

2

According to Derrida, we find the same "we," the same "eschato-teleological situation" in Heidegger. Yet according to Derrida, the question of the "we" in Heidegger is "the most difficult" (MP 147/123). It is the most difficult question because *Dasein* in *Being and Time* is not the metaphysical man, because the "The Letter on Humanism" delimits metaphysical humanism better than any other text, because Heidegger sketches out "the genesis of the concept and the value of man" with "archeological radicalness" (MP 153/128). Nevertheless, Derrida is going to "sketch out the forms of the hold [*la prise*] which the humanity of man keeps on the thought of being, a certain humanism on the truth of Being" (MP 148/123–124). This "hold," however for Derrida, is not "a mastery or an ontic relation in general" (MP 148/124). The relation of *prendre* is the subterranean necessity that, for Derrida, makes the delimitations of metaphysical humanism belong to the sphere of what they delimit. Nevertheless, Derrida calls it "a kind of magnetic attraction [*aimantation*]" between "the thought of what is proper to man" and "the question or truth of being" (MP 148/124). The "metaphor" of magnetism implies attraction, "action at a distance," and thereby anticipates the discussion of Nietzsche with which Derrida will conclude "The Ends of Man." Nevertheless, what is to be investigated now is "this magnetic attraction [in Heidegger] beneath the general concept of proximity" (MP 148/124).

In *Being and Time* (paragraph 2), Heidegger poses the question of the sense of being in its formal structure. For Heidegger, the inquiry into the sense of being is possible only because the sense of being is "always already" available to "us" in some way (quoted in MP 149/124). For Derrida, Heidegger most basically determines this "us" or "we" as the being who can always already understand being; this always prior understanding of being is the "fact" with which Heidegger starts (MP 149/125). The fact, however, according to Derrida, inscribes the formal structure of the ontological question "within the Indo-European linguistic milieu, to the possibility of which the origin of metaphysics is linked" (MP 149/125). Thus it seems that the Indo-European linguistic milieu is prior to and limits the ontological question; nevertheless, these limits do not eliminate the priority of the question: "the sense of these [Indo-European] limits is given to us only after the question of the sense of being" (MP 149/125). For Derrida, the relations of dependence between empirical facts and transcendental essences are far from linear; they define "the hold" (*la prise*).

For Heidegger, the always prior understanding of being makes "us" be the "exemplary being," or, as Derrida says, makes us be "the privileged text for a reading of the sense of being" (MP 149/125). Because our being is present to us, because we are close to ourselves, we interrogate ourselves about the sense of being. But for Derrida, what intervenes in the determination of the fact is "phenomenology's principle of all principles, the principle of presence and of presence in self-presence, such as it is manifested to the being and in the being that *we* are, . . . this self-presence, this absolute proximity of the (questioning) being to itself, this familiarity with itself of the being ready to understand being, . . . motivates the choice of the exemplary being, of the text, of the good text for the hermeneutics of the sense of being" (MP 150/125–126). Derrida immediately qualifies this connection of fundamental ontology to phenomenology by saying that *Dasein*'s self-presence "does not have the form of subjective consciousness, as in transcendental phenomenology" (MP 151/126). In other words, the *Da* of *Dasein* is something radically different from the form of subjective consciousness as well as from what the metaphysical predicate "human" might name. The *Da* of *Dasein* is prior to both man and subjective consciousness. For Heidegger, only after a re-reading of the question of being can one determine the *Da* of *Dasein* "as a presence near to itself" (MP 151/126). "Nevertheless," Derrida says, the question of the sense of being is defined as a making explicit of what is implicit.[5] Heidegger's reading of the text of *Dasein* is "a hermeneutics of unveiling or development"; his "style of reading . . . practices a continual bringing to light, something which resembles, at least a *prise de conscience,* without break, displacement, or change of terrain" (MP 151/126).[6] This "style of reading," according to Derrida, seems to make Heidegger's fundamental ontology again be dependent on or come after phenomenological consciousness and presence: the truth of being hidden in *Dasein*'s veils must be brought out, exposed, put in the light, held near, made present. This connection between being and presence, more precisely between being and truth and phenomenon, allows Derrida to identify ontology with phenomenology; it allows for any sort of dialogue between phenomenology and ontology.[7]

That Heidegger's hermeneutics of *Dasein* aims not at *Dasein* itself but at the sense hidden within *Dasein* implies that Heidegger does not fall into a "vicious circle," which "consists of first determining a being in its being, and then of posing the question of being on the basis of this ontological predetermination" (MP 151/126). "Nevertheless," Derrida says again (MP 151/126), because Heidegger must use the name "man" to speak of *Dasein,* it seems as though Heidegger falls precisely into such a vicious circle. The paleonym "man" "ties the analytic of *Dasein* to the totality of metaphysics' traditional discourse" (MP 151/127). While Heidegger wants to ascend back up to the far side of the metaphysical concept of *humanitas,* in fact, his discourse, using the name "man," enacting a repetition of the essence of man, remains dependent on this concept. As Derrida says, "We see therefore that *Dasein,* if he is *not* man, is *nothing other than* man" (MP 151/127, Derrida's emphasis).

The *value of proximity or of presence* in general therefore dominates "the equivocality of this gesture" in Heidegger, according to Derrida so that we see the early Heidegger, like Hegel and Husserl, remains caught (*pris*) in onto-theology. But the connection between the later Heidegger, the Heidegger of "The Letter on Humanism," and the early Heidegger is that

Heidegger in *Being and Time* says that, for *Dasein,* being is ontically closest but ontologically farthest. For Derrida, this claim implies not only that Heidegger's entire thought of the truth of being—both early and later— concerns itself with reducing the ontological distance; to have being ontologically close by is, for Heidegger, what is proper to man. It also implies that we must conceive the notion of proximity in Heidegger according to the ontological difference (MP 152/127). To conceive proximity ontologically means that one must recognize that being, in Heidegger, is nothing, is not a being, and is nameless. Nevertheless, being can only, that is, *must* be said in ontic metaphors (MP 157/131; cf. 153/128). This necessity to say "nothing" is why Derrida stresses Heidegger's metaphorics, in particular, his phenomenological metaphorics; *phainesthai,* shining, lighting, clearing, *Lichtung* as well as voice, listening are all attempts to say being, that is, presence in a more originary sense than its metaphysical or ontic determinations based on the present (MP 158/132).

These metaphors are supposed to lead us to conceive "the near" and "the proper" "before [*avant*] the opposition of space and time, according to the opening of a *spacing* which *belongs* neither to time nor to space, and which dislocates, while producing it, any presence of the presence" (MP 160/133, Derrida's emphasis). Being *before* any metaphysical sense, Heidegger's comments about the near and the proper of man cannot be taken (*pris*) or understood (*compris*) in the sense of "an essential attribute, the predicate of a substance, a characteristic among others, however fundamental, of a being, object or subject, called man" (MP 160/133). Minimally, however, the proper, the propriety of man and being, according to Derrida, means inseparability. Derrida says, "*But* [my emphasis] it is indeed as inseparability that the relations between being (substance, or *res*) and its essential predicate were thought in metaphysics *afterward* [Derrida's emphasis]" (MP 160/133). Not only does Heidegger's thought of the truth of being seem to depend on onto-theology—it belongs to onto-theology without belonging to it—it also seems again to depend on phenomenology, which reduces all things down to their sense. Although the relation of proximity between man and being cannot be described as a relation between two beings, it is a relation between two senses. As Derrida says, "The proper of man, his *Eigenheit,* his 'authenticity,' is to be related to the sense of being; he is to hear and to question (*fragen*) it in ek-sistence, to stand erect in the proximity of its light" (MP 160/133). Even the later Heidegger "can only metaphorize, by means of a profound necessity from which one cannot simply decide to escape, the language that it deconstructs" (MP 158/131).

3

It is well known that Derrida concludes this essay—here he is still trying to respond to the question the conference organizers asked him to address (MP 161/134)—with three comments; in fact, these are some of the most famous comments Derrida has ever made. We shall examine them briefly. In the first comment, Derrida claims that French thought (in 1968) is attempting to make "the security of the near," "the co-belonging of the name of man and the name of being" tremble by paying attention "to system and structure in its most original and strongest aspects" (MP 161/134).[8] According to Derrida, when structure is investigated in its most original and strongest aspects, it neither restores the classical, that is, onto-theological, interpretation of systematicity—an interpretation which claims that the value of *telos*, of *aletheia*, and of *ousia*, order the sense or direction (*sens*) of the system—nor does it destroy sense. This interpretation of a system keeps the system itself closed; instead, for Derrida, according to "the attention given to structure in its most original and strongest aspects," the structure is open. It is open because the system itself of sense is nonsense, not in the sense of absurdity or countersense ("the circle is square"), but in the sense of having no sense at all. This non-sense is why Derrida calls this first comment "The Reduction of Sense"; such a reduction of sense must "first [take] the form of a critique of phenomenology," which only enacted a "reduction to sense." (MP 162/134). Here Derrida is referring to what he had just shown a year earlier in *Voice and Phenomenon* (1967); as we shall see, the critique of the concept of sense, for Derrida, is really a critique of sense conceived as "relation to an object," that is, sense limited to knowledge. But, as we said, phenomenology does not hold center stage in "The Ends of Man." Therefore, this critique (which Derrida had already started in "Violence and Metaphysics") is really directed at Heidegger. So Derrida claims here that since Heidegger's destruction of metaphysical humanism "was produced initially on the basis of a *hermeneutical* question on the *sense* or the *truth* of being," the reduction of sense is going to have to work by means of "a sort of break with the thought of being, which has all the characteristics of a *relève* (*Aufhebung*) of humanism" (MP 162/134). As we shall see in Chapter 8, this critique of "the thought of being" which centers on *the question of sense* is crucial for determining all of Derrida's later work.

The similarity of Heideggerian destruction to the Hegelian *Aufhebung* leads to Derrida's second comment. The trembling of the near, which the attention paid "to system and structure in its most original and strongest aspects" brings about, "can only come from the outside" (MP 162/134). So the question is: how to exit to the outside? This is a pressing question for Derrida because "the 'logic' of every relation to the outside is very complex and surprising [*surprenante*]" (MP 162/135). This comment refers us back to the subterranean, structural, profound, or even "anonymous" (MP 161/134) necessity that is the topic of "The Ends of Man." One can always be taken, taken over, taken back, violated, in this "violent" relation between onto-theology or "the whole of the West" and its other (MP 162/134).[9] The violence of this relation is why it is necessary to strategize, to calculate probability, to take a chance. As is well known, for Derrida, this calculation involves two strategies. The first, the Heideggerian sort, attempts to exit without changing terrain; it is a continuous process of making explicit, which has the risk of "ceaselessly confirming, consolidating, *relever*, at an always more certain depth, that which one allegedly deconstructs" (MP 162/135). The second, "the one which dominates France today [in 1968]," is a decision to change terrain, "in a discontinuous and irruptive fashion," which always risks being "caught" (*pris*) by the simple practice of language and therefore reinstated on the oldest ground (MP 162–163/135).[10] The choice between strategies, of which Derrida speaks, does not derive (*relève*) from an *Aufhebung* of the two strategies but from a plurality of styles. This plurality is why Derrida turns to Nietzsche in the third comment.

This third comment is extremely important and we shall return to it in Chapter 8. It is extremely important not only for understanding Derrida's later philosophy (such as it is presented, for example, in *Specters of Marx*), but also for determining Derrida's uniqueness in the French philosophy of the sixties. At this moment in French thought, as is well known, there is a massive interest in Nietzsche coming from Deleuze, Foucault, and Klossowski. Like these three philosophers, Derrida too resorts to a reading of Nietzsche that does not characterize Nietzsche, as Heidegger's reading does, as "the last metaphysician." But, unlike them—and we could see this as well in *Spurs* if we were to investigate it—Derrida does not embrace *a* or *one* Nietzsche. For Derrida, there are two Nietzsches (as there are two Husserls). So Derrida speaks of "the distribution" (*le partage*) between two re-elevations of man in Nietzsche between the superior man and the superman (MP 163/135). The subterranean necessity which is the principal concept of this essay, and which we shall see developed fully in the *Intro-*

duction, implies that, in Nietzsche, the superior man, who is a humanist, and the overman, who is an anti-humanist, are inseparable. There is an inseparability between, Derrida says, "two ends of man" (MP 164/136). It is only through this inseparability of a double necessity that we can, for Derrida, conceive the end of man that would not be a teleology of the first person plural (MP 144/121).

4

This discussion completes our general investigation of Derrida's thought in relation to phenomenology and ontology. This general investigation has allowed us to see three aspects of Derrida's interpretation of Husserl. First, we were also able to see, through the investigation of "'Genesis and Structure' and Phenomenology," the type of critique on which deconstruction is based. On the one hand, there is always a kind of enlightenment in deconstruction that relies on presence, that relies on what Derrida will call "the violence of light" in "Violence and Metaphysics"; deconstruction, like phenomenology, criticizes dogmatic metaphysics. But there is another critique in deconstruction; this other critique we saw in particular in the revisions. This second critique is directed at the value of presence; but even here deconstruction, as we shall see, relies on a kind of experience and thus we can call it a kind of "super-phenomenological critique." As Derrida intimated in "'Genesis and Structure,'" this experience is an experience opened up by the Husserl who describes time and the other: the experience of language. This critique is going to bring phenomenology to an end for Derrida. But second, we saw in "The Ends of Man" that for Derrida the super-phenomenological critique also brings ontology to an end. The experience of language that supports the super-phenomenological critique is an experience of what Derrida here is calling "the subterranean necessity." By necessity, man and spirit, man and transcendental consciousness, man and *Dasein,* man and superman, man and the other man, and the two ends of man are for Derrida necessarily united. This necessity is more fundamental, deeper, below the ontology that asks the question of the sense of being. Moreover—but this turn is still far away for us—the end of the ontology also starts Derrida's turn from the question to the promise. In any case, we saw one more aspect of Derrida's interpretation of Husserl. So, third, through our investigation of Fink's famous *Kantstüdien* article, we were able to see that Derrida's reading of Husserl is not a renegade reading, but it rather stands within an incontestable tradition of Husserl interpretation that starts with Fink and then, as we are going to see now, passes through Tran-Duc-Thao and Cavaillès to Derrida;[11] this tradition orients itself toward paradoxes, paradoxes that arise from the basic problem of phenomenology: the problem of genesis.

Part Two.
The "Originary Dialectic" of Phenomenology and Ontology

4   Upping the Ante on Dialectic: An Investigation of *Le Problème de la genèse dans la philosophie de Husserl*

In Derrida's first investigation of Husserl, his *Mémoire* from the academic year 1953–54, *Le Problème de la genèse dans la philosophie de Husserl* (only published in 1990), his critique of phenomenology, his critique of its teleology and its archeology, is already in place. According to *Le Problème de la genèse*, the problem of genesis in Husserl's philosophy is the passage between "primitive existence" and "originary sense" (PGH 31). Derrida is going to claim that Husserl was able to conceive this passage only in terms of a "debate." He was not able to see beyond "alternation," "confusion," and "ambiguity." In turn, he was able to respond to the "dilemma" or "aporia" only with reconciliation and resolution; he could only decide. The hypothesis Derrida tries to confirm in "'Genesis and Structure'" (as we have seen) is here confirmed in detail. Even when Husserl seems most geneticist, in his last "historical" writings, the notion of an Idea in the Kantian sense tames the real. His "history of philosophy" is mixed with a "philosophy of history."[1] Husserl, for Derrida, remains therefore bound to a rationalist and idealist tradition (PGH 41, 217). Derrida's critique in *Le Problème de la genèse* is a phenomenological critique of a certain Husserlian dogmatism.

In 1953–54, the positive result of this critique is what Derrida calls an "originary dialectic" (PGH 9; cf. 166). Unlike the active, essential, ideal constitution at which Husserl aims his analyses, Derrida's originary dialectic is not pure. Derrida realizes that, no matter how complete, the transcendental reduction cannot completely eliminate the "already constituted" and reach the origin of the world. Indicated by the retentional phase of time-consciousness and by passive synthesis, a sensuous, empirical, actual kernel—in a word, history—is always "already there" before transcendental constitution. Thus, Derrida describes what is absolute as "an originary and dialectical synthesis of being and time" (PGH 40). Obviously, by utilizing a phrase like "being and time," already in 1954 a reading of Heidegger guides Derrida's critique of Husserlian phenomenology. Yet, apparently, this reading is not profound; it does not exhibit the deep understanding of Heidegger that appears in 1964 with "Violence and Metaphysics." In fact, Derrida's understanding of Heidegger here in *Le Problème de la genèse* seems virtually identical to the French humanistic readings discussed in "The Ends of Man." Therefore, Derrida's "originary dialectic of being and time" (PGH 40) is an originary dialectic involving the being named "man" (PGH 41).[2]

Although Sartre probably influenced Derrida's early reading of Heidegger (cf. PGH 2),[3] Derrida does not intend to "up the ante" on Sartre's dialectic of being and nothingness. Instead, he wants to up the ante on the dialectics proposed by two contemporary Husserl interpreters: Tran-Duc-Thao and Jean Cavaillès.[4] On the basis of the ambiguities found in Husserl's thought—ambiguities between the ideal and the real, essence and fact, logic and sensation—both Tran-Duc-Thao and Cavaillès, before Derrida, had already discovered basic dialectics. Remaining faithful to Fink's determination of Husserlian phenomenology's basic problem, Derrida claims that their dialectics are worldly. Derrida's dialectic therefore is "competitive." It does not reduce the ideal to the real like that of Tran-Duc-Thao's dialectical materialism; while recognizing the essential solidarity between logic and sensation, Derrida's dialectic does not succumb to empiricism. Derrida's dialectic is "adverserial." It does not absorb the real into the ideal like Cavaillès's theory of science; while recognizing the essential distinction between logic and sensation, Derrida's dialectic does not succumb to logicism. Instead, Derrida's dialectic "bids over" those of Tran-Duc-Thao and Cavaillès by simultaneously maintaining a distinction and a solidarity between the real and the ideal. Consequently, what one most sees in *Le Problème de la genèse* is "A 'dialectical' upping the ante (*une surenchère 'dialectique'*) beyond dialectical materialism (for example, that of Tran-Duc-Thao . . .) or beyond the dialectic that Cavaillès believes that he has to invoke against Husserl . . . " (PGH vii).[5] Undoubtedly, at this time, in the 1950s, Tran-Duc-Thao and Cavaillès provide for Derrida new ways to think beyond Husserl's phenomenology, but, as he penetrates more deeply into Heidegger and encounters Levinas, their importance wanes. Indeed, while one might make a case that Tran-Duc-Thao's Marxism distantly informs *Specters of Marx* and Cavaillès's mathematical reflections distantly inform Derrida's concept of undecidability, their importance is limited to this first period of Derrida's thought, prior to "Violence and Metaphysics" (1964). Nevertheless, since Derrida himself claims that, in *Le Problème de la genèse,* he was upping the ante on the dialectics of Tran-Duc-Thao and Cavaillès, we must investigate their respective dialectics. We shall begin with Tran-Duc-Thao.

1

In his 1949 "Existentialisme et matérialisme dialectique," Tran-Duc-Thao advocates a concrete philosophy in opposition to the then prevalent existentialist philosophy.[6] Abstraction dominates existentialist philosophy, according to Tran-Duc-Thao, because it adheres to phenomenology's theory. The cornerstone of Husserl's theory, the *epoché,* allows Husserl to posit the transcendental ego "outside of the world."[7] While Heidegger, in turn, makes progress over Husserl by recognizing that Husserl's transcendental ego is "a concrete and temporal self," by recognizing, according to Tran-Duc-Thao, that being-in-the-world has to be analyzed in terms of "human reality," Heidegger, for Tran-Duc-Thao, does not go far enough. Although identified with human reality, Heidegger's being-in-the-world is still subjective. Rather than the world founding the real human subject, *Dasein* founds the world.[8] Phenomenological theory's subjectivism, therefore, is why existentialism ends up conceiving human existence as "a nothingness."[9]

In contrast, however, to explicit phenomenological doctrine, phenomenological practice, according to Tran-Duc-Thao, can provide results different from subjectivism.[10] If pursued, such analyses, more faithful to phenomenology than its theory, would show that every human life, "my life," as Tran-Duc-Thao says, was conditioned by "a certain *milieu,* certain social structures, and a certain material organization, that [my life] is meaningful only within these conditions, and that I must protect them if I want my life to keep this meaning."[11] These conditions are not ones that I have chosen; the arbitrariness of a subjective decision cannot account for them.[12] Thus they are "objective," but not in the sense of a world of ideas existing in-itself; rather, these structures belong to this world.[13] What one must, therefore, investigate, according to Tran-Duc-Thao, is "a material world"; as he says, "material being envelops all the significations of life, as life in *this world.* The moment of materiality constitutes the *infrastructure* of human life, as the last foundation of every properly human meaning."[14] For

Tran-Duc-Thao, only dialectical materialism can analyze these real infra-structures.[15]

Carrying out what was only programmatically described in "Existentialisme et matérialisme dialectique," *Phénoménologie et matérialisme dialectique* presents (in particular, in Part I) a reading of Husserl's then-known works, both published and unpublished.[16] Everything turns, for Tran-Duc-Thao, on Husserl's Third Investigation notion of foundation (cf. PMD 25/4). Although, as Tran-Duc-Thao says, "[The concept of foundation in Husserl] is not a matter of deriving the intelligible from the sensible, in the manner of the empiricists, since it belongs to the essence of 'founded' acts to intend radically new objects" (PMD 47/17), nevertheless, the Third Investigation taken in conjunction with the Sixth Investigation's notion of categorical intuition shows that it is impossible to separate essences entirely from sensuous kernels (PMD 46/16, 31/8, 63/28). On the basis of this inseparability, Tran-Duc-Thao isolates three "ambiguities" within Husserl's phenomenological theory.[17]

The first, according to Tran-Duc-Thao, can be found within Husserl's notion of consciousness; Tran-Duc-Thao stresses that Husserl's presentation of this notion in the Göttingen lectures and in *Ideas I* combines both Kantian language—conditions for possibility of experience—and Cartesian language—the *cogito* (PMD 52–53/21–22).[18] This duality implies, according to Tran-Duc-Thao, that consciousness, for Husserl, is both "an absolutely original domain, posited outside of all worldly existence" (PMD 61/26) and "a concrete subjectivity" (PMD 58/25).[19] The second ambiguity, for Tran-Duc-Thao, lies within Husserl's notion of constitution. The doctrine of constitution simultaneously seeks to make transcendence relative to consciousness—this claim is based on the description of the thing in *Ideas I*—and—so it seems on the basis of the Fifth Cartesian Meditation and *Ideas II*—to keep the transcendence of others absolute to consciousness (PMD 96/48–49).[20] As Tran-Duc-Thao says, the notion of constitution in Husserl, therefore, is "obscure" (PMD 96/48–49).

Already indicated by the first two, the third ambiguity is the most basic, an ambiguity within Husserl's notion of an object. Traditional philosophy, according to Tran-Duc-Thao, establishes an opposition between the object of perception and the object (or content) of judgment (PMD 100/51). The object of judgment remains the same for everyone at all times. It is universal and eternal; it does not vary according to the situation of the self which posits it (PMD 104/54). In short, it is an ideal object (PMD 102/53). In contrast, the object of perception is real. It is a singular object possess-

ing a unique existence (PMD 102/52). The perceptual object is "what I perceive and whose singularity refers, in the final analysis, to my actual singularity" (PMD 102/53); it exists contemporaneously with my existence
(PMD 101/52). Despite the temporal nature of consciousness and, in particular, despite the role of memory, "the issue," according to Tran-Duc-
Thao, "is *this* singular existence, which, once past, can no longer be perceived but only remembered" (PMD 102/53). In regard to this traditional
opposition, Husserl's originality is based "precisely on a radically new conception of the relations of knowledge and (even more generally) of the
relation of thought to being" (PMD 98/50). What Husserl shows, according to Tran-Duc-Thao, is that the object of judgment is a claim that refers
back to its founding intentionality (PMD 104/54). Because the founding
act is a sensible intuition of a thing, universality refers back to singularity
and eternity refers back to what takes place in a moment. As Tran-Duc-
Thao says, and this is almost a rallying cry for him (one adopted from
Experience and Judgment), "omnitemporality is itself but a mode of temporality" (PMD 107/55). The perceptual object, therefore according to Tran-
Duc-Thao, is "an actuality . . . irreducibly in opposition to the ideality of
the object of judgment," but a judgment is nevertheless constituted only
on the basis of perception's original structure (PMD 100/51).

    The ambiguity within Husserl's notion of objectivity points to the heart
of the matter: the genesis of knowledge.[21] According to Tran-Duc-Thao,
what leads Husserl to the genetic problem is error's relationship to truth.
Just as there can be no thing-in-itself, for Husserl, there can be no truth-
in-itself. Although this denial is obvious—it defines phenomenology as
such—the lack of truth-in-itself implies that all truth arises out of experience or perception. Truth, therefore, for Husserl, is an achievement, performance, or, as Tran-Duc-Thao prefers to translate Husserl's *Leistung*, a
production (PDM 130–131/71–72).[22] The possibility of error resides in the
fact, according to Tran-Duc-Thao, that one can always characterize what
one perceives (PMD 145–146/78). Although arising in sensible perception,
characterization allows what is merely subjectively perceived to be made
into an object or noematic meaning; characterization permits the passage
from the sensible to the intelligible. This transition from the subjective to
the objective can be seen most easily, according to Tran-Duc-Thao, in the
case of ideal objects such as those found in geometry (PMD 155–157/83–85).
As in the perception of a sensible thing, the production of a geometrical
object starts from seeing something here and now, but, as Tran-Duc-Thao
says, "[the geometer] considers in the sensible given only what can be

construed through concepts" (PMD 154–155/83). The "originary creation" takes place when the geometer "projects an infinite horizon of possible operations in which geometrical being is defined as the *truth* of real forms" (PMD 155/83). This projection implies, as Tran-Duc-Thao says, "a negation of the sensible figure as such and the figure's absorption in a rational construction" (PMD 155/83). Absorbed, the figure becomes "independent of the acts of the consciousness which intend it" (PMD 152–153/83); it becomes an ideal object, universally and eternally valid, indefinitely repeatable, a permanent acquisition or possession (PMD 151–152/82, 155/83). Nevertheless, and this is true of a sensible object as well, independence permits the ideal object to pass over into symbolic representation. Separated from originary intuition, a verbal symbol can, as Tran-Duc-Thao says, "be reduced to a *flatis vocis*, which represents nothing of the object itself" (PMD 147/79). This is where error can occur: while representing nothing of the object itself, the empty symbolic representation can still function, things can still be proved on the basis of the empty theorems, even progress can be made in the geometrical science. Thus, a geometry student, for example, can be content with learning the mere manipulation of geometrical symbols without going back to geometry's originary acts of creation; but then, being distant from the intentions that originally animated the theorems, he can, during the course of a proof, mistakenly take the triangle's sensible representations for the triangle itself. Separation has enabled him to forget the very meaning of triangularity, its basic characteristic as intelligible or non-sensible. As Tran-Duc-Thao stresses, "such forgetfulness is not produced by simple oversight: the possibility of it is implicit in [the ideal object's] very meaning as *always valid*" (PMD 155/83). Therefore, for Husserl, error and truth are—this is Tran-Duc-Thao's word —"contemporaneous" (PMD 151/82).

The mere manipulation of symbolic expressions, in a word, error, necessitates then for Husserl that one reactivate the original act, which remains always present beneath its sedimentations (PMD 175/97). As Tran-Duc-Thao stresses, Husserl's well-known genetic descriptions—these descriptions would be genetic phenomenology's practice, not its theory—always uncover an irreducible relation of the ideal to what is sensible. Husserl's attempt, in *Formal and Transcendental Logic,* for example, to trace logic and mathematics back to pre-predicative experience implies that even the most abstract ontological regions are founded on sensible kernels (PMD 196/110–111, 208/117); similarly, Husserl's attempt to describe the genesis of judgments in pre-predicative experience, in *Experience and Judgment*,[23] implies that ideal significations come about through a passive preconstitution. For Tran-Duc-Thao, the ineradicable relation to sensation, described in these texts, implies that the ideal, abstract, or intelligible arises in a linear fashion from the sensible, concrete, or actual. As Tran-Duc-Thao says, "in the final analysis, it is always in *real sensible work* that the most elevated notions find the ultimate foundation of their intelligible meaning and their truth value" (PMD 208/117). The real is prior to the ideal, according to Tran-Duc-Thao, because "the identity of the two egos [that is, the transcendental ego and the empirical ego] is unquestionable" (PMD 204/115). Thus, the constituting, as Tran-Duc-Thao goes on to say, is "homogeneous with the sensible given from the beginning, which [this constituting] is going to raise to the level of intelligibility." To return to Tran-Duc-Thao's rallying cry, "omnitemporality is itself but a mode of temporality" (PMD 204/115). And not only for Tran-Duc-Thao is Husserlian temporalization centered around the actuality of the present, it is also itself an abstraction from the real world (PMD 143–144n1/230n5).[24]

Phenomenology's pursuit of genesis, therefore, results in an *aporia* which it itself cannot solve: how can pre-predicative experience extract a determination from the undifferentiated unity of a thing without already possessing a sense of this determination itself (PMD 219/124)? According to phenomenology's theory, pre-predicative experience is supposed to be basic, original, transcendental. Yet according to its practice, transcendental subjectivity always seems to presuppose what it is supposed to produce. For Tran-Duc-Thao, phenomenological analysis always shows that active constitution must presuppose the passive reception of a sensation, that active constitution must presuppose some sort of objective structure which serves as its guiding thread. According to Tran-Duc-Thao, we must ask: where do the sensation and the guiding thread come from? This *aporia* leads, according to Tran-Duc-Thao, to "insurmountable difficulties" for phenomenology, insurmountable difficulties resulting from phenomenology's subjectivism (PMD 219/124).[25]

For Tran-Duc-Thao, phenomenology's contradictions (PMD 217/123, 224/127, 5–6/xxi) can be resolved only by going back to constituting subjectivity's "actually real foundation" (PMD 223/127), that is, to "the technical and economic forms" which produce the conditions of human existence (PMD 220/125). As Tran-Duc-Thao says, "the description of pre-predicative significations refers back to the conditions of material existence and necessarily places the subject within the framework of objective reality" (PMD 219/124). As Tran-Duc-Thao realizes, phenomenology's actual result, that transcendental subjectivity is "the real man himself" (PMD 224/127), "contradicts the very notion of a '*transcendental constitution*,'" but, as he goes on to say, this "contradiction is only the fact of phenomenology itself" (PMD 221/126). There must therefore be, according to Tran-Duc-Thao, "a radical *dépassement*" of phenomenology by dialectical materialism (PMD 218/124). Only dialectical materialism can overcome phenomenology's "impasse" (PMD 218/124, 225/128).

It is easy to see that the reading of Husserl Tran-Duc-Thao produced in *Phénoménologie et matérialisme dialectique*, Part I, anticipates the one Derrida produced. Most obviously, because Tran-Duc-Thao, like Fink, establishes genesis as an unavoidable phenomenological issue, this issue dominates Derrida's entire reading of Husserl, from his *Memoire* to "Form and Meaning." [26] In *Le Problème de la genèse*, in the *Introduction*, and in *Voice and Phenomenon*, Derrida adopts Tran-Duc-Thao's rallying cry: omnitemporality is but a mode of temporality (PGH 184; LOG 165/148; VP 93/83). In all three, recognizing the irreducibility of the sensuous, Derrida focuses on the passage from the sensible to the intelligible. In *Le Problème de la genèse* and in the *Introduction*, Derrida focuses on the *aporia* Tran-Duc-Thao discovers in pre-predicative experience. [27] In both *Le Problème de la genèse* and in the *Introduction*, finally, genesis is defined by a dialecticism. Derrida's entire reading of Husserl carries out the task that Tran-Duc-Thao established: to overcome phenomenology's subjectivism with a type of dialecticism. In *Voice and Phenomenon*, this dialectic becomes the notion of *différance* (see VP 77/69).

A less obvious debt to Tran-Duc-Thao is Derrida's focus in both the *Introduction* and *Voice and Phenomenon* on the sign. Tran-Duc-Thao shows that the essential possibility of symbolic representation makes error contemporaneous with truth. Although Tran-Duc-Thao never draws this conclusion himself, the claim that error is contemporaneous with truth implies that absence always already contaminates presence; one can even say, according to Tran-Duc-Thao, at least implicitly, that something like a trace always already functions within perception. *Phénoménologie et matérialisme dialectique* even anticipates Derrida's own deconstructive methodology. As early as *Le Problème de la genèse*, Derrida focuses on the ambiguities and contradictions within Husserl's phenomenological theory. [28] And as late as *Voice and Phenomenon*, Derrida, just like Tran-Duc-Thao,

uses the contradictions discovered between Husserl's theory and his practice to criticize phenomenology as such. For Derrida ultimately, if deconstruction concerns these contradictions, difficulties, and problems, then
deconstruction aims at bringing about an experience of the problem. But
this focus on a kind of experience is still far away, after what we are calling
the "turn" in Derrida.[29] Indeed, that deconstruction aims at an experience
of the problem is still only intimated in *Voice and Phenomenon*. In *Voice
and Phenomenon,* unlike Tran-Duc-Thao, Derrida does not push his deconstruction beyond phenomenology to any sort of dialectical materialism. As Derrida says in his 1980 "The Time of the Thesis," Tran-Duc-
Thao's *Phénoménologie et matérialisme dialectique* "pointed to a task"—
overcome phenomenology's subjectivism with a dialecticism—"[but also
to] a difficulty, and no doubt to a dead end."[30]

The difficulty, for Derrida, lies within Tran-Duc-Thao's particular brand
of dialectic (cf. PMD 148/180, 157/85, 202–203/114–115). The problem of
genesis, in Tran-Duc-Thao, amounts to the problem of how to describe the
passage from the sensible to the intelligible. In order to describe it, Tran-
Duc-Thao utilizes all of Hegel's well-known terminology: the *Aufhebung*
as suppression, conservation, and elevation (PMD 240–241/137), a becoming conscious (*une prise de conscience*) (PMD 204/115), and a movement
from reality's in-itself to reality's for-itself (or truth) (PMD 143–144n1/
230n5). For Tran-Duc-Thao, this dialectical terminology is supposed to
avoid conceiving the genesis of knowledge either in terms of abstract conditions of possibility or in terms of psychological constructs. Nevertheless,
in *Phénoménologie et matérialisme dialectique,* when Tran-Duc-Thao defines dialectical materialism (or Marxism, as he also calls it [PMD 5/xxi]),
he denies himself "an ideal dialectic as we find in Hegel" (PMD 241/137).
Instead, the dialectic of his dialectical materialism is "the dialectic of scientific thought" (PMD 238/136) or, as he also says, "the movement of scientific explanation" (PMD 241/137). This dialectic in no way implies, for
Tran-Duc-Thao, a rejection or critique of the positivistic sciences. While
the positive sciences provide an account of life strictly in terms of its bio-
logical characteristics, namely, in terms of the physico-chemical (PMD
239/137), dialectical materialism, for Tran-Duc-Thao, interprets, compre-
hends, and understands the positive concepts (cf. PMD 218/124).[31] Dialectical materialism, in other words, "defines the truth of scientific concepts
insofar as it reproduces in consciousness the *real* processes by which life
constitutes itself in the general movement of material structures" (PMD

214/138). Even consciousness, a region apparently heterogeneous to the physico-chemical, presents no great difficulty for "the very movement of positive explanation"; as Tran-Duc-Thao says, "the act of consciousness in its lived meaning is defined exhaustively by the dialectic of behavior" (PMD 243/139). Transcendental structures such as temporalization "coincide in a strict manner" with real structures which merely precede them in real time; real time is the only type of priority for Tran-Duc-Thao. Dialectical materialism's subject matter, therefore, would be the "evolution of life leading to humanity" (PMD 235/134–135; cf. 252/145).

The difficulty is, as Derrida says in *Le Problème de la genèse*, that Tran-Duc-Thao's dialectical materialism "presupposes the problematic defined and resolved by Husserl" (PGH 226). Since Tran-Duc-Thao rejects Hegelianism and transcendental philosophy (cf. PMD 9/xxiii) and does not provide a more thorough explanation of his dialectical materialism,[32] it is hard to know how he can account for objective knowledge. On the one hand, as Derrida suggests in *Le Problème de la genèse*, it is possible that Tran-Duc-Thao is actually grounding objectivity on some sort of metaphysics of matter (PGH 257n8). A case can be made for this interpretation since, by rejecting phenomenology's subjectivism, Tran-Duc-Thao seems to appeal again to some sort of thing-in-itself. If this interpretation is correct, then Tran-Duc-Thao relapses into dogmatism. But, on the other hand, if Tran-Duc-Thao is not presupposing some sort of materialist metaphysics, then it must be the case that the natural sciences remain entirely ungrounded for him. Basing their priority entirely on real time, he does not provide the conditions for the possibility of the sciences. Without such a grounding, the truths of the sciences would have to appear arbitrary and accidental; the specificity of mathematical being, for example, would be entirely missed.[33] Tran-Duc-Thao's dialectic would be, as Derrida himself says, "a purely 'worldly' dialectic" (PGH 32; cf. also 231, 257n8). Tran-Duc-Thao's dialectical materialism, therefore, would fall prey to the same criticisms that Husserl leveled against Dilthey's historicism.[34] Indeed, if the real and ideal coincide "in a strict manner," then, as Derrida says in *Le Problème de la genèse*, "nothing more would allow us to distinguish between lived experience and natural facticity. No 'evidence' would be possible. We would entangle ourselves in a science of nature, of which the meaning and the condition of possibility would escape us. No access to objectivity would be able to be originally defined" (PGH 147). Tran-Duc-Thao's materialist dialectic would come to a dead end, a dead end that would make "Cavaillès's dialectical, dialecticist conclusions" interesting.[35]

2

Unlike Tran-Duc-Thao, who uncritically appropriates scientific results to support his dialectical materialism, Cavaillès, in "On Logic and the Theory of Science," investigates how actual science is constituted (LTS 40/383).[36] In fact, "On Logic and the Theory of Science" examines the modern history of scientific epistemology, from Kant to Husserl. Throughout this examination, Cavaillès utilizes three different criteria to evaluate each theory.[37] First, and most importantly, a scientific epistemology must be able to account for science's (or, more generally, logic's) necessity; this requirement, for Cavaillès, implies determining the conditions for the possibility of science. This requirement, however, also implies, for Cavaillès, that the theory recognize the heterogeneity between sensuous reality—when Cavaillès repeatedly speaks of ontology, he means an ontology of real things—and intelligible (or mathematical) reality. Second, a theory of science must be able to ground science; in other words, it must be able to account for its genesis. Logical forms cannot be self-constituting. Therefore, one cannot leave the question of the origin of logical forms unanswered. Third, a theory of science must finally account for science's progress. The test of this requirement always, for Cavaillès, lies in the way that a theory describes the interaction between logic or mathematics and the natural sciences. Do the natural sciences amount to nothing more than concrete matter for abstract forms? Is it possible for the natural scientist to choose merely pragmatically among all the possible mathematics or geometries, for example, when conducting experiments? Once more, the question of the difference between intelligible reality and sensuous reality plays an important role in Cavaillès's evaluation of how a theory conceives the relation.

The examination found in the first two sections of "On Logic and the Theory of Science" moves from what Cavaillès calls the "philosophy of consciousness," with Kant as its first proponent, to the "logicist position," that of the logical positivists. In the philosophy of consciousness, consciousness is absolute. Since all forms or laws always make a reference to an act, the genesis of logic is secured. Yet the problem for Cavaillès is that logical necessity is lost; it seems impossible to abstract entirely the universal form of consciousness from its sensuous, singular instantiation (LTS 3–5/359–360). That the philosophy of consciousness does not respect the difference between intelligible being and sensuous being can be seen in how it accounts for the relation between logic and the natural sciences; for the philosophy of consciousness, scientific progress takes place tautologically or analytically (mere internal necessity) (LTS 11–13/364–365; cf. 59/396). Inverse problems arise, according to Cavaillès, in the logicist position. While logicism, making form absolute, secures science's necessity, it cannot account for the constitution of logical forms (LTS 40/383). Indeed, when it turns to the relation between logic (or mathematics) and the natural sciences, it exhibits an empiricist prejudice; having no being of its own, logic provides no knowledge. In the logicist position, therefore, scientific progress takes place by contiguity or juxtaposition (no internal necessity) (LTS 41/385).

For Cavaillès, Bolzano holds the crucial transitional position between the philosophy of consciousness and the logicist position. Cavaillès says that Bolzano's "idea [of science as autonomous] is decisive for our problem" (LTS 21/371). Defining science as "demonstrated theory," Bolzano makes science into a reality independent from consciousness, intuition, and sensuousness (LTS 19/370; 25/374).[38] Science, for Bolzano, as Cavaillès says, is closed and total (LTS 22/371); it neither borrows from nor ends in anything other than itself (LTS 23/372).[39] Defined as demonstration, science's necessity is guaranteed. Moreover, Bolzano recognizes that, although total, science is by definition incomplete; the achievement of an empirical truth about this world does not exhaust it. Cavaillès himself characterizes demonstration as "a movement" (LTS 22/372), "a self-enclosed dynamism," "a growth in volume through the spontaneous generation of intelligible elements," "a conceptual becoming which cannot be stopped" (LTS 22/372). What is most important, therefore, for Cavaillès, is that "the philosophy of demonstration" alone therefore recognizes the heterogeneity between the logical entity and the sensuous entity.

Yet that Bolzano makes science autonomous implies, for Cavaillès, that he cannot account for its origin (LTS 26/374). Is science self-constituting? What is science's relationship to real sciences as they have developed historically? According to Bolzano, for Cavaillès, because the very essence of mathematics cannot be reconciled with a real origin, any claim to ground it there (in consciousness) is illusory. Given Bolzano's definition of science, it is impossible to found a theory of demonstration indirectly, that is, on the basis of what is exterior to demonstration. Conversely, because form always refers to something other than itself—forms cannot be self-constituting—any claim to ground demonstration from within itself is equally illusory. It is impossible to found a theory of demonstration directly, that is, on the basis of demonstration itself (LTS 43/386). It is against the backdrop of this problem—the genesis of knowledge—that Cavaillès turns to Husserl (LTS 44/386).[40]

Cavaillès bases his reading of Husserl almost entirely on *Formal and Transcendental Logic*. This text, according to Cavaillès, begins with the problems of the relation between formal ontology and apophansis (LTS 44/386). Without going into Cavaillès's summary of this relation, we can isolate a number of points that set up the criticism that follows. In regard to Husserl's theory of judgments, Cavaillès stresses that the notion of form determines everything (LTS 48/389). Husserl's formalism proceeds without concern for content (LTS 45/387); it privileges "non-contradictory statements" (LTS 46/388); and it establishes the general system, the theory of theories, as a nomology, closed and exhaustive (LTS 47/388). Husserl's formalism, for Cavaillès, therefore seems to preserve logic's autonomy.

Indeed, Cavaillès stresses that, in Husserl, one finds "a thematic separation" between apophansis and ontology. Apophansis always intends the structure of the judgment as such; conversely, independent from all logical development, a spontaneous general ontology, formal mathematics expanded into *mathesis universalis*, intends the properties of any object whatsoever (LTS 48/389). Nevertheless the "difference of orientation" between apophansis and ontology must not "mask"—this is Cavaillès's word —their "actual solidarity" (LTS 50/390). A judgment for Husserl always expresses a "state of affairs" and knowledge of objects always expresses itself in a judgment; the primacy of a state of affairs in Husserl is a primacy of the object. Apophansis, in Husserl therefore, is always oriented toward the object.

What is most important then, for Cavaillès, is the "principle of reducibility" (or "postulate of homogeneity" [LTS 68/403]) that Husserl formulates in *Formal and Transcendental Logic* (#42b). The principle of reducibility means, on the one hand, that the scope and true significance of every judgment must be led back to primary objects and, on the other hand, that homogeneity must be reestablished between judgments from various levels (LTS 50/391). In other words, this reduction always leads from abstract objects, which include the forms of judgments which have come about through nominalization, back to ultimate substrates, absolute subjects, or individual objects. Even if the mathematician, for example, claims self-sufficiency for his investigative domain, this claim, for Husserl, implies merely that the mathematician has forgotten his true vocation, which is to know the world (LTS 53/393). There is no mathematical knowledge, in Husserl, without application; the object must actually be attained. Thus, while Husserl claims that apophansis and ontology remain different in intention, the principle of reducibility implies, as Cavaillès says, "an equivalence of content between apophantic and formal ontology" (LTS 51/391). In fact, Cavaillès expresses this equivalence more strongly: "[logic and physics are] *one* and the same movement which, through mathematics, extends itself even to the realities of the world" (LTS 53/392, my emphasis); "to know has only *one* meaning, and that is to attain the real world" (LTS 53/392, my emphasis); and finally, "necessity is everywhere present and founded because it is *unique*" (LTS 55/394, my emphasis).

The undifferentiated character of the movements of logic and physics, the homogeneity of knowledge, of necessity, and even of truth (LTS 57/395), all of these claims in Husserl, according to Cavaillès, are based on "the primacy of consciousness" (LTS 55/394).[41] As Cavaillès says, "As far as their being in relation to consciousness is concerned, the independence of the objects is not an assertion of a *heterogeneity* which would involve subordination and, because of their diversity, a polymorphism of the corresponding knowledge. But consciousness is the totality of being; what it asserts is, only because it asserts it . . . " (LTS 55–56/394, my emphasis). Consciousness in Husserl is absolute being and being for him is "unique," singular and homogeneous. In other words, there can be in being "no unbridgeable gap (*d'hiatus infranchissable*) between two domains of knowing" (LTS 57/395). Although, for Husserl, sense experience and experiments of physics are particular modes of evidence, this diversity "does not involve a barrier" (LTS 57/395). Regardless of whether we have the sensory evidence of the historical perception of an object or the rational evidence of a mathematical demonstration, according to Cavaillès's analysis of Husserl, "there is the profound homogeneity of their both being the full insight of the same consciousness, so that relations of mutual conditioning are possible and justifiable through an analysis of the acts that secure both" (LTS 57/395). Formal logic has its foundation and conclusion in transcendental logic; the life of transcendental subjectivity develops itself in internal necessity (LTS 58/396).[42] Thus, Cavaillès sees that, on the basis of his principle of reducibility, Husserl's phenomenology turns out to be another version of the philosophy of consciousness, in a word, subjectivism.[43]

According to Cavaillès, Husserl's principle of reducibility implies that experience is logic's master (LTS 60/397). The priority of experience over logic can be seen, according to Cavaillès, in the transcendental analysis that starts from pure logic; it is always necessary to seek the justification of syntactic structures in their kernels or matter, in "the preliminary affinity of the experiential content which [they] organize" (LTS 61/398). Lacking definitive efficacy, categorial superstructures must reach back to "the individuals, the brute singularity of the experiential ground" (LTS 61/398). The priority of experience over logic—Cavaillès speaks of a "scandalous" logical empiricism in Husserl (LTS 66/401; cf. 60/397)—truly wreaks havoc for Husserl, according to Cavaillès, insofar as transcendental phenomenology is itself experiential and not logical, insofar as transcendental phenomenology is material and not formal.

Recognizing that transcendental analysis in Husserl is stratified, Cavaillès argues that there is a normative problem at each level (LTS 62/399). In order to determine each strata's own proper structure in distinction from the others, one must define its own conditioning norms. What is required is an apophansis and a formal ontology specific to each strata. The normative problem is so radical, according to Cavaillès, that Husserl needs to define norms "not only for the constitution of the constituted being but also for the constitution of the constituting being" (LTS 64/400). An enlargement of formal ontologies is required to reach "the unique domain of an absolute formal ontology which absorbs and totally realizes the prior investigations" (LTS 64/400). Husserl, according to Cavaillès, asserts that we can reach this homogeneous domain, but then raises the question of grounding it in absolute consciousness (LTS 64/400). For Cavaillès, one must then ask whether absolute consciousness can really be absolute: would it not also require a set of conditioning norms in order to distinguish it from other, more relative, conscious strata? Can this enlargement of formal domains and consciousnesses really stop itself without a "violent truncation"? Cavaillès recognizes that the only way to stop the regress is to conceive the absolute as a "coincidence between constituting and constituted moments."[44] Nevertheless, Cavaillès believes that phenomenology cannot admit such an "identification of planes," because in phenomenology all objectivities such as norms must be founded in relation to a creative subjectivity (LTS 65/400).[45] If subjectivity, however, is absolute, then formal logic would have to be conceived as relative to this one being known as consciousness; tied to something that is singular, logic would no longer be able to be conceived as universal. In short, it would lose its authority over different beings. Conversely, if logic is absolute, it would not be able to be identified with transcendental logic; having cut its ties to consciousness, logic would be ungrounded. In other words, the existence or appearance of logic would be inexplicable. As Cavaillès says in one of the most famous passages in "On Logic and the Theory of Science," "If transcendental logic really founds logic, there is no absolute logic (that is, governing the absolute subjective activity). If there is an absolute logic, it can draw its authority only from itself, and then it is not transcendental" (LTS 65/400–401).

Following directly from this first criticism of Husserl is a second, for Cavaillès: mathematics and therefore mathematical physics do not have their own proper content (LTS 69/403). Quoting Husserl's comment from *The Crisis*[46] that the truths of mathematical physics are merely well-tailored clothes for the life-world, Cavaillès claims that, in Husserl, physics is nothing more than a "shadow" of sense experience (LTS 67/402). What characterizes the "shadow's" difference from reality (that is, from what is given to the senses) is, according to Cavaillès, increased technicity and therefore greater facility. Mathematization intervenes, according to Cavaillès, only as the idealization of experience, smoothing over the extrinsic, removing the factual and arbitrary (LTS 68/402–403). For Husserl, mathematical physics, therefore, is nothing more than an art of prediction and probability; it is not a science of necessity (LTS 67–68/402). Making no real progress over experience, containing no "genuine speculative moment," as Cavaillès says (LTS 69/403), mathematics, for Husserl, must be defined as tautologous or nomological. As is well known, being nomological implies not only that mathematics' domain of objects can be exhaustively defined —as a formal system, mathematics is closed, saturated (LTS 70–71/404)— but also that the progressive increase of systems by establishing different levels can take place without contradiction (LTS 70/404). Indeed, according to Cavaillès, a nomological definition implies that the technique establishing something like a metamathematics can be stopped at any time, once the increased facility permits statements about reality to be obtained (LTS 71/404).

It is also well known that Gödel's ability to generate, by means of a technique, mathematical formulas about which no one can decide demonstrability questions Husserl's nomological definition (cf. LTS 72/405).[47] In regard to Gödel's proof, Cavaillès realizes that Gödel's new axiom, albeit undecidable, still represents an increase of knowledge. Referring to properties of integers, the undecidable turns out to be true. That the undecidable formula is legitimate implies, for Cavaillès, that formal systems possess their own proper content, different from experiential content. Moreover, that no one can decide whether the new formula follows from the basic set of axioms implies, for Cavaillès, that the expansion of formal systems does not take place in a predictable way; rather, based in its own sort of content, formal systems exhibit their own sort of necessity. Lastly, again, because formal systems possess their own sort of content, one cannot stop the technique that expands them simply because one can substitute empirical propositions for the formal ones. In short, and this is the obvious conclusion from Gödel's proof, formal systems, for Cavaillès, cannot be defined nomologically and cannot be closed.

There are two reasons, according to Cavaillès, why Gödel's result can overturn Husserl's definition of a formal system as tautologous so easily. Not only does Husserl fail, in fact, to examine the "logical entity itself" (LTS 58/396) but also, in principle, Husserl cannot do so (LTS 75/407). In principle, the phenomenological method ("archeology," as Cavaillès calls it [LTS 76/408]) always stops "before the simple elements, i.e., the realities of consciousness which refer to nothing else" (LTS 75/407). What phenomenology always wants, in Cavaillès's analysis, is to return across "the referential indicators [found in history] in order to bring out into the open the polished system of acts which 'no longer refer to anything'" (LTS 76/408). It questions back to the "lived impossibility," which, although originally producing the noema, is experienced as always the same (LTS 76/407). No matter how much the noema changes throughout history, the consciousness of this impossibility remains univocal; as Cavaillès says, "if there is a consciousness of progress [in Husserl], there is not a progress of consciousness" (LTS 78/409). What phenomenology always wants, in other words, is the one self-same source of evidence—and this is Cavaillès's phrase—it wants "immediate presence" (LTS 77/408). As we would say now, according to Cavaillès's analysis, Husserl's phenomenology turns out to be a "metaphysics of presence." The primacy of the reference to consciousness implies that Husserl's phenomenology overlooks the difference between science and experience, between the intelligible and the empirical.

The failure of all prior theories of science, including that of Husserl, is Cavaillès's most basic, negative thesis in "On Logic and the Theory of Science." What, however, would Cavaillès's positive thesis look like? In other words, if all prior theories amount to the abdication of thought (cf. LTS 77/408), then what would it mean, for Cavaillès, to remain steadfast to the *logos*? Unfortunately, Cavaillès does not provide a positive description of his scientific epistemology (cf. LTS 15/367). The well-known incomplete condition in which "On Logic and the Theory of Science" was published, moreover, makes any positive reconstruction at least questionable. Nevertheless, starting from the negative characteristics, we can construct something like the outline of Cavaillès's theory.[48]

First, and most importantly, because Cavaillès rejects Husserl's so-called principle of reducibility, we know that Cavaillès's theory of science could not be based in a metaphysics of presence; being, for him, would not be homogeneous, unique, or univocal (cf. LTS 78/409). Consequently, because Cavaillès recognizes both that logic cannot be self-constituting and that making logic refer to consciousness eliminates its necessity, his theory of science could neither be primarily a logicism nor primarily a philosophy of consciousness. In short, neither logic nor consciousness could be science's absolute, for Cavaillès. Only a theory that rejects both logic and consciousness could satisfy Cavaillès's triple requirement of necessity, genesis, and progress. Cavaillès's appropriation of Gödel's proof provides more negative determinations. For Cavaillès, it must be the case that a formal system such as mathematics, the inner "course" of science, develops neither by tautology nor by contiguity; it must develop discontinuously and unpredictably. Finally, since Gödel's proof demonstrates that a formal system is incomplete, Cavaillèsian science could not be finite.

Positively, Cavaillès says that only "a philosophy of the concept . . . can provide a theory of science" (LTS 78/409). Only a philosophy of the concept can satisfy the triple requirements for a theory of science.[49] Reversing the negative, neither-nor characterizations, we can say that concept, for Cavaillès, means both consciousness and logic (cf. LTS 78/409). The concept, for Cavaillès, refers to the inseparability between ideal form and empirical content (or matter), between mathematics and physics, between the intelligible and the real. In order to explain this "concept," Cavaillès says, in what must be the most famous passage in "On Logic and the Theory of Science," that "the generating necessity is not that of an activity, but of a dialectic" (LTS 78/409).[50] Cavaillès characterizes his dialectic by saying: " . . . progress itself [is] a perpetual revision of contents by deepening and erasure" (LTS 78/409).[51] Deepening and erasure imply, for Cavaillès, that science's movement, in a word, demonstration, does not proceed by analyticity or by contiguity; rather, the Cavaillèsian dialectic leaves and yet "intensifies" what went before (LTS 7/361). Each step that science takes is singular and yet revises what precedes. The necessity within this movement results from the very inseparability that defines the Cavaillèsian concept. Inseparability implies that the empirical history of scientific progress does not remain exterior to science's rational structure. The inseparable relation provides what Cavaillès calls, "a driving force," a driving force which is "the need to overcome each of them" (LTS 78/409). The dual need to overcome experience with thought and thought with experience implies that a development in empirical science functions as a sort of "catharticon" for a development in logic and vice versa (cf. LTS 18/369, 7/361). Indeed, being based in the inseparable relation, scientific developments are unpredictable; yet unpredictability does not imply, for Cavaillès, that scientific developments involve chance. Necessity, for Cavaillès, can always be recognized afterward, after science in fact has developed (LTS 74/406, 26/374).[52] No matter how surprising a development may be, retrospectively, for Cavaillès, one can always discover a "deduction" (LTS 74/406) or a "structure" (*enchaînement*).

Lastly, Cavaillès says positively that " . . . genuine mathematics begins with the infinite" (LTS 73/406). Here, it is necessary to return to Cavaillès's Gödel discussion.[53] Cavaillès recognizes that Gödel is able to generate the undecidable formula by a higher level reflection on formal systems; the undecidable comes about by superposition. Constructed out of the need for greater ease in dealing with metamathematical propositions, Gödel's technique, assigning his so-called "Gödel numbers," is one which can entirely mathematize the metamathematical. Cavaillès also recognizes that even the addition of a new undecidable formula to the basic axiomatic set will not result in a saturated system; by means of Gödel's technique, one can always generate more undecidable formulas. Therefore, the expansion from a smaller system to a larger one, from what Cavaillès calls a "restricted theory" to a "general theory" (LTS 71/404), is essentially infinite. As Cavaillès says, "Here technique takes its revenge by inverting the realized constructions into something abstract which surpasses it" (LTS 72/405). Yet since the permanent ability to generate more undecidable formulas is based solely on Gödel's technique, it must be the case that a system's openness, for Cavaillès, its infinity, is not only different from that of the mere infinite repetition of the same form—different from tautology— but also different from mere numerical difference without transformation of content—different from juxtaposition (cf. LTS 6/361). Cavaillès stresses the lack of closure—inexhaustibility—that results from Gödel's proof only in order to eliminate Husserl's (and indeed the philosophy of consciousness's and logicism's) conception of logic as an empty formalism; through Gödel's proof, Cavaillès seeks mathematics' proper content. Therefore, perhaps Cavaillès seeks a unity that reconciles form and content.[54]

Although it is not clear that this reconstruction of Cavaillès's positive thought is accurate—the best guess is that Cavaillès's positive thought would amount to a kind of Spinozism, "the absolute of intelligibility" (LTS 19/369)[55]—it at least allows us to see that certain elements of his thought already anticipate elements within that of Derrida. Most importantly, like Tran-Duc-Thao, Cavaillès attempts to move beyond Husserl's subjectivism toward a type of dialecticism.[56] Again, as we already stressed in our Tran-Duc-Thao discussion, the overcoming of phenomenology's subjectivism by means of a dialecticism is the philosophical task Derrida inherited. However, while Tran-Duc-Thao sees in Husserl a metaphysics of difference (ideality and matter) from which one must turn toward a metaphysics of identity (materialism), Cavaillès sees in Husserl a metaphysics of identity (consciousness) from which one must turn toward a metaphysics of difference (his theory of science). No matter how Cavaillès conceives the "unbridgeable hiatus" joining the different ontological regions of the scientific and the empirical, of the ideal and the real, of the logical and the conscious, his insistence on the gap between them, his insistence on ontological heterogeneity cannot be emphasized enough. Similarly, his recognition that Husserl's apparently homogeneous metaphysics can be overcome only by a consideration of logic as such—of the *logos*— already points toward Derrida's own reflections on language.[57] The metaphysics of presence can be overcome only by considering as such what the sign and, more precisely, writing represent: absence. Lastly, Cavaillès's utilization of Gödel's proof to disclose an essential inexhaustibility, especially insofar as Cavaillès stresses that this infinity arises out of a higher level of reflection, already contains the seeds of Derrida's concept of *différance*.

Despite the anticipation one can see in Cavaillès, Derrida "ups the ante" over the dialectic that we have been able to reconstruct on the basis of "On Logic and the Theory of Science." To reiterate, Derrida's dialectic, found in both *Le Problème de la genèse* and in the *Introduction*, is not that of Tran-Duc-Thao, who reduces the essential down to the factual in a "strict coincidence." In *Le Problème de la genèse*, Derrida insists that "the absolute beginning of philosophy must be essentialist" (PGH 226). In both of these texts, however, by pursuing the problem of genesis, Derrida discovers that one cannot eliminate the empirical from the ideal, existence from essence (PGH 227). Including actual genesis in its most "wild" form—and here we note again Tran-Duc-Thao's influence, even as Derrida explicitly rejects him—Derrida's dialectic does not equal Cavaillès's "coincidence of constituting and constituted," his "identification of planes."[58] On the basis of our reconstruction, it seems that Cavaillès's dialectic of "autonomous science," by stressing the heterogeneity of science in relation to the empirical, eliminates the empirical from the intelligible. Specifically therefore, Derrida's dialectic, recognizing a kind of complementarity between Cavaillès and Tran-Duc-Thao, differs from the dialectic of both, because it is empiricist in one case (Cavaillès) and essentialist in the other (Tran-Duc-Thao). More generally however, and more importantly, Derrida's dialectic differs because it is more basic. Being worldly, the dialectics of both Cavaillès (ideal) and Tran-Duc-Thao (real) remain, as Derrida says, at an "already constituted" level (PGH 8). Developed for the first time in *Le Problème de la genèse,* Derrida's dialectic "ups the ante" by attempting to articulate the absolute transcendental origin.

3

Being a "historical essay" concerning Husserl's then published works (PGH 1n1), *Le Problème de la genèse dans la philosophie de Husserl* begins with Husserl's *The Philosophy of Arithmetic.*[59] In this work, Husserl seeks an "absolute foundation" for mathematics; this task is one, according to Derrida, that Husserl will never give up (PGH 56). Connected to his permanent rejection of Kantian formalism is Husserl's attempt to discover the absolute foundation in the psychological subject. Kantian formalism must be rejected because, separating logical and mathematical forms from consciousness, it cannot explain the concrete or actual possibility of mathematical operations (PGH 55). How mathematical forms apply to the world can be explained only through an act of consciousness (PGH 55). Numbers, therefore, for Husserl at this early stage, are constituted by the act of counting multiplicities, an act which refers to a "temporal and intentional, constituting subject" (PGH 55).

Nevertheless, Husserl's prioritization of psychological genesis brings about an inverse problem. Since the conscious act is supposed to be concrete, real, and empirical (even historical, as Derrida says [PGH 72]), how can it guarantee the objectivity, the *a priori* necessity, of mathematics and logic (PGH 55–56)? According to Derrida, Husserl tackles this "dilemma" (PGH 52)—the inadequacy of both psychologism and logicism (PGH 52–53)—with the terms in which he inherited it (PGH 75). This failure to rethink the "antinomy" (PGH 71) results in the fact that Husserl "oscillates" (PGH 63) between logicism and psychologism in *The Philosophy of Arithmetic.* Examining *The Philosophy of Arithmetic* in detail, Derrida shows therefore, through several of Husserl's analyses, that the forms supposedly produced by psychological acts turn out to be "given," "already there," and "already constituted" prior to these acts. For Derrida, although Husserl claims priority for his genetic analyses, they in fact turn out to be superfluous, accessory, and secondary.[60] The most important of these analyses, for Derrida, is Husserl's "polemic" with Frege. As Derrida says, "All the paradoxes of genesis are present here" (PGH 70).

As is well known, Frege denies that psychology has any right to intervene in the arithmetical domain. He recognizes that, if one places the origin of numbers in an *a posteriori* system of concrete objects, then one can never explain numerical difference and numerical equivalence (or unity). An abstraction from such a system would provide nothing but an accumulation of accidental arrangements. Frege claims therefore that we must presuppose that the pure concept of number exists before the psychological operation which presents it or utilizes it. Responding to Frege, Husserl claims that if one makes the unity of a number independent of psychological acts, then one misses the original, concrete meaning of numbers, the fact that they are about real things. But, then, the *aporia* arises: how can such an empirical genesis produce numerical unity? According to Derrida, Husserl rejects this *aporia* because he realizes that concrete things are not arranged accidentally; he discovers at their base what he calls a "thing in general" (PGH 70-71). Consequently, for Husserl, abstraction not only produces mathematical unity—abstraction now no longer presupposes mathematical unity as in Frege—but also allows mathematical unity to have content. Abstraction intends both the suppression of the concrete thing's singularity and the concretion of the number's universality. Although Husserl's description apparently establishes the value of the genetic viewpoint, what actually takes place, according to Derrida, is that Husserl refers the entire problem of genesis to an *a priori*, ungenerated "thing in general" (PGH 71). The very notion of the "thing in general" "contradicts," as Derrida says, the priority of psychological genesis (PGH 74-75, 78). Therefore, Husserl's *Philosophy of Arithmetic* analyses, according to Derrida, are "ambiguous" (PGH 56).

The next historical phase that Derrida considers is Husserl's rejection of psychologism, his unrelenting "dissociation" of logic from psychology in the Prologomena to the *Logical Investigations*. Under critical pressure, Husserl quickly realizes that the psychological subject is insufficient to constitute logic and mathematics (PGH 79). Yet as Derrida stresses, while Husserl insists here that there is an "unbroachable discontinuity" between essence and fact (PGH 88), he also insists that essences bear upon facts (PGH 94). While appearing to be idealizing fictions, essences, Husserl says, are still "cum fundamento in re." For Derrida, "This *fundamentum in re* is very strange" (PGH 94; Derrida cites section 23 of the Prologomena). Indeed, as in *The Philosophy of Arithmetic,* the same "*aporia*" or "dilemma" arises here (PGH 95). If an abstraction from empirical facts produces the real determination and the real foundation of ideal possibilities, then essences can be neither pure nor rigorous. They must be vague; relativism and skepticism ensue. Inversely, as Derrida asks, "If the theories are 'pure,' if they are not constituted by abstraction and generalization, what is 'the *a priori* synthesis' which harmonizes them with natural experience, with the facts of which they are the essence" (PGH 95)? If this synthesis is itself ideal, then it is impossible to know how it can determine an empirical reality. If it is empirical, then Husserl's unqualified condemnation of psychologism tacitly appeals to the synthesis. Consequently, according to Derrida, it seems that just as the psychologism of *The Philosophy of Arithmetic* refers to logicism, the logicism of the Prologomena refers to psychologism. Thus, in Husserl, logicism and psychologism confuse themselves with one another (*se confondrent*) (PGH 95).[61]

According to Derrida, after the *Logical Investigations,* Husserl does not "eliminate the dilemma"; he merely wants "to illuminate the confusion" (PGH 103). Both logicism and psychologism appear to him as derived from a more originary domain, that of immanence or lived experience. In no way, however according to Derrida, can Husserl conceive lived experience genetically because all genesis, at this point for Husserl, is empirical and therefore cannot account for the validity of ideal objects (PGH 108). The method of the reduction is discovered therefore in order to determine this domain non-psychologistically (PGH 130–149).[62] Nevertheless, the already familar problem reoccurs, according to Derrida. If the immanent domain is static or structural, how can it be concrete? And if it is concrete, how can it be transcendental? Derrida demonstrates the reoccurence of the dilemma within two different texts: first, within *The Lectures on Internal Time-Consciousness;* here, he asks, "How can Husserl simultaneously conceive a history constituted in its very signification by something other than itself and an originarily temporal lived experience such as the one analyzed in *The Lectures on Internal Time-Consciousness*" (PGH 108–109)? Then within *Ideas I;* here, he asks, "Is the simple 'neutralization' of genesis, such as Husserl understands [the reduction] after a slow development, sufficient to found the descriptions of static constitution" (PGH 132)?

In the *Lectures on Internal Time-Consciousness,* Husserl seeks to disclose "the *a priori* of time" (PGH 114); his analyses therefore are eidetic. Objective, worldly, existential time must be "switched off." All reality, that is, all empirical reality, has to be bracketed, and with that all doubt. After the disconnection, what remains then is the immediate apprehension of time, the only possible and valid beginning, the only originary certitude of a reflection upon time (PGH 110). "This evidence," as Derrida says, "is purely immanent to subjectivity" (PGH 110). Within this evidence—what Husserl calls the "thick slice of time," the living present; what Derrida calls the "phenomenological *durée*" (PGH 110)—we see the pure temporal object being constituted on the basis of retention retaining a series of primal impressions and protention expecting another series (PGH 119). Husserl claims that what is retained in retention and what is expected in protention cannot be real; retention cannot be a sort of weakened impression (PGH 119-120). Otherwise, the most distant past would still somehow be present and retention would be equal to a psychological lived experience. Accordingly, Husserl defines retention as a "quasi-presence of the past" (PGH 120);[63] retention is a "non-present" (PGH 123; here, as later in *Voice and Phenomenon,* Derrida cites section 16 of the *Lectures*). Moreover, for Husserl, this "non-present" necessarily combines with the primal impression because primal impression cannot exist as a point. The primal impression has to have temporal density (PGH 120); otherwise it is nothing but an abstract limit point (PGH 127; here Derrida cites section 32). The inseparability of retention and primal impression, therefore, implies that the phenomenological present consists essentially in a synthesis (PGH 120).

For Husserl, the temporal synthesis is phenomenological or immanent and involves nothing ontological or transcendent. Yet Derrida raises the question that Husserl does not and seemingly cannot differentiate between the "already constituted" retention of immanent time and "already constituted" past of objective time, between the transcendence of moments constituted within the pure flux of lived experience and the transcendence of real objectivities of time. As Derrida says, "The empirical order is the always already constituted order" (PGH 111). Moreover, according to Derrida, because Husserl describes retention and protention as "intentional modifications," it is "inevitably" the case that primal impression is intentional (PGH 120). Being intentional means that primal impression must intend a real thing; primal impression must "announce" a real object (PGH 120). There must always be (as we saw in our discussion of Tran-Duc-Thao) a concrete kernel at the base of all of Husserl's analyses. Derrida claims therefore that the primal impression must originally be the impression *of* the sound as *real* (PGH 120). The irreality of the "quasi" sound in retention constitutes phenomenological temporality because it is originally founded upon "the *already constituted* reality (*real*) of the sound" (PGH 120). Indeed, if primal impression "announces" a given reality, then a passive genesis that produced the reality precedes the "primal constitution" of the present that Husserl describes in *The Lectures* (PGH 121). How else could one explain the real thing being "already there," ready for the idealization, ready for Husserl's very "exclusion" of objective time that allows the primal impression to be seen as such? Consequently, as Derrida says, "The temporality of immanent lived experience must be the absolute beginning of the appearance of time, but it appeared precisely as the absolute beginning thanks to a 'retention'; it inaugurates only in a tradition; it creates only because it has a historical heritage. It then seems illegitimate to exclude from the very beginning of the reflection all temporal transcendence and every constituted unity of time. The act of exclusion cannot be pure; it is originally retentional" (PGH 123–124). It is impossible, in other words, to exclude the real or the ontological completely from the *eidos* of time.[64]

For Derrida, the impossibility of exclusion explains why Husserl himself "oscillates" (again) in his descriptions (PGH 125,127), why there is "confusion" and "ambiguity" here (PGH 121, 125, 127). According to Derrida, given Husserl's descriptions, "we do not know where phenomenological time begins" (PGH 127). We cannot decide because Husserl "sometimes" (*tantôt*) calls the primal impression the "non-modified absolute" (PGH 127; Derrida cites section 31).[65] As a non-modified absolute, the primal impression would have to constitute time and constitute itself outside of any retention and protention. In this case, according to Derrida, the subjectivity of pure time would be prior to all synthesis and all genesis (PGH 127). "At other times" (*tantôt*), Husserl claims that the primal impression necessarily has its "before" and "after"; a present preceded by nothing, he says, is impossible (PGH 127–128; again section 32). As the edge of a temporal extension, the primal impression would be constituted by the entire process. It would always be subject to retentional and protentional modifications: "the phenomenological Present is pure and appears as such only genetically composed" (PGH 128).

In fact, according to Derrida, Husserl's "alternative" (PGH 128) appears as an *aporia* (PGH 129). Consciousness appears to constitute time and to be conditioned by it. In other words, immanent time-consciousness must somehow be both outside of time in order to constitute it and within time as subject to it; consciousness must both participate in it and remain foreign to it (PGH 129). As Husserl says, and Derrida underlines this famous passage from section 39: "The constituting and the constituted coincide and yet they cannot coincide in all regards" (PGH 129). As Derrida says therefore, "Precisely in terms of the descriptions of the originally immanent constituting consciousness of time, we recognize that the constituting 'overlaps with' [*recouvre,* conceals] the constituted" (PGH 129); the originary synthesis is *à la fois* constituted and constituting (PGH 123). Thus, since Husserl at the beginning wanted to reach the most originary, constituting domain freed of all constituted, his descriptions "contradict his very principles" (PGH 129; cf. 109, 121).

When Derrida turns to *Ideas I,* he claims that the "coincidence" between the pure "ego" and the actual "ego" causes all the problems found in this text, in particular, the problems of the status of *hyle* and that of temporality (PGH 150, 159). As is well known—and as we have seen already in our discussion of "'Genesis and Structure'"—Husserl describes the noetic-noematic correlation in terms of an intentional *morphe* or form (thought) and a non-intentional *hyle* or matter (sensation), both of which are *reell* components of every lived experience or perception (PGH 152–153). Here Derrida suggests a "contradictory" possibility. Despite the fact that, according to Husserl, the constitution of an object takes place when a conscious act animates *hyle* with a *morphé,* thereby endowing it with sense, it is possible that *hyle* is "already" endowed with sense because it must count as a *reell* part of consciousness. In other words, in order to be immanent to consciousness, as Husserl says it is, it seems that *hyle* must "already" be a lived experience before being animated (PGH 153). Yet, and conversely, because it is impossible, for Husserl, to have a non-animated lived experience, it seems that it must also be the case that *hyle* is a worldly reality before being animated (PGH 154). As Derrida asks, "consequently, as such and before being endowed with an intentional sense, is it not possible that *hyle* can be a worldly reality as well as a phenomenological reality" (PGH 154)? Indeed, as Derrida stresses, Husserl claims that *hyle* is the lived adumbration of the transcendent thing but is in principle different from the thing itself; Husserl claims that *hyle* is "neither the thing itself which is sketched nor an intentional projection at the thing" (PGH 155). Given its neither-nor definition, *hyle* appears to be a "mediation" between transcendent reality and immanent intentionality (PGH 155), between passive and active constitution. According to Derrida, Husserl could have dissipated the "mystery" surrounding this "relation" (PGH 152), only if he would have considered "formless matter" and "matterless form"; only such a consideration, according to Derrida, would have been able to determine whether consciousness consists in a "duality" or a "unity" of form and matter (PGH 156–157). Husserl, according to Derrida, at least in *Ideas I*, "accepts as such the ambiguity of a unified duality or of a plural unity at the level of an already accomplished constitution" (PGH 157). "The genetic synthesis is already complete when the analysis begins," because Husserl does not thoroughly consider temporality there.

In *Ideas I*, Husserl admits that his sparse descriptions of temporalization here are insufficient. Indeed, he even says (section 81), as Derrida quotes him, that the transcendental "absolute" reached by all the different reductions is not the final word. Although there is something which is self-constituting, time-consciousness, Husserl provides here merely "the form [of time] which connects lived experiences to lived experiences" (PGH 162–164). Derrida stresses that this form cannot be equivalent to the form of sensibility as in Kant; it cannot be the form that each lived experience possesses in a general way (PGH 165). The form itself must be a lived experience. Yet in order to maintain itself as a form, as a unity, it must somehow be distinct from the multiplicity of lived experiences and matter (PGH 165). Consequently, Husserl simultaneously (*à la fois*) describes the form as the punctual now through which flows ever new matter (PGH 167–168; here Derrida cites sections 81 as he will again later in *Voice and Phenomenon*) and claims that each now has its horizon of priority (PGH 168; here Derrida cites section 82). If the punctual limit, as Derrida says, is never really lived, then it is an *a priori* concept informing lived experience; if it is lived, then it cannot be punctual.[66]

One could however, as Husserl does, conceive the formal purity of time as the lived totality of real and possible nows (PGH 168–169). Husserl, as Derrida stresses, believes that one can even have an intuition of this totality. This intuition however is not that of a singular lived experience but that of an Idea in the Kantian sense (section 81 again). That Husserl can speak of an intuition here indicates his distance from Kant, but that this intuition cannot be that of a lived experience implies that he nevertheless is constrained to use "mediations, conceptual or otherwise, in order to reach a totality which is not 'given' to us" (PGH 170). The paradox therefore repeats itself once more in the Idea in the Kantian sense.

As Derrida stresses, this paradox keeps on reappearing in *Ideas I* because Husserl's analysis remains at the static or structural level. His analyses remain at a level "already constituted" (PGH 170). More basic is a "synthesis," according to Derrida, in which active form is essentially already material and in which matter is essentially already passively informed (PGH 171). This more "primordial synthesis" (mentioned by Husserl in section 81) must now be taken up (PGH 172). Constitution must be genetic; genesis must be transcendental (PGH 172). Indeed, according to Derrida, this "new foundation" is Husserl's precise concern in *Experience and Judgment* (PGH 173); as Husserl himself says, *Experience and Judgment* is "a genealogy of logic."

For Derrida, being a genealogy means that *Experience and Judgment* opens up *Ideas I*'s absolute, a self-enclosed subject. As Derrida says, "From *Experience and Judgment*'s first pages . . . we have left behind the project of *Ideas I;* the borders of the originary world are open" (PGH 180). As is well known (and as we know from our discussion of Tran-Duc-Thao), *Experience and Judgment*'s project is to trace predicative judgments back to pre-predicative experience. In fact, in contrast to genetic psychology which focuses on constructive acts, genetic phenomenology, as Derrida notes, "proposes to retrace the absolute itinerary which leads from pre-predicative evidence to predicative evidence" (PGH 181). Indeed, this return to evidence even means, for Derrida, that genetic phenomenology returns not to the eidetic structures of consciousness but to the purity of experience itself (PGH 181): "*a priori*, [genetic phenomenology] puts us in contact with the being as such (*l'étant comme tel*)" (PGH 181). As Derrida continues, "The abandonment of all formal *a priori* is total and complete; the pure, concrete and temporal, transcendental 'ego' gives way directly to the being as such" (PGH 181). It seems, therefore, that with *Experience and Judgment* we confront the actual genesis that passes from the pre-predicative reality to the predicative judgment, that passes from the being to what must be indefinitely valid and supratemporal (PGH 184).

Following Husserl, Derrida stresses that this transition occurs when the transcendental subject acts upon the world, which Husserl himself describes as "the universal soil of belief . . . always passively pregiven in certitude" (PGH 185; Derrida cites section 7). Again however, even here in *Experience and Judgment,* the paradoxes, dilemmas, and ambiguities recur, and in reference to Husserl's notion of world, for example, Derrida resorts to his "sometimes–at other times" explication (*tantôt-tantôt*) (PGH 187–194). "Sometimes," the world in Husserl equals the infinite totality of possible foundations of any judgment (PGH 187). In this case, the pre-

predicative amounts to a domain of "indefinite determinability" (PGH 187). Being indefinitely determinable, according to Derrida, means that the pre-predicative is an "empty totality" (PGH 190); it lacks all logical determination. Consequently, not only is it the case that transcendental passivity, which welcomes the pregiven world, is the formal condition for transcendental activity (PGH 187), but also it is the case that transcendental activity resembles the psychological construction of judgments. As Derrida says, "idealizations will be conceptual mediations" (PGH 188). Derrida also points out that this view of the world, as indefinite determinability, agrees with Husserl's claim that science is merely a sedimentation which must be stripped away in order to stand before the presence of the thing itself (PGH 189). "At other times," the world in Husserl is the pre-predicative in its actual reality; it is the preconstituted substrate of all signification. In this case, the world is that of experience in the most everyday sense: sensible, in which one sees something over there. Being based on complex experiences, predicative judgments would then be traced back to simple experiences. Every predication, according to Derrida, would be traced back to "the domain of passive belief" (PGH 191). In this case, in order to explain the generation of predication, of that which is supratemporal and indefinitely valid, Husserl would have to assume that within this domain there is either an idea or concept of the world which precedes *a priori* passive belief or one which succeeds it as a methodological idealization or as a useful formalization (PGH 191). In short, if the world is merely actual, a mere real substrate, then one must suppose either a formalism (a rationalism) or an empiricism (a constructivism). As Derrida says therefore, "In [Husserl's description of the world in *Experience and Judgment*], the actuality of existence as substrate and the infinite possibility of transcendental experiences oppose one another" (PGH 187). There is an "irreducible alternation" here; "genesis and absolute originality exclude one another mutually" (PGH 192). Either logic completely precedes genesis which makes genesis superfluous—formalism—or logic is generated which, conversely, makes logic a mere construction—empiricism. No matter what, however for Derrida, the reason that Husserl runs aground of this paradox is that he still remains, even in this most geneticist of books, at an "already constituted" level (PGH 186, 198, 205). As Derrida says, "The two worlds, real world and possible world . . . appear essentially to respond to the given definition of 'worldliness,' regardless of what Husserl says. 'Worldliness' is synonymous with 'constituted' and qualifies sensible realities as well as logical forms. Both depend on a transcendental constitution" (PGH 193).[67] Husserl, therefore, fails to reach the "primordial synthesis" promised in *Ideas I.*

According to Derrida, we can see Husserl's failure to reach this most basic level even in the very text that throws "the most light" on the genetic theme: *Cartesian Meditations* (PGH 216). After showing how Husserl's First Meditation discussion of science's teleological idea results in the same contradiction between formalism and empiricism that we have seen throughout *Le Problème de la genèse,* Derrida focuses on the Fourth Meditation.[68] This is a crucial discussion because, here in the Fourth Meditation, Husserl describes the ego's self-constitution (PGH 223–224). Somewhat paradoxically, as Derrida notes, Husserl himself stresses that even here, here where it is a question of the constituting and not the constituted, one must proceed eidetically. On the basis of the eidetic method, Husserl is able, according to Derrida, to claim that the universal principles of constitutive genesis present themselves under two forms: principles of active genesis and those of passive genesis (PGH 229; Derrida cites section 38). According to Derrida, an eidetic approach can capture active genesis. Active constitution is always guided by its intentional, reproducible sense. Thus, on the basis of the reproducible sense, one can always relive the acts which generated it (PGH 229).

Yet when one turns to passive genesis, which Husserl privileges saying that active genesis always and necessarily presupposes a passivity which receives the object and discovers it ready made (section 38), it is not clear that the eidetic method is applicable. "What will be the eidetic status," Derrida asks, "of passive genesis" (PGH 231)? Since every *eidos* will be the correlate of intentional activity, the essence of passive genesis too will be correlated to and constituted by intentional activity. As Derrida notes, all passive genesis will be recognized as such and originarily only through the activity of a subject. Yet since Husserl gives priority to passive genesis in all constitution, the very essence of passive genesis will itself refer to a prior passive genesis which will, in turn, have to be determined eidetically, and so on (PGH 231). Thus, as Derrida concludes, passive genesis will "always be understood with the sense of 'already there'" (PGH 232); active constitution will always by structured by "infinite references" and, within active constitution, history will announce itself.

According to Derrida, it must be the case that passive genesis must always already be there; in principle, history must be infinite (PGH 235). If one were able to assimilate completely passive genesis into transcendental activity, either one would arrive at a pre-existential foundation or at the end (*fin*) of transcendental activity's own becoming (PGH 232). As Derrida says, both of these consequences would be "mythical or metaphysical," and "would suspend intentionality and the originary temporality of lived experience" (PGH 232). Nevertheless, in order to be rigorous, an eidetic analysis must suppose that the absolute of sense is "*already* known*"; an eidetic analysis must "institute the absolute intentional sense and transcendental activity through a decree or through an exceptional and non-phenomenological type of evidence at the threshold of passivity itself" (PGH 235). Otherwise, it risks empiricism. As Derrida says, "this is the only way, for Husserl, to save the absolute rigor of his descriptions" (PGH 235). Indeed, at the end of section 38, Husserl speaks of the object as the final or goal form of all becoming. Although Husserl claims that this objective goal of being known as an abiding possession always refers back to an originary institution, which would yet be unknown and unpossessed, he also says that "what we call the unknown still has the structural form of the known, the form of the object. . . . " For Derrida, this claim reduces genesis to its intentional and eidetic signification and integrates passivity into transcendental activity; "whatever would be the product of any genesis, it will be understood and organized by the formal structure of the known" (PGH 236).

According to Derrida, this same reduction and integration of passive genesis can be seen in Husserl's last writings on history, in particular, the Vienna Lecture, *The Origin of Geometry,* and *The Crisis* itself. In fact, according to Derrida, the primacy of passive genesis is what leads Husserl finally to a consideration of history, to a consideration of what for him previously had only been the concern of empirical sciences. Because of its indefinite references, passive genesis forces Husserl to see history as the place where the transcendental ego intends the idea, its noematic correlate. The infinite idea of philosophy, for Husserl, becomes, as Derrida says, "the very being of transcendental subjectivity" (PGH 254). For Husserl, therefore, history is clarified by means of a teleology. For Derrida, two questions must be answered (PGH 248). What is the origin, the very birth of the idea? And, how is a crisis possible within the idea's becoming?

Derrida first examines the Vienna Lecture. After showing that Husserl's descriptions of the philosophical idea are contradictory—on the one hand, Husserl claims that the idea of philosophy is unlimited or infinite; on the other, he claims that only Europe has this idea (PGH 252–254)—Derrida considers two hypotheses concerning the idea's birth. First, he says, "the idea of philosophy is buried but present in the empirical becoming which precedes its advent" (PGH 253). This hypothesis itself can be interpreted in two ways. On the one hand, one can say that the idea is absolute. As buried and present in the empirical becoming, it in fact is not produced by empirical genesis; it precedes its anthropological incarnation. The advent is only revelation; the becoming is only spiritual. But if this is the case, then one must ask, as Derrida does, why does the idea appear at such a time and in such a place in human history, in Greece (PGH 254)? Indeed, "why does it have to appear at all" (PGH 254)? On the other hand, one can interpret this hypothesis as one in which the empirical event is absolute and essential. As Derrida notes, this interpretation seems warranted, since, for Husserl, transcendental subjectivity is not accidentally connected to anthropological subjectivity (PGH 254). Since the idea is transcendental subjectivity's very being, the idea's rootedness in the empirical also cannot be accidental. But if the idea's rootedness is essential, then we must admit not only that the idea lacks something that only the empirical can provide, some sort of content, but also that Husserl's own attempt in the Vienna Lecture to place European facticity between parentheses is itself at least questionable. If empirical rootedness is essential, European facticity would have to be irreplaceable. As Derrida concludes, either in the case where the idea is absolute or in the case where, making the empirical absolute, one nevertheless tries to strip facticity away, "[human becoming] remains then as such exclusively empirical and external to the life of teleology" (PGH 255). In either case, actual genesis of the idea appears accidental.

Derrida's second hypothesis suggests that "the idea does not exist outside of transcendental experience" (PGH 255). Here we return, according to Derrida, to the paradox already encountered in the previous discussion of passive genesis. Given the priority that Husserl has granted passive genesis, it must be the case that the idea produces itself first in a passive synthesis. If this is the case, then there are two possible ways to understand it. "Either," as Derrida says, "the passive moment of genesis is already animated by the idea" (PGH 256). In this case, passive genesis is integrated into a transcendental activity in general; the subject is not one ego, but an infinite totality of egos or even a superhuman ego. As Derrida notes, in this interpretation, Husserl's separation of European humanity from all others, Indian or Chinese, for example, makes no sense. "Or," as Derrida says, "the passive moment, and this is the most probable, refers to a pretranscendental domain" (PGH 256). But then finitude would be the origin of the infinite idea; that which is not infinite would produce it. But such a transition—from pure finitude to infinity—seems inexplicable, unless "the infinite idea was *already* present in human finitude" (PGH 256). Being already present in human finitude, the idea would again be animating the passive genetic moment.

If it is the case that the Vienna Lecture leaves the question of the birth of the idea unanswered—Derrida says that "the problem of genesis has still not been illuminated" (PGH 252)—*The Origin of Geometry,* according to Derrida, seems to promise an answer (PGH 260). As is well known, in *The Origin of Geometry,* by using geometry as an example, Husserl tries to reactivate, across tradition, the founding acts of transcendental subjectivity which have been forgotten due to the crisis of naturalist objectivism (PGH 262). According to Derrida, because Husserl conceives tradition not as a causal genesis but as a "continual synthesis," tradition functions as both the condition of possibility and the condition of impossibility for reactivation: "It is here that the *a priori* or in principle possibility of reactivation is converted into an *a priori* or in principle impossibility" (PGH 263). On the one hand, it is only because the tradition retains prior moments that we can reach back to the founding acts. Yet, on the other hand, precisely because all the prior moments condition the present, one must reactivate the totality of the past. If reactivation must be total, then, as Derrida asks, "on the basis of which moment is reactivation total and immediately explicated" (PGH 263)? To put this in another way, only because factual geometry is present to us now can we start our reactivation and proceed back; yet in order to reach the origin and overcome the totality, these facts must be reduced. One must do without sedimentations and yet it is impossible to do without them. That Husserl must resort to the "zigzag method," what he calls a "a sort of vicious circle" in *The Crisis* (PGH 263), implies that the possibility of reactivation always, irreducibly, presupposes some form of a constituted tradition; as Derrida says, "at the moment when we reach the most originary constituting source, the constituted is always already there" (PGH 264). Reactivation is therefore, according to Derrida, "indefinite" (PGH 264).

Husserl himself is unable to clarify the indefinite zigzag, according to Derrida, because once more Husserl's analyses remain at a post-genetic level (PGH 265). Once more, he oscillates between *a priori* formalism and absolute empiricism. This confusion, according to Derrida, can be seen in the fact that when Husserl actually describes the origin of geometry, "sometimes" (*tantôt*) he describes it as originary evidence; at other times (*tantôt*) he describes it as the development of a technique (PGH 266–267;

cf. also 265). Taken in isolation, both descriptions seem to deny entirely the initial movement of phenomenology toward concreteness and eidetic rigor (PGH 269). Unable to grasp the "continuity" (cf. PGH 269) between logicism and psychologism, Husserl resorts to a notion of reason, reason functioning in each human, as the origin of geometry (PGH 270–271). Derrida concludes his analysis of *The Origin of Geometry* by saying "Do not be surprised to see Husserl, after having invoked a *Reason hidden in history,* mix his project of a philosophy of history with a history of philosophy" (PGH 271). And this is precisely what Husserl does, according to Derrida, in *The Crisis.*

When he turns to *The Crisis,* Derrida primarily tries to determine exactly what Husserl is doing when he reconstructs the history of modern philosophy. According to Derrida, it is clear that the movement Husserl describes consists in an eidetic rigor; the movement and transitions follow a teleological necessity. Yet this eidetic appears strange insofar as Husserl not only compares his history of philosophy to a novelistic composition— suggesting at once falsehood and imaginative variation—but also interprets each figure in the history as one in which the infinite idea of philosophy is simultaneously (*à la fois*) concealed and revealed (PGH 278). Galileo, for instance, makes an eidetic infinity of nature possible and therefore accomplishes the idea of philosophy as an infinite task; yet this "invention" succumbs to "a simple empirical or psychological causality, [to the] technical, economic, or personal situation of the thinker" which keeps Galileo from recognizing the originary and teleological sense of his revolution (PGH 278). Mathematizing nature both reveals the infinite idea of philosophy and dissimulates the life-world. For Derrida, what is most troubling is that Husserl does not consider concealment (*recouvrement*) as "an internal necessity to history" (PGH 274). In fact, as we have seen all along in *Le Problème de la genèse,* Husserl seems to remain at an already constituted level of eidetics.

It is also clear that, because each figure in the history of modern philosophy conceals the idea, the idea as such is discovered as such only now, with Husserl's own phenomenology. While suggesting the possibility of a different reading—one in which phenomenology would amount to "an existential act and a *prise de conscience* of its finitude" (PGH 281)—Derrida claims that Husserl supposes that the sense of history is now "definitively constituted" (PGH 280). Only a complete constitution of the idea can justify a teleological reconstruction of the history of philosophy; only the last or final, terminal stage can allow us to understand the movement of the prior stages (PGH 275–276). This interpretation contains, however according to Derrida, two interrelated dangers (PGH 281). First, if the idea is definitively constituted, then it is no longer open to infinite, intuitive embellishment. It is closed upon itself; it is only a concept (PGH 281). Husserl's phenomenology, as Derrida says, would be "the last end of philosophy [la fin dernière de la philosophie]" (PGH 282). Second, it does not seem possible that the philosophy of history which phenomenology would now define or constitute is the end, because it bases itself on a constituted idea. It is only a "critical moment," which must return to originary, constituting evidence. As Derrida says, "we are thus at the opposed pole of a true, transcendental genesis as the authentic motive of all philosophy" (PGH 281). If this idealism is really what Husserl is advocating in *The Crisis*, then "this [project] is . . . essentially, from the viewpoint of the transcendental motivation itself, a failure of the objectivist or idealist type" (PGH 282).

4

Thus, in *Le Problème de la genèse*, Derrida's critique of Husserlian phenomenology is identical to the hypothesis posed in "'Genesis and Structure.'" In *Le Problème de la genèse*, we see that Derrida claims that an "*aporia*" animates the development of Husserl's thought; this "debate" (PGH 85) surrounds the very problem of genesis. The "paradox" arises from Husserl's original and permanent twofold rejection of Kantian formalism or logicism and of empiricism or psychologistic subjectivism: how to conceive the absolute origin of objective and ideal knowledge? In the pursuit of an answer to this question, Husserl invents the method of reduction and describes the essence of temporal experience, the absolute constituting source. But for Derrida, this description only makes the "dilemma" irresolvable (PGH 159; cf. 207). The irreducible inclusion of retention implies that the constituting is always preceded by a constituted, even though retention issues from the constituting of primal impression. Supposedly first, intentionality is already actual; supposedly original, consciousness is already invested with a sense; supposedly second, sense is already there. The reduction, therefore for Derrida, cannot capture, within temporal lived experience, the absolute constituting source: genesis. Hence, as Derrida says in "'Genesis and Structure'" (WD 232/157), every stage of Husserl's thought is left "unbalanced"; or, as he says repeatedly here, "ambiguity" and "oscillation" characterize Husserl's thought. In a word, for

Derrida, Husserl's thought is contradictory.[69] Yet Husserl's thought does not remain unbalanced and contradictory; Husserl decides for structure, form, and essence. As we know from both "'Genesis and Structure'" and from *Le Problème de la genèse*, the Idea in the Kantian sense, the infinite idea, the infinite task of philosophy, ultimately tames genesis for Husserl; as Derrida says, "Not having begun with a pure description of genesis, Husserl's methodological propaedeutic in fact betrays the presuppositions of an entire philosophy of genesis which assimilates the creative becoming of essences to an 'idea' or to a sense of becoming that Husserl will [eventually] mix with the very idea of philosophy. This teleological idea which will be revealed to us . . . as a genuine reduction of actual genesis to its purposiveness [*finalité*]" (PGH 207). Derrida's critique of phenomenology is a critique of its teleology and of its archeology. According to Derrida, Husserl lacks evidence—pure presence in a "theoretic view" (PGH 280)— for the Idea and for Reason. Therefore, because the idea is not given in a pure presence and yet it is posited as the end of history, because reason is not given in pure presence and yet it is posited as the origin of history, Derrida characterizes Husserl's thought as a "panlogicism" (PGH 16) or a rationalism (PGH 41, 217, 228, 235, 237–238, 282). In fact, as Derrida notes, Husserl's thought here resembles Hegel's "absolute idealism" (PGH 12, 224; cf. 41, 203, 207, 231, 238, 248, 275). In "'Genesis and Structure,'" as in *Le Problème de la genèse*, Husserl therefore falls prey to metaphysics (PGH 41, 232, 270, 271).

Derrida's use of the word "metaphysics" here does not exhibit Heidegger's influence and his allusions to Hegel here do not reflect Hyppolite's interpretations. Metaphysics, in 1954 for Derrida, is speculation without evidence or intuition; in other words, it is metaphysics in the Husserlian sense. Husserl himself succumbs to metaphysics in his last historical writings, because, according to Derrida, he feared a relapse into empirical skepticism. Through the analysis of time and especially passive synthesis, Husserl realized that the pursuit of the absolute origin could be achieved only by examining actual genesis. He tirelessly prepared the access, according to Derrida, to the domain of real history. This domain, however, is "barely accessible to phenomenological clarification" (PGH 206). Essentialism seems inappropriate here; as Derrida says, when confronted with such genesis, "one would expect a complete transformation of the method" (PGH 224). Nevertheless, while flirting constantly with concrete empirical description, Husserl always stops before actual genesis (PGH 203; cf. 98). Therefore, Husserlian phenomenology "must *really* coincide with ontology" (PGH 16, Derrida's emphasis); for Derrida, this co-incidence means that Husserlian phenomenology must pass into Heideggerian ontology (PGH 30n48).

In *Le Problème de la genèse*, Derrida does not cite one Heideggerian text, not even *Being and Time*. Yet Derrida says that "ontology" is "not an already constituted mundane science; it is precisely transcendental in the Husserlian sense of the term" (PGH 6). That Derrida makes a comment like this shows that for him in 1954—and we will see this move again in the *Introduction*—phenomenology's essentialism always has a priority over ontology even though ontology alone can raise the question of actual genesis. Thus Derrida says, "The absolute beginning of philosophy must be essentialist"; or, again, "All the critiques addressed to Husserl (those, notably of Tran-Duc-Thao and Heidegger, which are, moreover, very different from one another) tend toward a radical reversal about which one does not see that it presupposes the problematic defined and resolved by Husserl" (PGH 226). Being transcendental in a Husserlian, non-worldly sense, Heideggerian ontology concerns "an historical originary existence which is neither a psychic double, nor the constituted event, nor the empirical facticity of the transcendental 'ego.' It is the very existence of the subject. Insofar as being originarily temporal and finite, this existence is 'in-the-world'" (PGH 213; cf. 41n14). Because Derrida stresses that existence is transcendental and yet in-the-world, he defines ontology as an "existential analytic" and as "an anthropology (which obviously has nothing in common with the mundane science rejected by Husserl) in the Heideggerian sense" (PGH 251). Thus, Heideggerian ontology—and here we can see the Sartrean influence—concerns "'human reality,' whose essence is mixed with existence" (PGH 251); it concerns "human existence [which] is mixed dialectically with its essence" (PGH 41). In contrast, Husserl "reduces human finitude to an accident of history, to an 'essence of man'" (PGH 41).

For Derrida, therefore, Husserlian phenomenology is reduced "to being only a moment of the dialectic between phenomenology and ontology" (PGH 40). Derrida defines this dialectic very specifically; he says,

> The weakness of the great dialectics and great philosophies of becoming would be their formalism, their "worldliness": these would always be instituted on the basis of a "second" opposition, already formalized, between form and matter, sense and the sensible, etc., so that genesis, under the pretext of being perfectly intelligible or meaningful (in

a Platonism or a Hegelianism), perfectly historical or actual (in a dialectical materialism), cuts the connection which reattaches it to transcendental genesis; the latter, being "originary," is dialectical only in its constituted products. But so that a "non-dialectical" constitutes a "dialectic"—unless this constitution be a pure creation *ex nihilo* or a simple associative construction—must it not be the case that the "non-dialectical" be "already" dialectical? (PGH 8).

This "dialectic" of the dialectical and the non-dialectical, of the mundane and the transcendental, of being and sense (PGH 213), is "the originary absolute" (PGH 6). For Derrida, although the originary absolute cannot be characterized as an opposition, an alternation, an antinomy, or a duality, Derrida defines it by means of contradiction (PGH 150, 167, 252n3) and negation (PGH 197, 68, 168, 170, 217). Being defined by contradiction and negation, the originary absolute is—and these are the words Derrida uses here—"unity" (PGH 162, 167, 193), "identity" (PGH 128, 209, 251, 257), "synthesis" (PGH 222), "coincidence" (PGH 141, 150, 211), and "agreement" (PGH 150). For Derrida, however, the negation defining this specific dialectic is not logical negation restricted to the domain of judgment; it is based in nothingness, as Hegel and Heidegger have shown (PGH 196n47, 67n34, 216). As Derrida will say later, nothing separates the dialectical from the non-dialectical; nothing separates the transcendental from the mundane. The dialectical mixes itself with the non-dialectical; they are co-foundational (*se confond*). Thus, along with the first set of defining terms, Derrida also employs in *Le Problème de la genèse* phrases such as "à la fois" (PGH 8, 197, for example),[70] "solidarity and distinction" (PGH 123, 179, 198, 221, 257), "tension" (PGH 126, 167, 276), "complication" and "implication" (PGH 30, 233, 237, 251), borrowed from Husserl, "zigzag" (PGH 264, 266), and "recouvrement" (PGH 129, 211). "Recouvrement" is particularly interesting because it means not only "overlapping" but also "concealment," implying an originary dialectic of appearing and dissimulation. Perhaps, as Derrida himself notes in his 1990 Avertissement (PGH vii), the most important word he uses in *Le Problème de la genèse* to describe the dialectic is "contamination" (PGH 22, 28, 30). This word implies a relation in which what cannot be conceived as interior—the "outside" (*le "dehors*," PGH 275), as he says—is nevertheless found, with necessity, inside (*dans*, PGH 102–103, 249, 281). In other words, *contamination* suggests a relation in which what one cannot conceive as belonging to one thing is necessarily found to be part of it (*de*, PGH 102–103). Therefore, defined by contamination, this very specific sort of "dialectic" is why Derrida can say that, at the most basic level, "the word, *dialectic,* makes sense only analogically" (PGH 6; cf. 32). According to Derrida (perhaps anticipating *Voice and Phenomenon*), his dialectic is not even that of Hegel "which completes itself in absolute Knowledge" (PGH 257n8). Contamination therefore is why in his 1990 Avertissement, when Derrida speaks of *une surenchère "dialectique,"* the word *dialectique* is placed between scare quotes and merely modifies the word *surenchère.* What Derrida is really interested in finally is not dialectic but "upping the ante"; there is "more metaphor" (*plus de métaphore*), as Derrida will say in "White Mythology" (in *Margins of Philosophy*), or "more than one" (*plus d'un*), as he will say in *Specters of Marx.*

Nevertheless, this very specific dialectic refers to the very structure of genesis. For Derrida in 1954, as later, what is important about Husserl's descriptions of the Living Present is that it involves openness in regard to the past as well as in regard to the future; it is impossible therefore to have the infinite totality of time in "originary presence" (PGH 170). According to Derrida, "there is no actual intuition of the infinite totality of [temporal] connections but there is an actual intuition of the very indefiniteness of this totality of connections" (PGH 169). Derrida calls the intuition of the indefinite a "strange idea": for Derrida, this indefinite is an "inaccessible limit to every intuition"; it is "the unveiling of the absolute consciousness of an essential finitude," (PGH 169n89). The "toujours déja" (PGH 171n91) and "anxiety before the absolute indeterminate" (that is, before death) (PGH 169n89) constitute originary finitude appearing to itself. But even in 1954, Derrida distances himself from Heidegger by saying that "the possibility of an absolute purity of 'anxiety' suspends the dialectic of originary temporality. The latter, in fact, forces us to begin over again indefinitely—and this is where our finitude is—the movement towards the originary" (PGH 257n8). Not being pure, but contaminated with the inauthentic, the dialectic of originary temporality, for Derrida, is an "irreducible indefinite" (PGH 41).

Based in contamination, the structure of genesis, therefore, is such that "It will be constantly impossible to determine," as Derrida says, "the real beginning of this dialectic; we will be able to assert at once (*à la fois*) the distinction and the solidarity of the two movements without ever being able to reduce this simultaneity and this complexity to a pure and simple succession. In the final assessment, we will be unable to attach to any of the terms a chronologically, logically, or ontologically principial value" (PGH 6; cf. 166, 197). That the relations of priority are complicated can be seen in Derrida's interpretation of Husserl's Fourth Cartesian Meditation. There, as we have seen, Derrida argues, following Husserl himself, that every active constitution finds itself already conditioned by a passive genesis; in turn, every passive genesis finds itself referring to something already there, given to it; yet everything that is given must be actively constituted. Although active constitution will endow existence with sense, its endowment will not be able to eliminate its givenness. Although active constitution will assume formal priority, existence will maintain its temporal priority. Although the empirical, for example, "will always be understood *as such* and originally only by an activity of the subject, [it will] always be *understood with its meaning of 'already there'*" (PGH 232, Derrida's emphasis). The reversibility of these relations explains why Derrida stresses, repeatedly, in *Le Problème de la genèse,* that Husserl's most basic descriptions of constitution flounder on something "already constituted."[71] Being temporal, absolute consciousness always consists in a retentional phase, which is always already there prior to constitution; being a non-intentional part of consciousness, *hyle* is always already there prior to animation. Passive synthesis, therefore, implies that the world is always already there prior to active constitution. Throughout *Le Problème de la genèse,* Derrida calls this "already constituted" the empirical, the real, actual history, historical man (PGH 248; cf. 252n3). As Derrida says, " . . . this kernel of originary existence mixing itself dialectically with its essence [resists] all 'imaginative variation,' all eidetic reduction" (PGH 229–230); it is "wild" (as Derrida says in " 'Genesis and Structure' ") or better, "inert" (PGH 247); it is an "irreducible alterity" (PGH 29). The inert "always already there" will become for Derrida the trace.

As we shall see for Derrida, this "irreducible alterity" will grow in importance.[72] At the time of *Le Problème de la genèse,* intersubjectivity as well as *hyle* and as well as the objectivity of knowledge have their "common root" in temporality (PGH 239–240). As Derrida says here, "In fact, on the basis of the originary impression of time (and upon its foundation, that of space) theoretic transcendental subjectivity, the irreducible alterity of moments of time past and to come, retained and anticipated, of the surrounding world, of history, of 'egos,' appear to me in the experience of the Living Present. It is upon this foundation that transcendental intersubjectivity, the condition for the possibility of objectivity in general, is erected" (PGH 240). The reason time, for Derrida, is at the root of intersubjectivity, indeed at the root of every dilemma (cf. PGH 217), is that he has not yet considered the problem of language; yet here in *Le Problème de la genèse,* he is on the verge of considering it. In his discussion of the Idea in the Kantian sense, Derrida denies that an originary presence can fulfill it; instead of originary presence, Derrida claims that an Idea in the Kantian sense must include "mediations, conceptual or otherwise" (PGH 170).[73] This comment points in only one direction: the *logos*, voice, and, most precisely, writing.

5   The Root, That Is Necessarily One, of Every Dilemma: An Investigation of the *Introduction to Husserl's "The Origin of Geometry"*

In *Le Problème de la genèse,* Derrida asks the question that leads Husserl in "The Origin of Geometry" to a consideration of language: "How do we pass from an absolutely originary pre-predicative individual state . . . to the existence of a geometrical being in its ideal objectivity" (PGH 267)? In the earlier *Le Problème de la genèse,* however, Derrida pursues neither the question nor Husserl's answer to it. This happens in his 1962 *Introduction to Husserl's "The Origin of Geometry."* The *Introduction to Husserl's "The Origin of Geometry"* transforms the problem of genesis into the problem of the sign.[1] We are entering into what we might call Derrida's "linguistic turn." Only here, when Derrida pursues Husserl's answer to the question of the generation of ideal objects through *language,* does he discover that writing is an irreducible condition for sense and perception. Nevertheless, although a condition for knowledge, writing is not an intuition and cannot be determined by intuition. Through the *Introduction*'s analysis of writing therefore, Derrida is able "to approach something like the un-thought-out axiomatics of Husserlian phenomenology, its 'principle of all principles,' that is to say, its intuitionism. . . . "[2] But, more importantly, beyond the critique of phenomenology, the *Introduction* establishes an absolute unity—a "one"—in which all oppositions necessarily contaminate each other; the *Introduction,* therefore, sets up, as Derrida says in his 1966 essay "Freud and the Scene of Writing," "the originary concepts of 'différance' and 'delay.'"[3]

The absolute unity, which Derrida in the *Introduction* calls "passage," leads to the "difficulties" that Derrida locates in Husserl's "The Origin of

Geometry." Again, the reading of Husserl in terms of contradictions, difficulties, and problems ultimately for Derrida means that deconstruction is concerned to lead us to an experience. But here in the *Introduction* this aim is not yet clear. The reason why the *Introduction* exhibits a labyrinthine structure is due to Derrida's cataloging of these difficulties. As in *Le Problème de la genèse*, here in the *Introduction,* the difficulties require that phenomenology be completed with ontology. As in *Le Problème de la genèse,* Derrida here calls the absolute unity an "originary dialectic." But, unlike *Le Problème de la genèse,* the *Introduction* defines this dialectic in terms of "the originary difference of the absolute origin" (LOG 171/153). Derrida nearly has conceived *différance* because at this time he has a more profound understanding of Hegel. This more profound understanding of Hegel is due to Derrida's interaction with Jean Hyppolite. There are three reasons why Hyppolite's *Logic and Existence* is important for Derrida at this stage in his development.[4]

First, Hyppolite stresses the irreducible role that language plays in Hegel's dialectical genesis; consequently, Derrida investigates the role of language in Husserl. As we shall see, Hyppolite's consideration of language in Hegel opens up the question of memory in Derrida (which is one of his enduring concerns). Second, Hyppolite brings to light how Hegel's philosophy transforms metaphysics into logic; Hegel's philosophy, for Hyppolite, completes immanence without eliminating difference.[5] Consequently, Derrida seeks this difference in immanence in Husserl. As we shall see, this difference opens up for Derrida a new logic of totality (that he continuously employs in his writings). Third, Hyppolite conceives Hegel's philosophy in an anti-humanistic way; there is a transcendence of humanity in Hegel. Consequently, Derrida seeks in Husserl an anti-humanity in humanity, and the humanism of *Le Problème de la genèse* vanishes.

Hyppolite, however, defines Hegel's thought so that philosophers such as Derrida (and Deleuze and Foucault) seek ways to escape from Hegelianism.[6] First, although Hyppolite clarifies the relation between thought and being as "essential difference," he stresses that essential difference must, for Hegel, be conceived in terms of contradiction. Eventually, Derrida will conceive difference without contradiction. Second, although Hyppolite defines mediation as language, he conceives language as "living speech." Conceived as voice, language is equivalent to intellectual intuition. For Hegel, language is bound to knowledge. Hegel's thought, for Hyppolite therefore, is, as Derrida will say later, a logocentrism. And eventually, Derrida will depart from knowledge toward a notion of faith. Third, although

Hyppolite conceives Hegel's thought as an anti-humanism (unlike Kojève's humanistic conception), Hyppolite's reconception of difference leads Derrida not to an anti-humanism, but to a meta-humanism.

1

For Hyppolite in *Logic and Existence*, the problem of Hegel's philosophy is a problem of genesis (LE 177/137, for example); for him, the Hegelian question par excellence is: "How . . . is the passage from the Phenomenology to Absolute Knowledge brought about" (LE 31/27)? Hyppolite's response to this question revolves around three claims. First, the Hegelian enterprise, according to Hyppolite, consists in the attempt to transform philosophy into a logic (LE 5/5). Since the Logic is supposed to be, for Hegel, the very discourse of being "across" (*à travers*) man, in particular across the philosopher, one must, according to Hyppolite, explicate the "sparse philosophy of language [found] in Hegel's texts" (LE 5/5). Second—and this claim follows from the reduction of metaphysics to logic —like Nietzsche, Hegel eliminates the notion of another world behind this one. Since there is no ontological secret in Hegel, one must investigate, according to Hyppolite, the difference between the *Logos* and being, between absolute speculative life and empirical life (LE 71/59). Third—and this claim follows nevertheless from the elimination of the second world— Hegel's thought is not strictly a humanism. Since thought merely passes through man for Hegel, one must define, according to Hyppolite, the signification of the word "existence" as applied to human reality (LE 231/177).

The first claim in Hyppolite concerns language. For Hegel, according to Hyppolite, being itself expresses itself. In fact, it expresses its sense, its logic, its *Logos*, "through" man. By stressing the passage through man, Hyppolite raises the question of human language. He asks, "how can being say itself in man and man become through language universal consciousness of being?" In other words, "How can human language be 'this voice which knows itself when it no longer sounds like the voice of anyone'" (LE 6/5–6)? According to Hyppolite,[7] the *Encyclopaedia*'s "Philosophy of Spirit" shows how human language realizes the concept.[8]

"The Philosophy of Spirit" lays out a "dialectical genesis of language" starting with intuition. In intuition, the ego is affected. But what is given in intuition, under the forms of space and time, "is no longer there as soon as it is there." In order to apprehend a particular being, intuition needs to recognize. The ego needs to remember; the intuition must be internalized.

Internalization, for Hegel, means that intelligence—Hegel's name for the whole process of internalization and externalization through which self-recognition occurs—holds the sensible in an image which it can manipulate in the absence of the real thing. That the image can invoke the sensible in its absence implies that memory has negated the sensible's immediate existence; the sensible's particularity has been overcome. Consequently, memory raises the concrete determinations of intuition to the universality of pure knowledge. Memory therefore, according to Hyppolite, is "the essentialization of this immediate intuition" (LE 34/28; cf. LE 223/171, 225/173). The objective has become subjective.

Hyppolite employs a number of images to describe what memory is for Hegel; he calls it "the interior of being" or "the interior of things" (LE 34/28), "the night of conservation" (LE 34/28) and most importantly, "an undivided seed" (LE 34/28). (Hegel himself calls it a "pit" or a "mine.") Memory is the seed of exteriorization because, in memory, the ego, Hyppolite says, "by denying the sensible, still conserves it as an echo; it imagines the absence" (LE 34/28). Possessing only the echo, memory requires externalization; it needs to be present again. As Hyppolite says, "*Erinnerung* exists only through *Gedächtnis;* the interiorization of that about which we speak [exists] only through the complete exteriority of the one who speaks" (LE 34/29). Externalization then takes place through imagination.

Imagination produces two types of externalization: the symbol and the sign. What characterizes the symbol—symbolic writing or hieroglyphics —is the resemblance between the present intuition and what is symbolized; they have something in common. As Hyppolite says, "Intelligence is still prisoner of what is given in the exterior" (LE 36/30). A mediating step between the symbol and the sign is the enigma; what characterizes the enigma is the dissociation between the present intuition and that to which it refers. "The pyramid," Hyppolite says, "has no relation to the dead pharaoh; it invites imagination to surpass itself toward some sort of secret, but there is no particular secret" (LE 36–37/30). Although here, in the enigma, the sensible is not what it appears to be, in the pure sign—"in pronounced words or in written words which are signs of signs" (LE 37/30)—the sensible is reduced to the minimum. As such, the sensible counts for nothing. The representation bears no resemblance to its represented content; in the sign, the sign as such and that which it represents, signifier and signified, in no way agree (LE 37/31). In short, the sign is arbitrary. Although it remains an exterior being, the sign is intelligence's creation (LE 37/31).

Therefore, with the creation of the sign, the opposite of being, sense, interiority, is in a being; conversely, the being, the opposite of sense, exteriority, is meaningful. Intelligence has found an exteriority which is completely its own (LE 37/31); the subjective has become objective.

Despite the unity of sense and sensible found in the sign, Hyppolite stresses that the signified looks to be "an other" than the signifier or representation. Deriving from the sensible, the signified seems to preexist intelligence; it seems to remain external to intelligence. When the sign, however, becomes a permanent part of a language, when it is raised to the level of being universal, then this "difference" between sense and sign is suppressed (LE 39/32). The word is the thing, Hegel says. When confronted by the word "lion," for example, no one needs to have the intuition of the object or an image of it in order to understand the word. One merely thinks in the word. In fact, for Hegel, the word does not refer to the thing; rather the thing refers to the word, "to the universe of expressed and expressible significations" (LE 39/32). Language for Hegel, according to Hyppolite, is a system, a "space of names" (LE 40/33). Any one word-concept unit is determined (and enlarged) through its relations with other determinate units; the words in the system are not exterior to one another, but "structured" (LE 40/33). Discursive understanding, therefore, determines intuitive understanding, even though intuitive understanding produces discursive understanding. Instead of intuition being prior to thinking (or vice versa), intuitive understanding and discursive understanding are united (LE 40/33). This unity is why Hyppolite can say that "Language precedes the thought of which it would be the expression, or, thought precedes itself in this immediacy" (LE 38/31; cf. 40–41/33).

Language can be, according to Hyppolite, the milieu of dialectical discourse because of this contradiction: "language precedes and expresses thought" (LE 52/43). This contradiction "is the source of poetry and of the exaggerations of symbolic calculation" (LE 52/43). On the one hand, language, according to Hyppolite, exhibits the transition from the sensible to the sense; here, language is prior to thought. On the other hand, the understanding can turn language into a tool for its use; here language expresses thought, which precedes it. To say that language is prior to thought means, for Hegel, as is well known from his *Aesthetics*, that poetry precedes philosophy. More precisely however, and this is what Hyppolite stresses, the priority of language implies that "thought is not a pure sense which could exist in some unknown region, outside of its expression like an essence beyond appearance" (LE 52–53/43). Sense can never appear outside of language. In contrast to poetic thinking, the understanding takes into consideration only the expression of thought in language. The understanding acts as though sense could be an interiority without exteriority, as though thought did not precede or presuppose itself in being.

The understanding, however, suffers from an illusion (LE 57/47). If, like the understanding, we suppose "that sense can be separated from its sensible sign," language then would appear to be like clothing which can distort what is underneath; the exterior form of language would be something that could disguise thought (LE 56/46). Thought then could receive more appropriate articles of clothing. Conceiving language in this way, the understanding then pushes the negation of the sensible (found already in poetry) to the limit, hence understanding's symbolism. The discourse of the understanding aims for "a pure creation of a system of . . . symbols which would be better adapted to significations than verbal language" (LE 55/45). It wants to eliminate all equivocations and ambiguities already found in speech; it wants to be a "pure language, a system of symbols which remains absolutely invariant over the course of the diverse combinations they undergo" (LE 56/46). The purpose of such a project would be that, with an entirely univocal system of symbols, philosophic problems would be posed differently; they might even dissolve (LE 57/46). With such a conception of language, the understanding produces a discourse—mathematical demonstrations, in particular—that remains exterior to the content. What the symbols employed in pure language represent is not taken into consideration. Driven by the requirement of purity, the understanding settles for mere manipulation. Demonstration is mere tautology; it is entirely objective (LE 61–62/50). This externality is why, according to Hyppolite, the understanding's discourse is inauthentic (LE 49/41).

In contrast to such a discourse, dialectical discourse is neither mere tautology nor entirely objective. Dialectical discourse is internal to its content. As Hyppolite says, "the self of which Hegel speaks in the philosophical dialectic is the very sense of the content; it inhabits the determinations; it is these determinations in their becoming" (LE 62/50). Instead of being a formalism, philosophic dialectic is "a life already immanent to language as such where sense appears in the mediation" (LE 63/51).[9] This internality is why the word is indispensable (LE 58/48). The word is a "seed" (LE 58/48); therefore it never exists without a proposition and a proposition never exists without the set of propositions that reconstitutes the totality as result. The "word-concept," as Hyppolite says, "is what it is only in the predicates which confer upon it its content, only in its relations, but this means also that these relations constitute a totality, a sense which is a *support* and not a fixed and immobile being" (LE 58/47, Hyppolite's emphasis). By means of the relations (and varying contexts), the word is equivocal, but it maintains an identity as well. As Hyppolite says therefore, "the word is the concrete universal, the Hegelian concept which is totality" (LE 58/48). In other words,

> Language is the house (*la demeure*) of being as sense. The *Logos* is the primordial, originary voice (*verbe*) that is truly an exteriorization, but an exteriorization which, as such, disappears as soon as it appears. Hegel says that the only determination then is for this sense to hear itself (*s'entendre soi-même),* to understand itself. [The determination] is pure thought in which difference (the one that will be freed in exterior nature and in finite spirit) is the alterity that leads thought to overcome itself. (LE 215/166).

This difference between language and thought within thought implies the second claim that animates Hyppolite's answer to the genetic question: Hegel's elimination of the intelligible world different from the apparent one. Hegel's philosophy completes immanence (LE 230/176). According to Hyppolite, Hegel's critique of the second world is hard to "reconcile" with the fact that the *Logos* is supposed to be "distinct from nature and finite spirit" (LE 72/59). Hyppolite goes on: "Doesn't the *Logos* look like the essence of this existence actualized in nature and in history; doesn't speculative logic, that is, absolute knowledge, look like the essence of phenomenal or empirical knowledge?" (LE 72/59). What sort of relation exists between the *Logos* and nature and history, between essence and appearance? What sort of difference separates them but still allows them to be immanent to one another?

Hyppolite stresses that the understanding conceives essence as a second world behind the phenomenal one (LE 72/59). To empirical reflection, the objects apprehended appear to preexist the apprehension; they seem to be already "constituted" (LE 100/80); they are immediate (LE 96/77). When empirical reflection encounters error and illusion, a contradiction—the stick appears to be both crooked and straight—then empirical reflection attributes the contradiction to itself, to the subject, while the object, preexisting the apprehension and preconstituted, is non-contradictory. Empirical reflection, as Hyppolite stresses therefore, remains exterior to its object and the consequence is dogmatism and formalism (LE 98/79). Dogmatism arises because empirical reflection, or more precisely, external reflection, must presuppose an inaccessible essence behind the appearance, which is non-contradictory. Formalism arises because external reflection becomes totally subjective. It ends up describing merely the forms of possible experience; it leaves the content to the side. In both cases, the understanding wants only the positive and not the negative; its primary rule is the law of non-contradiction (LE 96/77, 99/79). Therefore, the understanding makes the truth of the phenomenon "a being beyond the phenomenon" (LE 72/59). The truth is conceived as an "essence distinct from the appearance and from the understanding itself" (LE 72/60).

Hegel refuses to be held to this "duality" of the relation as understanding conceives it. This "separation neglects the living relation which posits each term and reflects it into the other. The Absolute is mediation" (LE 74/61). This sentence, "the Absolute is mediation," means that, for Hegel, there is no preexisting base for reflection. There is no absolute beginning, for Hegel, no substrate prior to its predicates, no transcendent God; there is no immediacy that would not at the same time be mediated. Instead, the genesis of thought is necessarily circular (LE 84/68); the triad, for Hegel, is the rational minimum. What being presupposes in order to be understood can already be found in being. Although absolute knowledge starts from being, being is at the same time implicitly the knowledge of being. What is absolute therefore, for Hegel, according to Hyppolite, is the totality or total form (LE 78/64, 81/66).

The inability to determine priority in Hegel explains, for Hyppolite, Hegel's own statement that "the Absolute is subject." The activity of the subject, thought or reflection itself, is internal or immanent to being (LE 84/68; cf. LE 112/89). Since reflection is internal, then, according to Hyppolite, the moment of essence—an absolute world of essence, an intelligible world—"is a sort of inevitable illusion" (LE 77/63). Being itself divides itself; being appears and appears as different from the appearance. Every appearing—this defines essence, according to Hyppolite—refers or reflects one term into another. The "distinction" or "difference," however as Hyppolite says (LE 78/64), belongs to being's self; difference is "a concrete identity . . . , the self as itself [thus different] and the same (*autos* in its double sense, ipseity)" (LE 91/74).[10] Consequently, "appearance is not opposed to essence [as in the understanding]; it is essence itself. The essence is an appearance just as the appearance is the appearance of essence" (LE 78/64). Defining the living relation, this difference therefore is what Hegel calls the "essential difference." "Being which appears," as Hyppolite says, "is identical to itself in its difference, which is the essential difference, that is, the difference of itself from itself. It is different from itself in its identity; it contradicts itself" (LE 226/173; cf. LE 117/92, 172/133).

For Hyppolite, what is most important in order to understand essential difference is the distinction between empirical negation and speculative negation. Hyppolite isolates three characteristics of empirical negation. First, empirical negation consists in a duality of two terms external to one another (LE 125/98); finite determinations lie outside of one another. Second, empirical negation is mere negation; it does not determine the two terms positively. It leaves open the field of possibles; it says merely that "B is not A" without positively defining "A" (LE 130/101). Third, empirical opposition arises from an external reflection; there is a "third" which compares things or a genus, a preexisting base or common terrain, which contains the two (LE 129/100). Self-contradiction, therefore, does not occur.

Hyppolite stresses that originally Hegel (like Schelling) believed that one could only live and not conceive "the passage from the finite to the infinite" in which the Absolute consists (LE 124/97). When, however, Hegel realizes that "the passage to the limit"[11] must be translated into language in order to be philosophy, he also realizes that it cannot be conceived as empirical negation. If one conceives the relation between the finite and the infinite in terms of empirical negation, then the infinite can no longer be infinite; "[the infinite] would have the finite outside of itself as its border" (LE 124/97). Similarly, the relation between unity and opposition cannot be one in which unity would be beyond opposition. If it were, unity would be one of the opposing terms. In contrast, speculative negation is an internal negation. Speculative negation means that "each [opposing term] is," as Hyppolite says, "in itself the contrary of itself and represents . . . the other in itself" (LE 128/100). Determinations are internal to one another because, for Hegel, according to Hyppolite, every negation is a position. Since speculative negation does not leave the range of "possibles" be indefinite, it creates for each term *its* other. Therefore, when the Absolute negates the *Logos,* the only result can be Nature; Nature is for the *Logos its* other just as the *Logos* is for Nature *its* other (LE 130/101). Therefore, for Hegel, when the Absolute self-divides into the opposition—this is the absolute opposition, according to Hyppolite (LE 128/100)—between the *Logos* and Nature, no common terrain, no preexisting base or substance, supports the opposition (LE 129/101). The *Logos* and Nature are not species of one genus that contains them and on the basis of which they distinguish themselves (LE 128–129/101); there is no exterior "third." Rather, this negation is internal to the Absolute itself, the Absolute's own self-reflection. It is self-contradictory (LE 131/102).

Hyppolite further explicates the notion of speculative negation by focusing on Hegel's logic of diversity in the *Greater Logic's* doctrine of essence. Indeed, he says, "The problem of this distinction of things, of this diversity, is the very problem of the other" (LE 144/112). Being superabundant, nature throws a diversity of things before empirical thought (LE 147/114). All of these things appear to be different from one another and identical to themselves; in short, they appear to be ones. As Hyppolite says, "Just as light is dispersed in a prism, being shows itself broken into multiple fragments; difference which is the difference of identity gets scattered into a multiplicity of things external to one another. Difference realizes itself" (LE 146/114). Quantitative difference, however, is unessential difference, the mere surface of being (LE 153/118); these "atoms" are indiscernible (LE 150/116). The diverse things are in fact all alike. The negation between them is merely a pure positivity. In order therefore to render them different, a comparison must be made (LE 150/116).[12]

The knowing subject animating empirical reflection then takes it upon itself to compare the beings; it seeks out positive characteristics which in turn distinguish—negate—one thing from another. The identity of one thing is transposed into the likeness of things (similarity) and difference into not being alike (dissimilarity) (LE 150/116). When the knowing subject then compares, it realizes that like things are like in one regard and unlike in another. Then it must say that two things cannot be alike without also being different. As Hyppolite says, "in this case, the external difference sublates itself, because similarity is such only in relation to dissimilarity and vice versa" (LE 151/117). This contradiction, nevertheless, gets pushed back into "the subjective activity of comparison" (LE 151/117). For external reflection, things in themselves cannot be self-contradictory. When it encounters contradiction, it reduces it by, or attributes it to, a linguistic artifice (LE 151–152/117). External reflection remains beyond the things; it is merely subjective and the measure of comparison falls outside of the things themselves (LE 151/117).

Difference, however, according to Hyppolite, must be pushed up to contradiction (LE 157/121). In order to do this, empirical reflection must reflect upon itself (cf. LE 103/82). What it must realize is that its reflection is not only formal but also transcendental (LE 103/82). "Transcendental reflection," Hyppolite says, "grounds experience; it constitutes the content which presupposes it" (LE 103/82). External reflection then "has to take the appearance just as it is, and not as the appearance of a hidden being" (LE 113/89). When this happens, external reflection becomes internal reflection, empirical reflection becomes transcendental, or, more precisely, speculative. It sees the appearance as something it posits. Then, according to Hyppolite, "contradiction stops being formal and subjective when it is the contradiction of the things *themselves*"; "[the thing] *is* similar in its dissimilarity, dissimilar in its similarity" (LE 152/118, Hyppolite's emphasis).

Position occurs, according to Hyppolite, when reflection, now speculative, realizes that mere quantitative difference leaves things indiscernible (LE 153/118). In order to be discernible, each thing must differ from all the others; the quantitative negation must itself, in other words, be negated. Reflection then must discover what makes the thing what it is, the thing's "uniqueness" (*unicité*), its absolute characteristic (LE 153/119). Now however, because appearance is being taken as such, the absolute characteristic is not external to the thing. Instead, the absolute characteristic belongs necessarily to it (LE 153/119). This difference, internal negation, is what allows the thing to be different from all the others and consequently allows it to be itself (LE 154/119). Speculative negation makes the thing positive, posits it (LE 154/119).

Difference, therefore, according to Hyppolite, becomes the opposition of the positive and the negative (LE 154/119). Difference is no longer quantitative, but qualitative; it is essential difference. Essential difference provides a precise determination to each thing; it is not an opposition in which what is different stands over and against *an* other, but *its* very other (LE 155/119). In other words, each thing has its determination only in relation to a definite other, the one that belongs to it. As Hyppolite says, "the one, the positive, is what it is only because it excludes its other, the negative, and yet subsists only through it; the other, the negative, excludes the positive and likewise subsists only through it" (LE 155/120). Subsisting through the other, each thing represents the other in itself; it bears a mark of its other within itself. The thing, therefore, is self-contradictory. And this self-contradiction dissolves the thing into universal or infinite mediation, the Absolute or total form, in a word, the *Logos*.

Hyppolite insists upon the ontological significance of negation in the Absolute's opposing duplication. In Hegel, according to Hyppolite, position and negation are equally balanced and identified to one another. Nature and the *Logos* then must also be seen as equally balanced and identified to one another in the Absolute. As Hyppolite says, however, "Position appears to have a privilege because it is the indivisible self, but, to be precise, it is what it claims to be, it justifies this privilege, only when it recognizes itself as negation and negates this negation" (LE 130–131/101–102). For Hegel therefore, the absolute position is the negation of the negation; absolute position is the movement that achieves determination by reflecting its other in it (LE 131/102).

That absolute position is this movement means that "the *Logos* is the Whole in the determination of the concept of sense" (LE 131/102). The Absolute presupposes itself in the *Logos*, opposes itself to itself in Nature, posits itself concretely in spirit which is the identity of the opposed terms and this spirit itself becomes the *Logos;* it understands itself as presupposing itself (LE 131/102). The *Logos* is Nature's other; it is negative. The *Logos*, however, has the "power" to overcome itself. It is more than itself and can surmount this negation that is "its difference from itself" (LE 131/102). The *Logos* therefore conceives or finds the sense of Nature, turns it into *its* other, negates it. In other words, as Hyppolite says, "[the *Logos*] translates its very opposition with Nature into its determination; *contradiction is the logical translation of this opposition*" (LE 131/102). The *Logos* therefore contradicts itself; it is at once itself and its contrary.

According to Hyppolite, "Here perhaps we get to the decisive point of Hegelianism, to this torsion of thought through which we are able to think conceptually the unthinkable," through which we are able to conceive the other. "We cannot exit [*sortir*] from the *Logos*, the *Logos* exits [*sort*] from itself by remaining itself" (LE 131/102; cf. LE 75/61, 93/75, 95/76, 136/105–106). It becomes nonsense and the opacity of Nature. As thought's contrary, Nature, however, contains spirit in itself; it "points to the *Logos*, sense" (LE 132/102). Nature has a contradiction within itself; it is Nature and *Logos* at the same time. Nature, however, does not know that it contains this contradiction; instead, spirit knows it and conceives. Spirit's desire to know is why, Hyppolite says, "there are the natural sciences and a philosophy of science" (LE 132/102–103). By means of "the power of the negative" (LE 134/104), by means of "the pain, the work, and the patience of the negative" (LE 132/103), the *Logos* reflects nature's opacity into its contradiction. As Hyppolite says, "[the Absolute] raises thought, which would be only thought, over itself by obliging it to contradict itself; it turns this contradiction into the speculative means through which to reflect the Absolute itself" (LE 131–132/102). The *Logos*, therefore, as Hyppolite says, is "the authentic mediation" (LE 133/104). The *Logos* is both intuition and discourse, intellectual intuition (LE 66/53); as Hyppolite says, "Speculative

Logic is simultaneously the intuitive understanding that Kant attributed to God, and the discursive understanding that he reserved for man" (LE 86/69–70).

The authenticity of the logical mediation implies, and this is Hyppolite's third claim, that Hegel's thought is not strictly a humanism. As we have seen, for Hyppolite, Hegel's thought in general (and the *Phenomenology*, in particular) constantly criticizes the notion of another world beyond this one. As a result of this criticism, Hyppolite claims (in *Logic and Existence*'s final chapter) that one can extend Hegel's thought in two ways. The first is the one that Marx brought about in his *Economic and Philosophic Manuscripts of 1848*. (We shall return to Marx in Part IV, Chapter 8 where we discuss Derrida's *Specters of Marx*.) Here in the *1844 Manuscripts*, as Hyppolite stresses, Marx identifies universal self-consciousness with man (LE 233/178–179). According to Hyppolite, Marx's identification of universal self-consciousness with man has three implications. First and most importantly—Hyppolite says that "the whole debate is concentrated on this last point" (LE 238/182)—nature is taken as a pure positivity and therefore as a starting point, as primary. For Marx, when humans transform nature into products, their self-objectification merely extends or expresses nature (LE 237/182); humanity emerges out of nature in order to give nature a human face (LE 235/180). Their objectifications do not appear foreign to them. Hegel however, according to Marx, as Hyppolite stresses, confuses alienation (or more precisely, negation) with objectification. When Hegel according to Marx makes alienation fundamental, he transposes a particular historical process—the negation of natural man arising with capitalism (LE 237/181)—into speculative philosophy (LE 233/179, 236/ 181). Second, and this follows from considering nature as a pure positivity, death, for Marx (in the battle for recognition, for example), is the victory of the human species, of the Hegelian universal understood as society, and a return to nature (LE 235/180). Third, and this too follows from taking nature as a pure positivity, according to Marx, absolute knowledge is not something above man. Since absolute knowledge must appear in history, and since humans alone have a history, absolute knowledge is actually the realization of the human essence (LE 233/179). As the realization of humanity, absolute knowledge is, for Marx, "the end of history" (LE 233/179).

The second extension of Hegel's thought—"the one we have followed in this work," Hyppolite says (LE 231/177)—recognizes the fundamental and irreducible role negation plays in all the figures of spirit. As Hyppolite says,

"We must admit that Hegel went a lot farther upon this point than Marx. . . . [Hegel] has discovered this dimension of pure subjectivity *which is nothingness*" (LE 239/183, Hyppolite's emphasis). What Marx cannot explain is why man emerged into history and did not remain in nature (LE 238/183). In order to be able to explain why there is history, in a word, negation, one must see negation everywhere. Thus Hyppolite stresses that death in nature, the death of animals, is negation in itself (LE 239–240/ 184). Humans in turn make death for itself and thereby become aware of themselves as a void open to the future; they become aware of themselves as freedom (LE 240/185). This freedom, however, is not a pure self-negation. Man's negation is always the negation of a determination; negation is always launched into positivity (LE 242/186). Although unlimited, the desire to overcome oneself possesses a sense, but this sense, Hyppolite stresses, is not man (LE 242–243/186). The sense of history "is not the rational project of the individual; on the contrary, the individual learns to recognize a certain necessity in the destiny of history" (LE 243/186). This necessity is the *Logos,* which is the possibilities—indeed the chances and contingencies—of the existing being, comprehended or conceived contingencies (cf. LE 277/174–175). Such a necessity or destiny (cf. LE 33/28) implies that man in Hegel is an "intersection" (LE 243/186); the absolute Idea comes about across (*à travers*) existence (LE 231/177); or as Hyppolite also says, "man . . . becomes the house (*demeure*) of the Universal, of the *Logos,* of Being, and becomes capable of Truth" (LE 244/187).

No one can miss Hyppolite's allusion to Heidegger here; no one can miss all of the allusions to Husserl in *Logic and Existence.* When Hyppolite, for instance, speaks of Kant's contribution to the development of Hegel's thought, he says that Kant "ascends back up to the source of the constitution of the object" (LE 100/80; also LE 106/84, 183/141, 228/175). When Hyppolite speaks of Hegel's denunciation of the naive errors of empirical knowledge, he claims that this is done by a return to "the things themselves" (LE 3/4). When he speaks of speculative philosophy, he describes it as a "reduction" and a "bracketing" of the human condition (LE 50/42; also LE 177/136, 216/166). Finally, when Hyppolite speaks of the Hegelian logic, he describes it as a genesis of sense (*sens*) (LE 209/161). Hyppolite's surreptitious appropriation of Husserlian terminology to explicate Hegel's thought—Hyppolite never mentions the name "Husserl" in *Logic and Existence*—is why Derrida can say in his *Introduction* that *Logic and Existence* is "a work which, on a great many points, lets the profound convergence of Hegelian and Husserlian thought appear" (LOG 58n1/67n62).[13] In fact, Hyppolite's identification of the three great figures of phenomenology—Hegel, Husserl, and Heidegger—is why Derrida can move so seamlessly between them in *Voice and Phenomenon;* a seamless movement between Husserl and Hegel is especially obvious in *Voice and Phenomenon,* Chapter 6.[14]

More important, however, than Hyppolite's phenomenological identification is the fact that Hyppolite makes the problem of language unavoidable. Derrida can speak of language as the "ether" of thought in Husserl (LOG 34/49, 104/102) only because Hyppolite had done the same for Hegel (LE 86/69, 119/93, 233/179).[15] Hyppolite's elevation of the linguistic problem, in particular, his analysis of Hegel's dialectic of intelligence from *The Philosophy of Spirit,* is why Derrida at one point intended to write a thesis on Hegel's semiology.[16] But Hyppolite's recognition of the role of language in the Hegelian movement of idealization is crucial for Derrida; it is impossible to imagine Derrida having written a book called *Voice and Phenomenon* without the following quote (which we have already cited):

> Language is the house [*la demeure*] of being as sense. The *Logos* is the primordial, originary voice [*verbe*] that is truly an exteriorization, but an exteriorization which, as such, disappears as soon as it appears. Hegel says that the only determination then is for this sense to hear itself [*s'entendre soi-même*], to understand itself. [The determination] is pure thought in which difference . . . is the alterity that leads thought to overcome itself. (LE 215/166)

Here we have already the famous "hearing oneself speak" of *Voice and Phenomenon,* Chapter 6. Hyppolite's elevation of the linguistic problem results from another recognition, that Hegel transforms metaphysics into logic. This transformation in turn leads Hyppolite to consider the precise type of difference through which being distinguishes itself from itself as *Logos,* the type of difference through which appearance distinguishes itself from itself as essence, the type of difference through which the sensible distinguishes itself from itself as sense. It is Hyppolite who introduces sense, instead of essence, into philosophy, and with it the problem of difference.[17] Hyppolite's specification of this difference (LE 226/173; cf. LE 117/92, 172/133), then, is why Derrida can stress at the close of his *Introduction* "the primordial Difference of the absolute Origin" (LOG 171/153). Hyppolite's discussion of the essential difference in Hegel, moreover, is why Derrida can say in "Violence and Metaphysics" that

> Pure difference is not absolutely different (from nondifference). Hegel's critique of the concept of pure difference is for us here, doubtless, the most uncircumventable theme. Hegel thought absolute difference, and showed that it can be pure only by impure. (ED 271n1/320n91)

The very root of Derrida's law of contamination can be found here, in Hyppolite's Hegel. It is the source of the concept of *différance*. Finally again, in "Violence and Metaphysics," Derrida can stress in his critique of Levinas the confusion involved in the Greek word, "autos," between *idem* (identity) and *ipse* (self), only because Hyppolite had already noted how this confusion expresses being's own self-torsion (LE 91/74).[18] We cannot underestimate the importance of this confusion in the Greek word "autos": this confusion too is the basis of Derrida's concept of *différance* as it is presented in *Voice and Phenomenon*, Chapter 6, which concerns the operation of the voice as *auto*-affection (see especially VP 92/82).[19]

Although Hegel's transformation of metaphysics bases itself upon the elimination of a second world, his thought, for Hyppolite, is not strictly a humanism. Instead, the difference through which being produces its own logic is equivalent to the Husserlian reduction (LE 50/42; also LE 177/136, 216/166);[20] it is "a passage to the limit" which reduces humanity (LE 124/97).[21] Following Hyppolite, Derrida in the *Introduction* speaks of the reduction as "a passage to the limit" (LOG 127/119, 137/127).[22] Moreover, Derrida says at the close of the *Introduction* that "the absolute is passage" (LOG 165/149), because Hyppolite had already said that "the absolute is mediation." Finally, that Hegel's thought overcomes man is why Hyppolite can ask Father Van Breda at the 1958 Royaumont conference on Husserl the following question: "Doesn't this ambiguity [of Husserl's doctrine of the reduction] result at what we could conceive as a subjectless transcendental field?"[23] Derrida in the body of the *Introduction* quotes this exact comment (LOG 84–85/88). Nevertheless, Derrida separates himself from Hyppolite on precisely this question of a subjectless transcendental field. While Hyppolite determines the field as the *Logos,* or more precisely, as the voice, Derrida, as is well known, determines it as writing (*l'écriture*) (LOG 85/88). While a teleology of knowledge organizes the voice, something else organizes writing, something else that Derrida will, after *Voice and Phenomenon,* determine as faith. While the teleology of knowledge works by pushing difference all the way up to contradiction, writing, for Derrida, while still being called a "dialectic," works by not pushing difference all the way up to contradiction.[24] Instead, in the *Introduction,* we will see a new concept of difference that Derrida will eventually call *différance*. This new difference will include a negation, but the negation—the "non"—will be determined from finitude and death. This finitude, what Derrida already here in the *Introduction* calls "essential finitude" (LOG 151n1/138n164; see also LOG 28n1/44n37)[25], implies that what is other remain indeterminate and never can become *its* other through which contradiction and thus a positive infinity are constituted. What Derrida realizes is the *Logos* must pass through writing, and therefore reality, factuality, matter, in a word, history. Hyppolite himself is aware that the relation of history and the *Logos* presents "nearly insurmountable difficulties" (LE 243/186; also LE 244/187, 72/59). In the *Introduction,* Derrida will call this relation "the root that is necessarily one," and for him this "root that is necessarily one" remains difficult.

2

The Origin of Geometry is a fragmentary piece which belongs to a whole cluster of texts from the early 1930s associated with the incomplete *Crisis of European Sciences and Transcendental Phenomenology.* As is well known, in the thirties Husserl recognizes that tradition has led to a crisis in European science. Tradition has handed over truths, sentences, forms, formulas, symbols which scientists have manipulated validly without going back to the original experience which produced and endowed them with sense. These truths look to be separate from subjective experience. An "objectivist alienation" therefore threatens European science (LOG 10/31); a forgetfulness of the origin has occurred (LOG 13/33); European science and scientists have fallen into irresponsibility. Thus in the thirties phenomenology has the task, for Husserl, of regressively inquiring back into (*Rückfragen*) the original sense of European science, of reactivating its original experience, in order to reflect upon (Husserl uses the word "besinnen," which Ricoeur, for example, translates into French as "prendre conscience"[26]), in order to become conscious of, and take responsibility for scientific truths. Because Husserl's task in the thirties, which *The Origin of Geometry* exemplifies, lies in making oneself responsible for truth by regressively inquiring into its origin, one could call Derrida's *Introduction to Husserl's "The Origin of Geometry"* "The Origin of Truth" (following Merleau-Ponty)[27] or "On the Essence of Truth" (following Heidegger).

To provide a title for this book (which curiously bears no title) helps one come to understand it, but at first glance, Derrida's *Introduction* appears labyrinthine. There is, however, a key to it.[28] In the unnumbered paragraph with which the text opens, Derrida states that the "singularity" of Husserl's "The Origin of Geometry" among Husserl's writings lies in the fact that Husserl's "two denunciations of historicism and objectivism [have never] been so organically united" (LOG 4/26). This "strange" organic unity is Derrida's theme in the *Introduction*.[29] It consists not only in the unity of Husserl's twofold critique of historicism and objectivism, not only in the unity of Husserl's twofold notion of historicity, not only in the unity of Husserl's twofold notion of historical intuition, but also in the very unity of language and thought, of essence and fact, of *en droit* and *en fait*, of truth and non-truth, of philosophy and non-philosophy, of sense and non-sense. The organic unity is synonymous with what Derrida calls "the whole prize of our text": *Wechselspiel*, which Derrida translates as "un mouvement en vrille," literally, "a tendrillic movement" (LOG 14/33).[30] For Derrida, the tendrillic movement is an origin or an "in general" (to use genetic language [cf. LOG 60n1/69n66]) or a foundation (to use structural language [cf. LOG 79/83]), in short, a transcendental (cf. LOG 162n3/146n177). Derrida's entire *Introduction* is concerned with reconceiving the transcendental (cf. LOG 71/77, 123/117, 171/153) in terms of this new kind of "radical" ("radical" here intended in the literal sense). Thus, as Derrida himself says, "In the introduction we now attempt, our sole ambition will be to recognize and situate one stage of Husserl's thought, with its specific presuppositions and its particular unfinished state. Though this moment of Husserl's radicalism is ultimate in fact [*en fait*], it is perhaps not so in principle [*en droit*]" (LOG 5/27). When confronted with certain "difficulties," to which the new kind of root leads, Husserl resorts in *The Origin of Geometry* to procedures developed as early as the *Logical Investigations* (cf. LOG 124/117).[31] It is precisely on these difficulties that Derrida focuses his *Introduction*; as he says, "we will always try to be guided by [Husserl's] own intention, even when we get caught up in certain difficulties" (LOG 5/27).

The difficulties arise because, as Derrida stresses, the mathematical object has always been Husserl's "privileged example" of an object (LOG 6/27). Husserl's privilege of the mathematical object is the source of Derrida's concept of presence, being as presence, as it appears in *Voice and Phenomenon*: ob-ject that is close by or in front of a regard (a *Vor-stellung*) (cf. VP 59–60/53).[32] The mathematical object (and thus the geometrical object [cf. LOG 79n2/83n87]) holds the privileged position for Husserl because it is what it appears to be; it is ideal (LOG 6/27); it is pure truth (cf. LOG 66–68/74–75). As Derrida says, the mathematical object "is thoroughly transparent and exhausted by its phenomenality" (LOG 6/27). The mathematical object is, therefore, always already reduced to being a phenomenon. Being a phenomenon, it is defined by the dative; it is permanently available *to* a "pure regard" (*regard*) (LOG 72/78); it is a theorem in the literal sense of something "looked at" (cf. LOG 78/83). The being of the mathematical object then is being to a pure consciousness (LOG 6/27); its ontological sense is "object being" (LOG 6/27) or "perceived being" (LOG 78/83). Given the ontological sense of the mathematical object— ideality—more than any other object,[33] it would be most hostile to history, which is precisely what Husserl is trying to take seriously in the thirties; unlike the mathematical object, history is defined by uniqueness, irreversibility, and non-repeatability (LOG 9/30), in a word, factuality.

In our reading of the *Introduction,* we are going to divide Derrida's discussions into four parts, the first three of which will be organized around a difficulty: (A) the difficulty of tradition; (B) the difficulty of language; and (C) the difficulty of the Idea in the Kantian sense. Each difficulty will allow us to group certain paragraphs of Derrida's *Introduction* together. The first roughly corresponds to paragraphs 1 through 3; the second to paragraphs 4 through 7 (the second however focuses primarily on the *Introduction*'s two most famous paragraphs, 6 and 7); the last corresponds roughly to paragraphs 8 through 10. Eleven, which is the *Introduction*'s concluding paragraph, takes up the new sense of the transcendental that Derrida is trying to articulate and the definition of phenomenology as "lived anticipation"; we will designate it as (D).

(A) *The Difficulty of Tradition.* For Kant, the hostility between history and mathematical objects is so obvious that, for instance in the Preface to the second edition of *The Critique of Pure Reason,* he claims that geometry was revealed to and not created by the first geometer (LOG 21/39). Thus, for Kant, history is nothing more than an empirical embellishment of geometry; history remains and must remain an extrinsic circumstance because otherwise geometry would be relative, finite, bound to this earth. Like Kant, Husserl in *The Origin of Geometry* recognizes "geometry's truth, its normative value, is radically independent of its history" (LOG 26/43). According to Derrida, Husserl's recognition that history is external to geometry is why in *The Origin of Geometry* he starts out by reducing factual history: "in order to respect and show the normative independence of the ideal object . . . , in order to respect and show the unique historicity of the ideal object itself" (LOG 27/44). But Husserl also, according to Derrida, respects what history is: singular. For Husserl, now unlike Kant, geometry happened for a "first time" (LOG 31/47). Even though, as Derrida stresses, this "first time" act must include a strata of receptive intuition, it is still a production (*Leistung*) (LOG 22/40).[34] Even though, for Husserl, geometrical ideal objectivities such as triangularity must arise out of non-geometrical objectivities, they did not exist as such before this "experience." As non-revelatory, geometry's original experience cannot *not* be a "total fact." It must bear the characteristics of uniqueness ("unicité," as Derrida says), irreversibility, and irreplaceability (LOG 8/30, 31/47; cf. LOG 31n1/47n39); a creation happens only once. Although this "only once" would seem to preclude access for phenomenology to history, it does not, according to Derrida (LOG 31/47).

The non-repeatable fact must have in principle (*en droit*) brought into history what can be willfully and indefinitely repeated, an "essence-of-the-first time" (*Erstmaligkeit*) (LOG 30–32/46–48). Husserl, according to Derrida, describes this type of essence in *Ideas I* as ultimate material essences or eidetic singularities.[35] Such essences exclude empirical individuality, the *tode ti* of brute existence, while including the individuality in general of a particular thing; they refer to "the sense of the fact," the repeatability of the non-repeatable (LOG 33/48).[36] The essence-of-the-first time therefore consists in the exemplarity of the factual example. By creating in a singular historical event this very specific type of universal essence, "this experience," Derrida says, "remains, in principle as well as in fact, first" (LOG 29/46). But, while in *Ideas I* the status of eidetic singularities was already "delicate," according to Derrida, here the status of eidetic singularities is "really more difficult to solve" (LOG 33/49). It is more difficult to solve because unlike *Ideas I* in which "the clue . . . is the immanent lived experience of the sensible thing perceived *originaliter . . .* always present" (LOG 33/49), in *The Origin of Geometry* the "first time" is not present; historical distance seems to have been interposed always already.

For Derrida, Husserl's designation of his investigation in *The Origin of Geometry* as a *Rückfrage* implies the irreducibility of the "always already" interposed historical distance. Derrida translates Husserl's "Rückfrage" into French as "question en retour" (LOG 36/50)[37]—currently Husserl translators render "Rückfrage" into English as "regressive inquiry"[38] —because "question en retour" (return inquiry) captures "Rückfrage's" "postal and epistolary reference or resonance of a communication at a distance" (LOG 36/50). As Derrida says, "Like *Rückfrage*, return inquiry is asked starting from [*à partir de*] a first sending [*envoi*]. Starting from a received and *already* readable document, the possibility is offered me of asking again, and *in return,* about the originary and final intention of what has been delivered to me by tradition" (LOG 36/50). These postal analogies, Derrida says, are "at the metaphorical focal point of [*The Origin of Geometry*]" (LOG 36/50). The postal analogies imply that, in order to inquire back, one must begin with a delivered letter; *Rückfrage* immediately implies a necessary lateness or delay and makes us confront the tendrillic movement.

Husserl must start with the static reduction of the current, factual, and therefore contingent state of geometry (LOG 34–35/49–50). Thus whenever Husserl uses the word "must" in *The Origin of Geometry,* this "must," as Derrida says, "marks the necessity of an eidetic pre-scription and of an *a priori* normalcy recognized now in the present [*présentement*] and timelessly [*intemporellement*] assigned to a past fact" (LOG 34/49). For Husserl, according to Derrida, the phenomenologist can state the value of *a priori* necessity independently of all factual knowledge; for Husserl, although this necessity is recognized only after the fact of the event—after someone has, so to speak, "written and mailed" geometry—this "after" is "not the indication of a dependence" (LOG 35n1/49n42). For Derrida *in contrast,* the "after" indicates an irreducible necessary dependence; "intemporellement" and "présentement," "eidetic pre-scription" and "fact" are bound together. For Derrida, I must start with "ready-made geometry" (*la géométrie tout-prête*) or with the geometry currently in circulation, with factual geometry (LOG 35/50). As Derrida says, "There must *always already* [my emphasis] have been the fact of a history of geometry, so that the reduction can be performed. I must already have a naive knowledge of geometry and must not *begin* [Derrida's emphasis] at its origin. Here the juridical necessity of the method conceals [*recouvre*][39] the factual necessity of history" (LOG 20/38). Therefore, the necessity of starting with the factual is nothing less than an "accidental and exterior fatality" (LOG 35/50). For Derrida, at once internal and necessary and external and accidental, this unity makes the order of dependence in history reversible and not linear; as Derrida says, " . . . the architectonic relations . . . are complicated, if not inverted. This would demonstrate . . . at what point the juridical order of implications is not so linear and how difficult it is to recognize the starting point" (LOG 14/33–34; cf. 33–34/49). The difficulty of recognizing the starting point implies for Derrida that geometrical truth has never and will never—it can never and must never—unconceal itself as such.

Although Husserl must start with factual geometry, Derrida stresses that Husserl's return inquiry is not bound by the notion of truth associated with deductive or axiomatic systems (LOG 43/56). If Husserl's return inquiry were bound by such a notion due to his starting point in ready-made geometry, then his inquiry would have been almost immediately invalidated by Gödel's discovery of undecidable propositions, which calls deductivity itself into question (LOG 39/53).[40] Therefore, the unity of the originary sense of mathematico-geometrical truth in general does not permit itself to be bound by the alternative of "true" or "false," determinate or indeterminate (LOG 43/56); the unity of geometry's sense is nothing but, as Derrida says, "the pure openness and unity of an infinite horizon" (LOG 44/56). Concealed within factual geometry, geometrical truth can always exceed the facts, and this unconcealment of geometrical truth is just as necessary as its concealment in facts.

Besides the postal metaphorics, there is another metaphorics at work in Derrida's *Introduction:* the metaphorics of economy. When Derrida claims that Husserl recognizes the independence of the value of geometrical ideal objectivity in relation to empirical history, he quotes the following passage from *Ideas I,* paragraph 25 (LOG 27/43):

> Instead of philosophizing and psychologizing about geometrical thought and intuition from an outside standpoint, we should enter vitally into these activities, and through direct analyses determine their immanent sense. It may well be that we have inherited dispositions for knowledge from cognitions of past generations; but for the question of concerning the sense and value of what we cognize, the history of this heritage is as indifferent as is that of our gold currency to its real value.

But then after Derrida introduces the postal analogies, he alludes back to *Ideas I,* paragraph 25 by saying:

> Return inquiry, reactionary and therefore revolutionary moment of this *Wechselspiel,* would be impracticable if geometry were essentially something which stops circulating in the ideality of value. Undoubtedly, 'no more than the history of its transmission grounds the value of gold' can any mundane history provide the sense of this circulation, since, on the contrary, history presupposes it. It is rather the maintenance of the circulation which allows the neutralization of mundane history. This neutralization opens then the space of an intentional and intrinsic history of circulation itself and allows one to understand how a tradition of truth is possible in general. (LOG 36–37/51)

Finally Derrida says,

> Since the opacity of the fact has been able to be reduced immediately by means of the production of ideal objects, historical structures are structures of sense and value which can never stop circulating, while capitalizing to infinity, according to an original mode, their sedimentary deposits. A possibility but not a necessity is there, for the interest and the difficulty of Husserl's analysis holds to what it [Husserl's analysis] is developing on two planes at once. (LOG 44/56)

"Value" here (and throughout the *Introduction*) renders the French "valeur"; "valeur" in turn renders the German "Geltung," which also means validity or acceptance. But it is significant to render "Geltung" as "valeur" and then in English as "value" in order to be consistent with the whole metaphorics of gold that Derrida is developing here. According to Derrida, that Husserl's analysis develops on two planes at once implies that the tradition of truth, exemplified by geometry, is "sometime" in Husserl merely one form, among many, of the cultural world (LOG 44/56). As such, it is transferred like all these forms. It is transferred therefore according to "the retentional power of living consciousness" which is finite (LOG 45/57). This finitude is why the tradition can be subject to loss and forgetfulness. But "at other times," according to Derrida, Husserl describes the tradition of truth, science, as "a unique and archetypal form of traditional culture" (LOG 46/58). Here science is the very idea of culture, an infinite idea. This infinity is why the tradition is open to capitalization and memory; infinity guarantees that "no signification ceases to circulate at any moment and can always be reconceived and reawakened in its circulation" (LOG 47/59). We should notice how the wording of this comment matches that of the passage quoted above from page 44/56. But, as Derrida stresses on page 44/56, Husserl's analysis accrues on two levels *at once* (*à la fois*); the unity of these two planes results in "the culture and tradition of truth" having a "paradoxical historicity" (LOG 48/59); it seems to have broken with all empirical content of real history and yet it seems to be irreducibly connected to history since it is the only means by which real history has continuity.

(B) *The Difficulty of Language.* The metaphorics of letters and gold coins implies that tradition for Husserl is defined by language. This claim becomes explicit in *The Origin of Geometry* when Husserl answers the following question—Derrida calls this question a "detour" in Husserl's text, because Husserl seems to be avoiding describing the origin of geometry for which he prepared himself (LOG 51/62)—"how can the subjective ego-logical evidence of sense become objective and intersubjective?" (LOG 52/63) by saying "literature in the broadest sense" (LOG 56–57/66). Ini-tially, according to Derrida, language allows Husserl to consider the nature of ideality. In reference to *The Origin of Geometry* discussion, Derrida ap-propriates the terminology of bound and free ideality that Husserl devel-ops in *Experience and Judgment* (LOG 52/63).[41] Although linguistic units possess a degree of ideality—their phonetic and graphic forms and their intentional content are repeatable (LOG 58/67)—they cannot be under-stood without referring to facto-historical linguistic systems and to real sensible things in this world (LOG 62/70). A geometrical object such as circularity, however, is intelligible, entirely noetic, and thus not bound to the real and contingent world; geometrical objects are entirely free ideali-ties. Geometrical propositions then, like the Pythagorean theorem, can be translated an infinite number of times; they are supra- or a-temporal and supra- or a-spatial. Geometrical ideality seems to lie beyond all language and sense content as such; it is absolutely true (LOG 68/75). This absolute truth of geometrical ideality is why Derrida calls Husserl's redescent to-ward language a "surprising turnabout" (LOG 69/76).

It might seem that Husserl's "coming back" to language implies that now he must take the brackets off the facts and plunge into real history, but, as Derrida says, "In reality . . . Husserl does exactly the opposite" (LOG 69–70/76).[42] Here (at the beginning of paragraph 6), Derrida is stressing that Husserl's redescent toward language "brings to its final completion the purpose of the reduction itself" (LOG 70/76). Husserl is bracketing con-stituted or empirical languages and cultures in order to let the originality of constitutive or transcendental language come to light (LOG 72/78).[43] The objectivity of geometrical truth could not be constituted without "an in-formation within a pure language in general" (LOG 70/77). Without this pure and essential linguistic possibility, geometrical truth would re-main ineffable and solitary.[44] As constitutive, speech is no longer expres-sion (*Ausserung*) in the sense of putting on the outside something already complete as an object on the inside; speech is the concrete, juridical con-dition of truth (LOG 71/77). Derrida says, "The paradox is that, without the apparent fall back (*retombée*) into language and thereby into history, a fall which would alienate the ideal purity of sense, sense would remain an empirical formation imprisoned as fact in a psychological subjectivty—*in the inventor's head.*" (LOG 71/77, Derrida's emphasis). This paradox, a redescent into bondage which is simultaneously a liberation, is "the most interesting difficulty" of *The Origin of Geometry* for Derrida (LOG 69–70/76).

What makes this paradox the most interesting difficulty for Derrida is that the possibility of transcendental language is the same as the possibility of intersubjectivity (*des possibilités solidaires*) (LOG 73/79). As Derrida says, "in its foundation, the problem of geometry's origin puts the problem of the constitution of intersubjectivity on the same level with that of the phenomenological origin of language" (LOG 73/79). According to Derrida, for there to be a universal or pure language, there must be consciousness of being-in-community, and for there to be consciousness of being-in-community there must be a universal or pure language (LOG 74/79). In turn, both being-in-community and a universal language suppose the horizon and unity of one and the same world. The world for Husserl, according to Derrida, is not understood as a system of facts but as "the one, but infinitely open, totality of possible experiences" (LOG 74/79).

Derrida proposes (in paragraph 6) five criticisms of Husserl's claim, in *The Origin of Geometry*, that being-in-community and pure language are possible.[45] First, according to Derrida, Husserl privileges mature, normal mankind as the horizon of civilization and as the linguistic community (LOG 74/79); certain men and certain speaking subjects are "good examples," while others such as children and madmen are not. For Derrida, Husserl's privileging implies that one empirical and factual modification—adult normality—is pretending to be a universal transcendental norm (LOG 74/80). Second,[46] the possibility of a universal language presupposes that "the perilous problem concerning the possibility of a 'pure grammar' and 'a priori norms' of language is resolved"; yet Husserl never resolved this problem (LOG 75/80).

The next three criticisms all are reducible to the following: Husserl's phenomenology falls prey to what he himself would call objectivism. As Derrida says, "The profound rhythm of [the] tension between objectivism and the transcendental motif, a tension so remarkably described in the *Crisis*, also puts phenomenology in motion" (LOG 78/83). So, third, according to Derrida, a universal language presupposes that everything is nameable in the broadest sense. Since names require a referent, they require an object given in intuition. A universal language then presupposes that, no matter how heterogeneous several constituted languages or cultures may be, "translation in principle is an always possible task"; as Derrida says, "two *normal* men will always have *a priori* consciousness of their belonging together to one and the same humanity, living in one and the same world" (LOG 75-76/81, Derrida's emphasis). This consciousness of belonging together to one and the same humanity and world requires that these two normal men be able to strip off cultural predicates and be together before "the same natural being," which then serves as "the ultimate arbitrating agency for every misunderstanding" and as "the permanent chance for the reinvention of language." As Derrida says, "Consciousness of being before the *same* thing [Derrida's emphasis], an object perceived *as such* [my emphasis], is consciousness of a pure and precultural *we*" (LOG 76/81; cf. LOG 76n1/81n84). The pure and precultural "we"—pure community, absolute translatability, universal language—therefore depends on "this purely natural objective being," which is the being of the sensible world, the earth itself, "the element which is the one most objectively exposed before us" (LOG 76/81). But, as Derrida says, "preculturally *pure* nature is always already buried" (LOG 77/81, Derrida's emphasis). There are no absolutely or purely objective objects, no objects *as such,* because the return to preculture is a "reduction of a determinate culture, a theoretical operation which is one of the highest forms of culture in general" (LOG 76/81). We must always start with culture; there is always already the mediation of technics. As we have seen and as we shall see again, the necessity of the reduction and *Rückfrage* implies the necessity of objects as such being always already concealed. Due to the intractable necessity of the "always already buried," a pure and precultural "we" can never be established; we can never overcome cultural, indeed singular, differences; we can never be before one and the same world. So, for Derrida, non-communication and misunderstanding are the very horizon of culture and language (LOG 77/82). As Derrida says, "although [the infinite pole of a sound intelligence (*une bonne intelligence*)] is always heralded so that language can begin, is not finitude the essential which we can never radically overcome?" (LOG 77/82).

The fourth criticism makes the tension of objectivism and the transcendental motif in phenomenology itself explicit. For Husserl, every meaning that cannot be led back to the model of an objective and sensible being "would remain marked by the empirical subjectivity of an individual or society" (LOG 77/82). In other words, such a meaning would never achieve universality if it could not be fulfilled by the intuition of a precultural, purely natural object. That this is the case for Husserl has the consequence of depriving Husserl's own phenomenology of universality. Husserl's own thought, as Derrida points out, is a penetration not of objectivity in general but of subjectivity in general (LOG 77/82). In other words, not being an object as such, subjectivity in general must be for Husserl fundamentally ineffable and inaccessible to "a direct, univocal, and rigorous language" (LOG 77/82). For Husserl, according to Derrida, a poetic language, which would be expressive of subjective experience and therefore equivocal, has no transcendental value; as Derrida says, "For Husserl, the model of language is the objective language of science"; " . . . language, tradition, and history exist only insofar as objects break the surface" (LOG 77–78/82).

The fifth and last criticism concerns the privilege of space in Husserl's thought. As the infinite horizon of every possible experience, the world (which supports there being a "we" and a pure language) is "the infinitely open common place for everything we can encounter before us and for us" (LOG 78/82–83). For Derrida, "before us and for us" means "given as an object" (LOG 78/83). As we have already seen in our discussion of Husserl's privilege of the mathematical object, an object is defined by its relation to a regard (*regard, Blick*) and thus is a sort of theorem related to the theoretical attitude. Here however, Derrida relates the object as theorem to the theorem in geometry. The privilege of geometry in Husserl as "the exemplary index of scientific being" (LOG 54/64) derives from the fact that geometry deals with "the spatiality of bodies [*corps*] (which is only one of the body's eidetic components), that is, deals with what endows the notion of horizon and of object with sense" (LOG 78/83). As the investigation of the spatiality of bodies, geometry gives the world and objects their ontological sense. So, as Derrida continues, the science of geometry deals with what is absolutely objective in the objects—spatiality—but it is the "Earth" (Derrida's capitalization) which provides these "earthly objects" (LOG 78/83). As the ground and foundation of objects, the Earth is transcendental. But as the place on which or in which the world is set, "the Earth is not an object and can never be one" (LOG 79/83). The ontological sense of the Earth is not therefore that of perceived being; it cannot be intuited as an object, it is never before us and for us. Therefore, its spatiality must differ from that studied in geometry, and there could never be a "geo-logy," that is, there could never be a *logos* of the Earth in the sense of both science and language. As Derrida says, "an objective science of the Earth itself . . . is as radically impossible as that of transcendental subjectivity" (LOG 79/83).

The five criticisms that we have just considered concern the fact that for Husserl, according to Derrida, the possibility of language is on the same level as the possibility of intersubjectivity. Not only, however, is the possibility of language on the same level as the possibility of intersubjectivity—both of which are spatial—but also both are dependent on temporalization. Anticipating the *Introduction*'s conclusion, Derrida claims (here at the end of paragraph 6) that "preobjective and preexact temporality . . . is . . . the *root* of transcendental intersubjectivity" (LOG 83n1/86n90, my emphasis; cf. LOG 129n2/121n134). Husserl's order of description in *The Origin of Geometry* seems to support this claim because he turns to time within his description of language (LOG 82/86). But, of course, in the Fifth Cartesian Meditation, which Derrida cites here, Husserl appeals to temporalization to explicate the constitution of another monad in mine (LOG 83n1/86n90; cf. LOG 46/57–58, 49–50/60–61). The recognition and communication "of the same" (*du même*), according to Derrida, occurs first within individual consciousness across finite retentions, and afterward it is reproduced as the "same" in the act of recollection (LOG 82/85). In an egological subject, therefore, ideality is heralded before being the ideality of an identical object for other subjects. For Derrida, this internal generation across other moments of the same subject implies that "intersubjectivity is first in a certain way the nonempirical relation of Ego to Ego, of my present to other presents as such, that is, as others and as presents (as past presents), of one absolute origin with other absolute origins which are always mine despite their radical alterity" (LOG 82/86).[47] Derrida calls this auto-affective relation a dialectic, but he qualifies it by saying that this dialectic "permits the reduction, without negation, of all alterity" (LOG 83/86). The qualification "without negation" implies that alterity is within the same, but it is not identified with the self. Alterity is merely reduced, meaning that mundane relations with others have been put out of circuit so that the transcendental relation between same and other can come to light. Therefore, concluding this brief discussion of temporalization—a theme to which we shall return below—Derrida says, "The Living Present constitutes the other as other in the self and the same as the same in the other" (LOG 83/86). In other words, *auto* and *ipse* do not bear the same, identical sense as *idem*.

Paragraph 6, which we have just completed examining, and paragraph 7, to which we are now turning, are the most famous of Derrida's *Introduction*. Both concern pure or transcendental language. They differ, however, insofar as paragraph 6 concerns speech—the "speaking subject"—while paragraph 7 concerns writing—a "subjectless transcendental field." But while their concern with language probably accounts for their fame, what makes them important is that paragraph 6 contains Derrida's discussion of "the most interesting difficulty" of *The Origin of Geometry* (LOG 69-70/76)—truth's bondage to spoken language being paradoxically truth's liberation—while paragraph 7 contains his discussion of "the most difficult problem" of *The Origin of Geometry* (LOG 91/93)—the determination of the sense of truth's disappearance due to its paradoxical bondage in and liberation through writing. This "most difficult problem" is one that appears only, according to Derrida, in Husserl's later philosophy of history, and especially in *The Origin of Geometry,* although nothing in Husserl's earliest works, works such as the *Logical Investigations,* "prohibits or contradicts" this difficulty (LOG 90-91/92-93; LOG 90n2/92n95). Derrida frames this difficulty in the opening pages of paragraph 7.

In these opening pages, Derrida says, "by itself the speaking subject, in the strict sense of the term, is incapable of absolutely grounding the ideal objectivity of sense" (LOG 83/87). Oral language only frees the ideal objectivity of sense from individual subjectivity, but leaves it bound to the institutive community. To be absolutely ideal, the object must be freed from actual subjectivity in general, freed from actual evidence for a real subject, and freed from actual circulation within a determinate community (LOG 84/87). As Derrida says, only "the possibility of *writing* will assure the absolute traditionalization of the object, its absolute ideal objectivity—that is, the purity of its relation to a universal transcendental subjectivity" (LOG 84/87, Derrida's emphasis). In other words, only by means of writing does a truth achieve "perduring presence" (LOG 83/87). "La présence perdurante" is Derrida's translation of Husserl's "das verharrende Dasein"; this translation already indicates the connection between presence and existence or being on which Derrida will soon focus after the *Introduction.* Moreover, this translation shows that truth *lacks* persisting presence or persisting existence. This lack—Husserl himself says "es fehlt"—is why writing is necessary; it "supplements," to use terminology Derrida will not develop until *Voice and Phenomenon,* the lack of presence or existence and at the same time it comes to produce this very presence or existence (cf. VP 98-99/88-89). This supplementarity means, according to Derrida, that writing is no longer a mnemotechnical aid to truth; this necessary supplementation is why Husserl calls the "body" of writing "a flesh, a body proper (*Leib*), or a spiritual corporeality (*geistige Leiblichkeit*)." Truth can no longer do without what Derrida calls "consignment" (*consignation*) (LOG 86/89; cf. LOG 72/78). The French word "consignation" means the depositing of money toward a debt, but it also contains the word "sign" within it. Truth's ontological sense is such then that it can no longer dispense with signs (LOG 90–91/92).[48] Being incarnated in a "graph" is no longer extrinsic to ideal objectivity, according to Derrida; written incarnation is no longer a system of signals (*signalisation*) or an article of clothing thrown over the truth. It does not "advent" (*advient*) upon ideal objectivity, nor does it "fall upon" or "overcome" (*survient*) ideal objectivity (LOG 87/90). As Derrida says, "The act of writing is therefore the highest possibility of all 'constitution'" (LOG 86/89). The constitutive role of writing does not imply however, for Derrida, that truth's ontological sense now derives from its factual linguistic incarnations, that truth is now relative in the worst sense of the word. Indeed, that truth must still be free in regard to all linguistic facticity in order to be itself refers us once more to the paradox that we saw in our examination of paragraph 6; as Derrida says in 7, "paradoxically, the graphic possibility permits the ultimate freeing of ideality" (LOG 88/90).

The graphic possibility, however, adds a new characteristic to this paradox. This new characteristic is death. By constituting truth as an ideal objectivity, writing can free the ideal object from all factual or actual subjects. As Derrida says, "By absolutely virtualizing dialogue, writing creates a kind of autonomous transcendental field from which every actual subject can be absent" (LOG 84/88). For Derrida, the possible freeing from all actual subjects means that writing is a transcendental field in which the conditions of subjectivity would appear and where the subject would be constituted (LOG 84–85/88). By being able to do without every actual or factual subject, every actual reader or writer, writing opens up the possibility of transcendental subjectivity. Therefore transcendental subjectivity depends on the possibility of writing; as Derrida says, "a subjectless transcendental field is one of the 'conditions' of transcendental subjectivity" (LOG 85/88). But, according to Derrida, although writing can function without all actual subjects, it still must be related purely to a consciousness which assures its functioning (LOG 85/88). If writing were not related purely to consciousness in general, it would be totally insignificant. "In its sense," writing can do without every actual reading in general, but, "in its sense," it is also dependent upon a writer or reader in general (LOG 85/88). It must be "haunted by a virtual intentionality" (LOG 85/88).

These non-linear relations of dependence which define writing for Derrida bring us to what must be the most obscure sentence in the *Introduction:* "The silence of prehistoric arcana and buried civilizations, the entombment of lost intentions and of guarded secrets, the illegibility of lapidary inscriptions disclose the transcendental sense of death, in what unites it to the absolute of intentional right in the very agency of its failure" (LOG 85/88).[49] This sentence means that inscriptions left behind by prehistoric (that is, dead) civilizations tell us what death is for, that is, what death means, that to which death is directed ("sens," like "Sinn," means both sense and direction). Death is for the transcendental. The reason we die is for the transcendental "we" (LOG 91/92); the reason we die is for an absolute liberation (LOG 93/94). And we saw this connection between death and the transcendental in our brief investigation of Derrida's later "The Ends of Man."[50] Moreover, as the condition for the possibility of ideal objects, writing unites death to the transcendental ("to the absolute of intentional right"). Since ideal objects cannot remain bound to actual subjects, in other words, since the transcendental requires this freedom in regard to all actual subjects in order to be itself, it is impossible to conceive the transcendental apart from the possibility of the death of all actual subjects. But yet, writing is the very agency of the transcendental's failure. This part of the sentence makes sense only if we realize that Derrida (following Husserl, but especially Fink) takes seriously the fact that in phenomenology the transcendental is immanent to the mundane even as it differs from the mundane. Therefore, if all factual subjects were to die—an apocalypse—in other words, if writing completely freed itself from the factual, the transcendental would be constituted as such and, as well, the inscription would be unreadable. This very unreadability would be the failure of the transcendental. In its very *absoluteness* of intentional right, writing would become "a chaotic literality" (LOG 85/88). Without any factual subjects, writing would be deprived of its transcendental function. The "soul" of the written body would flee and *never return*. The transcendental must appear in the factual and, as well, it must be freed from the factual.

This opaque sentence therefore refers to what Derrida calls writing's "ambiguous value"; writing makes communication and memory virtual, but "by the same blow," it "makes passivity, forgetfulness, and all the phenomenon of *crisis* possible" (LOG 84/87, Derrida's emphasis; cf. LOG 90/92). The transcendental sense of death rebounds on all language, including speech. According to Derrida, "writing imputes and completes the ambiguity of all language. As the movement of the essential and constitutive capacity for incorporation, language is also the place of factual and contingent incorporation for every absolute ideal object, that is, for the truth" (LOG 90/92). Every expression of ideal objectivity is also an empirical fact (LOG 90/92). In the sign, the truth becomes capable of suffering change.

Language, as Derrida says, is the "mundane and exposed residence [*résidence*] of a non-thought truth" (LOG 90–91/92). In other words, for Derrida, language is the house of truth, but an unsafe house. Through its incorporation in language, truth is guarded and put in danger (LOG 91/92). Writing's "equivocation" (LOG 91/93) therefore refers to the possibility of truth's disappearance in its very appearance. Derrida selects the word "disappearance" (*disparition*) in order to discuss the ambiguity, because "disappearance" means both "what is annihilated" and "what ceases, intermittently or definitely, to appear *in fact* without affecting its ontological sense" (LOG 91/93, Derrida's emphasis). For Derrida—and here again we see why his *Introduction* could be called "On the Essence of Truth"— since the problem of writing's ambiguous value is one of dis-appearance, it is the very question of phenomenology: what is the sense of appearance (LOG 91/93)? Even more for Derrida, now in *The Origin of Geometry* we can see the possibility of truth's disappearance appear in Husserl's philosophy, a philosophy which in certain respects is the opposite of an empiricism; until *The Origin of Geometry,* for Husserl the possibility of truth's disappearance, for example in the *Logical Investigations* (cf. LOG 90n2/92n95), agreed only with empiricism or non-philosophy (LOG 91/93; cf. LOG 128/120).

In three ways, Derrida determines this most difficult problem of truth's disappearance. The first determination is that, for Husserl, this possibility does not arise within individual consciousness. As Derrida says, "let us rule out the hypothesis of a *death of sense* in general within the individual consciousness" (LOG 92/93, Derrida's emphasis). For Husserl, once sense appears in egological consciousness, its total annihilation becomes impossible. Despite the vanishing of retentions, there is no profound forgetfulness of the presence of a sense within the monadic subject. But "the permanence and virtual presence of sense within a monadic subject" only heralds absolutely ideal objectivity, which requires speech and writing. Absolutely ideal objectivity is found menaced as truth in the world (LOG 92/93). Therefore, as Derrida says, "Profound *forgetfulness* . . . extends into the spaces of intersubjectivity and the distance of communities. *Forgetfulness* is a historical category" (LOG 92/93).

The second determination concerns the *factual* destruction of the "guardian sign," that is, the sign that guards sense (LOG 92–93/94). Husserl, according to Derrida, is unconcerned about such destruction because, "in its sense," absolutely free idealities are not bound to their factual exemplars (LOG 93/94). If all published representations of triangles were destroyed today, that event would have no effect on triangularity, for Husserl. Even if "a burning of the world-wide library" were to make absolute ideality disappear from the surface of the world, "its ontological sense as truth, which is not in the world—neither in our world here, nor any other—would remain intact in itself" (LOG 94/94). To think that such extrinsic conditions could affect absolutely free idealities intrinsically, for Husserl, would be to plunge into the most serious confusions of significations and regions (LOG 94/95). Only such events can affect bound idealities that are "in their very sense" connected to their factual instantiations (LOG 93/94). For Husserl, only bound idealities can be reduced to ashes. But Derrida stresses that Husserl conceives sense entirely as an object (LOG 93/94). That sense must be an object (and not an "in-itself" or a "pure spiritual interiority") means that it must be exposed to intersubjectivity. Because the corporeality of signs is such that everyone can perceive them without mediation, sense defined in this way is "con-signed" to signs and thereby made available to communities (LOG 93/94). The apparently irreducible bond between sense and signs seems to imply that the destruction of a factual sign would affect all senses, bound and free with forgetfulness. Yet Derrida suggests that perhaps corporeality may not constitute what the sign is. As he says, "Corporeal exteriority undoubtedly does not *constitute* the sign as such but, in a sense that we must make clear, corporeal exteriority is *indispensable* to it" (LOG 93/94, Derrida's emphasis).

The third determination continues this reflection on the essence of the sign. Derrida says, "We would be fully convinced, if here . . . Husserl had considered writing to be a sensible phenomenon" (LOG 97/97). If it were, then the bond that sense has to it could be broken. Yet writing, for Husserl in *The Origin of Geometry*, is "simultaneously" (*à la fois*) a constituted sensible body (*Körper*) but also a constituting body proper or flesh (*Leib*). This simultaneity makes it difficult to understand how writing would save its *Leiblichkeit* from corporeal disaster (LOG 97/97). But, according to Derrida, Husserl is not going to immobilize his analysis within this "ambiguity"; he is going to dissociate *Leib* from *Körper* (LOG 98/97). As Derrida says, "Although, in the word, *Körper* and *Leib*, body and flesh, are in fact numerically one and the same being, their senses are definitively heterogeneous and nothing can come to the latter through the former" (LOG 98/98, Derrida's emphasis). Dispensing with the *Körper*, Husserl locates the danger to sense in the *Geistigkeit* of the *Leib*, in the intentional act (LOG 98/98). Forgetfulness of truth for Husserl, according to Derrida, therefore is nothing but the abdication of responsibility (LOG 98/98).

As one of the ego's intentional modifications, forgetfulness for Husserl is never radical. The investigator (or reader) must overcome his initial passivity when confronted with sedimented sense and actively re-produce the originary evidence in which the ideality was produced. Describing this process, Derrida says, "I make myself fully responsible for and conscious of the sense over which I take control. In the domain of ideal objectivities, *Reactivierung* is the very act of all *Verantwortung* and of all *Besinnung*" (LOG 100/99). For Husserl however, responsibility is a co-responsibility, engaging not only the one who receives the sense but also the one who creates and expresses it (LOG 101/100). Sedimentations come to be deposited, for Husserl, only if the writer has provided "surfaces" for them, in other words, only if he has expressed the sense equivocally (LOG 101/100). In response to the irresponsibility of equivocity—here Derrida uses "equivocité" and "plurivocité" interchangeably—Husserl, according to Derrida, imposes an imperative of univocity on readers and writers (LOG 101/100).

Derrida explains the scientist and philosopher's obligation to univocity in terms of its superficiality. Husserl wants to reduce plurivocity because a univocal expression "breaks the surface totally" (*fait totalement surface*); it emerges completely from all change. But it also makes a perfectly smooth surface; a univocal expression offers no folds or creases (*repli*) into which intentions (being formed over the course of a culture) could deposit more or less virtual significations (LOG 103/101). More importantly, having no creases, a univocal expression harbors no depth (LOG 103/101). As Derrida says, "[univocal language] gives everything over in order to be seen in an actual evidence, . . . nothing is hidden there or nothing is heralded there in the penumbra of potential intentions, . . . it has mastered the whole dynamics of sense" (LOG 103/101). This superficiality is why a univocal expression remains the same and preserves its ideal identity across the whole becoming of the culture. Remaining the same, univocity, as Derrida stresses, assures communication across generations and the exactitude of translation. Therefore, as univocity subtracts sense from historical modifications, it alone makes pure history possible; as Derrida says, "[univocity] is only the index of the limpidity of the historical ether" (LOG 103–104/102). The superficiality of univocal expression is pure phenomenality or pure appearance; and, although Derrida does not say this, it is the mode of expression appropriate to mathematical objects, which are also pure phenomenality. So univocal expression is an intellectual intuition, the *logos*.

It is important to recognize here (toward the end of paragraph 7 [cf. also LOG 51–52/62]) that Derrida is endorsing Husserl's imperative of univocity. He says, "Such a reduction [to univocity] *must* (*doit*) be recommenced indefinitely, for language neither can nor *must* (*doit*) be maintained under the protection of univocity" (LOG 104/102, my emphasis). The sentence's first clause clearly states that we *must* start a reduction to univocity over and over again. But the second clause tells why it is necessary to start the reduction over indefinitely. Language cannot become univocal; there is an irreducible inadequation between possibility and necessity. Moreover, the second clause provides a second imperative, an imperative of plurivocity. Since language can become plural, for Derrida it *must* become plural. So, in the same sentence, there is a disjunction between possibility ("can") and necessity ("must") that leads to a double necessity or a double imperative (or a double injunction). Obviously, everything here turns on the word "devoir" (and on the expression "il faut") which, for Derrida, cannot be determined as either theoretical or as ethical. We are not going to explore these crucial terms—"devoir" and "il faut"—more right now; we shall return to them later.

Nevertheless, here Derrida provides examples of the imperative's duplicity. Derrida says, "Facing equivocity (which testifies to a depth of becoming and the dissimulation of a past), we have the choice between two attempts, when we want to take the memory (*la mémoire*) of a culture up in a sort of Hegelian *Errinerung* and interiorize it" (LOG 104/102). As is well known—indeed this is one of the most famous discussions from Derrida's *Introduction*—the first attempt would resemble that of James Joyce in *Ulysses*.[51] According to Derrida, in *Ulysses* Joyce attempts to re-collect all empirical and cultural meanings, all equivocities, in one book; he focuses on the passive associative resonances and ignores the translatable cores. The second attempt would be that of Husserl. In contrast to Joyce, Husserl attempts to impoverish factual or empirical language down to its translatable cores in order to remember the pure structure of history. So Joyce's attempt would "preclude history by plunging it into the nocturnal and ill-transmissible riches of 'bound' idealities"; similarly, Husserl's attempt "would itself have no other consequence than to sterilize or paralyze history in the poverty of an indefinite iteration" (LOG 104/102). So, as Derrida stresses, there must be a "relativity" between the two projects (LOG 105/103). Joyce's project depends upon that of Husserl because there could be no recollection of empiricity without a structure supporting transmission; Husserl's depends upon that of Joyce because his memory would not be historical without testifying to some genesis. Husserl, according to

Derrida, "had to admit an irreducible, enriching, and always renascent equivocity into pure historicity" (LOG 105/103).

Here Derrida criticizes Husserl's imperative of univocity, showing that it must include an imperative of plurivocity; moreover, this critique shows that memory in the sense of Hegelian *Erinnerung* must include forgetfulness. According to Derrida, there are only two limit cases in which absolute univocity can be imagined (LOG 105–106/103). The first case concerns propriety or the proper. We could imagine that the designated thing was singular or unique, precultural or natural. A singular name then could correspond to it and be univocal. As Derrida stresses however, the word itself must be ideal or universal. The notion of univocity itself implies that the sense must remain the same across a transmission; the characteristic of univocity is translatability. The project of univocity itself then necessitates the word's utterance; if the word is not communicated, I would never know that it was univocal. Sharing places the singular word, as Derrida says, "in a culture, in a network of linguistic relations and oppositions, which would load the word with intentions or with virtual reminiscences" (LOG 106/103). Thus in this first limit case (which resembles what Derrida says about a pure, precultural object in paragraph 6 [cf. LOG 75–77/81–82]), absolute univocity defeats itself.

In the second, Derrida starts from universality, not singularity. Here the chance for univocity does not lie in a precultural object but in a transcultural one, an absolutely ideal objectivity such as a geometrical object. Derrida argues however that an ideal object in principle is "always inscribed within a mobile system of relations and takes its source in an infinitely open project of acquisition" (LOG 104/106). In other words, an object is indefinitely iterable. Indefinite iterability implies that an ideal object is irreducibly relational; a true proposition can always fall into "some singular placings in perspective, some multiple interconnections of sense, and therefore some mediate and potential aims" (LOG 104/106). An ideal object can be singularly recontextualized, mediated by lateral relations, animated by unforeseen intentions. Iterability of course defines all language, not just absolutely ideal objectivities. Thus as Derrida says,

> If, in fact, equivocity is always irreducible, that is because words and language in general are not and can never be absolute *objects*. They do not possess any resistant and permanent identity that is absolutely their own. They have their linguistic being from an intention, which traverses

them as mediations. The "same" word is always "other" according to the always different intentional acts which thereby make a word significative. There is a sort of *pure* equivocity here, which grows in the very rhythm of science. (LOG 106–107/104, Derrida's emphasis)

This analysis (in paragraph 7) completes Derrida's reflection on the essence of the sign (in the *Introduction*). This analysis amounts to a sort of paradox since the very possibility of univocity is the possibility of equivocity: "the same word is always other," as if every word were a kind of indexical. We must keep this paradox in mind when we turn to *Voice and Phenomenon;* the theme of the sign and voice—uni-vocity and equi-vocity—and the word—indication understood as "l'indice"[52]—are already at work here in the *Introduction.* Combining this analysis, which shows that univocity is impossible, with the constitutive role of the sign, we can see that Husserl's definition of sense as object, which bases itself upon his privileging of mathematical objects, fails. Since all objects must be con-signed, they can never be pure objects, can never be purely objective, purely phenomenal, purely present. The disappearance of truth—truth understood as the pure immediacy of an object in intuition—cannot be an "accidental aberration" (LOG 108/105); it has always already disappeared, because "words and language in general are not and can never be absolute *objects.*" Without such an absolute object, there cannot be pure translatability and therefore pure community; in other words, if we adopt the Hegelian language that Derrida employs (the discussion of memory here at the end of paragraph 7 being probably the clearest *hommage* to Hyppolite in the *Introduction*), spirit can never be absolute; there is always more—*une surenchère*—indefinite mediation (LOG 106n1/104n113).

Nevertheless, as Derrida stresses, Husserl believes that the phenomenologist can idealize away from the relativity of univocity and plurivocity; so Husserl installs absolute univocity as an "infinite idea," as an infinite task, as a *telos,* as an Idea in the Kantian sense (LOG 107/104). In fact, although here at the end of paragraph 7 and throughout the next three paragraphs, Derrida's *Introduction* continues to follow the order of Husserl's text, these three paragraphs (8, 9, 10) concern primarily Husserl's concept of an Idea in the Kantian sense and the type of idealization that produces it, which Husserl also calls Reason. Husserl utilizes this idealization and Idea not only to handle the problems of equivocity and finitude in reactivation, but also to describe the very origin of geometry. As Derrida says, "This idealization, which has for its correlate an infinite idea, always decisively intervenes in the difficult moments of Husserl's description" (LOG 106/109). Derrida's analysis of idealization—the passage to the limit—and the Idea in the Kantian sense—totality—leads to "one of the most difficult" motifs in Husserl's thought: that constituting historicity may itself be constituted (LOG 129/121). In other words, and we have seen this criticism above, the "starting point" of idealization cannot be determined in an intuition.

(C) *The Difficulty of the Idea in the Kantian Sense.* Following Derrida's reconstruction (LOG 136/127), we can easily see how Husserl determines the preconditions of the origin of geometry. For Husserl, the origin of geometry lies in the invariant structures of the lifeworld; within the lifeworld, things are laid out in "anexact" space and time. While things consist in a number of determinations, things are also corporeal and have spatial shapes. Under the pressure of pragmatic needs, these shapes can be perfected; imaginative variation produces morphological shapes such as roundness. The art of measurement must also have been developed. This art, according to Husserl, points the way to univocity and exact objectivity. The origin of geometry itself then starts from these lifeworld structures. The passage away is prepared, according to Derrida, by "a *philosophical* act" (LOG 136/127, Derrida's emphasis). The philosopher, according to Husserl, inaugurates the theoretical attitude that "overcomes" (LOG 136/127), "tears" (LOG 143/131–132), or "cuts a hole" (LOG 148/135) through finitude. Under the influence of Platonism (LOG 137/127), some ideal "Euclid" opens up the horizon of knowledge as an infinite task. The theoretical attitude, Derrida says, "makes idealization's decisive 'passage to the limit' possible, as well as the constitution of the mathematical field in general" (LOG 136/127).

As the word "field" suggests, the inaugural infinitization encloses mathematics with a limit. As Derrida says, "The very infinity of the content of the [inaugural infinitization] will be confined within an *a priori* system which, for the Greeks, will always be *closed*" (LOG 138/127, Derrida's emphasis). In other words, it establishes a totality within which infinite developments are possible. Derrida suggests that we need to distinguish in Husserl between two types of infinitizations (LOG 138/128). On the one hand, there is the inaugural infinitization which establishes "mathematical aprioriness"; on the other, there is the infinitization which enlarges apriori systems (LOG 138/128). So, while the second type of infinitization will overthrow an apriori system such as Euclid's geometry, it "will take place only *within* infinity as the possibility of mathematical apriori in general"

(LOG 138/128, Derrida's emphasis). The Greeks simply did not become conscious of all the possibilities contained in mathematical aprioriness; in other words, "the infinite infinity of the modern revolution" was heralded "within the finite infinity of Antiquity's creation" (LOG 140/130). These two types of infinitizations therefore imply that the passage to the limit sets up a limit, but a limit that is traversable without taking a step outside that totality.

On the basis of these two types of infinitizations, Derrida criticizes Husserl's notion of origin. Derrida recognizes that Husserl must consider the lifeworld invariants not as immediate conditions for the origin of geometry, but as pre-conditions. If they were conditions, Husserl would fall into an infinite regress of origins (LOG 134–35/125). Derrida however also recognizes that the inaugural infinitization based in the theoretical attitude which opens up mathematics is only the first type and stage of infinitization; in the Modern age, there is the second type and stage of infinitization. According to Derrida, this second infinitization is a "resurrection" or "rebirth" of geometry because it starts from—Derrida uses the phrase "à partir de" frequently in this discussion—because it "starts from" the first. But there are other possibilities still hidden or indicated in the origin. For instance, philosophy being transformed into phenomenology itself "starts from" the inaugural infinitization. Phenomenology however thematizes subjectivity's anexact essences. Why have, as Derrida asks then, the origin of geometry begin with the idealization of exactitude; why not place the origin in the imaginative variation producing morphological shapes (LOG 142/131)? Each revolution based on geometrical or mathematical infinity then implies that we must rethink the origin's composition in terms of what was previously concealed there. And because the development itself is infinite, we must conclude that the origin recedes further into absence with every revolution. The infinite openness of the geometrical tradition itself implies an infinite regress of origins. Derrida therefore wonders "if it is legitimate to speak of *one* origin of geometry" (LOG 141/131, Derrida's emphasis). The reciprocal implication of end and origin implies that the geometrical traditional line, for Husserl, is only a fragment of and relative to the absolute, "universal teleology of Reason" (LOG 142/131). The idealization that Husserl describes therefore as the specific origin of geometry—the passage to the limit—is the general origin of all knowledge, tradition, and culture; it is Reason.

The general origin brings us to Derrida's analysis of Husserlian idealization. Derrida claims—we must always keep in mind that, in 1962, Derrida did not have access to all the *Husserliana* documents—that Husserl has never investigated this idealizing activity as such. Minimally, it must be defined, according to Derrida, as "starting from an *anticipatory* structure of intentionality" (LOG 146/134, Derrida's emphasis). As anticipatory, the act must therefore already be ideal. As Derrida says, "the presence to consciousness of an Idea in the Kantian sense at once [*à la fois*] authorizes and commands this idealization of anticipation" (LOG 147/134-135). Like a *Wesensschau* (which determines an object in intuition), idealization cannot be arbitrary and go in any direction (LOG 147/135). As Derrida says, "the originary passage-to-the-limit is possible only if it is guided by an essence that can be anticipated, then 'recognized' . . . " (LOG 147/135). In the idealization, I must be able to anticipate recognizing the same essence over and over again. The anticipation of re-cognition implies that the idealizing activity is defined by the iterative "immer wieder" and the "und so weiter" (LOG 146-48/134-135, 148n1/135n161). And thus, as Derrida says, "a privilege must be acknowledged to the protentional dimension of intentionality and to the dimension of the future . . . " (LOG 148/135).

For Derrida, the privilege of the protentional dimension in idealization leads back once more to temporalization in Husserl (LOG 148-150/136-137). The question for Derrida (here in paragraph 10) is not the nature of temporalization, but rather whether the Idea of the living present (that is, the total flux of lived experience) can appear as such. If the Idea of the living present, which is the Idea in the Kantian sense, cannot appear as such, then what one re-cognizes in idealization is not grounded in intuition. Without the intuition of it as such, the Idea looks to be a structure always already constituted. The question of its appearance as such is crucial for phenomenology, according to Derrida, because the Idea is that "starting from which a phenomenology is set up to achieve the final intention of philosophy" (LOG 155/141). So the question for Derrida is whether the Idea of what he calls "the indefinite *Maintenance*" of the "double envelopment" of retentions and protentions can appear as such (LOG 149/137). There is no good way to render "maintenance" in English, a word which Derrida capitalizes throughout this discussion. We are going to utilize the French word, although *maintenance* implies, of course, that the living present, for Derrida, is the indefinite "maintaining" or "nowing" of the double envelopment. Derrida says,

> . . . this *Maintenance* itself appears *as such*, it is the *Living* Present, and it has the *phenomenological* sense of a *consciousness*, only if the unity

of this movement is given as *indefinite* and if its sense of indefiniteness
is *heralded* [*s'annonce*] in the Present, that is, if the openness of the
infinite future is, as such, a possibility *lived* [*vécue*] as sense and as right.
(LOG 149–150/137, Derrida's emphasis and capitalizations)

This complicated sentence means that, in order for the Idea of the living
present to appear *as such,* the infinite openness of the future must not appear *as* something or *as* someone; in other words, it cannot be relative. But
in order for the Idea of the *living* present to be non-relative, the lived experience of it must be absolutely open or alive, that is, it must have no
intrinsic relation to death or closedness. Thus Derrida continues, "Death
will not be understood as sense but as a fact extrinsic to the movement of
temporalization" (LOG 150/137). If death is understood as an extrinsic fact,
then the temporal movement of all lived experience will be absolutely alive
or open; it will never come to an end. But death cannot be understood as
a mere extrinsic fact because, as we have seen in the discussion of writing,
death is constitutive for every ideal object. The Idea must be relative to
death in general. This relativity is so necessary that the only condition under which the Idea could become absolutely alive would be the death of
every human in general. But then the Idea would be absolutely dead at the
same time, because there would be no human consciousness to experience
or live it. Thus the *Maintenance* cannot appear as such; it can only appear
as something or as someone and therefore it can only be thought and never
intuited as such. Derrida concludes,

> The unity of infinity, the condition for that temporalization, must there-
> fore be *thought,* since it is heralded [*s'annonce*] without appearing and
> without being contained in a Present. This thought unity, which makes
> the phenomenalization of time as such possible, is therefore always the
> Idea in the Kantian sense which never phenomenalizes itself. (LOG
> 150/137, Derrida's emphasis)

From the non-appearance of the Idea as such, Derrida turns to the type
of evidence that the Idea in the Kantian sense might have. He refers to
Husserl's *Ideas I* "principle of all principles"; according to him, "implicitly"
the principle's thing itself given "in person" means "finite thing" (LOG
151/138; cf. LOG 51/62). Immediately we can see consequences of this interpretation of the phenomenological principle of all principles: if the Idea in
the Kantian sense is infinite, and if evidence is always finite, there can

be no evidence of the Idea as such. In other words, we have access to the finite form of the Idea but not to its content (LOG 153/139). As such—and here Derrida borrows from Husserl's discussion of the Idea in the Kantian sense from *Ideas I* (LOG 152–153/139)—the Idea can only be an "X." We must keep in mind that the "X" is a chiasm or a cross, as in the sign of the cross, because we can simplify the above complicated argumentation concerning the Idea of the living present in the following manner: the only way Husserl can have the Idea of the living present—the total flux of lived experience—appear as such and not as a human finite idea is to posit a divine consciousness existing separate from human consciousness. Apparently Husserl never falls into such a Platonistic dualism, although we can say that his phenomenological philosophy is a sort of Christianity. So to speak, for Husserl, God becomes man and appears in person. But appearing in man, God appears as man and not as such. Moreover, appearing as man, God can die on the cross, on the "X." In other words, the Idea of the living present must appear as man—immanence—and thus as a finite form (cf. LOG 153/139).

Derrida himself compares the Idea to God in paragraph 11 (LOG 163–164/147–148), and we shall see how important this comparison is when we turn to our reading of "Violence and Metaphysics."[53] But here in paragraph 10 he calls it "the invisible milieu of seeing analogous to the diaphaneity of the Aristotelian Diaphanous, the elemental third but one provenance of the seen and visible" (LOG 152/138). Because the Idea is invisible, we can only think about it or speak of it; it is the *Logos*. Therefore, there can be no phenomenology of the Idea (LOG 151/138). As Derrida says, "That a phenomenological determination of the Idea itself may be radically impossible . . . means perhaps that phenomenology cannot be reflected in a phenomenology of phenomenology, and that its *Logos* can never appear as such, can never be given in a philosophy of seeing, but, like all Speech, can only be heard across the visible" (LOG 155/141). The "across" (*à travers*) here indicates that we are still talking about the origin of geometry, about space, even about mathematical space (cf. LOG 148/136), and not merely time. But this space, for Derrida even in the *Introduction*, is not entirely diaphanous; he says,

> [Husserl] locates the *space* [Derrida's emphasis] where consciousness signifies [*se signifie*] to itself the Idea's prescription and thus is recognized as transcendental consciousness through the *sign* [my emphasis]

of the infinite: this space is the *interval* [Derrida's emphasis] between the Idea of infinity in its formal and finite yet concrete evidence and infinity itself of which one has the Idea. (LOG 140/154)

Thus, the *Logos,* for Derrida, is not intellectual intuition because it is consigned. Across the interval of space, the finite form of the sign indicates the Idea's infinite content. The sign, not intuition, defines the Idea's "original presence" (LOG 152/139), its "mysterious evidence" (LOG 109/106). The analysis of the Idea's evidence shows, therefore, that phenomenology's final foundation can never measure up directly to a phenomenology. We lack the infinite intuition of it. But, as Derrida says,

> At least this *Endstiftung* can give access to itself in a philosophy, insofar as it is *heralded* [*s'annonce*] in a concrete phenomenological evidence, in a concrete *consciousness* which is made *responsible* for it despite the finitude of that consciousness, and insofar as it grounds transcendental historicity and transcendental intersubjectivity. Husserl's phenomenology starts from this *lived anticipation* [*anticipation vécue*] as a radical responsibility. . . . (LOG 155/141, Derrida's emphasis)

(D) *The New Sense of the Transcendental.* Lived anticipation as a radical responsibility is, as Derrida says at the very beginning of paragraph 11, the "prise de conscience of the Idea's profound historicity" (LOG 156/141). As we noted above, due to Ricoeur, the phrase "la prise de conscience" is at this time the standard French translation of Husserl's "Selbstbesinning," the word found in *The Crisis* fragment "Philosophy as Mankind's *Selbstbessinnung.*" This fragment, the closing comments of *The Origin of Geometry*—Derrida's *Introduction* is still following the order of Husserl's text—and some late fragments on God (to which we alluded above) play a crucial role in determining what phenomenology means for Derrida in 1962. In the closing comments of *The Origin of Geometry,* Husserl speaks of a teleological Reason traversing all historicity from one end to another (LOG 161/145); in "Philosophy as Mankind's *Selbstbesinnung,*" Husserl speaks of *Selbstbesinnung* as the constant movement of the self-elucidation of historical rationality (LOG 161/146). Husserl's fragments on God describe God sometimes as the one who speaks in us, sometimes as the one toward whom I am on the way (LOG 163/147). According to Derrida, these descriptions present us with a "paradox" (LOG 159/144) or a "dilemma" (LOG 164/148). It seems that teleological reason for Husserl merely traverses factual types of humanity (LOG 161/145); that human consciousness is merely the mediation of a *Logos* retaking possession of itself across this consciousness (LOG 162/146); that the essential and actual plentitude, God, would be deployed merely in a historical discursivity from which it would let itself be derived (LOG 164/147–148). God, Reason, the Idea, the *Logos* would be *beyond*, even beyond historicity understood as the condition for the possibility of factual histories. If the Idea for Husserl is truly beyond— and we have encountered this problem in Husserl before in our analysis of Derrida's essay "'Genesis and Structure' and Phenomenology" (Chapter 2)—then Husserl's phenomenology collapses into "a speculative metaphysics or an absolute idealism" (LOG 164/147). It looks to be a Platonism. But such an interpretation of Husserl's comments about the Idea and Reason, as Derrida notes, goes against his doctrine of the noema and his critique of psychologism (LOG 159–160/144–145). In short, for Husserl, as actual, the Idea looks to be beyond factual history and beyond historicity as the possibility of history, and yet the Idea is nothing outside of historicity and history.

Confronted with this dilemma, Derrida says, "Instead of frantically investigating the choice, it is necessary to strive toward the root that is necessarily one of every dilemma" (LOG 164/148). This root is so "one"—"the elemental third but one provenance"—such a "profound unity" that, starting from it, one must say "both at once [*les deux à la fois*]" (LOG 164/148). Indeed, Derrida says, "both at once" is "perhaps the only response to the question of historicity," a question which has produced so many difficulties, paradoxes, and dilemmas (LOG 164/148). So God, Reason, the *Logos*, or the Idea passes "across" and is "beyond" constituted, that is, factual history; but *as well*, God, Reason, the *Logos*, or the Idea is nothing but the pole of constituting historicity (LOG 164/148). The profound root, of course for Derrida (in the *Introduction*), is the Living Present. For Husserl, "supratemporal" and "intemporal," terms by which he determines the Idea and which suggest the eternal, are actually characteristics of the Living Present, which is omnitemporality (LOG 165/148). Therefore, Derrida says, "The hidden temporal unity of 'dia-', 'supra-', or 'in-'temporality on the one hand and *omni*temporality on the other is the unitary foundation of all the agencies dissociated by the various reductions: factuality and essentiality, worldliness and nonworldliness, reality and ideality, *empeiria* and transcendentality" (LOG 165/149, Derrida's emphasis).

As throughout his *Introduction*, Derrida notes again that temporalization is the "root" of historicity (LOG 166/150). But historicity involves language and therefore spatialization. So, Derrida says, " . . . historicity can be only the passage of a Speech, the pure tradition of an originary Logos towards a polar Telos" (LOG 165/149). But the "two at once," "the one" implies that there can be no being that makes sense outside of this passage; so, as Derrida stresses, "the Absolute is Passage" (LOG 165/149). The "movement" (cf. LOG 150/137, 159/144, 161/145, 165/148) implied by this sentence is a circularity, but a circularity without end since the "originary Logos" and "polar Telos" *are* nothing outside of the circulation (LOG 165/149). Moreover, since the origin and end are mutually dependent—teleological actualizations tell us what was originally possible and the original possibilities tell us what we should actualize—"their reciprocal inspiration" (LOG 165/149) implies that the movement is endlessly back and forth. Therefore, Derrida is suggesting for historicity the image of a, so to speak, straight-line circularity, what he called earlier in the *Introduction* a "mouvement en vrille" (LOG 14/33): "every adventure is a conversion [*conversion*] and every return [*retour*] an audacious move toward the horizon" (LOG 166/149). But even more, the tendrillic movement is labyrinthine because sense can always be lost "en route" due "to the inauthenticity of a language and . . . the abdication of a speaking being" (LOG 166/149). So, as Derrida says, "this movement is also the Absolute of a Danger" (LOG 166/149).

This entire movement determines, for Derrida, phenomenology's most basic definition: "first of all *Selbstbesinnung* and *Verantwortung*" (LOG 166/149). In the labyrinthine movement, "consciousness invents its way [*chemin*] in an indefinite reduction which has always already begun" (LOG 166/149). This reduction is always a reduction to sense, one in which one freely resolves "to take up again one's own sense"; Derrida here uses the phrase "reprendre son sens" which is similar to "prendre conscience." To become conscious of one's own sense, according to Derrida, is "to make oneself accountable, through speech, for an imperiled way [*chemin*]" (LOG 166/149). The speech "is always already a response," because the sense has lapsed into unconsciousness or disappeared; the way is imperiled. But, for Derrida, being always already a response, the speech is responsible, which means "to take upon oneself [*se charger*] a word that is heard, to take [*prendre*] upon oneself the exchange of sense in order to watch over its waymaking [*cheminement*]" (LOG 166/149). All of Derrida's uses of the word "chemin" here refer to the literal sense of "method" as "way" (*hodos*). So the primary definition of phenomenology for Derrida is "Method of Discourse" (LOG 166/149; cf. LOG 20/38). And the discourse is the reduction always already begun, always already a response to a lost sense, a response through which one makes oneself responsible for the sense continuing on its way. The response therefore is "a teleological affirmation" (LOG 168/151), a "yes" for the adventure to continue, a "yes" of the future.

The tendrillic movement, however, shows the inadequacy of phenomenology as such because the movement implies not that historicity has a sense but that it is sense (LOG 166/150). Derrida's entire analysis in paragraph 11 depends, not surprisingly, on the word "sens."[54] As is well known, "sens" is ambiguous between sense as "meaning" and sense as "direction"; thus sense implies both immanence to experience and language and transcendence beyond experience and language. As immanence, sense is appearance or phenomenon—being—and yet, as transcendence, it is the possibility of appearance or phenomenon—sense is both non-*reell* and non-real. To stress the transcendence of sense to reality, Derrida appropriates Plato's "epekeina tes ousias" (LOG 159/144). Derrida recognizes that Husserl's (and indeed the entire phenomenological tradition's) use of the word "sense" stems from the attempt to reconceive the Platonic or metaphysical notion of Idea, *eidos,* form, or essence; "sense" replaces "essence" in order to deprive essence of transcendent existence.[55] Thus the word "sense" allows phenomenology to be vigilant against Platonism or against speculative metaphysics (cf. LOG 167/150). To say that "historicity is sense" means therefore both at once "history's *appearing* and the *possibility* of its appearing" (LOG 167/150).

But to say the *appearing* of history means the appearing of a "Geschehen"; it means the "gathering [*rassemblement*] of what advents" (cf. LOG 165/149). Derrida is not using these terms, "Geschehen" and "rassemblement" (which translates the German "Versammlung"), arbitrarily; they are obviously Heideggerian. To assert that "historicity is sense" (meaning the appearing of history and the possibility of the appearing of history) means, for Derrida, that

> phenomenology can be articulated without confusion with a "philosophy" posing the question of Being or History. This "ontological" question ("ontological" in the non-Husserlian sense of the term, which alone can be, and today often is, opposed to Husserl's phenomenological ontology) cannot arise from phenomenology as such. (LOG 167/150)

While this comment seems to imply a priority of ontology in a non-Husserlian sense, that is, in a Heideggerian sense, over phenomenology, Derrida immediately qualifies this by saying, "we do not believe either that this question can ever, *in philosophical discourse, simply precede* transcendental phenomenology as its presupposition or latent foundation" (LOG

167/150, Derrida's emphasis). For Derrida in the *Introduction,* since the question of being asks for a *decision* concerning the sense of being, phenomenology always has priority over ontology. Since phenomenology determines the conditions for the possibility of appearance, that is, the conditions for Being, phenomenology is the philosophical propaedeutic for the philosophical decision concerning the sense of being. But since the propaedeutic is always heralded as infinite, the completion of the propaedeutic is ideal, not factual. So phenomenology never gives up its juridical right. Only phenomenology can, again for Derrida in the *Introduction,* give us knowledge of sense as the possibility of the appearing of Being or History. In paragraph 11, here at the very end of the *Introduction,* Derrida describes this knowledge as "light," as "certainty" and as "apriori security" (LOG 168–171/151–153). Only the phenomenological light allows us to speak. If ontology is not supposed to be empiricism or non-philosophy, if it is to complete philosophy (LOG 169/151), if it is to be discourse, it must first know that of which it speaks (*en sachant de quoi l'on parle*) (LOG 167/150; cf. LOG 168/151). Without this propaedeutic of method which gives us knowledge of sense as possibility, ontology remains in silence (LOG 169/151). Ontology, according to Derrida, only has the right to the question of Being as History; but "every response to such a question can resurface only in a phenomenological process" (LOG 169/151). Only on the condition of phenomenology can we ask not just the "how" of history, but the "why" (LOG 167/150). Only on that condition can we ask "in clarity why there is a history rather than nothing" (LOG 168/151). No matter what, as Derrida says,

> The "why" can emerge only from the *possibility* (in the metaphysical
> or ontological sense, and not in the phenomenological sense) of the non-
> being of historical factuality; and nonbeing *as* nonhistory only unveils
> its contingency [*eventualité*] starting from a consciousness of pure sense
> and pure historicity, that is, starting from a consciousness of possibility
> in the phenomenological sense. (LOG 167–168/150)

We shall return to this logic of possibility, contingency, and necessity in a moment, but the point we should recognize here is that, for Derrida, the "metaphysical or ontological possibility" depends on "possibility in the phenomenological sense." We shall return to this relation of dependence between metaphysics and phenomenology when we turn to "Violence and Metaphysics" below.[56]

As we have seen throughout our analysis of Derrida's *Introduction,* the relations of dependence are far from linear. For Derrida, phenomenology, as the philosophy of sense as the possibility of the appearing of history, and ontology, as the philosophy of sense as the appearing of history, are "irreducibly joined [*solidaire*]" (LOG 167/150). Just as ontology must presume phenomenology, phenomenology must presume ontology. As Derrida says, "Being itself must always already be given to thinking, in the pre-sumption—which is also a resumption—of Method. And undoubtedly an access to being *and* being's advent must already be *contracted*, when phenomenology begins by claiming the right to speak" (LOG 169–170/152, Derrida's emphasis). The phenomenological method must start from the constituted; therefore, it must presume the advent of being and that an access to being—language—has already been given; otherwise, phenomenology would not be able to begin. But, as Derrida stresses, this starting point in being and not in pure sense implies that phenomenology is always already late (*en retard*) (LOG 170/152). The lateness, however, is not "a simple and faulty misery" of thought as phenomenology, because phenomenology itself prescribes historicity for being; only phenomenology can give us access to the consciousness of the Living Present.

As always for Derrida in the *Introduction*, the Living Present is the root; here it necessitates delay. But it does this because "the auto-temporalization" of the Living Present is linked with intersubjectivity (LOG 170/152). Derrida says,

> The discursive and dialectical intersubjectivity of Time with itself in the infinite multiplicity and infinite implication of its absolute origins, justifies [*donnant droit à*] every other [*toute autre*] intersubjectivity in general and makes the polemical unity of appearing and disappearing irreducible. Lateness is here the philosophical absolute, because the beginning of methodical reflection can be only the implication of an *other* absolute origin, prior and in general possible. (LOG 170/152)

We should note the wording of this comment. At issue is *auto*-temporalization, but *auto* is not the same as *idem* (identity). So, within the dialectical movement of time with itself, there is always the possibility of an other. In retention, there is always already another past present, which must be a Living Present and thus another absolute origin. But then since this movement is already the movement of intersubjectivity, the other absolute origin must involve absence because, according to the Fifth Cartesian Meditation, I can never have a *Gegenwärtigung* of the other's psychic life; I can only have a *Vergegenwärtigung* of it. So the absolute origin is always already other and has always already disappeared. This is why the "polemical unity of appearing and disappearing" is irreducible. Understood through intersubjectivity, the consciousness of the Living Present is a consciousness of "impossibility," according to Derrida (LOG 171/153). It is impossible for this consciousness "to rest in the simple *maintenance* of *one* Living Present" (LOG 171/153). It is always other in its self-identity. Nevertheless, the living present has, as Derrida says, "a strange style of unity," without which "nothing would appear." The very impossibility of being at rest and yet still unified, the impossibility of being open and yet still being one—"the pure and interminable disquietude of thought working to 'reduce' Difference by exceeding the factical infinity toward the infinity of its sense and of its value, that is, while maintaining Difference" (LOG 171/153)—this disquietude, therefore, is the origin or condition for the possibility of anything appearing. In other words, as Derrida says, "Difference would be transcendental" (LOG 171/153).

3

Thus, in the 1962 *Introduction to Husserl's "The Origin of Geometry,"* due to Hyppolite, Derrida poses for the first time the question of language.[57] But Derrida does not seem to understand what writing's essential role in the constitution of ideal objects implies—nonpresence or death—since he only speaks of speech in the *Introduction*'s last paragraph. Nevertheless, that language is a central concern makes Derrida for the first time utilize the concept of intersubjectivity to clarify the living present. As in the earlier *Le Problème de la genèse* (PGH 239–240), Derrida says in the *Introduction* that "preobjective and preexact temporality . . . is . . . the root of transcendental intersubjectivity" (LOG 83n1/86n90; cf. LOG 129n2/121n134); indeed, as we have just seen, the living present is "the root, that is necessarily one, of every dilemma" (LOG 164–165/148–149). As far as we can determine, Derrida never eliminates this fundamental role of the living present (cf. SM 15/xix). Nevertheless, we can see a transition coming about here in 1962 for Derrida. In *Le Problème de la genèse*, Derrida never cites Husserl's Fifth Cartesian Meditation; but in the *Introduction*, he cites it twice explicitly (LOG 50n1/61n55, 83n1/86n90) and alludes to it once (LOG 109/106). More importantly, Derrida says that there is an irreducible "polemical unity of appearing and disappearing" in the living present because of "the discursive and dialectical *intersubjectivity* of Time with itself" (LOG 170/152, my emphasis). To be as precise as possible, Derrida here is interpreting retention in terms of what Husserl shows in the Fifth

Cartesian Meditation, that is, that there is no presentation (no *Gegenwärtigung*) of the other's lived experiences; there is only a *Fremderfahrung* which includes *Vergegenwärtigung*. Being a transcendental ego, the alter ego is another absolute origin within what is most mine, the living present; similarly, having the form of the living present, each retention is another absolute origin within what is most mine, the living present. The descriptions of *Fremderfahrung* will become increasingly important for Derrida and remain so. As we shall see when we turn to *Voice and Phenomenon*, the irreducible absence included in the experience of the alien ego will determine how Derrida conceives retention (and not vice versa), the result being that he will not conceive retention as a past present, nor will he conceive protention as a future present. Retention and protention *herald* without presenting. Already therefore in 1962, we can see the outline of Derrida's concept of the trace whenever Derrida uses the verb "s'annoncer."

We can see another sign of Derrida's shift to "a common structural root" of time and the other when he discusses the "we." The concept of the "we" links alterity directly to the question of language and, of course, anticipates the 1968 essay "The Ends of Man" (see Chapter 3 above). As we have seen here, in the *Introduction*'s sixth paragraph, Derrida argues that in order to have a pure community and pure communication—in other words, in order to have absolute translatability—we must have access to a preculturally pure nature. Since, however, we must always start from culture, from the phenomenological reduction which is the highest form of culture, "preculturally *pure* nature is always already buried" (LOG 77/81, Derrida's emphasis). This analysis of the relation between culture and nature implies that I do not have unmediated access (a *Gegenwärtigung*) to the alien ego's singular lived experience of nature. So I can never confirm that he has the same experience of the object as I do. But the analysis also implies that there is mediation between him and me; I have the possibility of a *Vergegenwärtigung* of the alter ego's lived experiences of the object. Since I can use mediation, I am always already in a sort of community with the alien ego, a community, however, that is never pure. There is always already culture, but never one pure culture. In other words, all of us share the form of the living present, which makes mediation possible, but each of us has a singular stream of content, which makes mediation necessary.

The impurity of the community implies that the structure of genesis is incomplete. As we just saw, "the polemical unity of appearing and disappearing" implies "the absolute of delay." Within the living present, retention and protention are necessary. Consequently, in every experience, retention has always already occurred, making the origin disappear; we must start therefore from what derived from the absent origin; hence the necessity of memory. Similarly, protention has always already occurred, making the end disappear; we must start from what is to come from the absent future; hence the necessity of anticipation. As we saw above, the incompleteness of the living present implies non-linear relations of dependence. Starting from the factual or constituted, the reduction's results are second; yet what is discovered through all of the reductions is essential and therefore first. For Derrida, as we saw already in *Le Problème de la genèse*, it is impossible to determine which, the factual or the essential, is genuinely original. In the *Introduction* however, the relations of dependence are even more complicated. The tendrillic movement arises because, since the origin and the end have always already disappeared, a movement toward one necessitates a "conversion," a turning back toward the other. An actualization in the future implies that that possibility was latent in the past; a possibility discovered in the past implies its future actualization. But, again, retention and protention—both understood through *Vergegenwärtigung*—imply that the tendrillic movement is endless; the movement, therefore, cannot be totalized.

Derrida's entire analysis in the *Introduction* depends on an instability in the concept of totality (and with the word "totality" we must still think of Hyppolite's Hegel). This instability provides Derrida with a new "logic."[58] By definition, a totality must be finite because a total brings things to an end; it must enclose things within a limit. But also, by definition, a totality must be open to everything and therefore be endless and unlimited; otherwise, it would not be a total. The *Introduction*'s concept of totality will define Derrida's concept of *différance*. Derrida anticipates this concept, which is developed for the first time in *Voice and Phenomenon*, when he speaks of phenomenology being "stretched" [*tendue*] between the infinite and the finite (LOG 151/138; cf. LOG 127/119, 171/153). Because the logic of *différance* is one of totality, it is extremely powerful. Its power, however, comes from an "impuissance."[59] This impotence means, Derrida tells us, that consciousness cannot enclose itself; it cannot come to a rest or to an end; it cannot be finite. But, as an *impuissance* to rest, consciousness *must* exceed the limit. So the *impuissance* to rest is a necessity of movement. This *impuissance* had already appeared in paragraph 7, when Derrida said that we are unable to maintain language in univocity; it must be equivocal (LOG 104/102). But also in paragraph 7, as we noted, Derrida states that language must be univocal; in other words, it cannot be equivocal. So there is a second necessity based on a second impotence. Derrida states this second impotence when he says that "the Living Present is the phenomenological absolute from which I can never exit [*dont je ne peux jamais sortir*]" (LOG 149/136). The impotence to exit from the living present means that I must stay within the limits of the living present. But, conversely, the impotence to rest means that I must exceed the limits of the living present. The absolute of the living present is such that this double necessity, this double imperative, this double injunction is always "out of joint." The root that is necessarily one is two; the root that is necessarily two is one. Always being out of joint implies that the living present is "stretched" between two possibilities: unable to enclose myself, I can still exit; unable to exit, I can still enclose myself. For Derrida, these necessary possibilities of exiting and enclosing are not abstract, because "they are lived [*vécue*] under the form of *horizon*" (LOG 123/117, Derrida's emphasis). While Derrida will eventually abandon the phenomenological notion of horizon, we see why it is crucial for him now. The phenomenological notion of horizon means that necessary conditions of possibilities are experienced (unlike Kantian transcendental conditions of possible experience). But as concretely lived, the necessary possibilities also include contingency. There can be as many ways to exit or to enclose oneself as there are facts. Now we can start to see the extreme power of the Derridean notion of necessity: no fact can be excluded as a possible, finite place from which the infinite can be liberated; all facts are needed as possible, finite places in which infinity can be enclosed. But the Derridean notion of necessity is even more powerful because it is both theoretical and ethical; as Derrida says in a footnote, "the Idea is the common root of the theoretical and the ethical" (LOG 149n1/136n162; cf. LOG 17n1/36n21). Whenever therefore Derrida uses either "devoir" or "il faut," he means both "must" and "should." Every fact must be; every fact should be.

That Derrida reconceives the transcendental in terms of this extremely powerful logic of totality demonstrates his indebtedness to Hyppolite's interpretation of Hegel as a thinker of the whole (*du tout*) (cf. LE 131/102). Indeed, in the *Introduction*, Derrida is still trying to up the ante on the dialectic over those of Cavaillès and Tran-Duc-Thao (cf. especially LOG 157–159/142–144). In the attempt to up the ante, Derrida transforms the concept of the dialectic so radically that the word "dialectic" loses its traditional sense and becomes inappropriate. Derrida, however, does not seem to realize that the word is inappropriate, which shows us the inchoate character of Derrida's thought in 1962; he says—and we have quoted this passage already—"By its very dialecticalness, the absolute primordiality of the Living Present permits the reduction, *without negation,* of all alterity [*toute alterité*]" (LOG 82–83/86, my emphasis; cf. LOG 126/119). This passage implies that Derrida is separating alterity from negation (as the stranger does in Plato's *Sophist*);[60] in other words, Derrida is not allowing alterity to be pushed all the way up to contradiction or to be deepened down into opposition. But this comment, as we shall see, does not mean that Derrida is not maintaining some sort of concept of negativity. Separating alterity from opposition and contradiction but not from negativity, one cannot really speak of a dialectic as Derrida does in this passage. The word "dialectic" therefore will be virtually absent in Derrida's "Violence and Metaphysics"—but here we shall see "negativity"—and in *Voice and Phenomenon,* and, by the time of "The Ends of Man" in 1968, it will have completely disappeared from Derrida's lexicon of positive terms. Instead, the words "undecidability," "contamination," and, of course, "différance" will replace it.

Derrida's logic of totality—now understood through alterity—transforms the meaning of the words "unity" and "one," and, of course, it transforms the meaning of the word "negation" and "position." As we have seen, the living present, for Derrida in 1962, is the one root; the living present includes negative aspects—the "not yet" of protention and the "no longer" of retention—but these negatives are merely others. As mere others, they are not negated, but rather they are affirmed insofar as the living present is totally open. The living present is the necessary *affirmation* of all possible things, even those that have not yet happened and those that are no longer happening (cf. LOG 168/151). Position in Derrida does not mean the positive characteristics of all things; it means the affirmation of all things. Therefore all the negative terms that one can find in the *Introduction*—"non-problematicity" (LOG 111/107); "non-historicity" (LOG 120/114); "non-modifiable" (LOG 112/109); "non-sense" (LOG 37/51); "non-dialectical" (LOG 158/143); "non-philosophy" (LOG 91/93)—terms, like "in-finite," must be understood in terms of the affirmation of alterity. Although inchoate, Derrida's thinking in 1962 already implies that when he speaks of a "subjectless transcendental field," of transcendence, of "epekeina tes ousias," of a "beyond," he is speaking not of a negation but merely of an other. Unlike that of Hyppolite, Derrida's thinking therefore is not *anti*-humanistic, which implies negation, opposition, and contradiction, but "meta-humanistic."

The "meta-humanism" of the *Introduction* transforms the notion of ontology that Derrida utilized in *Le Problème de la genèse,* where he, probably under the influence of Sartre's reading of Heidegger, associated it with anthropology. In the *Introduction,* while "ontology" still means Heidegger, now Derrida equates it with metaphysics (LOG 167/150). Ontology, for Derrida in the closing pages of the *Introduction,* concerns "the surging forth of naked factuality" (LOG 169n1/151n184). "Pure existentiale facticity as wild singularity" is, for Derrida, outside the scope of all eidetic subsumption (LOG 169n1/151n184) and therefore outside the scope of phenomenology. But, for Derrida, if we prioritize the surging forth of factuality, of "Being as History" (LOG 169/151, Derrida's capitalization), then we would mix "transcendental idealism and speculative metaphysics" (LOG 167/150). For Derrida in 1962, phenomenology must remain "pure" (cf. LOG 170/153).[61] That Derrida uses the word "pure" so frequently in these closing pages shows again that he has not yet in 1962 understood the implications of the word "contamination," despite the fact that he used it already in *Le Problème de la genèse.* Indeed, in these closing pages Derrida does not seem to understand the logic of totality that he himself develops in the *Introduction.* In these closing pages we see once more what the original version of "'Genesis and Structure'" expressed. For Derrida, there must be a "juridical priority" given to phenomenology (LOG 169n1/151n184) in order to be vigilant against speculative metaphysics. Still maintaining the "hypothesis" of "'Genesis and Structure,'" Derrida shows that Husserl flirts with metaphysics (and ontology) whenever he speaks of the Idea or reason (or of God in the fragments); Husserl himself seems to posit the *arche* or the *telos* without intuition. To speak of the *arche* and *telos* of history or of being goes beyond the limits of finite, phenomenological evidence; Husserl seems not to obey his own principle of all principles (cf. LOG 151/138; cf. LOG 51/62). Here Derrida is applying a classical phenomenological critique; he has not yet developed what we are calling a "super-phenomenological" critique. Thus, for Derrida, "Phenomenology alone can make infinite historicity *appear*" (LOG 170/152, my emphasis). This appearing is the basis for phenomenology's right to respond to every ontological question. Phenomenology alone provides evidence; it alone makes sense; it alone knows. As Derrida says—and we have already quoted this passage—"we can pass from the [phenomenological] question of 'how' to the [ontological] question of 'why' by *knowing* that of which we speak" (*en sachant de quoi l'on parle*) (LOG 167/150). That Derrida conceives responsibility in terms of a response to a question shows that epistemology—even absolute knowledge—still orients him in these closing pages. If, as

Derrida says at the very end of the *Introduction*, difference is transcendental, then difference is "beyond being." Unlike in *Le Problème de la genèse*, here in the *Introduction* Derrida directly appeals to the Scholastic notion of a transcategorical in order to define his new sense of transcendental (LOG 162n3/146n177). But if difference is beyond being, if difference is originary, then how is it possible to conceive it? Will we not find ourselves caught in the same?

Part Three.
The End of Phenomenology and Ontology

6   More Metaphysical than Metaphysics: An Investigation of "Violence and Metaphysics"

We now enter the most crucial period in the development of Derrida's early thinking, the mid-sixties.[1] Four things seem to happen during this period. First, Derrida deepens his understanding of the dialectic between phenomenology and ontology with which he closed both the 1962 *Introduction to Husserl's "The Origin of Geometry"* and the 1954 *Le Problème de la genèse*; in particular, he understands more fully the implications of his discovery of *écriture*. The problem of language, indeed the problem of the sign, becomes more intense. Second, there is an investigation of Levinas's writings up to approximately 1963.[2] In this investigation Derrida discovers that Levinas's thought "calls us to depart from the Greek site" (ED 122/82), the site which is the source of the thought of both Husserl and Heidegger, of both phenomenology and ontology (ED 120/81). When Derrida adopts the Levinasian experience of the other as outside of Greek philosophy, both phenomenology and ontology, in a sense, come to an end in Derrida's thinking. All of Levinas's questions to Husserl and Heidegger become Derrida's questions. But third, Derrida adopts Levinas's thought of the other within the structure of the dialectic between phenomenology and ontology. Derrida substitutes Levinas's thought of the other for the human existence, the surging forth of naked factuality, wild singularity, the Being as history of both *Le Problème de la genèse* and the *Introduction*: in other words, the experience of the other, which Levinas calls metaphysics, replaces what Derrida had called in his earlier Husserl books "ontology," "ontology in a non-Husserlian sense," that is, it replaces Heideggerian ontology.[3] This replacement pushes ontology over onto the other side of the dialectic with phenomenology. There is now a dialectic between what Levinas calls "metaphysics," where metaphysics holds the side of non-presence, transcendence, and genesis, and onto-phenomenology, where onto-phenomenology—"violence"—holds the side of presence, im-

manence, and structure. The result of this new dialectic—Derrida's terminology now is going to be "system" or "economy" (ED 117/79, 163/110–111,
226/152)—is a critique of Levinas from the onto-phenomenological side
of the dialectic. But fourth, at the same time as Derrida is investigating
Levinas's thought of the other, he is investigating Heidegger's thought of
being. In this simultaneous investigation, Derrida discovers that Heidegger's thought of being pursues the origin of philosophy, Greek philosophy, in his investigations of pre-Platonistic thinkers; this origin is the same
that is not identity but difference. This realization transforms the dialectic
between metaphysics and onto-phenomenology into a dialectic between
alterity and difference, between Levinas's thought of God and Heidegger's thought of being. Although quickly after 1967 Derrida will start to
question Heidegger, and first of all from a Nietzschean standpoint,[4] this
complicated "dialectic" defines Derrida's later thought;[5] it defines deconstruction. Originally published in 1964 in *Revue de métaphysique et de morale*, "Violence and Metaphysics: An Essay on the Thought of Emmanuel
Levinas" represents Derrida's first attempt to "amalgamate"—in a sort of
alchemical or magical relation (cf. MP 141/119)—the non-Greek genetic
thought of the transcendence of the other with the Greek structuralist
thought of the immanence of the same (which is not identity but difference). It is the first deconstruction. Because deconstruction consists in this
amalgamation, we can say—appropriating the idea of an "upping of the
ante"—that deconstruction is "more metaphysical" than Levinas's metaphysics. We shall return to this "amalgamation" in Part IV, Chapter 8. We
must say therefore that Derrida's own thinking begins with "Violence and
Metaphysics": deconstruction begins when phenomenology and ontology
come to an end.[6] Unlike "'Genesis and Structure' and Phenomenology,"
which has an unrivaled privilege in regard to a specific phase of Derrida's
thinking, his interpretation of Husserl,[7] "Violence and Metaphysics" has
an unrivaled privilege in regard to the general development of Derrida's
thought. No serious investigation of Derrida's interpretation of Husserl
can avoid this essay.

1

It is clear that the idea of deconstruction is on the horizon in "Violence and Metaphysics" since Derrida uses the word "destruction" a number of times.[8] The word "destruction" however—more than the word "deconstruction," which does not occur in "Violence and Metaphysics," not

even in the revisions Derrida made for its inclusion in *Writing and Difference* in 1967—suggests violence, as in the essay's title, "Violence and Metaphysics": the essay could have been called "Destruction and Metaphysics." This transformation of the title shows us immediately how much this essay concerns a confrontation between Heidegger and Levinas. Where Heidegger had had the impulse (*motif*) to reduce metaphysics and show its dependence on fundamental ontology, Levinas has the opposite impulse to raise metaphysics up again and to make metaphysics more fundamental than ontology (ED 119–120/81). Where Heidegger had had the impulse to make ethics secondary in relation to being or fundamental ontology, Levinas has the opposite impulse to make ethics be fundamental: ethics understood as the experience of the other is the sole means of opening up metaphysics (ED 122–23/82–83). These impulses can be found in Husserl as well, of course, and Levinas takes up his opposite impulses in response to phenomenology; but, as we shall see when we return to Husserl below, the well-known difference between Heidegger's thought of being and Husserl's thought of the phenomenon—Husserl does not ask the question of being—is now for Derrida crucial. In any case, these comments concerning the relation of metaphysics and ontology (which come from the Introduction to "Violence and Metaphysics") show us that what is at stake in this essay is a question of precedence, fundamentality, or presupposition. We must keep in mind throughout our reading of "Violence and Metaphysics" the new concept of the transcendental Derrida developed in the *Introduction*. In "Violence and Metaphysics," Derrida says (alluding to Fink) that what both metaphysics and ontology concern themselves with is an "origin," a "depth," which is not "in the world"; rather, this depth is "the possibility of our language and the nexus of our world" (ED 122/82). He continues,

> It is at this depth that the thought of Emmanuel Levinas can make us tremble. . . . This thought, which fundamentally no longer seeks to be a thought of being and phenomenality, makes us *dream* of an unheard of demotivation and dispossession. (ED 122/82, my emphasis)

The words "demotivation" and "dispossession" also suggest deconstruction. Indeed, Derrida calls Levinas's thought a "destruction" of phenomenology and ontology (ED 127/85). Undoubtedly this Levinasian "dream" is Derrida's dream as well: deconstruction fundamentally seeks no longer to be a thought of being and phenomenality. This is why Derrida says that his interrogation of Levinas is "anything but an objection" (ED 125/84).

But at the Conclusion of "Violence and Metaphysics," Derrida also says that this Levinasian *dream*—and this is why we italicized the word "dream" above—of an unheard-of demotivation and dispossession is a "*dream* because it must vanish *at daybreak,* as soon as language awakens" (ED 224/ 151, Derrida's emphasis). This quote implies that Levinas's metaphysics is a kind of nighttime, dark thinking, as opposed to "the violence of light" (this phrase is the title of the first section of "Violence and Metaphysics"). The most basic question of "Violence and Metaphysics"—the question, Derrida says, Levinas is posing to us (ED 125/81)—is the question of the origin of language. We can express this question in other ways: the question of the relation of thought to language, experience to discourse, silence to speech, or even the relation of genesis to structure. The relation of genesis and structure is still at the heart of Derrida's thinking here in "Violence and Metaphysics." But if *Derrida's* (not Levinas's) thought concerns both the dream and the waking, then we must say as well that deconstruction concerns a level more fundamental or more general, wider, than Levinas's metaphysics. This greater fundamentality is why we have been able to insist on deconstruction being a critique of—being more fundamental, it includes or possesses—the thought of Levinas (or that of Heidegger or that of Husserl, etc.). Deconstruction is "more metaphysical" than Levinas's metaphysics; if Levinas's metaphysics is a "meta-phenomenology" or "meta-ontology" (ED 127/85), deconstruction is "meta-metaphysics."

To understand what it means to say that deconstruction is more metaphysical than metaphysics, we must, of course, investigate what Derrida says about Levinas's metaphysics. Since we are on the verge of considering *Voice and Phenomenon,* we must keep in mind here the phrase "metaphysics of presence," a phrase Derrida coins on the basis of his investigation of Heidegger. The phrase occurs in "Violence and Metaphysics," but each time it occurs it is a 1967 revision; only once does Derrida associate the phrase with Levinas's thought (ED 225/152). Our question now, we might say, is: is Levinas's metaphysics for Derrida a metaphysics of presence? Most generally, the metaphysics of presence is defined as a valorization of perceptual presence over any type of non-presence *and* a lack of an ontological reflection on the "ens" of "praesens." We shall return to this phrase below and provide a more specific definition of it. But the question is: does Levinas's metaphysics fit this general definition? Metaphysics, of course, for Levinas—and this means his ethics as well—is the discourse of alterity. According to Derrida, alterity in Levinas is defined by two characteristics. On the one hand, "the other," for Levinas according to Derrida, "is other only if its alterity is absolutely irreducible, that is, infinitely irreducible . . . " (ED 154/104); it must be an absolute alterity, "an exteriority which can be neither derived, nor engendered, nor constituted on the basis of anything other than itself" (ED 156/106). In other words, as Derrida also says, Levinas conceives the other "without relation to the same" (ED 224/151).[9] This first characteristic means that the other is without relation to violence (or war), or to totality, or to language, if language means any sort of formality (the Greek *logos*). The other is relationless, infinite; it is peace and silence. On the other hand, alterity, for Levinas according to Derrida (who here quotes *Totality and Infinity*), is defined by "the saying to the other, this relationship to the other as interlocutor, this relation with an existent" (ED 146/98). In fact, Levinas says, "Discourse is discourse with God. . . . Metaphysics is the essence of this language with God" (ED 159/108). The second characteristic means that alterity is defined by language, by speech, and by a dative relation (ED 141/95), a relation *to* the existent, God; "existent," as is well known, is Levinas's translation of Heidegger's "Seiend," being. In other words, defined by the dative relation of dialogue, the other is not, for Levinas, defined by intuition (ED 142/96). According to formal logic, which, as Derrida notes (ED 142/95, 131/88, 187/128), Levinas rejects, these two characteristics of alterity form a contradiction. The reading according to contradictions, difficulties, and problems that we saw in *Le Problème de la genèse* and in the *Introduction* is still functioning in "Violence and Metaphysics."

If we focus only on the first characteristic—"without relation to the same"—we are led into what Derrida calls "the classical difficulties of language" ("classical" meaning here not ancient Greek philosophy but modern philosophy from Descartes to Kant) (ED 170/116). Because classical, that is, modern philosophy conceived God as a positive infinity, it confronted the difficulty of how to express this positive infinity linguistically (ED 168/114). Because the other for Levinas is conceived, thought, or experienced "without relation to the same," the other's translation into language, which includes negativity, form, and the logic of non-contradiction, "betrays" the other (ED 224/151; see also 135/91, 187/128). For instance, the infinite is betrayed by the word "in-finite," which is a negative term. For Derrida, by conceiving the other "without relation to the same," Levinas has given up the right to speak about the other, and yet Levinas speaks about it; therefore Levinas "reverts . . . to a pre-Kantian style of infinitist dogmatism" (ED 191/130). On the basis of the first characteristic of alterity alone, Levinas's thought, for Derrida, consists in "the classical schema" of the relation of thought to language, that is, an external relation (ED 224/151, 169/114).

We have seen this critique of dogmatism—thus a critique in the Kantian sense—in Derrida's earlier writings on Husserl; it implies that Levinas does not have the evidence—in a word, *the presence*—for the claims he is making because he conceives the other "without relation to the same." Below, we shall examine more closely the relation between Levinas's metaphysics and Husserl's phenomenology (in order to make the transition to *Voice and Phenomenon*). It is important to note now however that this critique is based on the fact that it is impossible to conceive alterity without it having a relation to presence, or, more precisely, to "the intentional phenomenon in which the other appears as other, and lends itself to language, *to every possible language*" (ED 184–85/125, Derrida's italics). Levinas's statements are limited by experience. But this critique also implies that Levinas's metaphysics is *not* a metaphysics of presence. *Metaphysics in the Levinasian sense* does not rely on presence for its claims about alterity, while Husserl's phenomenology does, implying that phenomenology turns out to be a *metaphysics of presence*. The alterity of the other is precisely a non-presence. Derrida's 1967 revisions concerning Levinas's notion of the trace—"The Trace of the Other" appears only in 1963—suggest as much (ED 190/129, 160/108). But even if metaphysics in the Levinasian sense is not a metaphysics of presence, the critique that Derrida is leveling here against Levinas still holds: Levinasian metaphysics must find itself *taken* by the metaphysics of presence, most generally, by the Greek *logos* (which implies that Levinas should not have called his thought metaphysics, which is a "Greek notion" [cf. ED 123/83]). For Derrida, the metaphysics of presence is violence in the Levinasian sense—the relation to the same—and without this relation to violence metaphysics in the Levinasian sense would be defined by *pure* non-presence, *pure* alterity, and thus *pure* non-violence (or peace).[10] This determination of Levinas's metaphysics means that now the title of "Violence and Metaphysics" could have been "The Metaphysics of Presence and Metaphysics in the Levinasian Sense."

The first characteristic of alterity, "without relation to the same," therefore implies that Levinas's thought consists in the "classical schema of the relation of thought and language," a relation of exteriority. When Levinas, however, defines alterity in terms of dialogue, he in effect is making language and thought identical, giving up thereby this classical schema. Yet, for Levinas, the definition of alterity as speech does not put the other into relation with the same; dialogue is teaching, not enslavement. This exteriority of alterity from the same, even though alterity is now identified with language, implies that Levinas is describing a language, a speech, which would be "non-violent language" (ED 218/146–47). According to Derrida, if Levinas is trying here to conceive a "non-violent language," it would have to be a language "which would do without the verb *to be*, that is, without predication" (ED 218/147). "Predication is the first violence" (ED 218/147). Levinas's language would have to be a sentenceless speech (ED 218/147). Derrida tells us what this language would look like:

> Since the verb *to be* and the predicative act are implied in every other verb, and in every common noun, nonviolent language, in the last analysis, would be a language of pure invocation, pure adoration, proffering only proper nouns in order to call to the other from afar. (ED 218/147)

But such a speech consisting of only proper nouns would not be a language as the Greeks knew it, "the Greeks who taught us what *Logos* meant" (ED 219/147); as Derrida says, "there is no *Logos* which does not suppose the interlacing of nouns and verbs" (ED 219/147).

We have not seen this critique in Derrida before, a critique of linguistic naivety. It derives from Derrida's first investigation of language in his *Introduction to Husserl's "The Origin of Geometry."* We recall that, when Derrida investigates the language through which ideal objects are constituted, he realizes that this "transcendental language"—indeed all languages—must be at once equivocal and univocal. The non-violent language that Derrida describes for Levinas would be equivocal or poetic; yet this language would not be possible—no communication would take place—without a kernel of sameness, univocity. Yet this critique of equivocity implies, yet again, that Levinas's metaphysics is not a metaphysics of presence. In *Of Grammatology* in 1967, Derrida identifies the metaphysics of presence with what he calls "logocentrism," that is, a conception of language as formal and non-contradictory, consisting in predication which allows truth value to be determined, in a word, a conception of language as univocal. If metaphysics *in the Levinasian sense* consists in a "non-violent language" which is non-logistic, and if the metaphysics of presence is a metaphysics of the *logos,* then Levinas's metaphysics is something different from a metaphysics of presence, from logocentrism: the alterity of the other is "nothing less than irrational" (ED 187/128). Derrida's 1967 revisions concerning Levinas's notion of the trace again suggest as much (ED 190/129, 160/108). But even if metaphysics in the Levinasian sense is not a logocentrism, the critique that Derrida is leveling here against Levinas still holds: Levinasian metaphysics must find itself taken by the Greek *logos*. Without this relation to the violence that is the *logos*, metaphysics in the Levinasian sense would be defined as a *pure* non-violent language, as pure speechlessness. Again, we must say that Levinas cannot say how, without the relation to formality and predication, without relation to the copula which joins and differentiates a subject and an object, this non-violent language would be able to say, show, or give anything. It would not be able to teach.

As we have just noted, Derrida's first investigation of language had just occurred in the 1962 *Introduction*. The revisions Derrida made for the inclusion of "Violence and Metaphysics" in the 1967 *Writing and Difference* indicate a growing awareness of the results of this first investigation. For instance, the following passage is a 1967 insertion:

> . . . an *inscribed* origin. The *inscription* is the written origin: traced and henceforth *inscribed in* a system, in a figure it no longer governs. Without which there would no longer be any one's own body [*de corps propre*]. (ED 169/115, Derrida's italics)

Moreover, in the 1967 version, Derrida changed "Language, son of earth and sun" to read "Language, son of earth and sun: *writing* [*écriture*]" (ED 166/112–113, my emphasis). These revisions indicate that Derrida now sees that what he was calling "writing" in the *Introduction, écriture* (which also means "scripture"), precisely provides the conception of language that Levinas needs. On the one hand, writing, for Derrida, is a *speechless* speech, since it is silent, voiceless or equivocal, outside of the Greek *logos*, since it is "prehistoric arcana"; and yet, on the other hand, since writing is formed —"the persisting existence or presence" of the words on the page—it is within the Greek *logos*: it is speechless *speech*. This duality of writing is why Derrida says, "by neutralizing the demands of empirical 'economy,' writing's essence is more 'metaphysical' (in Levinas's sense) than speech" (ED 150–151/102). *Writing is more metaphysical in Levinas's sense than Levinas's metaphysics precisely because writing is metaphysical in the Greek sense.*

We can now formulate the schema of the relation of thought to language that Derrida sees in Levinas's philosophy (at least up to 1963). If Levinas had remained within the classical schema of the relation of thought to language according to the first characteristic of alterity, Levinas would have had available to him the resources that negative theology and Bergsonism had available (ED 170/116). Because Bergson, for example, conceived intuition as alien to philosophical discourse, he gave himself "the right to speak . . . in a language resigned to its own failure" (ED 170/116). Bergson, according to Derrida, has the right to "denounce" and to have "disdain" (*mépris*) for discourse as a betrayal of intuition (intuition in the Bergsonian sense).[11] This denunciation of the betrayal of discourse is "the classical resource" for this "classical difficulty." According to Derrida, Levinas cannot provide himself with this resource; he has given up the right to speak in a language resigned to its own failure, because, according to the second characteristic of alterity, "the possibility of metaphysics [in the Levinasian sense] is the possibility of speech" (ED 171/116). In other words, for Levinas, thought does not "travel through philosophical discourse as through a foreign medium" (ED 171/116). With Levinas, therefore, we have, according to Derrida, "a classical schema," that is, a kind of dogmatism based on the fact that Levinas conceives the other "without relation to the same," "a classical schema here complicated by a metaphysics of dialogue and teaching, of a demonstration which contradicts what is demonstrated by the very rigor and truth of its structure" (ED 224/151). Unlike Bergson, for example, who resolves himself to the denunciation of language for its betrayal of intuition (ED 171/116)—this resolution could be described as a resolution in favor of incoherent coherence—Levinas, for Derrida, "resolves himself to betraying his own intentions in his philosophical discourse" (ED 224/151), a resolution Derrida himself calls "incoherent incoherence" (ED 224/151).[12] In relation to both of these choices— the resolution of Bergsonism (or negative theology) for the denunciation of the betrayal of language and Levinas's resolution for the betrayal of one's own intentions in discourse without being able to denounce this betrayal—Derrida says, in the Introduction to "Violence and Metaphysics," that "We will not choose" (ED 125/84); in fact, he says, "We will not choose between the opening [*l'ouverture*] and totality," where the "opening" refers to the first characteristic of alterity, that is, that the other is without relation to the same; and where "totality" refers to the second characteristic, that is, that the other is language, which cannot be conceived without relation to the same, to presence. Derrida continues, "Therefore we will be incoherent, but without systematically resolving ourselves to incoherence" (ED 125/84). Thus Derrida's non-choice, or, perhaps better, his undecidability is a coherent incoherence, which he calls "the impossible system" (ED 125/84). In order to conceive this impossible system, Derrida says in the Conclusion to "Violence and Metaphysics" that "it is necessary, in a certain way, to become classical once more, and again find other impulses for the divorce between speech and thought. This path is quite, perhaps too, abandoned today. Among others by Levinas" (ED 224/151). These impulses are, for Derrida, both Jewish and Greek; hence Derrida's famous invocation of Joyce at the very end of "Violence and Metaphysics."

2

On the basis of our brief discussion of writing above, we already have a sense of that in which this "impossible system" consists. It defines deconstruction (even in Derrida's later writings). Since Derrida's impulses in this impossible system are double, both Jewish and Greek, the purpose of this system is "to attempt a breakthrough to the beyond of philosophical discourse . . . *within language*" (ED 163/110, my emphasis). According to Derrida, the only chance we have of succeeding at this breakthrough is by "posing *formally and thematically the problem of the relation between the belonging and the breakthrough*" (ED 163/110, Derrida's italics). "Belonging" (*appartenance*) refers to philosophy, the Greek, totality, and "the breakthrough" (*percée*) refers to non-philosophy, the non-Greek, the opening. Derrida explains here in "Violence and Metaphysics" that "formally" means "in the most formalized way," not in "a logic" of the opening and totality, but in an "unheard of graphics," "within which philosophical conceptuality would be no more than a *function*" (ED 163/110–111). This comment is a 1967 addition which indicates yet again that Derrida is recognizing the importance of his discovery in the *Introduction:* writing. This use of the word "writing" implies that Derrida's thought, deconstruction, is always a kind of formalism. Writing always suggests the shaping and outline, indeed, the drawing, of letters: hence a form. Here, what Derrida is calling a "graphics" refers to what we were calling "the logic of totality" earlier.[13] We can no longer, however, call this logic a "logic," because logic is a philosophical concept; what we call "logic" is nothing but a function of this system.

While we cannot call this system a logic, we can continue to use the word "totality." In "Violence and Metaphysics," Derrida calls the graphics a "structural totality"; Derrida says, "A *system* is neither finite nor infinite. A structural totality escapes from this alternative in its play" (ED 180/123). Repeatedly, Derrida says that, although Levinas assumes that totality means finite totality, this determination of finitude is "in no way inscribed in its concept" (ED 180/122; 176/119). Yet also throughout "Violence and Metaphysics," Derrida also speaks of an "originary finitude" (ED 152/103, 167/113, 169/114, 192/131). In the *Introduction,* Derrida called this "essential finitude."[14] These two comments—that totality is not necessarily only a finitude and that finitude is essential or originary—imply that there is an ambiguity in the concept of totality (or in the concept of in-finity). As we recall from the closing discussion of the *Introduction*, by definition, a totality must be finite because a total brings things to an end; it must enclose things within a limit. But also, by definition, a totality must be open to everything and therefore be endless and unlimited; otherwise, it would not be a total. This ambiguity, or better, undecidability, or better still, this "difference between totality [understood as finite] and infinity [understood as totality]" (ED 180/123) defines the impossible system for Derrida. If this difference is one that breaks through to the other as other —finite and not the same—and also at the same time one that makes the other be the same—infinite and not not the same—then this difference must be understood as a negativity. "A system is *neither* finite *nor* infinite" (cf. ED 135/90). In other words, what lies over the limit of totality cannot be the same: it must be other. But also at the same time, insofar as the totality must be infinite sameness, it must negate what is not the same (not not the same). The same, therefore, as Derrida says, is "in strange complicity with negativity" (ED 175/119). We are obviously very close to Hegel here and to the concept of internal difference that we discovered in Hyppolite (cf. ED 139/93).[15] Although we quoted this comment above, we believe it is so important that we must quote it again; it comes from a footnote to "Violence and Metaphysics":

> Pure difference is not absolutely different (from nondifference). Hegel's critique of the concept of pure difference is for us here, doubtless, the most uncircumventable theme. Hegel thought absolute difference, and showed that it can be pure only by impure. (ED 227n1/320n91)

This comment is the source both of Derrida's concept of "différance" and of "contamination."[16] It means that there can never be pure or absolute alterity, or pure or absolute difference. Nevertheless, this comment does not mean—despite the fact that Derrida has not explicitly demarcated his concept of *différance* from Hegelian contradiction in "Violence and Metaphysics" (cf. POS 59-60/44)[17]—that Derrida is here speaking of a positive infinity, of the Hegelian "absolute position." We must recognize that what Derrida is here calling "originary finitude" implies that there is a necessary indetermination in the other. For Derrida, even though the other must be in relation to the same, the other can never entirely become *my* other (or *its* other as Hegel would say), which would allow the other to be a contradiction and thus be completely included in the same. This is impossible because the other belongs to the same as a form that can be iterated indefinitely. Derrida's thought is a thought of the indefinite; he says, "The infinitely other would not be what it is, other, if it was a positive infinity, and if it did not maintain within itself the negativity of the indefinite, of the *apeiron*" (ED 168/114; see also ED 175/119, 170/115).

Even with this idea of negative alterity, an impure difference—*différance*—we are still not at the most fundamental level of what Derrida is calling the impossible system. According to Derrida:

> We are wondering about the sense of a necessity: the necessity of lodging oneself within traditional conceptuality in order to destroy it. . . . Is it an extrinsic necessity? Does it not touch upon only an instrument, an "expression," which can be put between quotation marks? Or does it hide, rather, some indestructible and unforeseeable resource of the Greek *logos* . . . Some unlimited power of envelopment by which he that attempts to repel it would always already be *overtaken* [*surpris*]. (ED 165/111–112)

We must hear in the word "indestructible" the word "deconstruction." The necessity of lodging oneself within traditional conceptuality is not an extrinsic necessity. The resource—as we shall see, the word "resource" appears in *Voice and Phenomenon*[18]—the resource and power of the Greek *logos* cannot be deconstructed.[19] We are now at the most fundamental level, the level of an indestructible necessity. As we saw in our reading of the *Introduction,* the power (*la puissance*) of this necessity, for Derrida, is based on an impotence (*une impuissance*). So, in "Violence and Metaphysics," he says,

> For egological life has as its irreducible and absolutely universal form the living present. There is no experience which can be lived other than in the present. The absolute impossibility of living other than in the present, this eternal impossibility, defines the unthinkable as the limit of reason. (ED 194/132; see ED 188/128)

There is an absolute necessity that all experience occur within this form; I am powerless to make them occur otherwise. This comment utilizes the language of Husserlian phenomenology. Derrida also expresses it in the language of Heideggerian ontology: "Being is necessarily dissimulated" by the existent (ED 221/149). For Derrida, this necessary dissimulation of the other in the existent, that the other cannot appear as what it is but only as a phenomenon, "these necessities are violence itself" (ED 188/128; also ED 195/133, 221/149). There is always *le surpris, la prise,* and *comprendre,* both in the sense of understanding and inclusion. But as we also saw in our reading of the *Introduction,* the indestructible necessity is double for Derrida. In "Violence and Metaphysics," he says,

> . . . the Idea in the Kantian sense designates the infinite overflowing of a horizon which, by reason of an absolute and essential *necessity* which itself is absolutely principial and irreducible, *never can* become an object itself, or be fulfilled, equaled, by the intuition of an object. (ED 177/120, my emphasis)

There is an absolute necessity that all experience exceed intuition whose form is always the living present. We know what this comment means. It is impossible for an experience not to be in the form of the present (because of the finitude of experience); therefore it must be included in the form of the present. Yet it is impossible for an experience to be in the form of the present (because of the openness of the infinite idea); therefore it must be excluded from the form of the present. We can reformulate this double necessity in the language of Heidegger's ontology. It is impossible for being not to be an existent (because of the dissimulation of being); therefore it must be included in the existent. Yet it is impossible for being to be in the existent (because being is not an existent); therefore it must be excluded from the existent. According to this double necessity, for every *prise* therefore there is a *mépris,* violence and non-violence (ED 188/129), or better, "violence against violence" (ED 172/117).

There is one last consequence of Derrida's impossible system. Here we return to the dialectic between phenomenology and ontology that we saw in *Introduction:* the relations of dependence are far from linear. On the one hand, Levinas's metaphysics in its very critique of phenomenology—because of the first indestructible necessity of totality—must presuppose phenomenology insofar as there can be no access to the sense of the other except on the basis of an intentional modification of my ego (ED 188/128); similarly, Levinas's metaphysics in its very critique of ontology—again because of the first indestructible necessity of totality—must presuppose ontology insofar as the being of the other would make no sense without what Heidegger called the pre-understanding of being (ED 206–208/140–141). On the other hand, however, there is the second indestructible necessity of the opening: phenomenology and ontology must presuppose Levinas's metaphysics. As we saw in the *Introduction,* phenomenology is always late;

being has always already advented so that phenomenology can begin its work. The question of being precedes phenomenology—although phenomenology retains the right to answer the question, by knowing that of which it speaks, by its light (the first indestructible necessity). In "Violence and Metaphysics," however, in contrast to the *Introduction,* Derrida speaks of a question that is not philosophy's question, that is, that is a question of non-philosophy, the question of the origin of philosophy (ED 118/79). This non-philosophical question's "silent opening escapes phenomenology, as the origin and end of phenomenology's *logos*" (ED 195–196/133). It is important to note (especially as we approach *Voice and Phenomenon*) that this question of origin in "Violence and Metaphysics" is genetic; it seems to be the same question of "why" as we saw in the *Introduction.* But here Derrida does *not* call it an "ontological question." This opening of the question of philosophy's origin now for Derrida is a question that could be asked only of God, or perhaps better, *to* God. Unlike the *Introduction,* where the question of being precedes phenomenology understood as a method or propaedeutic, here in "Violence and Metaphysics," God "would precede every 'method'" (ED 223/150). Derrida says,

> . . . it is infinity—as nondetermination and concrete operation—which would permit the thinking of the difference between being and ontic determination. The ontic content of infinity would destroy ontic closure. Implicitly or not, the thought of infinity *would open the question,* and the ontico-ontological difference. Paradoxically, it would be this thought of infinity (what is called the thought of God) which would permit one to affirm the priority of ontology over theology, and to affirm that *the thought of being* is presupposed by *the thought of God.* (ED 222/150, my emphasis)

Although an existent thing, God's ontic content—His attributes—for Derrida, transcends every existent thing. He is nothing, as Derrida says, "nothing determinate" and thus "God means death" (ED 170/115). Again we see the deepening of the *Introduction*'s discovery of *écriture,* "the transcendental sense of death." Given this deepening, it is not surprising that, for Derrida in "Violence and Metaphysics," the relation between creatures and God is at once univocal (ED 222/150) and equivocal (ED 221/142). God, for Derrida, is a transcendental in the Scholastic sense, "transcategorical" (cf. ED 205–206/140), or, as Derrida says in *Voice and Phenomenon,* "ultra-transcendental" (VP 14/15). Univocal means that God and man are the same, that God is immanent in man; equivocal means that God and man are other, that God transcends man. This "at once" univocal and equivocal God, which is merely another expression of the double necessity, is why Derrida can say that, without the ontic content of infinity, without God's transcendence (equivocal) and immanence (univocal), there could be no question *either* about being *or* about the existents. The infinite alterity called God opens up the very difference between being and the existent. So, theo-logy, the thought of God, presupposes ontology, insofar as God is an existent, the most excellent existent; we could not understand the being of this existent without ontology. *And* the thought of being presupposes the thought of God, only because God (in His infinite transcendence) allows us to have the difference between existents and what transcends existents, being. We could, of course, characterize this double presupposition as a chiasm, the chi (X); it means that the title of "Violence and Metaphysics" could have been "The Thought of Being and the Thought of God."

3

It is only now, when we see how Levinas's metaphysics, understood as a kind of theology of the existent God, presupposes the thought of being, that we get the sense that Derrida considers Levinas's metaphysics to be a metaphysics of presence (cf. ED 209/142). We cannot say anything more than "we get a sense" because Derrida only associates Levinas's metaphysics with the metaphysics of presence indirectly, through the word "empiricism" (ED 225/152). Instead, in the 1967 revision for the inclusion of "Violence and Metaphysics" in *Writing and Difference*, Derrida directly associates the phrase, "the metaphysics of presence" with Husserl's phenomenology. Clearly, he is trying to reconcile this essay with the conclusions of *Voice and Phenomenon*. At the beginning of "Of Ontological Violence" in both the 1964 and in the 1967 version, Derrida says,

> In order to speak, as we have just spoken, of the present as the absolute form of experience, one must already understand what time is, must understand the *ens of the praes-ens,* and the proximity of the *being of this ens.* The present of presence and the presence of the present suppose the horizon, the pre-understanding anticipation of being as time. (ED 196/134, Derrida's italics)

Derrida then inserts the following in the 1967 version:

> If the sense of being always has been determined by philosophy as presence, then the *question of* being, posed on the basis of the transcendental horizon of time . . . is the first tremor of philosophical security, as it is of self-assured presence. Now, Husserl never unfolded this question of being. If phenomenology carries this question within itself each time that it considers the themes of temporalization, and of the relationship to the alter ego, it nonetheless remains dominated by a metaphysics of presence. The question of Being does not govern its discourse. (ED 196–97/134, Derrida's italics)

We can already see the thesis of *Voice and Phenomenon* in this revision. *Voice and Phenomenon* "deconstructs"—again this word does not occur in "Violence and Metaphysics"—Husserl's phenomenology insofar as it is "dominated by a metaphysics of presence."

We must now make this concept of the metaphysics of presence as precise as possible. For Derrida, two characteristics define it. On the one hand, the metaphysics of presence consists in experience being defined as "an encountering of an irreducible presence, the perception of phenomenality" (ED 225/152).[20] These two phrases are not accidental: on the one hand, the metaphysics of presence is the encounter in the sense of the "counter" or the "over and against" of an object, a metaphysics of objectivity; on the other, the metaphysics of presence is perception of the phenomenon in the sense of proximity to self in interiority, a metaphysics of subjectivity (cf. VP 83–84/75). Phenomenology is precisely the attempt to reconcile these two senses of being, subjectivity and objectivity. And, as we saw in our investigation of the *Introduction,* this conception of presence derives from Derrida's realization that the mathematical object is Husserl's privileged example.[21] Yet Derrida says,

> In another way, one could certainly show that Husserl silently presupposes a metaphysical anticipation or decision when, for example, he asserts being (*Sein*) as the nonreality (*Realität*) of the ideal (*Ideal*). Ideality is unreal, but it *is*—as object or as thought-being. Without the presupposed access to a sense of being that reality does not exhaust, the entire Husserlian theory of ideality would collapse and with it all of transcendental phenomenology. (ED 197/134, Derrida's italics)

This passage is probably the idea that became *Voice and Phenomenon.* The decision mentioned in this passage is different from the one Derrida points to in his earlier works; this decision is ontological (and not a decision to favor structure over genesis). This decision brings us to the second characteristic of the metaphysics of presence, that phenomenology is a discourse "not governed by the question of being" (ED 197/134). In other words, the metaphysics of presence is a discourse that presupposes a sense of being, the sense as presence. Insofar as it does not take up the question of being, the metaphysics of presence has either "decided" that being's sense lies in presence or "anticipates" that its sense will be determined as presence, any kind of absence being but a modification of presence (ED 197/134). In other words, the metaphysics of presence is a dogmatism (the decision) or a teleology (cf. ED 172/117) (the anticipation) of presence. We have seen this dogmatism and this teleology before: in short, the metaphysics of presence takes presence as an irreducible value. If we combine these two characteristics, we can define the metaphysics of presence in the following way: it is a discourse which values ontic presence (either the subject or the object) as being irreducible to anything else that could be characterized as non-presence. We must add one qualification to this definition: because the metaphysics of presence values presence, it determines language in terms of its ability to present (logocentrism). As we shall see when we turn to our reading of *Voice and Phenomenon,* this qualification means that the metaphysics of presence values the medium of voice. Nevertheless, in general, the metaphysics of presence is what Levinas would call violence.

Derrida must reconcile the conclusions of *Voice and Phenomenon* with those of "Violence and Metaphysics" because "Violence and Metaphysics" contains Derrida's longest positive or non-critical interpretation of Husserl; it occurs in the section of "Violence and Metaphysics" called "Difference and Eschatology," in a subsection called "Of Transcendental Violence."[22] We must examine this section if we want to understand *Voice and Phenomenon.* It presents us with two Husserls. The first Husserl is the Husserl of the metaphysics of presence, and perhaps we have to call this Husserl "the superficial Husserl." As we saw above, Levinas's metaphysics must presuppose phenomenology as the source of presence for its claims about alterity: "metaphysics . . . always supposes a phenomenology in its very critique of phenomenology, and especially if, like Levinas's metaphysics, it seeks to be discourse and instruction" (ED 173/118). There can be no discourse of alterity, of course, for Derrida, without "the passage to essentiality" (ED 197/134); without "the ultimate jurisdiction of evident truth"; "the layer of phenomenological evidence in general"; "the possibilities of essence which guides all concepts," including ethical concepts; "sense for concrete consciousness in general" (ED 178–79/121). In a word, metaphysics in the Levinasian sense requires phenomenal presence.

The second Husserl, however, is a Levinasian Husserl, and perhaps we have to call this Husserl "the deep Husserl" (cf. VP 114/101). In "Of Transcendental Violence," besides criticizing Levinas for his unacknowledged presupposition of phenomenal presence, Derrida also defends Husserl from the charges Levinas levels against his Fifth Cartesian Meditation. The result is that "Levinas and Husserl are quite close here" (ED 183/125). Derrida summarizes the Levinasian critique of Husserl:

> . . . according to Levinas, by making the other, notably in the *Cartesian Meditations,* the ego's phenomenon, constituted by analogical appresentation on the basis of belonging to the ego's own sphere, Husserl allegedly missed the infinite alterity of the other, reducing it to the same. To make the other an alter ego, Levinas says frequently, is to neutralize its absolute alterity. (ED 180/123)

Derrida's defense of Husserl from this charge consists in three steps. First, Derrida argues that what Husserl is particularly "sensitive" to in the Fifth Meditation is the "singular and irreducible style" of evidence or phenomenon or appearance within which the other is given to an ego, to a "me," to me (ED 181–82/123). As Derrida says, "One could neither speak, nor have any sense of the totally other, if there was not a phenomenon of the totally other, or evidence of the totally other as such" (ED 181/123). In short, for there to be any discourse of the other, the other must appear to me. But, as Derrida says, this appearance is of a "singular and irreducible style," which brings us to the second step.

So second, following Husserl's explicit intentions, Derrida argues that the intentionality aiming at the other is "irreducibly mediate" (ED 182/123). We cannot stress this aspect of Derrida's argumentation enough: the mediate nature of this experience, of the phenomenon of the other, is the direct link to the question of the sign in *Voice and Phenomenon;* what Husserl calls analogical appresentation is the basis for what Derrida calls the trace. What Husserl calls analogical appresentation, for Derrida, implies, not an analogical and assimilatory reduction of the other to the same, but rather "the unsurpassable necessity of . . . mediations" (ED 182/124); these mediations make the other be other. Analogical appresentation is therefore for Derrida "nonviolent respect for the secret," that is, respect for the fact that the other is never given to me immediately and originally in communion with my own lived experiences. Analogical appresentation, for Derrida, implies that the other consists in an "originary non-presence," an "original non-phenomenalization" (ED 181/123). The originality of this non-presence, which must not be confused with mere absence, is due to the fact that the interiority of others cannot be given to me immediately, cannot be my interior life, is never my own. There is, in other words, an originary non-propriety (ED 183/124). Yet, while original, that is, singular and irreducible, the alterity of others, for Derrida, participates in a more general alterity, that of the thing, which too hides sides and profiles. Here Derrida is alluding, of course, to Husserl's famous descriptions of the perception of things in *Ideas I* in terms of adumbrations. The other is first of all a body and therefore involves profiles. Without this adumbrating, the other's original non-presence would not be able to appear. Husserl therefore, according to Derrida, in the Fifth Meditation "describes the phenomenal system of non-phenomenality" (ED 183/125).

This phenomenal system of non-phenomenality brings us to the third step, which concerns what Husserl himself calls "archi-factuality" (*Urtatsache*), non-empirical factuality, or transcendental factuality (ED 192/131). Derrida quotes this passage from *Formal and Transcendental Logic*: "This *I am* is for me, for the I who says it and understands it accordingly, the *primordial intentional foundation of my world*" (ED 193/131). This comment means, according to Derrida, that "nothing can appear outside of its belonging to 'my world' for an 'I am'"; in other words, "*my world* is the opening in which all experience occurs" (ED 193/131). I, the factual "me," am the origin of the world and therefore at the same time the transcendental ego, but also other "me's" are other origins of the world and therefore at the same time transcendental egos. For Derrida, with the structure of this transcendental factuality, with this relativity of all experience to me, we are at the heart of Husserl's theory of intersubjectivity. According to Derrida, for Levinas, Husserl's determination of the other as an alter ego in the Fifth Cartesian Meditation is violence, since alter *ego* implies that the other is the same as or like me (ED 184/125). Levinas, however, is treating the expression "alter ego" as if *alter* were the epithet of a real, that is, factual or pre-eidetic subject (ED 187/127). In contrast, Derrida stresses that the expression "alter ego" consists in a "strangeness": " . . . the transcendental syntax of the expression *alter ego* tolerates no relationship of substantive to adjective, of absolute to epithet, in one sense or in another" (ED 187/ 127). In other words, as we have noted already,[23] "ipse," that is, self or ego, and "idem," that is, identity, do not mean the same thing (ED 162/100, 185/126). So what Husserl does in the Fifth Meditation, according to Derrida, is describe the experience by means of which—analogical appresentation —the other is other because he has the form of an ego, that is, because he is another "origin of the world" (Fink), another transcendental ego (ED 184/125). But as another origin of the world, the other constitutes me as other. So, for Derrida, following Husserl, *ipse*, or egoity in general, includes alterity or difference: my ego is mine for me and other for the other and the other's ego is his for him and other for me. Derrida calls this relationship "transcendental symmetry" (ED 185/126). The point Derrida is making here is that the alterity of the other is impossible without this transcendental symmetry or transcendental sameness (ED 190/129). Without it, the other would be "entirely in the world," and therefore would be the same as me understood now as a factual or empirical person. And it is from this factual or empirical symmetry that empirical dissymmetries can arise like the master-slave relation (ED 185/126). In other words, the transcendental symmetry makes ethical or empirical or real violence possible. So we must conclude that this transcendental symmetry is the irreducible violence of the relation to the other—since it is symmetry or sameness—and yet it is at the same time non-violence—since it alone maintains the alterity of the other, since, in other words, it is dissymmetry or difference (ED 188/128–29). Derrida concludes this third step by briefly repeating this analysis of egoity as transcendental archi-factuality "in the direction of the archi-factuality of the 'living present'" (ED 194/132). Here we find the comments about the form of all experience having the form of the living present that we quoted above. We shall not analyze them again.

What is significant therefore about Derrida's interpretation of Husserl in "Of Transcendental Violence" is that it presents us with the structure of the interpretation of Husserl in *Voice and Phenomenon*. We have one Husserl, the Husserl of the metaphysics of presence, focusing on truth, essence, and evidence: the superficial Husserl. But then we have a second Husserl, one quite close to Levinas, thanks to the themes of alterity and temporalization: the in-depth Husserl. Borrowing the wording from the end of "The Ends of Man," this is the Husserl who "abruptly changes terrain from" Western metaphysics. The two Husserls give us the double necessity of the impossible system: "the phenomenal system of non-phenomenality." As we are going to see now, in *Voice and Phenomenon*, Derrida will test one Husserl with the other. Can the Levinasian Husserl escape from the "catch" (*la prise*) of the metaphysics of presence? Does not the metaphysics of presence find itself "worked over" (ED 178/121) by the themes of nonpresence, the alter ego and temporalization? *Voice and Phenomenon* is entirely about this test, or, more precisely, this experience (*cette épreuve*) (VP 111/99).

7   The Test of the Sign: An Investigation of *Voice and Phenomenon*

We now enter the climax of our investigation. When one is investigating *Voice and Phenomenon*, it is always important to keep in mind its subtitle: "Introduction to the Problem of the Sign in Husserl's Phenomenology." The problem of the sign has come to replace, for Derrida, the problem of genesis. We could see this replacement approaching on the basis of our investigation of the 1962 *Introduction to Husserl's "The Origin of Geometry."* The *Introduction* could have been called "The Origin of Truth," since Derrida was concerned with the difficulties into which Husserl was led when he described the genesis of ideal objects. The problem of genesis is that truth itself, phenomenality, requires what Derrida called there "consignation" (LOG 86/89; cf. LOG 72/78). Truth itself cannot dispense with signs (LOG 90–91/92). Yet, it is the sign, *écriture*, which brings about the crisis for Husserl; and this crisis is why Husserl in *The Origin of Geometry* calls for an imperative of univocity. The problem, however, is that the sign is always at once equi-vocal and uni-vocal. Already therefore the problem of the sign is the problem of voice: the *Introduction to Husserl's "The Origin of Geometry"* could have been called *Voice and Phenomenon*. A 1967 addition to "Violence and Metaphysics" tells us precisely the thesis that both the *Introduction* and *Voice and Phenomenon* share: "the phenomenon supposes originary contamination by the sign" (ED 190/129).

It seems therefore that the difference between these two Husserl studies is only that, while the *Introduction* specifies this problem within Husserl's last great work, *The Crisis* and the texts associated with it, in particular, *The Origin of Geometry*, *Voice and Phenomenon* specifies the problem of the sign within Husserl's first great work, *Logical Investigations*. But we know that this specification is not what makes *Voice and Phenomenon* both a great and controversial work. In *Voice and Phenomenon*, Derrida engages in a deconstruction of Husserl's phenomenology. As the title indicates, it concerns the very nature of phenomenology: *logos* (voice) and *phaino-menon* (phenomenon). But here we must be careful: insofar as *Voice and Phenomenon* is a deconstruction, it works to expose the double necessity that functions at the deepest level. So, of course, Derrida claims in *Voice and Phenomenon* that Husserl's phenomenology is "taken" (*pris*) by "the metaphysics of presence"; the first necessity is inescapable: all experience must occur within the form of the living present. Yet to say that Husserl's phenomenology "belongs" (*appartient*) to the metaphysics of presence also means that Husserl's phenomenology *does not* belong to the metaphys-ics of presence: the second necessity, the second Husserl, the "in depth" Husserl (cf. VP 114/101). The Husserl who describes the themes of non-presence, that is, alterity and temporalization, this Husserl amounts to— here borrowing the wording from the end of "The Ends of Man"—"a dis-continuous and irruptive change of terrain from Western metaphysics." As Derrida says in "Violence and Metaphysics," "phenomenology carries [the question of being] within itself each time that it considers the themes of temporalization, and of the relationship to the alter ego" (ED 196–97/134). Yet we also know from our investigation of "Violence and Metaphysics" that Derrida replaces the question of being with a question that is not phi-losophy's question, the question of the origin of philosophy itself. Al-though Levinas's name does not appear in *Voice and Phenomenon,* Heideg-ger's question of being, mediated by the investigation of Levinas, becomes now "an unheard-of question." And this question is opened, for Derrida, only through the test (*l'épreuve*) of the sign from within a certain inside of the metaphysics of presence.

Because *Voice and Phenomenon* is a small book, really not much more than an extensive essay about the same length as "Violence and Metaphys-ics," it is quite easy to overlook its important claims and argumentation. Therefore, we are going to proceed by presenting in the first section the problem that Derrida confronts in *Voice and Phenomenon,* his general ar-gumentation, and what he calls "the object and nerve [*nerf*] of the demon-stration" that he finds in Husserl's First Logical Investigation (VP 53/48). Then, in the second section, we shall examine the specific arguments found in Chapters 4 and 5. Then, in a third section, we shall examine Chapters 6 and 7, which amount to the presentation of Derrida's own philosophy. In-deed, the title of the book comes from Chapter 6 (VP 87/78). Finally, we shall investigate the final six pages that are the Conclusion to *Voice and Phenomenon.* Here we shall divide the final six pages into two parts: (1) the experience of the *aporia* of *différance,* and (2) the thought of *différance.*

Voice and Phenomenon deserves this kind of attention first and foremost because it constitutes a new way of thinking in the history of philosophy: deconstruction.

1

The Problem. The problem that Derrida confronts in *Voice and Phenomenon* consists in determining "the phenomenological project in its essence" (VP 23/22) or in determining "the irreducible specificity" of phenomenology (VP 48/44). By means of a sort of reversal, the title of this book means "phenomeno-logy" itself, the *logos* and the *phainomenon*. For Derrida, the essence of phenomenology can be determined from the "essential distinction," which opens the First Logical Investigation;[1] the difference within the sign between indication (*Anzeichen*)[2] and expression (*Ausdruck*) provides, as he says, "the germinal structure of the whole of Husserl's thought" (VP 1/3).[3] But the problem being confronted in *Voice and Phenomenon* is broader than the determination of the whole of Husserl's thought: Derrida says, "our problem" is "the historical destiny of phenomenology" (VP 26/27). Concerning the problem of phenomenology's historical destiny, we must make three points.

First, historical destiny means both the origin and the end of phenomenology; so, Derrida says, "What would be at issue would be . . . to begin to verify that the resource of the phenomenological critique is the metaphysical project itself, in its historical completion and in the merely restored purity of its origin" (VP 3/5). In other words, "phenomenology repeats the original intention of metaphysics" (VP 8/9). The historical destiny of phenomenology therefore consists in the repetition, restoration, and completion of the origin of metaphysics, that is, the *Greek* origin, that is, Greek metaphysics (cf. VP 70/63). As we saw in "Violence and Metaphysics," Greek metaphysics is for Derrida the metaphysics of presence. Just on the basis of *The Crisis,* the claim that phenomenology completes the original intention of philosophy does not seem controversial. For Derrida, it is even less controversial if one looks at *Cartesian Meditations,* section 60, where Husserl describes phenomenology's results as metaphysics, but not in the degenerative sense (VP 4/5). According to Derrida—but this claim also seems obvious—for Husserl, "the unique and permanent impulse [*motif*] of all the faults and perversions that Husserl denounces in 'degenerate' metaphysics . . . is a blindness before the authentic mode of ideality" (VP 4/6).

Two characteristics define the "authentic mode of ideality." On the one hand, ideality is a form that is not real in the sense of factual or worldly existence, but still *is*, that is, it possesses ideal existence; because ideality is *ideal*, it "can be indefinitely *repeated* in the *identity* of its *presence*" (VP 4/6, Derrida's emphasis). But, on the other hand, ideality's second characteristic is that, although authentic ideality is non-worldly, it does not consist in "another worldliness"; instead, "its origin will always be the possible repetition of a productive act" (VP 4/6). This second characteristic is content. By avoiding degenerate metaphysics (that is, Platonism), Husserl can assure only the *indefinite* repetition of the form, since the real subjects who perform the acts of repetition can die. Therefore, in order that the repetition can be open to infinity *ideally*, there must be, as Derrida says, "one ideal form" that "assures the unity of the indefinite and the ideal": "this is the present or rather the presence of the *living present*" (VP 4/6). The living present is "the ultimate form of ideality." Derrida continues:

> Presence has always been and will always be, to infinity, the form in which—we can say this apodictically—the infinite diversity of content will be produced. The opposition—which inaugurates metaphysics— between form and matter finds in the concrete ideality of the living present its ultimate and radical justification. (VP 5/6)

We must recognize here, as we stressed earlier in our investigation of "Violence and Metaphysics," that presence for Derrida is both formal and intuitive, objective and subjective; presence is the unity of the two characteristics.[4] The living present provides the "ultimate and radical justification" of the form-matter opposition because the living present is both a form—the ultimate justification—and an intuition (or content)—the radical justification. The living present therefore unifies the two "impulses" which define phenomenology: "the purity of formalism and the radicality of intuitionism" (VP 16/16). According to Derrida, these two defining impulses provide the two possible ways in which one can interpret the opening move of Husserl's First Investigation. On the one hand, Husserl is basing his dissociation within the sign between indication and expression on an essence of the sign. Derrida interprets the fact that Husserl does not investigate this general essence as dogmatism (VP 24/23).[5] Yet if Husserl were to investigate the essence, he would end up "adhering" to classical ontology (VP 27/26), submitting the sign to truth (VP 25/24): this submission is the purity of Husserl's formalism (cf. VP 24/23). On the other hand, we can interpret his dissociation as being based on the reduction of naïve ontology, a reduction that returns us to the active constitution of truth across its signs; this reduction is "critical vigilance" (VP 26–27/25). It corresponds to the "radicality of intuitionism." While the first interpretation is structural, the second is genetic. In this second interpretation, Derrida, of course, refers to *The Origin of Geometry*. The second interpretation is based on the realization, Husserl's own realization, that,

> since the possibility of constituting ideal objects belongs to the essence
> of consciousness, and since these ideal objects are historical products,
> only appearing thanks to acts of creation or intending, the element
> of consciousness and the element of language will be more and more
> difficult to discern. (VP 15/15; cf. 26/25)

If Husserl wants to maintain both impulses, both the *purity* of formalism and the *radicality* of intuitionism, in light of the growing indiscernibility between language and consciousness, then he is going to have to have a concept of language, that is, a concept of the sign, which harmonizes these two impulses, a sign that is purely formal, that is, non-mundane and structural, and radically intuitive, mundane, and genetic. The sign itself, for Husserl, would have to provide the "ultimate and radical justification of the inaugural opposition of metaphysics." This indiscernibility between consciousness and language is why the problem of phenomenology, its historical destiny, is for Derrida the problem of the sign.[6]

The second point in relation to the problem of the determination of phenomenology's historical destiny is: Husserl's repetition, restoration, and completion, in short, the purification, of the original intention of Greek metaphysics consists in "explicitly (*expressément*) taking up (*assumer*) the decision" with which Greek philosophy started; he explicitly takes up "the heritage and validity" of this decision (VP 6/7; see also VP 59/53). The problem of phenomenology, for Derrida, is that Husserl does not make the decision himself; for Husserl, the origin of Greek metaphysics is itself Greek. And this decision means, as we have seen before, that Greek metaphysics values presence either as pure form or as radical intuition (cf. VP 59/53). Most generally, as we have noted, Husserl's phenomenology attempts to complete this decision, unify the two kinds of presence. But, specifically, according to Derrida, this decision is one that "subordinates a reflection on the sign to a logic" (VP 6/7). This subordination implies that Husserl is determining "the essence of language"—the sign—on the basis of logicity, one part or kind of language; the norm for all language, in other words, will be the purpose or destination of one specific use of language, logic. And this purpose is presentation, presence or truth (VP 6-8/8-9). The determination of logic in terms of logicity means that Husserl conceives language as voice (VP 9/10). Of course, there is no concept of the voice as such in Husserl. We must recognize that, in *Voice and Phenomenon*, Derrida is importing a certain Hegelian radicalism into Husserl. Such an importation is not unusual if we keep in mind both Fink's interpretation of Husserl and Hyppolite's interpretation of Hegel. The justification for importing Hegelianism into Husserl comes, it seems, primarily from paragraph 124 of *Ideas I* where Husserl describes the movement from sense to concept through a *medium*. Derrida sees in Husserl's descriptions here what Hyppolite had called the movement from sensible to sense and thus to thought, the movement of mediation. Another reason for the importation is the concept of the flesh in Husserl, the "geistige Leiblichkeit," *spiritual* flesh (VP 15-16/16). The use of the word "Geist" obviously suggests Hegel. Spiritual flesh is a body, but the body reduced, that is, a body that is still alive "in the absence of the world" (VP 16/16). This definition of the flesh means that the flesh is formal, structural, and transcendental; it is not *Körper*, that is, physical body. But also—and, of course, we know this best from Merleau-Ponty—the flesh is the body alive with intentional animation, the body breathing, animated "by *Geist*, that is, the will" (VP 37/35). This intentional animation is why Derrida suggests that one translate "Bedeutung" into French as "vouloir dire" (which means of course "meaning," but literally "wanting to say" or even "willing to say"; this translation is also important for Derrida's conception of deconstruction) (VP 18l/18). The body of expression of presence—its "substance" or "element"—is the spirituality of the breath as *phone* (VP 9/10). This definition of the flesh means that the flesh is intuitive and genetic; in a "certain sense" it is still a body. Here we see again the two characteristics that define authentic ideality for Husserl, and, like the living present, the flesh is what assures their unity. Living speech is what best preserves ideality and living presence. "The voice," as Derrida says therefore, "hears itself" (VP 16/16), meaning that it goes out of itself while remaining inside of itself (VP 34-35/32-33; see also 22-23/22), or, better, the voice ex-presses itself without exiting the ideal. As Derrida stresses, in the First Logical Investigation, when Husserl turns—Derrida, of course, calls this turn a "reduction"—to the solitary life of the soul, one seems able to have "the unity of the word" without "the multiple sensible events of its employment" (VP 45/41). In interior monologue, the "form" of the word is ideal and it does not exist in the sense of factual existence, yet it is still animated by a "vouloir-dire"

(VP 45/41). As Derrida says, "In 'the solitary life of the soul,' we no longer use *real* (*wirklich*) words, but only *imagined* (*vorgestellt*) words" (VP 47/43). These imagined or represented words are unities, unities that "join the signified concept to the signifying 'phonic complex'" (VP 16/16). Derrida says that this conception of language in terms of unities—"the language of unities" (VP 16/16)—is "perhaps naïve" (VP 16/16).[7]

Our third point in relation to the problem of phenomenology's historical destiny is: while Husserl only takes up—hence the naivety—the decision that inaugurates metaphysics, Derrida's most general purpose in *Voice and Phenomenon*—his deconstruction—lies in bringing us to the moment prior to this decision. This metaphysical decision, as we saw in our investigation of the *Introduction,* is based on a question. This is the question of the sense (*sens*) of being; the decision was to define the sense of being as presence. As we shall see, this response to the question is what Derrida calls voice, which always attempts to restore presence. For Derrida, this decision produces a "schema" of the metaphysics of presence (VP 57/51; 114/101; 115/102; cf. also 64n1/57n6), and with the word "schema" we should indeed hear Kant's schematism since what Derrida intends with this term is a passage from a certain inside to an outside. The schema is that, with the decision in favor of presence (ideality), metaphysics tries to make the sign and difference "derivative" (VP 57/51). Yet if one tries to restore the originality and non-derivative character of the sign and difference against metaphysics, one finds that the concept of the sign and difference are marked by the history of metaphysics: difference and the sign are metaphysical concepts. So the mere reversal of terms, from presence to the sign, does not free one of metaphysics; indeed, one finds oneself constrained to work "within" (*à l'intérieur*), "from a certain inside of," metaphysics. To work "within," "inside," "interior to" metaphysics requires for Derrida that we determine the sense of this sense of being. In the Introduction to *Voice and Phenomenon,* Derrida says, "From what *question* are we to receive and read this distinction [between indication and expression], whose stakes appear to be quite high?" (VP 2/4, my emphasis). This question will turn out to be the question of the will of saying "to infinity," of the meaning (*vouloir dire*) of "to infinity" (VP 114/102). All of *Voice and Phenomenon* unfolds within this question, which is not explicitly stated until its Conclusion. The answer to this question leads us to an experience. Even though the word "experience" obviously means presence (cf. ED 225/152), we can use it here.[8] The use of the word is justified by the following claim from the

Introduction to *Voice and Phenomenon,* in which Derrida specifies his intention:

> What is only at issue is to make the original and non-empirical space of non-foundation appear over the irreducible void on the basis of which the security of presence in the metaphysical form of ideality is decided and raised up. It is within this horizon that we will here interrogate the phenomenological concept of the sign. (VP 5–6/7)

The wording of this passage is important. In *Voice and Phenomenon,* Derrida is trying to "make appear" (*faire apparaître*); thus he is trying precisely to bring something to presence, to an experience, for us. And what he is trying to bring to presence for us is what can never be presented: the irreducible void. Thus *Voice and Phenomenon*—deconstruction—concerns the precise moment when what can never be presented comes into presence, the point "over" (*sur*) the void and thus "below" metaphysics. This is the moment or point of insecurity "within," "inside of," "interior to" metaphysics. Appropriating terminology that Derrida had not yet developed, this moment (or point) could be described as the moment of undecidability: the *aporia.* Thus *Voice and Phenomenon* concerns the undecidable moment right before the decision is made about the security and assurance of presence in the metaphysical form of ideality (that is, in Husserl's phenomenology). In other words, it concerns the moment right before the question of the sense of being is answered, the moment of responsibility (cf. VP 15/15). Derrida's deconstruction is trying to bring us to the moment when the question can be asked and answered again, and this moment in fact opens up a different question, an unheard-of question, the question that Derrida, in "Violence and Metaphysics," called the question of the origin of philosophy, the non-philosophical question.

The Basic Argumentation. In regard to the argumentation, we must state immediately that *Voice and Phenomenon* does not consist in any sort of refutation of phenomenology. Indeed, nothing in *Voice and Phenomenon* is supposed to "impugn" or "injure" the founding validity of presence or the apodicticity of phenomenological-transcendental description (VP 5/7). In fact, as Derrida says, "we must first yield" to "phenomenological necessity" (VP 2/4). As we saw in "Violence and Metaphysics," for Derrida, the "principle of all principles" as stated in *Ideas I,* the present or presence of sense to a full and originary intuition, is necessary. It is, as we have seen in our investigations of the *Introduction* and "Violence and Metaphysics," one of the two necessities, the Greek necessity. For Derrida, the "phenomenological critique" is valid (VP 2–3/4–5); presence must be presupposed (a "metaphysical presupposition" [VP 2–3/4–5]). There must be descriptive vigilance (VP 15/15). There can be no retreating from the radicality of transcendental phenomenology (VP 49n1/45n4). Indeed, Derrida says that we must pass through the transcendental reduction in order to grasp what he calls "différance" (VP 92/82). Yet, as we have already seen, Derrida also says in *Voice and Phenomenon* that Husserl's phenomenology is "dogmatic" or "speculative" or "naïve" (VP 3/4, 15/15, 26/25). Derrida can say this because Husserl only took up the decision that inaugurated metaphysics; he himself did not experience the paradox that opens the question. Although this critique is different from Derrida's earlier critique of Husserl (which we called a "phenomenological critique" since it amounted to enforcing Husserl's "the principle of all principles" against Husserl himself when he lapses into a philosophy of history, and against Levinas when he conceives the other without relation to the same), we could call the *Voice and Phenomenon* critique a "super-phenomenological critique" because it refers us to an experience. But, although this experience cannot be called intuition, it is based on Husserlian insights, insights from the second (non-Greek or Levinasian) Husserl. In *Voice and Phenomenon,* as we saw in "Violence and Metaphysics," the themes of temporalization and intersubjectivity bring us to this experience. In temporalization and intersubjectivity, there is always not only *Gegenwärtigung* but also *Vergegenwärtigung* (VP 5/7). Because these themes always include *Vergegenwärtigung,* we find that an "irreducible nonpresence," a "nonlife," a "nonself-belonging of the living present" which is a "non-primordiality" has "a constitutive validity" (VP 5/6). Thus the experience that opens the question of metaphysics is the experience of the unity of *Gegenwärtigung* and *Vergegenwärtigung;* as Derrida says, "everything 'begins' with 're-presentation'" (VP 49n1/45n4). Every claim, for Derrida, metaphysics itself, is to be measured against this experience of re-presentation. This experience cannot be deconstructed.

Because this experience cannot be deconstructed, Derrida calls it, following the Scholastic tradition, the "ultra-transcendental concept of life" (VP 14/15).[9] For Derrida, life (which he also calls "psyche") is "the self-relation, whether or not it takes the form of consciousness" (VP 14/14). Life for Derrida is the voice that hears itself. But we need to recall here, as we saw in "Violence and Metaphysics," that for Derrida *ipse* and *idem* do not have the same meaning; the self-relation is not identical. The voice hears itself and hears another. In *Voice and Phenomenon,* Derrida says that this self-relation consists in a "focal point" (*foyer*) (VP 9/10) or a "kernel" (*noyau*) (VP 14/14), or even a "unity" (VP 14/14, 9/10). This unity leads Derrida to Husserl's concept of the parallelism between transcendental life and empirical life (VP 10/11). What is crucial for Derrida in this concept is that, while the parallels must be heterogeneous, the parallels must be the same since their difference cannot be an ontic duplication; the transcendental ego and the empirical ego cannot be two beings (VP 11/12). The parallels therefore are differentiated, as Derrida says, by "nothing," by "the nothing" (VP 12–13/13). Because the ultra-transcendental concept of life consists in this heterogeneity which is the same, in this difference that is a unity, Derrida says,

> . . . the strange unity of these two parallels, which relates one to the other, does not let itself be distributed by them and dividing itself joins finally the transcendental to its other; this is *life.* . . . "Living" is thus the name of what precedes the reduction and escapes finally from all the distributions [*les partages*] that the reduction makes appear. But this is because it is its own distribution and its own opposition to its other. By determining "living" in this way, we just named the resource of the insecurity of the discourse. . . . (VP 14/14–15, Derrida's emphasis)

Life, for Derrida, precedes the reduction because it is the unity from which the reduction makes its division into transcendental life and empirical life. But what is even more important is that life does not follow the distributions that phenomenology establishes after the reduction. All of the argumentation in *Voice and Phenomenon* depends on the fact that, as Derrida says here, life "is its own distribution and its opposition to its other."

This non-regulatable concept of life results in three aspects of the discourse in which *Voice and Phenomenon* consists. First, all of the "difficulties" (VP 15/15), "paradoxes" (VP 23/22), "enigmas" (VP 32/30, 5/6), and "aporias" (VP 113/101) in Husserl's thought that Derrida catalogs here (and in his earlier works on Husserl) result from life's self-distribution. Because life distributes itself, Husserl's own descriptions contradict his explicit distribution of phenomena (see, for example, VP 76/68). While Husserl's distributions occur "expressément"—this is what he wants to say on purpose —life's distributions occur, we might say, "non-expressément," involuntarily in Husserl's descriptions (cf. VP 36–39/34–36, 58/52). In *Voice and Phenomenon,* whenever Derrida moves from what he calls "commentary" to what he calls "translation" (VP 18/18) or "interpretation" (VP 32/33, 59/53, 98/88), he is moving from Husserl's express intentions to what life itself distributes as it is found in Husserl's own descriptions. Indeed, as we shall see in *Voice and Phenomenon*'s sixth chapter, beyond commentary, Derrida himself engages in what we can only call a genuine phenomenological description of life, that is, a genuine phenomenological description of the voice.

Second, life's self-distribution results in all the contaminations that made *Voice and Phenomenon* famous. Like "the impossible system" that we saw in "Violence and Metaphysics," the ultra-transcendental concept of life consists in a double necessity—life must be itself (it must be held in life) and it must be other than itself (it must be taken by death)—that "hold" and "take" define what Derrida always means with contamination. As Derrida says in *Voice and Phenomenon*: "Taken: that is, contaminated" (*Pris: c'est-à-dire, contaminé*) (VP 21/20). The entire discourse of *Voice and Phenomenon* concerns this necessary mutual contamination, *la prise* (as we saw in "Violence and Metaphysics"). In general, in *Voice and Phenomenon*, contamination means that Husserl must be "held" (*pris*) by presence; Derrida says, "another necessity also confirms the metaphysics of presence" in Husserl (VP 27/25). But contamination also means that one must be "taken" (*pris*) by non-presence; this "take" occurs, of course, when Husserl describes temporalization and intersubjectivity. Specifically however, contamination develops in four themes throughout *Voice and Phenomenon*. First, contamination means, for Derrida, that indication (or the index) and expression are not just in fact *interwoven*—"interweaving" and "contamination" are synonymous terms for Derrida—but also are always interwoven (VP 21/20). The interweaving of the parallels means that indication (or the index) and expression cannot be separated. This inseparability is why Derrida stresses that Husserl's distinction between the indication (or the index) and expression is "more *functional* than *substantial*" (VP 20/20, Derrida's emphasis); just like the parallels, this distinction is not an ontic distinction (VP 32/30): "the totality of discourse is *caught* [*prise*] in an indicative web" (VP 33/31, my emphasis). Moreover, this interweaving of the two functions is evident, according to Derrida, in the general terms that Husserl uses to describe the functions: "Zeigen" (showing) (VP 24/23) and "Weisen" (monstration) (VP 31/29). Second, the contamination means that all of Husserl's ontological differences are interwoven. Just like the parallels, the noema or ideality must not be posited as an ontic duplicate of mundane beings (like a Platonic idea [cf. VP 59/53]). In other words, the noema or ideality must have ideal being and not real existence, that is, *Sein* or *Bestand* and not *Dasein* or *Realität* (VP 29/28). While however ideality must not be *real* (factual), it also cannot be *reell* (that is, part of consciousness); it must be *irreelle* (cf. VP 59n1/53n3) As ir-real, ideality is neither of consciousness nor of the world; or, reversing the "neither-nor," we can say that ideality is both of consciousness and of the world, both *real* and *reelle*. This "both-and" is what Derrida called in "'Genesis and Structure' and Phenomenology" "the anarchy of the noema" (ED 243/163).[10] Third, the contamination means that the inside and outside are interwoven. The language of inside and outside that Derrida is employing throughout *Voice and Phenomenon* does not imply that Derrida conceives "the whole of Husserl's thought" as a return to "a simple inside" (VP 23/22). Derrida knows that the reduction reveals a "relation to the object," a dative relation, the intention of an objective ideality (VP 22/22). What he is interested in throughout *Voice and Phenomenon* is that in Husserl "meaning [that is, *Bedeutung, vouloir-dire*] would isolate the concentrated purity of its *expressiveness* just at that moment when the relation to a certain *outside* has been suspended" (VP 22/22, Derrida's emphasis). But a certain *outside* must still be outside; it must not be purely inside. And a *certain* outside is different from other kinds of outsides; it must not be purely outside. Fourth, everyone knows that in *Ideas I* (section 43) Husserl says that "between perception on the one hand and the symbolic representation by means of images or signs on the other, there is an unbridgeable essential difference" (cited in VP 67n1/60n1). Therefore contamination means that perception and the sign, silence and voice, are interwoven (VP 14–15/15; also 67/60). As the last sentence of *Voice and Phenomenon* says, "Contrary to the assurance that Husserl gives us . . . 'the regard' [*le regard, Blick*] cannot 'abide' [*demeurer*]" (VP 117/104). And, of course, we must keep this word, "Blick," in mind since it is connected to the word "Augenblick," blink of the eye, which, as is well known, is so crucial for *Voice and Phenomenon*, Chapter 5.

The third aspect in which life's self-distribution results is the polemics we find in *Voice and Phenomenon*.[11] Here we must recall that in "Violence and Metaphysics" Derrida says that "it is necessary, in *a certain way,* to become classical once more, and again find *other impulses* for the divorce between speech and thought" (ED 224/151, my emphasis). This "in a certain way" means that the polemics take two forms. On the one hand, because there is a divorce between speech and thought, there are denunciations. The first sentence of the first chapter says: "Husserl begins by denouncing a confusion" (VP 17/17). Husserl is able to denounce the confusion in the sign, to show "disdain" (*mépris*) for language, because he conceives the transcendental as heterogeneous to the world, because he conceives indication as exterior to expression. For Derrida too, the *ultra-transcendental* concept of life is external and heterogeneous to the world (even though the ultra-transcendental concept of life implies a sameness between empirical life and transcendental life). The *ultra*-transcendental life corresponds to no-thing and tolerates no analogy with mundane things (VP 13/13); it is "refractory to the category" (cf. ED 205–206/140). It travels through language as through a foreign medium (cf. ED 171/116). It is inexpressible since language is, according to Derrida, analogical or equivocal or metaphorical (VP 13/13); it is, as Derrida says in "Violence and Metaphysics," "the unthinkable, impossible, unutterable beyond (the tradition's) Being and *Logos*" (ED 168/114). Without this heterogeneity of ultra-transcendental life, it would be impossible to provide, as Derrida says, a transcendental "explication, that is, no language could be deployed freely within truth" (VP 12/12). In short, the ultra-transcendental life (perhaps we must call it "God") is *the truth,* and without its heterogeneity the discourse, that is, Derrida's discourse about the ultra-transcendental life, could not be true, since it would have no distinct referent (VP 12/12). Thus, like Husserl, but also like Bergson (as we saw in "Violence and Metaphysics"), Derrida too can denounce the "betrayal" of the concept (or intuition) in language, in "conceptless verbalities" (VP 25/24). As he says, "All the concepts of metaphysics—in particular those of activity and passivity, of will and non-will, and therefore those of affection or auto-affection, of purity and impurity, etc.—*conceal* the strange 'movement' of this difference" (VP 95/85, Derrida's emphasis). But the polemic takes a second form because "consciousness and language are more and more difficult to discern" (VP 15/15). Here, of course, Derrida rejoins what he discovered in *The Origin of Geometry.* In *Voice and Phenomenon,* Derrida says that the activity of signification conditions "the movement and concept of the truth"; therefore the activity of signification has no truth in itself (VP 25–26/24–25). This conditioning means that language itself brings forth the truth, the truth against which a statement could be compared, through which one could determine a true discourse. This divorce between thought and language "in a certain way" is why Derrida says in *Voice and Phenomenon* that "language guards the difference that guards language" (VP 13/14). In other words, language produces the difference between language and its exterior (the truth) which makes true language possible. But if language produces the truth, for Derrida, and language is always analogical, equivocal, or metaphorical, then no *simple* "disdain" (*mépris*) of language is possible.

What is heterogeneous to language is always already "archived" there (cf. VP 15/15). In order to express, or better, in order to indicate, or even better, in order "to point the finger at the invisible" (*montrer l'invisible du doigt*) (cf. VP 24/23), at what is heterogeneous to language but always already in language, one has to take up (and thus be taken by) the metaphors, equivocities, and analogies which are language, and oppose them to one another: for instance, light against blindness. One has to work "the language of metaphysics from the inside" (VP 57/51). Therefore, as Derrida says, it is necessary to "take up freely the destruction [of language] and cast metaphor against metaphor" (VP 13/13). This "war of language against itself" defines the discourse of *Voice and Phenomenon.*

"*The Objective and Nerve of This Demonstration.*" The demonstration to which Derrida is referring here (in the opening sentence of the fourth chapter), of course, is Husserl's "demonstration" in the First Logical Investigation: "The 'solitary life of the soul' was to prove that such an expression without indication is possible" (VP 53/48). According to Derrida's commentary on Husserl's First Investigation distinctions, a demonstration (*Beweis*) "gives us to see in the evidence of the proof (*la preuve*)" (VP 31/31), as opposed to *Hinweis,* which "points the finger at the nonseen" (VP 31/31).[12] What this proof aims to make us see, in other words, its "objective," consists, according to Derrida, in showing "the *exteriority* of the index to expression" (VP 28/27, my emphasis). As Derrida says, "It is necessary to push to the side [*écarter*], abstract, and 'reduce' indication" (VP 28/27). The possibility of the index being exterior to expression is, for Derrida, "inseparable from the possibility of all the reductions to come, whether they are eidetic or transcendental" (VP 31/30). Everything that Husserl uses to define indication in the First Investigation, according to Derrida, includes all of what will be on the outside in the reductions: "factuality, worldly existence, essential non-necessity, non-evidence, etc." (VP 32/30). "The index," as Derrida says, "falls outside of the content of absolutely ideal objectivity, that is, the truth" (VP 31/30). Yet, specifically, indication (or the index) must be pushed aside, must fall outside, because of the "nerve" of the demonstration. Here we start to see the impact of Derrida's encounter with Levinas; as in "Violence and Metaphysics," here in *Voice and Phenomenon,* Derrida takes very seriously Husserl's description in the Fifth Cartesian Meditation that " . . . I only have relations of *analogical appresentation, of mediate and potential intentionality,* with the other's ownness, with the self-presence of the other; its primordial presentation is closed to me" (VP 42/39). We cannot underestimate the importance of this Husserlian insight for Derrida: we can have "no primordial intuition of the presence of the other's lived experience" (VP 43/40). The sign in its indicative function is the "*mediation of any appresentation in general*" (VP 44/40). In communication to another, there is what Husserl calls the "manifesting function" (*kundgebende Funktion*) (VP 41/38).[13] I aim at making my lived experience manifest to another and this manifestation must pass through the mediation of the physical side of language, through the body, and not merely in the flesh, not "in person" (VP 41/38). Here we have the "root" of indication, according to Derrida: "indication takes place whenever the sense-giving act, the animating intention, the living spirituality of the meaning-intention is not fully present" (VP 41/38). In contrast, "pure expressivity will be the pure active intention (spirit, *psyche*, life, will) of a *bedeuten* that animates a discourse whose content (*Bedeutung*) will be present" (VP 43–44/40). We now see the "nerve" of the demonstration: it is presence (VP 43/40). Presence is the "fiber" that ties all the parts of the demonstration together, the "thread" guiding the descriptions. But presence is also the "nerve" in a second sense; it is the *boldness* of the demonstration, since pushing indication to the outside amounts to pushing death and the other to the outside of the solitary life of the soul, leaving behind pure self-presence, pure life:

> [*Bedeutung*] therefore would be *present to the self* in the life of a present, which has not yet exited [*sorti*] from itself into the world, into space, into nature. Since all of these "exits" exile this life of self-presence into the index, we can be assured that indication ... is the process of death at work in the signs. And as soon as others appear, indicative language—another name for the relation to death—will not allow itself to be erased. (VP 44/40)

2

We turn now to Derrida's specific argumentation found in Chapters 4 and 5. At the beginning of Chapter 4, Derrida tells us that, in order to support the demonstration of indication being exterior to expression, Husserl appeals to two types of arguments (VP 53/48). Chapter 4 concerns the first argument, while Chapter 5 concerns the second.

First Argument. This is Derrida's summary of the first type of argument:

> In interior discourse, I am communicating nothing to myself. I am indicating nothing to myself. At best, I can imagine myself doing this; I can only represent myself as manifesting something to myself. Here, there is only a *representation,* and *imagination.* (VP 53/48)

According to Derrida, this first argument (as well as the second) concerns the status of representation in language, representation in all the senses of representation that are relevant to Husserl's thought: representation as the locus of ideality in general (*Vorstellung*); representation as repetition or reproduction of presentation (*Vergegenwärtigung* as modifying *Gegenwärtigung*); and finally representation as taking the place of another *Vorstellung* (*Repräsentation*) (VP 54/49). The first argument concerns representation because in interior speech, one really communicates nothing to oneself; one merely imagines or represents oneself as a speaking and communicating subject. Therefore, in this first argument, it seems as though Husserl applies the fundamental distinction, "an essential distinction," "a simple exteriority," between reality as factuality and representation as ideality to language (VP 54/49). This distinction implies, according to Derrida, that representation in every sense of the word is neither essential nor constitutive but merely an accident contingently adding itself to the actual or factual practice of discourse (VP 55/49), a "simple exteriority" (VP 54/49).

But, as Derrida points out, when I actually use words, that is, when I consider the agency of signs in general, without any concern for the purpose of communication, "I must from the outset operate (within) a structure of repetition whose element can only be representative" (VP 55/50). Relying on his analysis of the word from section seven of the *Introduction,* Derrida says, "A phoneme or grapheme is necessarily always *other,* to a certain degree, each time that it presents itself in an operation or a perception; but it can function as a sign and as language in general only if a *formal identity* allows it to be re-issued and re-cognized" (VP 55–56/50, my emphasis and hyphenation). In other words, the sign in general must be an empirical event—"necessarily always other"—and it must be a "formal identity." As Derrida will say slightly later in "Signature Event Context," "everything that follows may be read as the exploration of the logic which links repetition to alterity," that is, the logic of iterability (MP 375/315). This definition of the sign in terms of iterability (a sign consists in a minimally iterable or re-presentable form) means that actual language is just as representative or imaginary as imaginary language and that imaginary or representative language is just as actual as actual language. If imaginary also means fictive, then we can also say, "the sign is worked by fiction" (VP 63/56). Whether representative—"I think that I'm speaking when I speak to myself" (*Je me représente ou je crois que je parle quand je me parle*)—or actual—"I am actually speaking when I speak to someone else"—the sign in general is re-presentational. As Derrida says, "discourse represents itself, *is* its representation. Better, discourse is *the* representation of itself" (VP 64/57, Derrida's emphasis). This definition of the sign in terms of re-presentation (iterability), therefore, casts doubt on Husserl's attempt to distinguish essentially between imagined speech as in interior monologue and actual or empirical speech as in communication.

As is well known, on the basis of the discussion of the status of representation in language, Derrida draws the famous ontological consequence that the relation to being as presence is the relation to my death; the drawing of this consequence does not amount to a digression since, for Husserl, "the structure of discourse can be described only in terms of ideality" (VP 58/52). As *Vor-stellung*, ideality is the determination of being as presence: present before or in proximity to—that is, as an ob-ject—a regard (*un regard*)—that is, as a phenomenon. The sense of representation, however, that the definition of the sign makes fundamental in language is not *Vor-stellung* as the locus of ideality or being as presence, but *Vergegenwärtigung* as modifying *Gegenwärtigung*, that is, re-presentation or presentification (as this term is also sometimes translated) implying an absence. As Derrida stresses, a sign never takes place "once" (VP 55/50), which implies that the sign's event *disappears* with the sign's repetition. Or we must say that sign is defined by the possibility of its own disappearance as an empirical event. The possibility of the sign is the relationship, therefore, with death (VP 60/54). But, *similar to the sign*, ideality in Husserl (as we have already noted) does not exist in the world—indefinite iterability—and it does not come from another world—empirical event (VP 58/52). Yet no matter how often an ideality is repeated, to infinity, it will have the form of the present, the living present. I can empty this form of all content and still I will know with certainty that before my birth and after my death the present is. In other words, when I relate myself to "the presence of the present as ultimate form of being and of ideality," I transgress "empirical existence, the facticity, the contingency, mundaneity, etc. And first of all *mine*" (VP 60/54). Therefore, within this determination of being as presence, being as ideality, the absolute possibility of repetition, "the relationship with *my death* (my disappearance in general)" is hidden (VP 60/54). And this relation to my death is a necessity found in the determination of being as presence. As Derrida says,

> If the possibility of my disappearance in general must in a certain way be lived so that a relationship with presence in general can be instituted, we can no longer say that the experience of the possibility of my absolute disappearance (my death) comes [*vient*] to affect me, happens [*survient*] to an *I am* and modifies a subject. (VP 60/54)

On the basis of this necessity, Derrida draws several famous conclusions. Being lived only as an "I am present," Descartes's "I am" depends on a relation to presence in general, to being as presence. "The appearing of the *I* to itself in the *I am* is therefore a relation to its own possible disappearance" (VP 60/54). Thus, "I am" fundamentally means "I am mortal," and, as Derrida says, "I am immortal" is a self-contradictory proposition since "I am" means "I am mortal." Derrida extends this thinking farther: when Yahweh says "I am the one who is," this statement is "the confession of a mortal" (VP 61/54). We should keep this comment in mind since Derrida will return to this statement in *Voice and Phenomenon*, Chapter 7: it implies that God is dead, or that God is death (cf. ED 170/115). But Derrida's most general conclusion here is that "the move that leads from the *I am* to the determination of my being as *res cogitans* (thus, as immortality) is the move by which the origin of presence and ideality steals itself away in the very presence and ideality that it makes possible" (VP 61/54–55). Being repetition and my disappearance in general, this origin of being as presence, as *Vor-stellung* is *Vergegenwärtigung*.

Second Argument. We come now to the second type of argument Husserl presents in order to support the demonstration of indication being exterior to expression. While Derrida's critique of this argument occurs in Chapter 5, he summarizes it at the beginning of Chapter 4:

> In inward speech, I communicate nothing to myself *because there is no need of it;* I can only pretend to do so. Such an operation—the communication of the self to itself—cannot take place because it would not make sense. And it would make no sense because it would have *no purposiveness* [*finalité, Zweckmässigkeit*]. The existence of psychic acts do not have to be indicated (remember that only an existence can in general be indicated) because it is immediately present to the subject in the present instant. (VP 53/48)

In other words, signs are useless (*zwecklosig*), that is, the manifestation of the self to the self through the delegation of an indicative sign is super-fluous, since lived experience is *immediately* self-present in the mode of certitude and absolute necessity. There is no need for or purpose to indicative signs here, since there is no alterity, no difference in the identity of presence as self-presence. Because Husserl says (in section 8) that "the acts in question are experienced by us at that very moment [*im selben Augenblick*, literally "in the blink of an eye"]" (cited in VP 54/49), Derrida claims that Husserl's immediate self-presence has to depend on the present taken as a now and dependence on the now leads Derrida to investigate briefly Husserl's *Lectures on Internal Time Consciousness* (VP 68/61). The argumentation that Derrida presents in Chapter 5 has created a lot of controversy. Most generally, or most minimally, Derrida is trying to show here that, in the *Lectures*, in sections 16 and 17 in particular, Husserl's descriptions of absolute temporal consciousness are, at least, confusing and a little less than consistent, that his definition of retention borders on being contradictory and is at least perplexing. At the very least, it seems plausible to argue that Husserl's definition of retention is perplexing (or complex). If one can plausibly argue that Husserl's definition of retention is perplexing, then one can investigate the definition and, as Derrida is doing here, discover another "logic" going on, so to speak, below it. This other "logic"—which is the "impossible system" of "Violence and Metaphysics," and what we were calling "the logic of totality" in the *Introduction*—is *Voice and Phenomenon*'s genuine contribution to philosophy; it defines, of course, what Derrida here calls "the trace" and "différance."[14]

Specifically, Derrida draws three "benchmarks" (*repères*) on the basis of the *Lectures* in order to determine Husserl's descriptions of the consciousness of time in relation to the historical destiny of phenomenology (VP 68/61). The first benchmark is that, in the *Lectures*, "the concept of *punctuality*, of the *now* as *stigme*, plays a role that is still major" (VP 68/61). According to this "benchmark," temporality in Husserl has "a non-displaceable center, an eye or living nucleus, the punctuality of the actual now [*le maintenant actuel*]" (VP 69/62). To support this claim, Derrida cites in particular section 11 of the *Lectures*, where Husserl speaks of the now-apprehension being "the nucleus of a comet's tail of retention" (see VP 69/62). Derrida also cites sections 10 and 16 of the *Lectures* and section 81 of *Ideas I*, where Husserl speaks of the actual now being "a form that persists through continuous change of matter." According to Derrida, in the First Investigation Husserl is referring to this self-same identity of the actual now; this actual now is what Husserl refers to throughout his writings as a beginning, a *principium* (VP 69–70/62). It is "the primal form" of consciousness (VP 71/63). For Derrida, the now in Husserl locates the problematic which brings us closest to the genuine stakes and the profound agency of Husserl's taking up of the decision which opened Greek metaphysics; this problematic is the concept of time. Through it one can bring phenomenology into confrontation with any thought of non-presence or non-consciousness (like that of Freud). And, as we saw in "Violence and Metaphysics," the "non" of "non-presence," for Derrida, must not be understood in the sense of a contrary or a negative absence (VP 70/63); here we have a kind of negativity which cannot be reduced to that of a mere counter-concept or opposition. Therefore, this first benchmark allows us to enter into "the debate," which is "unlike any other," between philosophy and non-philosophy. "Within philosophy," Derrida says, there is no possible objection to the privilege of the present-now since it is the element of conscious thought and evidence itself (VP 70/62). But if we start to suspect this privilege, we are no longer "within philosophy": "we begin to enucleate [literally, to remove the core or even to remove the globe of the eye from its socket] consciousness itself from somewhere other [*ailleurs*] than philosophy, which removes from the discourse all *security* and every possible *foundation*" (VP 70/62, Derrida's emphasis).

Since the argumentation in the second "benchmark" is well known, we can summarize it in three claims. First, for Husserl himself, retention is not an accidental modification of the present, but a constitutive part. Second, Husserl says in section 16 that retention is a "non-perception." Third, as soon as we have these two claims, we must conclude, as Derrida does, that the now phase of the present, that the present itself, "is *composed continually* with a non-presence and a non-perception" (VP 72/64, Derrida's emphasis). What is not well known here is that the second "benchmark" concerns the *content* of Husserl's descriptions in the *Lectures*, while the first concerned the *form*, the now as the primal form of consciousness (VP 71/63). This content is Husserl's descriptions that accommodate the original "spreading out" of the present, its thickness, that forbids any isolated now (VP 68–69/61). What is also not well known is that at stake in this second "benchmark" is *the kind of difference* that one can establish between the retentional phase of the present, of the spreading out, and secondary memory. In other words, what is at stake is the kind of difference we can establish between *Gegenwärtigung* and *Vergegenwärtigung*, between presentation and re-presentation. While Husserl, of course, shows in *The Lec-*

tures the irreducibility of *Vergegenwärtigung* to *Gegenwärtigung,* Derrida neverthless interrogates—without questioning the demonstrative validity of this distinction—"the evidential soil and the *milieu* of these distinctions, what relates the distinguished terms to one another and constitutes the very possibility of the *comparison*" (VP 72/64, Derrida's emphasis). Derrida is not claiming therefore that there is no difference between retention and secondary memory or *Vergegenwärtigung.* Instead, because Husserl in section 16 calls retention a "non-perception," Derrida is arguing that there is a *continuity* between retention and secondary memory such that it is impossible to claim that there is a *radical discontinuity* or a *radical difference* between retention and re-presentation, and therefore between re-presentation and presentation or perception (VP 72/64). As Derrida says,

> as soon as we admit this continuity of the now and the non-now, of perception and non-perception, we welcome the other into the self-identity of the *Augenblick:* non-presence and non-evidence into the *blink of the eye of the instant.* There is a duration of the blink of the eye, and it closes the eye. This alterity is even the condition of presence, of presentation and therefore of *Vorstellung* in general, before all the dissociations which could be produced there. (VP 73/65)

The Bergsonian language here—the *durée*—is obvious and perhaps Derrida is even using a Bergsonian philosophic method of differentiation. But Bergson would not have utilized the language of alterity as Derrida is doing here and throughout all of his later writings. Within what Derrida calls the *durée,* there is an alterity, a heterogeneity between perception and non-perception which is also a continuity; but between retention (understood as a non-perception) and re-production, there is only a difference between two modifications of non-perception (VP 73/65). This alterity of the blink of the eye not only "shakes what we could call the metaphysical assurance par excellence," but also the "im selben Augenblick" of the First Investigation. It not only "radically destroys" every possibility of self-identity within simplicity (VP 73/66), it also "cuts at the roots" of the argument concerning the uselessness of the sign in the self-relation (VP 74/66).

If the first benchmark brought us into the debate between philosophy and non-philosophy, and if the second brought us to what in non-philosophy shakes metaphysical assurance, then the third brings us to what non-philosophy precisely concerns: what Derrida in the Introduction to

Voice and Phenomenon called "the irreducible void" below metaphysical security. Therefore, the third benchmark concerns the root deeper than the argumentation Husserl is presenting, the "ineradicable origin" (VP 76/68), which is older than "phenomenological originariness" (VP 75/67), older than "the axiomatic *principium* of phenomenology itself" (VP 74/66). In order to preserve this axiomatic *principium,* that is, presence, Husserl, despite the fact that the content of his own descriptions implies a continuity between retention taken as a non-perception and the living now, wants to shift the boundary between originariness and non-originariness from the boundary between actuality and non-actuality within the present to the boundary between two forms of re-turn, that is, between re-tention and re-production. This shift would keep retention within the sphere of originary certitude. According to Derrida however, "we must be able to say *a priori* that the common root [of re-tention and re-production, that is] the possibility of re-petition in its most general form, . . . the constitution of a trace in the most universal sense, is a possibility which must not only inhabit the pure actuality of the now, but also constitute the pure actuality of the now through the very movement of the différance that the trace introduces into it" (VP 73/67). Although we have seen that Derrida was already using the verb "differer" in the *Introduction,* here in *Voice and Phenomenon,* chapter 5, we have Derrida's first introduction of the term as such, "différance," along with the term "the trace." These concepts refer to the irreducible void, to the logic that lies below Husserl's perplexing definition of retention. Most generally, *différance* and the trace mean that something like the sign or something like *Vergegenwärtigung* or something like a memory, a lateness, an alterity, conditions every experience, every presentation, every perception, every "me." Derrida argues that we must have this kind of conditioning by something like an *a priori Vergegenwärtigung* because without it we would not be able to explain why Husserl himself says that reflection and re-presentation essentially belong to every lived experience (VP 76/67–68). Playing on the literal meaning of the word "reflection," Derrida describes this originary *Vergegenwärtigung* as a "fold" (VP 76/68). And he calls this other within me, within "the solitary life of the soul," a "dialectic." As we have noted before, Derrida does not abandon the word "dialectic" until after *Voice and Phenomenon;* we can even say that he is still trying to "up the ante" on the dialectics of Tran-Duc-Thao and Cavaillès. But we can see Derrida's growing reservations about this word. Chapter 5 concludes with him saying that,

Does not this "dialectic"—in every sense of the term and before any speculative reconquest—open up living to différance, and constitute, in the pure immanence of experience, the *divergence* [*écart*] involved in indicative communication and even in signification in general? (VP 77/69)

3

We now come to the climax of *Voice and Phenomenon* itself, Chapters 6 and 7, in which Derrida presents his own, positive thought. His thought concerns, as we have noted, the ultra-transcendental concept of life, the self-relation that makes its own distributions (VP 14/14), "the *divergence* [*écart*] involved in indicative communication and even in signification in general" (VP 77/69), "the intimacy of life to itself" (VP 87/78). For Derrida, life is voice. As we have also noted, the voice is equivalent to intentional animation in Husserl, the giving of sense, sense-donation (*Sinngebung*), literally the breathing of life into a body to make it flesh (*Leib*). As we enter Chapter 6, we must recognize here that all of Derrida's most famous concepts—which we are now going to see developed: *différance;* the trace; the supplement—all of these Derrida develops on the basis of a reflection on life and that means on the voice. The voice is, for Derrida, a "paradox" (VP 81/72) or an "enigma" (VP 84/75); it is "the unnameable" (VP 86/77). This claim, of course, is not intended to contest the most popular views of Derrida, that he is a philosopher of writing. Of course, he is; but we must recognize that what is central to Derrida's thinking is the self-relation, and in connection to the self-relation here—in his deconstruction—Derrida is providing a genuine phenomenological description of the voice: "It is necessary therefore . . . to specify this pure concept of auto-affection [that is, the voice] and *describe* what in it makes it appropriate to universality" (VP 88/79, my emphasis). Finally, we must recognize that, while Husserl's examples of interior discourse in the First Investigation form Derrida's starting point here, Derrida is relying heavily upon *Ideas I*, especially section 124. Thus, Derrida refers to his contemporaneous 1967 essay on section 124 ("Form and Meaning: A Note on the Phenomenology of Language," which was collected in *Margins* in 1972).[15] He is relying on section 124 because it provides a view of expression in light of idealization, moving from a pre-expressive stratum of sense to the expression of *Bedeutung* in conceptual and universal form. This pre-expressive stratum—"the absolute silence of the self-relation" (VP 77/69)—is life for Derrida.

In Chapter 6 then, the starting point is the examples Husserl provides of interior discourse in the First Investigation. As is well known, the examples belong to the order of practicality (VP 79/71): "You have gone wrong, you can't go on like this" (VP 78/70). It is hard not to see, once again, Levinas in the background here, especially when Derrida, alluding to Heidegger, questions the privilege of being (VP 82–83/74; see also 82n2/74n4). The example on which Derrida focuses is an *ethical* statement; the voice is not only the voice of consciousness but also the voice of conscience. For Husserl, that the examples of interior soliloquy are axiological or axiopoetic is supposed to show us that this case of language is not indicative: nothing is shown here directly or indirectly; the subject learns nothing about himself; his language refers to nothing that exists. As Derrida stresses, these examples do not mean that Husserl thinks that all interior discourse is practical. Husserl always maintains the reducibility of the axiological to its theoretical-logical core; for Husserl, all language is ordered more or less immediately by the possibility of a relation to the object: *theorein* and thus light, in a word, presence (or "violence," to use the terminology of "Violence and Metaphysics") (VP 80/71). This reduction of the practical to the theoretical would seem to imply that Husserl's examples are expressive. But the examples are not expressive, since, as Derrida says, "they are not immediately in the form of predication. They do not utilize immediately the verb *to be* and their sense, if not their grammatical form, is not in the present; they are the observation of a past in the form of a reproach, exhortation to remorse or to change" (VP 81/72–73). For Derrida, the only conclusion one can draw is this: "*Paradoxically,* [the example] is not indicative because, insofar as being non-theoretical, as being non-logical, as being non-cognitive, it is also not expressive" (VP 81/72, my emphasis). This comment anticipates where Derrida concludes the description of the voice, in a paradox. But what is important for Husserl is that this sort of example in which one exhorts oneself to change one's ways is not expressive because it does not possess "the irreducible and pure core of expression": the third-person present indicative of the verb "to be" (VP 82/73). As Derrida says, "The 'speaking to oneself' that Husserl here wants to restore is not a 'speaking to oneself about oneself,' unless that takes the form of a 'speaking to oneself that S is P'" (VP 82/74).

Because the verb "to be" is at the core of expression, Derrida can turn to the question of ideality, being as ideality, and thus to *Ideas I* section 124 (VP 83/74). As we just noted, section 124 is important for Derrida because, here, Husserl is speaking of the transition from pre-expressive sense to expression and thus to conceptualization; thus it concerns, like *The Origin of Geometry*, idealization. Insofar as it concerns idealization, it allows Derrida to associate Husserl's phenomenology with Hegelianism. Derrida says here in Chapter 6 between parentheses, "Hegel was more attentive to [the complicity between sound or voice and ideality] than any other philosopher, and, from the viewpoint of the history of metaphysics, this is a noteworthy fact . . . " (VP 86–87/77).[16] For Derrida, when Husserl in section 124 speaks of expression as a "medium" through which or by means of which sense passes into a universal and conceptual form, he is describing the torsion of the self, thought thinking itself, what Hyppolite called the movement from sensible to sense and thus to thought.

So Derrida is arguing here that the medium Husserl mentions in section 124 could only be verbality, the voice. It *must* be the voice—Derrida says in Chapter 6: "il faut parler" and "il faut s'entendre" (VP 82–83/74)—because of how Husserl conceives the "objectivity of the object," ideal objects (VP 84/75). As Derrida says, "the complicity between idealization and voice is indefectible" (VP 84/75); there is "an essential connection between expression and the *phone*" (VP 85/76). Given the descriptions Husserl provides in section 124, expression is supposed to restore the totality of a sense actually given in intuition, restore it within the form of presence (VP 83/75). So we are talking here about a passage from the object given in intuition to subjective meaning, from sense to thought. Although we have discussed this before, the following definition of presence is crucial: according to Derrida,

> the medium of expression must protect, respect, and restore the presence of the sense *simultaneously as the being-before of the object*, available for a look and *as proximity to self in interiority*. The "pre" of the *present object* now-before is an *against* [*contre*] (*Gegen*wart, *Gegen*stand) simultaneously in the sense of the *wholly against* [*tout-contre*] of proximity and in the sense of the *encounter* [*l'encontre*] of the op-posed. (VP 83–84/75)

In expression, sense must be simultaneously present in the sense of an object (the relation to the ob-ject as over and against) and present in the sense of the subject (the proximity to self in identity, as close as possible). In other words, on the one hand, an ideal object can be repeated "to infinity" while remaining the same; since "its presence to intuition, its being in front of the look, essentially depends on no mundane or empirical synthesis, the restitution of its sense within the form of presence is a universal and un-limited possibility" (VP 84/75). But also, on the other hand, an ideal object is nothing outside of the world. So, as Derrida adds,

> [an ideal object] must be constituted, repeated, and expressed in a medium which does not cut away at the presence and the self-presence of the acts which intend it: a medium which preserves *simultaneously* [my emphasis] the *presence of the object* [Derrida's emphasis] in front of intuition and the *self-presence* [Derrida's emphasis], the absolute prox-imity of the acts to themselves. (VP 85/75-76)

This simultaneity of the presence of the object (infinite iterability) and self-presence (proximity) requires the voice. The voice is the element of consciousness, the element of the self-presence of the acts of repetition, and it is the element which nevertheless does not have the form of mun-daneity; it is the element of infinite iterability, of presence.[17] "*The voice is the name of this element. The voice hears itself*" (VP 85/76, Derrida's italics).

In order to determine this element—it is phenomenal and therefore not outside the world and yet it has a form that is non-mundane—Derrida en-gages in what we must call a "phenomenological description of the voice." Throughout these pages (VP 84-90/75-80), he italicizes the verb "se don-ner" (VP 85/76; 87/78; 89/80). How is the phenomenon of the voice *given*? What happens when "I am hearing myself during the time that I am speaking" (VP 87/77)? Hearing-oneself-speak is, according to Derrida, an "absolutely unique type of auto-affection" (VP 88/78).[18] The phenomeno-logical essence of this self-relation seems to consist in three moments, ac-cording to Derrida (but these also seem to be self-evident). First, whether I actually use my vocal cords or not, there is forming either in my head or in my mouth sound; the sound is produced in the world (VP 89/79). So the voice is nothing outside of the world. Nevertheless, as Derrida stresses, this mundaneity of the sound does not mean that an objective, mundane sci-ence can teach us anything about the voice (VP 89/79). A mundane sci-ence cannot teach us anything about the voice because, second, hearing-oneself-speak is temporal, i.e., the sound is iterated across moments. This temporal iteration is why sound is the most ideal of all signs (VP 86/77). Third, in hearing-oneself-speak, one still exteriorizes one's thoughts or "meaning-intention" or acts of repetition in the sound. This exteriorization —ex-pression—seems to imply that we have now moved from time to space. But since the sound is heard by the subject during the time he is speaking, the voice is in absolute proximity to its speaker, "within the absolute proximity of its present" (VP 85/76), "absolutely close to me" (VP 87/77). The subject lets himself be affected by the signifier (that is, hears his own sounds, his own voice) without any detour through exteriority or through the world, or, as Derrida says, without any detour through "the non-proper in general" (VP 88/78). Hearing-oneself-speak is absolutely pure auto-affection (VP 89/79). In this auto-affection, one stays within what Husserl in the Fifth Cartesian Meditation called "the sphere of ownness." This sphere of auto-affection is so close that it does not even require the interior space or extension that we require when we try to experience or imagine our own body (VP 88–89/79). What makes it be a pure auto-affection, according to Derrida, is that it is "a self-proximity which would be nothing other than the absolute reduction of space in general" (VP 89/79). This absolute reduction of space in general is why hearing-oneself-speak, the unity of sound and voice (or meaning-intention), is so appropriate for universality (VP 89/79). Requiring the intervention of no surface in the world, the voice is a "signifying substance that is absolutely available" (VP 89/79). Its transmission or iteration encounters no obstacles or limits. The signified or what I want to say is so close to the signifier that the signifier is "diaphanous" (VP 90/80). Therefore, *the phoneme gives itself as the mastered ideality of the phenomenon*" (VP 87/78, Derrida's italics), hence the title of this book, "voice and phenomenon." As Derrida says,

> . . . the unity of the sound (which is in the world) and the *phone* (in the phenomenological sense), which allows the latter to be produced in the world as pure auto-affection, is the unique agency which escapes from the distinction between intra-mundaneity and transcendentality. And by the same token, this unity is what makes the distinction possible. (VP 89/79)

The voice therefore for Derrida is ultra-transcendental. It is the very element and means of consciousness: "The voice is the being close-by itself in the form of universality, as con-science. The voice *is* consciousness" (VP 89/79–80, Derrida's italics).

For Derrida, this voice functions even at the most fundamental, pre-expressive level, at the very root of transcendental experience, in absolute silence; this insinuation of the voice is why Chapter 6 is called "La voix qui garde le silence," "the voice that keeps quiet." The voice functions here because its primary determination is temporality (VP 93/83). According to

Derrida, the living present in Husserl, originary temporalization, is auto-affection. As he says, the "source-point," the "primordial impression" of the living present, described in *The Lectures,* "is pure auto-affection" (VP 93/83). It is pure auto-affection because, as Derrida says, for Husserl, temporality is never the predicate of a real being or existent. On the one hand, this non-reality of time means that the intuition of time cannot be empirical (VP 93/83). The intuition of time is a receiving that receives nothing: "The absolute novelty of each now is therefore engendered by nothing. It consists in a primordial impression which engenders itself" (VP 93/83). On the other hand, the non-reality of time means that, just as the receiving receives nothing, this production produces nothing; it does not generate a being or existent. Temporalization is a "pure movement" producing itself: spontaneous self-generation (VP 93/84). According to Derrida, this transcendental temporalization, transcendental auto-affection, supposes that "a pure difference . . . divides self-presence" (VP 92/82), the pure difference between receiving and creating (VP 92/82). This pure difference originarily introduces into self-presence all the impurity that we believed we had been able to exclude: space, the outside, the world, the body, etc. (VP 95/85, 92/82). We must assume that there is a difference, which divides the self, which divides the *auto* (VP 92/82): "It produces the same as the self-relation within the difference with oneself, the same as the non-identical" (VP 92/82). We see once again the importance of Hyppolite's realization that confusion within the Greek word "autos" between *idem* (identity) and *ipse* (self) expresses the self-torsion of thought.[19] This self-torsion is the concept of "différance" that we saw Derrida introduce in Chapter 5 (VP 92/82).

As we saw then, this concept refers to the irreducible void, to the logic that lies below Husserl's perplexing definition of retention. So, as in Chapter 5, here in Chapter 6, Derrida says, "The living present springs forth on the basis of its non-self-identity, and on the basis of the retentional trace. It is always already a trace" (VP 95/85). The trace implies that there is a repetition that is prior to any present impression. For Derrida, we can say in the most general terms that memory precedes perception. A memory in turn implies that there is a lateness and therefore distance from what is remembered, which is no longer present. This identity, in Derrida, of the trace with memory is very important for Derrida; it will allow Derrida to develop, quickly after *Voice and Phenomenon,* the concept of the simulacrum. For example, already in the 1968 "Différance" essay, Derrida says, " . . . the trace is not a presence but the simulacrum of a presence . . . " (MP

25/24). Nevertheless, as we are going to see in Part IV, Chapter 8, the simulacrum or trace does not include the memory of a "who," a person; this inclusion of a "who" in memory, for Derrida, will be at the center of his concept of the specter. In any case, what is important here is that Derrida is prioritizing memory over perception. When I *hear* myself speak, the hearing is a repetition of the speaking that has already disappeared; representation (*Vergegenwärtigung*) has intervened, and that intervention means, in a word, space. As Derrida says, "the 'outside' insinuates itself in the movement by which the inside of non-space, what has the name of 'time,' appears to itself, constitutes itself, 'presents' itself" (VP 96/86). In other words, in silence, when time generates a new impression for itself, the generator has already disappeared; the impression therefore is a trace, spatialized, distanced, from the outside (even though it came from me). Within time, there is a fundamental "spacing" (VP 96/86). We must notice that these formulations so far imply a movement *in*—"s'est insinué dans"—we cannot leave the interiority of the living present but the outside comes in (into immanence). But, with the repetition there is in time a "pure exit of time out of itself" (VP 96/86). This exiting occurs because the repetition can go to infinity, beyond the present, distance itself, and be different. And as we know from the *Introduction,* this "exiting" needs writing (cf. VP 90–91/80–81). When I hear myself *speak,* the speaking can go far beyond my own hearing by being written down. So Derrida calls this movement of the retentional trace "archi-writing" (VP 95/85) (as in tracing) since "when I see myself *writing* and when I signify by gestures, the proximity of hearing myself speak is broken" (VP 90/80, my italics). Because the infinite repetition needs writing or more generally language, Derrida says that this movement is "the root of a metaphor which can be only originary" (VP 95/85). This comment means that language is originary, that there is no experience, not even silent transcendental experience that does not participate in the order of signification. We have no choice but to metaphorize. In temporalization, we have a trans-fer, a *meta-phora,* of the same across difference.

We can explain this *différance* one other way. In temporalization, in auto-affection, one is differentiated into receiver and creator, hearer and speaker by means of the repetition: I say something; *then* in my hearing of it, I repeat it just as I had made it. Yet this difference is not a difference between two beings; there is no ontic duplication that would place this auto-affection outside of the world. Thus, while the transcendental reduction attempts to take us into the transcendental ego, which is non-mundane, which is outside of the world, it cannot purely do this since it does not make the transcendental ego into an ontic double. Here we have the same and yet different, and yet not a *substantial* difference. This sameness within two is why Derrida says that,

> As the relation between an inside and an outside in general, an existent and a non-existent in general, a constituting and a constituted in general, temporalization is simultaneously the power and the limit of the phenomenological reduction. The hearing-oneself-speak is not the interiority of an inside closed upon itself. It is the irreducible openness in the inside, the eye and the world in speech. *The phenomenological reduction is a stage.* (VP 96/86)

The image of the stage—Derrida also calls temporalization or auto-affection an "archi-stage" (VP 94n1/84n9)—implies that the movement always involves re-presentation (as in a stage representation), *Vergegenwärtigung*. On the same stage, there are always several personas, other egos (VP 94n1/84n9).

For Derrida, the inclusion of the voice that keeps quiet in temporalization, of the voice that indeed defines consciousness in general, is not an accident that befalls self-presence. In fact, indication is not an accident that befalls expression and, as is well known, writing is not, for Derrida, an accident that befalls speech. These are not contingent associations (VP 97/87). There is already, for Derrida, a lack that *needs* their addition. This question of necessary "supplementation" brings us to the concluding Chapter 7 of *Voice and Phenomenon*. The last sentence of Chapter 6 says,

> And if indication, for example, writing in the popular sense, must necessarily "be added on" to speech in order to complete the constitution of ideal objects, if speech must "be added on" to the thought identity of the object, this is because the "presence" of the sense and of the speech had already started to be self-deficient [*se manquer à elle-même*]. (VP 97/87)

This sentence recalls what we saw in section 7 of the *Introduction.*[20] The ideality of sense lacks "persisting presence"; "la présence persistante," we recall, was Derrida's translation of Husserl's "das verharrende Dasein." This lack, this "manque," this "irreducible void" is the basis for what Derrida now in *Voice and Phenomenon*, Chapter 7, calls "supplementarity": "The supplementary difference vicariously stands in for presence in its originary self-deficiency [*dans son manque originaire à elle-même*]" (VP 98/88).

As is well known, supplementarity is a term roughly synonymous with *différance*—"So understood, supplementarity is really *différance*" (VP 98/88)—and *différance* is defined by the ambiguity in the French verb "différer," between "fissure and making late," between "division and delay" (VP 98/88; cf. ED 314/211–212; MP 8–9/7–8). The "logic" of supplementarity or *différance*, which we have discussed earlier (the "logic" of totality in the *Introduction* or the "impossible system" of "Violence and Metaphysics"), is "complex" (VP 99/89). First, as we just saw in auto-affection, a difference necessarily divides the self; the difference between speaker and hearer means that I cannot have the presence of my self immediately; there is an impossibility of immediate presence here; the difference is non-presence; always already, presence had started to be deficient in relation *to* itself. So, as Derrida says in Chapter 7,

> ... this concept of originary supplementarity not only implies the non-plentitude of presence (or in Husserlian language the non-fulfillment of an intuition), but also it designates this function of substitutive supplementation in general, the structure of "in place of" (*für etwas*) which defines every sign in general. . . . (VP 98/88)

According to Derrida, the deficiency to itself, "à elle-même," this self-difference is the structure of the sign in general (cf. VP 24–25/23–24); it is the "dative dimension" of self-presence: "présence à soi" (VP 98–99/88–89). Second, since the difference is the difference of substitution, of a going across from me *to* me, from me as the speaker *to* me as the hearer, the dative dimension is the possibility of iteration; and it is this possibility or power of iteration that produces self-presence: I iterate my self in order to send it back *to* me and have thereby my self more fully; or, as in idealization, the power of iteration produces ideal objectivity by going beyond psychological and subjective sense. As we saw in the *Introduction*, my access to presence is always late (there is always already non-presence) and thus presence, for Derrida, always comes later, after iterability. So, third, since there is self-presence *now*, or since there is ideal objectivity *now, later as a product*, the difference of iterability looks to be a *mere* supplement, contingently "added on" to presence; now it looks as though the contamination of iterability is an after-effect or delayed reaction, a *Nagträglichkeit* (to use Freudian terminology; see VP 71/63 and again ED 314/211–212), an *après coup* of presence itself. Iterability or writing in the "popular sense" seems to come after presence. But actually the contamination was, as the title of Chapter 7 says, "le supplément d'origine," "the supplement-origin." The logic or structure of *différance* shows that the possibility of iteration produces both non-presence and presence; it is at once the condition of the possibility and impossibility of presence. As Derrida says, "a possibility produces that to which it is said to be added onto" (VP 99/89).

Because of this necessary lack of presence or intuitive plentitude—and this demonstrates the overall coherence of *Voice and Phenomenon*—Derrida in Chapter 7 returns to the two "impulses" of phenomenology mentioned at the end of the Introduction to *Voice and Phenomenon*: "the purity of formalism and the radicality of intuitionism" (VP 16/16). In light of the structure of supplementarity, the purpose of Chapter 7 lies in discovering—Derrida says that "this is the most important" (VP 99/89)—"the way in which expression itself implies, in its structure, a non-plenitude" (VP 99/89). This non-plenitude is the lack, the non-fulfillment by intuition. According to Derrida, Husserl's concept of language—"pure logical grammar" or "pure formal semantic theory" (VP 100/90)—liberates or emancipates the pure forms of expression from intuition: "Against the whole tradition, Husserl demonstrates that speech then is still speech with its full set of rights provided that it obey certain rules which are not immediately given as rules of knowledge" (VP 100/90). As we shall see in a moment, Husserl's epistemological project nevertheless determines the concept of language, but Derrida's "interpretation" of Husserl's concept of language allows us to see Husserl's "whole originality" (VP 99–100/89–90).

What Derrida says here is based on section 9 of the First Logical Investigation. Two comments by Husserl there are crucial: on the one hand, Husserl says that the acts of expression divide into the acts which give it meaning "und eventuell die anschauliche Fülle"; Derrida's French is "et éventuellement la plénitude intuitive" and the standard English translation is "and *possibly* also intuitive fullness (VP 101/90, my emphasis in the English translation). On the other hand, Husserl says, still in section 9, that the objective something can be made present and when this happens the relation to the object is realized; then he says, "Oder dies ist nicht der Fall; der Ausdruck fungiert ist sinnvoll"; Derrida's French is "Ou bien ce n'est pas le cas; l'expression fonctionne avec sa charge de sens" and the standard English translation is "Alternatively this need not occur: the expression functions significantly" (VP 101/91). What is important here, for Derrida, is that Husserl says that the act of intuitive plentitude is "eventuell," that is, possible, eventual, or contingent; Husserl does not say that intuitive plentitude is necessary for the sign to be meaningful. Derrida concludes, "La plénitude est donc seulement éventuelle" (VP 101). Thus intuitive plentitude is not an essential component of expression, and, in fact, when it happens that there is no intuitive plentitude—"or it is not the case"—then the expression still functions meaningfully. In order to be meaningful, in order to be what it is, expression does not essentially require the intuition of the object, but must "dispense with the full presence of the object aimed at by intuition" (VP 100/90). The essential necessity of non-fulfillment does not mean, for Derrida, that expression must dispense with intuitive presence; instead, it means that necessarily an expression must *possibly*, eventually, do without it. If it *could not* dispense with a here-and-now intuition, the expression would not be ideal, which, for Husserl, is the primary determination of expression.

On the basis of what we see in section 9 of the First Investigation, we have the essential non-plentitude, the lack, which defines expression. Derrida says, "the whole purpose of this chapter is to accumulate the proofs [*les preuves*] of this difference between intention and intuition" (VP 101/91). We shall return to this idea of "proofs" or "tests" in a moment, but for now we must note that the proofs Derrida accumulates are, first, the case of a statement about perception and, second, writing. The case of a statement about perception is obvious. If I state, "I see a particular person by the window," while I actually do see that person, it looks as though "I have an intimately blended unity" of intention and intuition. But in order that what this statement expresses be ideal, it is necessary that the non-perception of the person not impair that ideality. In other words, what Derrida is pointing at is a necessary possibility. If the statement is to function, it must not require the here-and-now intuition; the lack of intuition is necessarily possible. Derrida concludes,

> The absence of intuition—and therefore of the subject of intuition—is not only *tolerated* by speech; it is *required* by the general structure of signification, when considered *in itself.* It is radically requisite: the total absence of the subject and object of a statement—the death of the writer and/or the disappearance of the objects he was able to describe—does not prevent a text from "meaning" something. (VP 104/93)

This comment leads to Derrida's "proof" of non-plentitude by writing (*l'écriture*). In writing, the word "I" functions even when the author is "unknown" (*inconnu*: the lack of knowledge, and thus without sense), "fictitious," or even "dead" (cf. VP 107/96). What Derrida is trying to show here is that this normal case in writing—which Husserl considers abnormal (VP 107/96)—is the normal case for all personal pronouns, or for all occasional expressions, to use Husserl's terminology, or for all indexicals, to use the common linguistic term. While this might look to be a quite limited issue, we know from the *Introduction* that the question of writing for Derrida is really a question of transcendental subjectivity. Husserl distinguishes indexicals from objective expression whose model would be "mathematical expressions" which are univocal (VP 105/94). These objective expressions are, for Husserl, "absolutely pure expressions, free from all indicative contamination" (VP 105/94). Because the word "I" is an indexical—and this connection to subjectivity, to the ego, is why it is important to realize that frequently Derrida uses the word "l'indice" to translate "Anzeichen" in Husserl (cf. MP 381/320)—we might say that we are dealing with absolutely pure indication; we are here dealing with *subjective* expressions that are equivocal. We can see already the complication. Husserl thinks that, when the word "I" functions in solitary discourse, I have a fulfilling intuition of the meaning of "I" in an immediate representation of my personality (VP 106/94–95); this fulfillment implies a sort of pure self-presence and pure expression. In solitary discourse, the indexical becomes objective and univocal, since now it refers only to *my* personality. But, since the indexical now refers only to *my* personality, the pure self-presence must be conceived as a factual or empirical self-presence. If the self-presence is only factual, then the *pure* self-presence and expression are not possible: the "I" must also be ideal if it is to function at all. Insofar as it is "ideal," the "I" must be able to function without my intuitive presence, and then indication contaminates, but this contamination is necessary, necessary for the "I" to function ideally. Indication understood as "eventual" intuitive non-fulfillment or "eventual" non-presence is necessary for ideality to be, for Derrida. This "eventual" lack of fulfillment (or plentitude) means, paradoxically, that insofar as they are ideal and univocal and expressive, indexicals are factual, equivocal, and indicative; the very possibility of a proper or literal meaning of the word "I" (ideality) is at the same time the possibility of its impropriety or metaphoricity (VP 108/97). We have seen this kind of paradox before in Derrida, in section 7 of the *Introduction,* when he says that a word is not an absolute object.[21] This paradox is the "normal situation," according to Derrida (VP 108/97).

Indeed, unless the indexical "I" was also ideal, there could be no discourse of transcendental phenomenology (VP 106/95). One would be unable to make any "general" phenomenological claims about subjectivity unless this particular indexical, the "I," were also ideal, and not requiring a fulfilling intuition in order to function or be meaningful (VP 105/94). Here, at the transcendental level, understood as the possibility of non-presence, indication is not added on to expression, but rather "dictates" it (VP 108/97), as if indication were, to use a term Derrida introduces here, a "franc-parler" (VP 108/97), meaning a frank or honest discourse as well as a discourse unconstrained by presence and knowledge, as if indication were a "testament" (VP 108/96), a last will and testament which we assume to be honest but do not *know* if it is true. We shall return to this honest testament in a moment. But what we must see here is that this "eventual" non-presence (this "eventual" lack of knowledge) is the normal situation, according to Derrida. The normal situation is that the empirical subject *must be capable* of dying—Derrida here is speaking of a necessary possibility—in order that the objective ego, the general ego, the *eidos* ego, is possible. As Derrida says, "My death is structurally necessary to the pronouncing of the I" (VP 107/96). While earlier Derrida had been able to reach the "I am mortal" on the basis of the "I am," now he is able to understand the "I am" on the basis of the "I am dead" (VP 108/97). At the very moment that I make a statement such as "I am alive," my "ontic death" (*être-mort*) must be possible.

According to Derrida, although the premises of this argument are present in Husserl, Husserl himself does not draw the consequences that my death must be possible in order for an expression to function, that the "normal situation" occurs whenever the word "I" is separated from the person, whenever the person is unknown (VP 109/97). Husserl cannot recognize that "non-knowledge" (*non-savoir*) is the norm because "the impulse of full 'presence,' the intuitionistic imperative, and the project of knowledge continue to command . . . the whole of the description" (VP 109/97). Husserl limits the "originality" of the concept of *Bedeutung* with the radicality of intuition. Indeed, according to Derrida, "in order to be radical," intuition must be the *telos* of meaning or sense; meaning must, for Husserl, always be "pro-visional," that is, it must always be directed toward a vision, which fulfills the meaning-intention. For Derrida, this determination of the essence of meaning by the *telos* of presence means that the sign is constituted as a "lack" (*manque*) of truth, as if the lack were temporary and contingent (VP 109/97–98). Husserl has determined sense as "a relation to the object" (*rapport à l'objet*). This "relation to an object" means that any expression which does not point to a possible object—expressions such as "abracadabra" or "Green is or"—must for Husserl be defined as "non-sense" (*Unsinn*). Obviously, expressions such as these do not make sense; they are "non-sense."[22] Yet they function, as if their author were unknown or dead; for example, "Green is or" or "le vert est ou" could function in poetry (see MP 380–381/319–320). The relation to an object, therefore, for Husserl, is an epistemological criterion and this criterion of presence is what, according to Derrida, Husserl means by "normality": "The norm is knowledge (*connaissance*), the intuition that is adequate to its object, the evidence that is not only distinct but also 'clear.' It is the full presence of sense to a consciousness that is itself self-present in the plentitude of its life, its living present" (VP 109–110/98). This norm of knowledge, in its radicality, limits the purity of Husserl's formalism. As Derrida concludes Chapter 7, "[To recognize that Husserl determines sense as relation to an object] is to recognize the initial limitation of sense to knowledge [*savoir*], the *logos* to objectivity, language to reason" (VP 111/99).

4

The Experience of the Aporia of Différance. Already in *Voice and Phenomenon*, Derrida is defining deconstruction in terms of an experience. This is the first sentence of *Voice and Phenomenon*'s Conclusion: "We have experienced [*éprouvé*] the systematic solidarity of the concepts of sense, objectivity, truth, intuition, perception, and expression" (VP 111/99). In reference to this comment, we must recall that earlier in Chapter 7, Derrida had said that, "the whole purpose of this chapter is to accumulate the proofs [*les preuves*] of this difference between intention and intuition" (VP 101/91). Deconstruction is a putting to the test of this difference. Derrida also says here in the Conclusion that the experience is one of the systematic solidarity of these Husserlian concepts (sense, ideality, objectivity, truth, intuition, perception, expression) whose "common matrix" is "presence" (VP 111/99). Presence must be understood in terms of the living present and the living present is "the founding concept of phenomenology as metaphysics" (VP 111/99). As we have seen, the living present is the foundation of the inaugural opposition of metaphysics, form and matter, or, in other words, form and intuition, or meaning-intention and intuition. The experience Derrida is pointing us toward is indeed one of presence; after all, Derrida ends "Violence and Metaphysics" (in a 1967 revision) by asking: "is not experience always an encountering of an irreducible presence . . . ?" (ED 225/152). But we must also recall that, in the Introduction to *Voice and Phenomenon*, Derrida says, "What is only at issue is to make the original and non-empirical space of non-foundation appear over the irreducible void" (VP 5–6/7). The experience that Derrida is trying to bring forth is an experience—the "making appear" or the presence—of the irreducible void, of the difference or lack, which is original and yet not a foundation. So the experience of deconstruction must be conceived as the presence of the non-foundation.

As we have already seen,[23] presence, for Derrida, is,

> the absolute proximity of self-identity, the object being in front of as available for repetition, the maintenance of the temporal present whose ideal form is the self-presence of transcendental *life* whose ideal identity allows *idealiter* the repetition to infinity. (VP 111/99, Derrida's emphasis)

We should note here that this definition of presence consists in three aspects (indicated by the three clauses). First, presence is proximity of the self; second, presence is the object over and against and therefore available for repetition. These first two aspects are respectively subjective (intuition) and objective (form), as we have stressed above. Then the third is transcendental life in the present that allows for the unification of the first two aspects of presence. As we noted above, this "transcendental life" is the voice. Encountering no obstacle or limit, the voice is the element of universality, infinite repetition; it maintains, as the quote above suggests, the present. The object can be repeated to infinity and its form will always, ideally, be that of the present, that of life. But, as Derrida stresses in this quote, the entire structure of presence is *idealiter*. For Husserl, according to Derrida, *idealiter*, the repetition to infinity of the object, will always have the form of the living present. In other words, the repetition of the object will never allow the object, now idealized, to die. Ideally, we can "substitute" the objective for the subjective (VP 112/100), that is, we can supplement, that is, repeat the intuition that always lacks persisting existence and thereby give it persisting existence. Ideally, we can substitute equivocal expressions such as indexical with an objective content which is univocal. In section 28 of the First Investigation however, Husserl says that we are infinitely far from this ideal. On the basis of this comment from section 28, Derrida says, " . . . all of what is thought *purely* in this concept, being by the same blow determined as *ideality*, the living present is *in fact* really, actually, etc. deferred [*différé*]. This *différance* is the difference between ideality and non-ideality" (VP 111–112/99).

Here Derrida is defining *différance*, not in terms of its double sense of difference and delay, but rather in terms of the difference between *en fait* and *en droit*, *de jure* and *de facto*, essence (or principle) and fact. Anticipating this comment about *différance*, earlier in *Voice and Phenomenon* (Chapter 1), Derrida says,

> The whole analysis will therefore advance in this divergence [*écart*] between *de facto* [*le fait*] and *de jure* [*le droit*], existence and essence, reality and intentional function. . . . We would be tempted to say that this divergence, which defines the very space of phenomenology, does not exist prior to the question of language, nor does the divergence enter into language as into one domain or as one problem among others. On the contrary, the divergence opens itself up only in and through the possibility of language. And its juridical validity, the right to a distinction between fact and intentional right, depends entirely on language, and in language, on the validity of a radical distinction between indication and expression. (VP 21/21)

We can see already that, in this quote, Derrida is presenting a paradoxical structure. Language is the condition for the possibility of the distinction between fact and right. But the juridical validity of language as this condition depends on the validity of the distinction between indication and expression. But this distinction, Husserl tells us, does not hold in fact. So the distinction between indication and expression is an ideal distinction and thus depends on the very distinction that it is supposed to justify. The condition for the possibility depends on the very thing it is conditioning. Thus, the condition for the possibility is at the same time the condition for its impossibility. This paradox or *aporia* is *différance*.

We can put this *aporia* in another way. The very possibility of differentiating between ideality or essence and fact is iterability: an ideality can be repeated to infinity, while a fact is singular. But, insofar as being iterable, an ideality can never in fact be given as such in an intuition; it can always be repeated beyond the limit of this intuition. In other words, because an ideality can be iterated, we can have the difference between *de jure* and *de facto*. Anything that is "in principle" can be iterated. Yet precisely because it can be iterated, it can never be given in a real intuition. So the very condition for the possibility of the *de jure–de facto* difference—iterability—makes the distinction impossible to maintain as an opposition. In other words, because a form can be iterated, it is different from its content; but because it is different in this way, through iterability, a form can never be given as such; thus we are never certain that there is really is a difference. The only way we could be certain that the form is different from the content would be if the form were a content, were an intuition; but if the form were an intuition, then the difference would be erased: the principle would be a fact. Here, in this difficult discussion, Derrida is repeating what we saw in the *Introduction* concerning the Idea in the Kantian sense (cf. VP 112/100). We can have infinity under the conditions of a finite intuition, but then we do not have given to us infinity itself. And this difference is necessary for us to be able to talk about there being anything like an ideality; an ideality must be repeatable beyond, to infinity, any given intuition of it. But because we do not have the intuition of infinity itself—it is a non-presence and non-being—the difference is erased. There seems to be only the finite intuition; infinity must present itself, if it is to be. As Derrida says, the very possibility of the difference between fact and principle (*droit*, in French)—this possibility is iteration—is the impossibility of the difference—since being iterable, the right is not present as something different *as such*. This *aporia* is precisely what deconstruction is supposed to lead us to experience.

The Thought of Différance. The experience of *différance*—the *aporia* that the condition of possibility being at the same time a condition of impossibility—takes place "within," or it constitutes a "certain inside of the metaphysics of presence," which "attempts to produce a kind of insecurity within it" (VP 64n1/57n6), and thus constrains us to think. So, at the close of *Voice and Phenomenon*, Derrida addresses precisely how "this différance is given to thought [*se donne-t-elle à penser*]." Precisely, Derrida asks: "what does 'to infinity' mean? What does presence as différance to infinity mean? What does the life of the living present as différance to infinity mean?" (VP 114/101). Here we should also note that each time Derrida says "mean," the French verb, of course, is "vouloir dire," "vouloir" expressing a kind of wanting or will. The question is: what does presence as *différance* to infinity *want* or *will* in saying? Phrased in this way, the question concerns the fulfillment or accomplishment of this will.

Derrida has already provided the schema for this will (as we discussed in the first section of this chapter). The will of metaphysics wants to make difference and the sign *derivative*. Derrida stresses that, because Husserl relies on the Idea in the Kantian sense "as the indefiniteness of a 'to infinity'," "we are led to think that he never *derived* difference from the plentitude of a *parousia,* from the full presence of a positive infinite, that he never believed in the accomplishment of an 'absolute knowledge' as presence near to the self in the Logos, that he never believed in the accomplishment of an infinite concept" (VP 114/101, my emphasis). Yet it is precisely because Husserl never "believed in the accomplishment of absolute knowledge" that he "indefatigably runs out of breath [*s'essouffle: exhausts* himself literally]" trying to make difference derivative from presence. The Idea in the Kantian sense is the "immer wieder" of trying to make the ideal itself appear, but this appearance never occurs for Husserl. So, Derrida says, "*Within this schema* [*A l'intérieur de ce schème*], Hegelianism looks more radical" (VP 114/101, my emphasis). We must recall that the Husserl of *Ideas I*, paragraph 124, is quite close, for Derrida, to this Hegelian radicalism; so we are following here at the Conclusion to *Voice and Phenomenon* the development already laid out in Chapter 6. Within the schema of the metaphysics of presence, Hegelianism, for Derrida, looks to be more radical when it shows (in its critique of Kant) that we must think the positive infinity. Unlike Husserl, who remains Kantian in his resistance to think the infinite as such (except in section 124 and in his descriptions of absolute consciousness in the *Lectures*), Hegel thinks the infinite and therefore "the indefiniteness of différance appears *as such*" (VP 114/102). The positive infinite, that is, totality, is a process of self-relation and self-differentiation; auto-affection, thought thinking itself, shows that difference is irreducible. In the "Différance" essay, Derrida indeed identifies *différance* with the Hegelian concept of difference (found in the Jena Logic) (MP 15/14) and we have already cited the quote from "Violence and Metaphysics" concerning Hegelian difference (ED 271n1/320n91). In Hegel, the Idea or what Derrida calls "the Ideal" appears as such. "But," as Derrida says,

> this appearing of the Ideal as infinite différance can produce itself only in a relation to death in general. Only a relation to my-death can make the infinite différance of presence appear. By the same blow, compared to the ideality of the positive infinite, this relation to my-death becomes an accident of finite empiricity. The appearing of infinite différance is itself finite. Henceforth, différance, which is nothing outside of this relation, becomes the finitude of life as the essential relation to the self as to its death. We can no longer conceive it within the opposition between finite and infinite, absence and presence, negation and affirmation. (VP 114/102)

For Derrida, the Ideal of *différance* can appear only in relation to death, as we have seen. And, as the relation to death makes the infinite *différance*

appear, "du même coup"—here we have the structure of supplementarity
—the relation to death becomes an accident of finite empiricity. *After* making the ideal possible, the relation to death becomes an accident. Nevertheless, *différance* is nothing outside of this relation; it is the finitude of life
understood as the essential self-relation in which death is a necessary possibility. Indeed, we can say that the infinite *différance* is finite, but, for Derrida, the subject and the predicate here do not form an opposition or an
identity. We have indeed "upped the ante on dialectic."

But, Derrida repeats the "à l'intérieur." The radicalism of Hegel is, as
in Husserl, the radicality of intuition and knowledge; *différance* is still
thought in Hegelianism on the basis of presence (VP 115/102). So, "within
the metaphysics of presence" "absolute knowledge is," as Derrida "believes," "the closure if not the end [*fin*] of history" (VP 115/102). The
schema of the metaphysics of presence is the will to make difference and
the sign derivative from presence. Thus Derrida says, of course, "the history of metaphysics is the absolute will to hear-oneself-speak" (VP 115/
102). Hegelianism's radicality is that it fulfills or accomplishes the "vocation of infinity as absolute self-presence in con-sciousness [*con-science*]"
(VP 115/102). Here Derrida introduces the language of the call of conscience to suggest the ambiguity of the word "fin," meaning both "end"
and "purpose," both death and life. Insofar as Hegelianism answers this
call, it reaches the end (*la fin*) of the infinite and it reaches the purpose or
telos (*la fin*) of the infinite. The purpose—what it willed—would be "the
unity of the concept, of the logos, and consciousness in a voice without
différance" (VP 115/102). Such a unity—the ideal—would have no relation
to the distance and absence and death of empiricity so that it would be
absolutely alive. But also, since such a unity could be produced only on the
basis of a relation to death in general, it is absolutely dead. In other words,
absolute knowledge would be absolute spirit and absolute or pure spirit
could be conceived only as absolutely alive and as absolutely dead. As Derrida says, "[The history of metaphysics] is closed when this absolute infinity appears to itself as its own death. *A voice without différance, a voice
without writing, is simultaneously absolutely alive and absolutely dead*" (VP
115/102, Derrida's emphasis).

Despite appearances, this comment does not imply any sort of apocalypse. Instead, what Derrida is expressing here is a new kind of eschatology.
The end in which life is absolved from death or death from life *must* not
happen; the double necessity that we have seen Derrida develop in the *In-*

troduction forbids it. Life must be itself (it must be held in life) *and* it must be other than itself (it must be taken by death). These two necessities are absolutely inseparable. What is absolute is passage or the relation. Absolute life or absolute death cannot happen; this absoluteness is impossible; in fact it is *the worst* that could happen. The end, for Derrida, must always be done over again, beyond absolute knowledge. It will be done over within "the openness of an unheard-of question that opens neither upon knowledge nor upon non-knowledge that is knowledge to come. In the openness of this question, *we no longer know*" (VP 115/103, Derrida's emphasis). We cannot underestimate the importance of this comment—and we shall return to it in Part IV, Chapter 8—it indicates clearly what we had already seen, that is, that Derrida is conceiving genesis, the problem of the sign, in terms of the structure of the question. Yet we cannot even say that this question is the question of being, since it does not ask about presence; it is the question of non-philosophy that we saw in "Violence and Metaphysics." Because, however, it is not a question of sense, because it is beyond absolute knowledge, this unheard-of question does not "will to say" (*ne veut pas dire*) anything (VP 116/103). The response that it demands, therefore, is not the fulfillment of intuition. We can see already that Derrida has really stopped describing a question here. He is really describing some other structure than a question; he is anticipating the turn to the promise. In any case, the response that the unheard-of question is demanding is "the memory of old signs [*la memoire des vieux signes*] (VP 115/102). This is a very specific memory. If I remember the old name "différance" and conceive it on the basis of presence, this old name remains an old name. If I remember it "otherwise" (*autrement*), then the name is another name (*un autre nom*); it is "older" (*plus vieux*). We know from Derrida's later writings how important this word "plus" is; it always suggests that we are upping the ante. The memory to which Derrida is alluding here in the Conclusion to *Voice and Phenomenon* is "older" (*plus 'vieux'*) than presence (VP 116/103). Derrida puts scare quotes around *vieux* to indicate its strangeness. "Plus 'vieux'" suggests the threshold. When one is older, one is both before those who are younger (one was born before the younger ones) and ahead of those who are younger (one will die ahead of the younger ones); one is both closer to the beginning and closer to the end. Older is a life on the threshold of death, relating death and life to one another. This older name recalled in an older memory is at once before and after presence. Such an older name is the one that opens out onto what

Derrida calls "the phenomenon of labyrinth" (VP 117/104). It is the name mentioned in the famous quote from Husserl (*Ideas I,* section 100), with which Derrida ends *Voice and Phenomenon:*

> A *name* [my emphasis] mentioned reminds us of the Dresden gallery. . . . We wander through the rooms. . . . A painting by Teniers . . . represents a gallery of paintings. . . . The paintings of this gallery would represent in their turn paintings, which on their part exhibited readable inscriptions and so forth. (quoted in VP 116–117/104)

This older and other name is perhaps "the specter," and perhaps the painting by Teniers opens out onto a portrait gallery, or, better, a gallery of religious paintings.

Part Four.
The Turn in Derrida

8   Looking for Noon at Two O'Clock: An Investigation of *Specters of Marx*

Voice and Phenomenon brings Derrida's formative period to a close.[1] As is well known, from 1967 on, Derrida's thought will develop in many directions and into many domains. In general, however, the concepts forged during this first period (from 1954 to 1967) remain in place in the later writings. In fact, the most remarkable thing about Derrida's vast corpus is its continuity; Derrida's thought does not, as one might think, shift *all of a sudden* from metaphysical issues to ethico-political issues. *Différance* and supplementarity continue to be basic concepts in the later writings, and in the early writings the ethico-political issues make an appearance (the "we," for example in the *Introduction*). Nevertheless, it is undeniable that during this formative first period, the problem of genesis dominates; the deconstruction of metaphysics—this claim is very obvious—defines the early Derrida; and the ethico-political issues are generally in the background. As Derrida's ethico-political issues, however, gradually move to the foreground, these issues—the decline of communism, for example—require new concepts. This gradual shift of emphasis from metaphysics to ethics and politics results in one major conceptual event: the "turn" from the question to the promise.[2] If we must say that the basic problem of phenomenology is the problem of genesis, then now (after 1967) we must say that Derrida conceives genesis not in terms of the question, but in terms of the promise. What Derrida realizes is that a question, interrogation, does not have the power to necessitate change; a response to a question only explicates the implicit sense of the question. When someone, however, says to me, "Swear!" and I swear to do what he or she commands, I must believe that I understand the command and I must believe that I can do what is commanded of me. The trace that poses a question does not have the force to necessitate such a change in me because the trace in the early Derrida is merely an impersonal "what." Derrida therefore must—although this change as well is more a shift in emphasis than a conceptual break—transform the trace into the "revenant," the "returning" or "the ghost," that is, into the specter; the specter is a personal memory *who* commands me to change. While in the formative first period, Derrida conceived deconstruction as responding to a question posed within (*à l'intérieur*) metaphysics in order to go outside, now he conceives deconstruction as the keeping of a promise to a specter who needs to come inside, and thereby form a community. Either way—toward the outside (exiting the metaphysics of presence) or toward the inside (hospitality)—deconstruction concerns itself with the limit or the threshold.

Thus, in order to conclude this investigation of Derrida's interpretation of Husserl, we are going to investigate *Specters of Marx.* Such an investigation can not only demonstrate the continuity of Derrida's thought with his early interpretation of Husserl, but also define precisely the "turn" in Derrida's thinking. Only such an investigation can demonstrate the genuine stakes of this new kind of thinking called deconstruction. This concluding investigation will consist in two steps. First, we are going to assemble three points from the formative period where the turn starts to be made. Then, in a second step, we are going to reconstruct the logic of the promise on the basis of *Specters of Marx;* this logic will be divided into three moments: the disjunction of the promise; the injunction of the promise; and the keeping of the promise. Derrida's new concept of the promise stems, in general, from the recognition that Heidegger's conception of the question, which had formed the frame for Derrida's thinking from 1962 to 1967, is inadequate to the requirements of ethics and politics. Turning from the question of being and even from the question of non-philosophy and turning to the promise of justice, Derrida combines Levinas's thought with that of Nietzsche.[3] Derrida's interpretation of Husserl concludes, as we are now going to see, with an "amalgamation" of Levinas and Nietzsche,[4] an amalgamation that we can characterize with the common French saying, "chercher le midi à quartorze heure" (literally, "looking for noon at two o'clock"), which means, of course, to seek to do the impossible.[5] This search is a new problem, beyond the problem of genesis, beyond the problem of the sign, beyond the basic problem of phenomenology: the problem of the promise.

1

At the edge of his formative period, we can locate three points where Derrida starts to turn from the question to the promise. First, as we noted, Derrida's 1968 essay, "The Ends of Man," starts Derrida's turn from Heidegger;[6] it also begins the turn from the structure of the question.[7] In "The Ends of Man," Derrida initiates a debate with Heidegger that continues into the later works, a debate over the concept of history. As early as 1954, Derrida was concerned, as we have seen, with conceiving genesis non-teleologically and non-archeologically; in other words, he was looking for a way to escape the type of *absolute* termination of a development in presence that the ambiguity of the French word "fin" and the German word "Zweck" suggest. What Derrida realizes is that the Heideggerian question is still connected to an archeological and teleological concept of genesis; the question is not as open as he thought it was in *Voice and Phenomenon*. The Heideggerian question privileges the being that *we* are, Dasein, and it is based in sense. Therefore a response to a question is nothing more than the making explicit of what was implicit in the question; the response brings the sense to presence and therefore makes it available for knowledge. Here we see the result of Derrida's reflection on death and sense in Chapters 4 and 7 of *Voice and Phenomenon*. Because my death, as an empirical or ontic being, is a possibility structurally necessary for the functioning of any sense, the sense is based in "non-sense" and therefore goes beyond "the relation to an object"; it goes *to* the other. Most importantly, Derrida realizes therefore that, because of the concept of sense, the Heideggerian question does not involve a moment of rupture, a moment of change through action, that would make a response outside and otherwise. Derrida is calling the entire structure of Heidegger's hermeneutic circle into question. This can be seen by comparing Derrida's discussion of the Heideggerian question in the section entitled "Reading Us" (MP 150–151/125–126) to his famous concluding comments on deconstruction (MP 162/135). We recall from Chapter 3, in our investigation of "The Ends of Man," that Derrida had criticized Heidegger's hermeneutics because it had not reduced sense. Now we must see that, in 1968, Derrida's debate with Heidegger takes place over Nietzsche.[8] What is most important in this brief discussion is that when Derrida mentions the "Great Noon," he is evoking Nietzsche's saying, "God is dead." Everything in these final comments therefore unfolds from a reflection, albeit tacit, on God's death. Derrida explicitly mentions the overman and says that his laughter will explode out toward a "return" (*un retour*) (MP 163/136), and thereby evokes Nietzsche's doctrine of eternal recurrence. Derrida also says that the overman "will dance at the 'active forgetting' and the cruel . . . feast of which the *Genealogy of Morals* speaks" (MP 163/136). As is well known, Nietzsche discusses active forgetting in paragraph 1 and the cruel feast in paragraphs 6 and 7 of the *Genealogy of Morals*' second essay. The second essay, of course, opens with the comment, "To breed an animal with the right to make promises"; it shows that promising and, especially, the keeping of the promise is based on sovereignty. And sovereignty—without a master over, Godless—is a sign, for Nietzsche, of the overman.

While Nietzsche is one source of Derrida's conception of the promise, the other is clearly Levinas, in particular, his concept of messianic eschatology in the Preface to *Totality and Infinity;* thus our second point where we can see Derrida starting to turn from the question to the promise.[9] On the basis of our investigation of "Violence and Metaphysics," we can see that Derrida is criticizing Levinas's notion of messianic eschatology (ED 191/130, 213/144).[10] The keeping of the promise of Levinas's messianic eschatology implies, according to Derrida, that the infinitely other appear as such, thereby rupturing being and history.[11] But, for Derrida, there is a necessity—the first necessity of *différance*—that demands that the infinitely other appear and to appear means to be finite (ED 188/128; cf. MP 27/25). This necessity is, of course, a formalism: the infinitely other must appear in a finite form such as that of intuitive presence (Husserl) or that of a being (Heidegger). This finite appearance is the onto-phenomenological presupposition of Levinasian ethics. This first necessity is a necessity, therefore, of anti-Platonism, a necessity of immanence consistent with the Nietzschean death of God (ED 221–223/149–151). There can be no separation between a finite form and its infinite iterability, and insofar as there can be no separation, we know that there is a second necessity of *différance*, that the infinitely other exit from the form or from totality. For Derrida also however—this point was definitely only in the background in the formative period since it appears only once in these writings, in a footnote (LOG 149n1/136n162; cf. also ED 179–180/122)—this double necessity that requires the infinitely other to appear in intuitive presence or as a being and to exit from intuitive presence or from a being is *both theoretical and ethical.* For Derrida, we must recognize that it is not only the case that the infinitely other *must* appear and dis-appear, but also that it *should* appear and dis-appear. In other words, there is an "injunction" (ED 19/80) that the infinitely other appear and that it dis-appear. But now, since we can see that the double necessity is theoretico-ethical, we can also see that the double necessity of *différance,* the injunction of *différance,* consists in a disjunction: the exiting always demands an entering and the entering always demands an exiting; singularity limits generality and generality de-limits singularity. There is therefore an originary disequilibrium or inadequation that we can characterize with ethical terms: for Derrida, always already, there has been violence, inequality, or injustice between a finite form and its infinite iterability. Therefore we should give justice. The infinitely iterable form *should* de-limit any finite form and it *should* be limited to a finite form. In other words, the infinitely other must and should be emancipated from any totality and must and should be welcomed into my home. We must be hospitable to the other man.

The third point where we can see Derrida turning from the question to the promise concerns knowledge. We recall, at the close of Chapter 7, that Derrida was discussing how Husserl "limits" the purity of his formalism with sense understood as "relation to an object." As Derrida says, Husserl defines form "always as the form of a sense, and sense opens up only in the knowing intentionality with an object" (VP 110/98). For instance—this is Husserl's own example, which Derrida quotes—the form "abracadabra" has no relation to an object because it does not have the form "S is P"; therefore, for Husserl, it has no sense (VP 111/99). But, as Derrida stresses, this "abracadabra" still functions. Derrida therefore is not defining the concept of form in terms of "une intentionalité connaissante." We know, however, that *différance* derives from the Husserlian concept of intentionality; we have already seen the importance of the dative relation; it defines *différance*. While the dative relation in Derrida is not limited by knowledge or intuition, by presence, it is still defined as a "relation to." This "relation to" is not a sending out to a fulfillment in a vision, an intuition, or a regard; it does not give us knowledge or knowledge to come. If it does not give us knowledge—beyond absolute knowledge—then we must say it gives us non-knowledge. And the only way we can conceive this non-knowledge is as faith. To think otherwise than presence and knowledge is to have faith. The word "foi" does not occur once in *Voice and Phenomenon*. But Derrida repeatedly uses the verb "croire"—"Nous y croyons littéralement" (VP 115/102, for example)—in the Conclusion concerning absolute knowledge. Perhaps we have to say that with Derrida there is no knowing intentionality but there is an intentionality of faith (*une intentionalité croyante*); the "unheard-of question" that Derrida mentions in the Conclusion to *Voice and Phenomenon* is fulfilled in faith. Yet if the response to the question is one of faith and not knowledge, and if there is a theoretico-ethical double necessity in the unheard-of question—"il faut l'entendre ainsi *et* autrement"—then it is clear that something other than a question is happening here. "Abracadabra," as we said, functions; in fact, it has a sense in a non-epistemic context; it has a magical sense: "abracadabra" is an incantation in the conjuring up of ghosts. Faith, for Derrida, can be the only response to a ghostly presence. The unheard-of question is fundamentally what Derrida had called a "frank speech" like a "testament" that commands me to promise to do something.

2

We are now ready to reconstruct the logic of the promise as it appears in the 1993 *Specters of Marx*. The Derridean promise has three moments, the first of which is the disjunction we were just discussing. Second, there is the injunction of the promise; third, there is the keeping of the promise. Here in the first moment, disjunction, we must take our lead not from *Specters of Marx* but from Derrida's 1987 *Of Spirit*.

Disjunction. As earlier in "The Ends of Man," in *Of Spirit*, Derrida questions Heidegger's "long unquestioned privilege of the *Fragen*" (OS 24–25/9). As in "The Ends of Man," in *Of Spirit*, Derrida connects the structure of the Heideggerian question of Being to the "we," to hermeneutics, to sense, and to knowledge (OS 36/17, 87/56, 59/35). The Heideggerian question always demands a response that makes a sense (which was implicit in the question itself) visible. Therefore, in *Of Spirit*, to move away from the question, Derrida transforms Heidegger's famous formula "Die Sprache spricht" into "Die Sprache verspricht sich."[12] Focusing on the reflexive, Derrida interprets this sentence to mean that nothing precedes language (OS 147/94). It is not the case that first a group of people mutually promise to one another to use the same conventions, thereby creating language; instead, as the sentence literally says, language promises itself, promises to work, to communicate in order that people might speak. But the priority of the linguistic promise implies for Derrida that, since the question of being takes place in language, it is dependent on the promise as its condition (OS 147/94, 147n1/94n5). By asserting the priority of the promise over the question of being here in *Of Spirit*, Derrida is stressing what we saw in his *Introduction to Husserl's "The Origin of Geometry"*: language is the condition for the possibility of knowledge. This point is perhaps more obvious as we recall what is well known from texts such as "Signature Event Context": linguistic codes precede and make possible any speaker's particular utilization of them. As a speaker, I must swear my allegiance to these codes in order to communicate with someone else; I must affirm them and obey them if I want to ask a question, even the question of being.

But Derrida also stresses in *Of Spirit* that the sentence "Die Sprache ver-spricht sich" means that language mis-speaks, makes a slip of the tongue, and undoes itself. Language, and these are Derrida's words in *Of Spirit,* "becomes undone or unhinged, derails or becomes delirious, deteriorates" (OS 93/146). In short, language is "out of joint." And here we shift from *Of Spirit* to *Specters of Marx.* As *Specters of Marx* shows, the most basic feature of the Derridean promise is that it is a disjunction (SM 39/16). The promise is disjoined because it is based in the structure of *différance.* We know what "différance" means: the promise is disjoined because it is based in originary iterability; therefore dissymmetry is first. We also know that since the promise is based in originary iterability, it implies that neither presence nor sense nor being define it. In addition to this well-known Der-ridean concept, there is, however, a new one, that of the specter. But here too, in the concept of the *revenant,* Derrida maintains continuity with his most famous work. Most generally, the specter has the same structure as the trace or the simulacrum. As we already noted, in the "Différance" essay, Derrida says, " . . . the trace is not a presence but the simulacrum of a presence . . . " (MP 25/24). Since iterability defines the *revenant* (SM 32/11, 255/161), the ghost refers to possibility just as the trace or simulacrum does (SM 33/11, 34/12; cf. 70/38). Moreover, like the simulacrum or trace, in-corporation, immaterial materiality, non-sensuous sensuousness, in-visible visibility, general singularity, all of these terms define the *revenant.*

But for Derrida—and this is truly where the turn from his early work lies—the specter consists in a tri-partite distinction that distinguishes it from the concept of the trace or the simulacrum.[13] First, the *revenant* is distinguished from the simulacrum because it is a ghost of a "dead hu-man" or of a dead animal (SM 32/10, 154/93; GT 181/143). It does not mat-ter whether we say human or animal here, as long as the ghost is a "who" and not merely a "what" (SM 268/169). In short, the ghost is like an "auto-biography," memoirs. That the ghost must be understood as a "who" trans-forms the notion of singularity that Derrida uses throughout his early writings; instead of being a brute, empirical fact, the ghost, for Derrida, must be a persona, a character (*un personage*), a person (SM 250/157). This is why the word "autonomy" keeps coming up in *Specters of Marx* (SM 244/153, for example). In other words, for there to be a ghost, there must be flesh (SM 202/126).[14] But, second, the *revenant* must also be a body, more precisely, a prosthesis, an artifact, a machine; the ghost is a reminder, a sort of "memo." In the case of Derrida's favorite ghost, the ghost of Ham-let's father, we know that he wears a helmet with a visor—and we shall return to this visor in a moment. So, combining memoirs and memorandum, the *revenant* combines both autonomy and automaton. But, third, the *revenant* is, as Derrida says in *Specters of Marx*, "of spirit" (SM 201/125–126). We come back again to Hegel; Hegel, of course, associates spirit with memory. Being memory, spirit allows for the inward feeling of unity with others that constitutes a community. But, for Derrida, since the *revenant* is based in originary iteration, the memory that it represents is an absolute memory—*une memoire*—one not relative to a present; the *revenant* is a past that has never been present, an immemorial or eternal past. So, following the same logic as Hegel, this memory also constitutes a community. When the ghost of Hamlet's father says, "swear!" Derrida stresses that "*they* swear" (SM 57/29); in other words, the ghost constitutes a "we." But the spectral, for Derrida, implies, on the one hand, that the mechanism of the *revenant*—its generality—exceeds the boundary encircling any community, and, on the other, that the flesh of the *revenant*—its singularity—always conceals spirit. In short, the *revenant* constitutes a community, we might say, without community.[15]

That spirit never can appear as such refers us back to the helmet, to what Derrida calls in *Specters of Marx* the "visor effect" (SM 26–27/7, 164/100). The "visor effect" implies that the *revenant* looks at us (SM 165/101),[16] but we cannot see its face or its skin; there is no epiphany of the other here because of the helmet. The "visor effect" implies, therefore, that the *revenant* remains a secret (SM 28/7). The secret, Derrida tells us in his 1990 essay "Donner la mort," is based on Husserl's insight from the Fifth Cartesian Meditation that the psychic life of an other can never give itself in a presentation but must involve appresentation (AEL 96/51–52).[17] Without presentation, there is no knowledge of the *revenant* for us to whom it comes; but also, there is no self-presentation for the *revenant* itself since the psychic life of every other must be structured, of course for Derrida, by *différance*. That there is no self-presentation for the *revenant* itself means that the *revenant* harbors no secret in the sense of a presence; there is no presence hidden behind the helmet; as Derrida would say in *Voice and Phenomenon*, the ghost does not want to say (*ne veut pas dire*).[18] We are blind to the ghost and the ghost is blind to itself.

Therefore, although Hamlet and his little community swear to the ghost to wreak vengeance on the murderer of his father, Hamlet does not really know what this "thing" called the ghost is; he does not really know what it is commanding. Since the *revenant* is clad in "visored armor," Hamlet cannot see the face of the other. Thus, lacking a presentation, anyone who responds to a ghostly injunction cannot conceive the commandment as a program (SM 126/75; GT 156/122–123); one cannot calculate its fulfillment (SM 217–218/136). A response to it cannot *not* involve unpredictability. No one can predict the end of the promise because there was no beginning to the promise. Hamlet cannot calculate the keeping of the promise, because the ghost of Hamlet's father himself does not know what will fulfill the command. The promise in Derrida is an-archical; it is what he called in *Voice and Phenomenon* "the phenomenon of the labyrinth." There is not even something like an inchoate sense at the origin that could be made explicit. Since there was no *arche*, we cannot balance a *telos* against it. This lack of balance—the disjunction—brings us to the second moment of the Derridean promise, the injunction.

Injunction. For Derrida, the fundamental lack of balance at the root of the promise is the only way that justice is possible. Justice, for Derrida, is the relation to the other, and as such it implies that there is always already dissymmetry, disharmony, and a memory without anteriority.[19] So one never had justice in the first place. Never having justice originally is why one can try to rectify the disjointure; it is why one can promise to give justice. Derrida insists on using the word "give" instead of "render," because the promise is also always a promise of a gift (SM 254/160; cf. GT 39/24). Since there is no primordial jointure, to give justice is to give what one does not have (SM 55/27); since there is no primordial jointure, to promise to give justice is to promise too much.[20] Since one has promised too much—to give what one does not have—one can never stop fulfilling the promise; there is no way ultimately to pay off the debt. Although a promise of justice, the promise, for Derrida, is not a promise of revenge (SM 53/25).

Because the promise is not vengeful, the redemption, which one can promise to the *revenant,* is not eschatological (SM 100–106/58–61). The promise, as Derrida says in *Of Spirit,* is one of spirit (OS 147/94), but its fulfillment can never ultimately bring about an emancipation of spirit from the body or from the flesh. Spirit can never appear as such. There is no second coming of a heaven on earth—be it capitalism or communism— no promised land, no heaven in heaven. But the unfulfillability of the promise, for Derrida, is still messianic (SM 124/73). Derrida's concept of the messianic is based on the concept of formal necessity that we saw him develop in the formative period. Between infinite iterability and finite form, there is a dis-junction, at once a joining and disjoining, so that not only must and should the infinitely iterable form appear in a finite form but also the infinitely iterable form must and should be liberated from the finite form. Because this at once ethical and theoretical necessity is formal, the content, for Derrida, does not matter. As Derrida says in *Specters of Marx*, in the "devoir" or the "il faut" of the injunction there is a sort of "epoche" of the content (SM 102/59), a sort of indifference to the content (SM 123–124/73; AEL 199/115). This indifference is why Derrida calls his concept of the messianic "messianic without messianism" (SM 124/73; cf. AEL 121/67, 204/118–19). But the indifference to the content is, for Derrida, actually an interest in all of the content, in all kinds of injunctions and promises; as Derrida says repeatedly in *Specters of Marx*, there is more than one of them. The pluralism of the promise makes the urgency of fulfillment more imminent, more impatient (SM 60/31). No matter what the promise is, we have to keep trying to keep it just simply because it can never be kept. The ghost, therefore, has to have faith in me—that I will keep trying—just as I have to believe in the ghost—that it is something. And this faith brings us to the third moment of the Derridean promise, the keeping of it.[21]

The Keeping of the Promise. The keeping of the promise is the decisive moment. Just as the promise's moment of disjunction marked a turn with Derrida's best-known concepts, the moment of keeping the promise marks a turn with Derrida's best-known formulations of deconstruction. In 1993, the dialectic of ontology and phenomenology of the formative period finally turns into "hauntology" (SM 31/10). In the moment of keeping the promise, the ghost *selects*. Because of the visor, Hamlet cannot see the face of his father's ghost, but the dead father can see Hamlet. Hamlet feels himself (*se sent*) being looked at (SM 216/136); in other words, Hamlet feels himself being selected by the *revenant*. Selected, Hamlet swears that he will keep the memory of his father; in effect, Hamlet is saying "Yes"—and this "Yes" is a reply to the injunction (AEL 53/24)[22]—he is saying, "Yes, I promise to remember to do what you are asking me to do" (OS 147/94).[23] But the *revenant* does not just select Hamlet. Hamlet, Horatio, and Marcellus swear together, and, by doing so, they indeed form a little community (SM 73–74/40–41). They are friends insofar as they are swearing to keep the memory of the ghost. But also they are allies insofar as they are conspiring against a common enemy to bring about justice. The conspiracy against the superior power must be kept secret.[24] The conspirators must guard the secret from the enemy, if the conspiracy is to succeed; but, more fundamentally, they must keep the secret since the conspirators never *knew* the *revenant*'s secret in the first place; what unites them is their *belief* in the *revenant*.[25] So when Hamlet, Horatio, and Marcellus swear together, they are forming a sort of religion.[26]

But, for Derrida, this religion is not a religion in the normal sense;[27] as he says in *Specters of Marx,* the promise is "in principle non-religious in the positive sense of the term" (SM 149/91).[28] Instead, this "quasi-religion" is an experience; Derrida says, "we prefer to say messianic rather than *messianism,* so as to designate a structure of experience rather than a religion" (SM 266/167–168). We saw this experience in the Conclusion to *Voice and Phenomenon.* Here in *Specters of Marx* Derrida defines the experience as the experience of death; this experience is not a Husserlian lived-experience, not *un vécu.* Therefore, it is important to keep in mind that the *revenant* is dead, even murdered; it is just as important to remember, however, that the appearance of the deceased as a ghost means that it is, as Derrida says in *Specters of Marx,* "a quasi-divinity" (SM 245/153). The friends believe in this quasi-divinity, despite its being dead (SM 245/154). Their belief therefore indicates what for Derrida is the essence of belief: to believe in the unbelievable (SM 227/143).

In *Specters of Marx,* Derrida calls these believers in the unbelievable "scholars to come," which he distinguishes from "traditional scholars" (SM 33–34/11–12, 234/146). "Traditional scholars" require proofs, vision, representations, in short, knowledge, before they believe in anything (SM 33–34/11–12, 234/136). The traditional scholars want to question the *revenant* and know what it is, that it is real, that it *is.* In contrast, Derrida's new scholars (or perhaps, new theologians) have promised, and believe in a God who does not exist (at least in the sense of perfect presence). In other words, they believe in a God beyond being, otherwise than essence, wholly other (*tout autre*). So, to the traditional scholars, what the scholars of the future believe in is a paradox.[29]

While Derrida's new scholars do not require proofs of God's existence (SM 227/143),[30] they nevertheless put the paradox to the test, experiment with it. The new scholars put the paradox to the test by addressing themselves to the specter, in other words, by addressing themselves to God.[31] They conjure the dead God up with a formula: "tout autre est tout autre." This formula is Derrida's most fundamental expression of the paradox of the *revenant.* In *Specters of Marx,* Derrida mentions this formula only once (SM 273/173; cf. SM 229–234/144–146), but he analyzes it in "Donner la mort."[32] The key to this formula lies in the copula, which is both predicative and existential. What is wholly other *is* and thus is not purely wholly other than being—the existential copula—and yet what is wholly other *is* wholly other—the predicative copula and thus is wholly other than being. That is, the quality of "wholly-other" is attributed of the wholly other, and yet the wholly other exists, exists as a being. The formula "tout autre est tout autre" is, therefore, first of all a tautology: "every other is every other." In other words, there is no difference between anything. In this interpretation, the formula is an expression of absolute immanence: there is no "beyond being"; everything is the same. But there is a second way of understanding the tautology: "wholly other is wholly other." In this case, we have an expression of absolute transcendence: the "beyond Being" is wholly beyond Being; it is entirely other. But there is even a third way to read the formula: each and every other is wholly other. This way of reading the formula introduces heterology and makes the sentence very strange, even uncanny. It is now an expression of pantheism; each and every other, even those others known as animals, conceals spirit and therefore is a sort of divinity. Because this formula "tout autre est tout autre" expresses pantheism, it is probably the most welcoming sentence that Derrida has ever written.[33]

But, as Derrida says in *Specters of Marx*, "hospitality and exclusion go together" (SM 223/141). With formulas, we conjure the ghosts up, and with formulas we conjure some of them away. In other words, if the religious conspiracy is to have effects, the secret has to be *both* kept or guarded from some, the enemies, *and* divulged or shared with others, the friends (PS 550–551, 557). Since it seems that we are able to conjure up the *revenant* with the formula "tout autre est tout autre," an affirmation, we can conjure some ghosts away only with a negation. The only way we can speak of the *revenant* in order to keep it and share it is by saying that it is neither this nor that (cf. ED 135/90).[34] And, in order to formulate such negative formulas, critique is required.

In *Specters of Marx*, Derrida says that critique must be "self-critique," if it is to be radical (SM 145/88). To be self-critical, Marxism, for example according to Derrida, must isolate one of its spirits "from all its other spirits" (*tous ses autres esprits*) (SM 146/89). To select one spirit from all the other spirits is to distinguish "between everything and almost everything (*entre tout et presque tout*)" (SM 146/89). Everything, that is, every concept, every idea, every ideology, is spiritual, but almost all of them are not faithful to the *revenant*. As Derrida says in *Of Spirit*, "thought is fidelity to [the] promise" (OS 150/94). Being faithful to the *revenant* means being faithful to this rule: like the *revenant* who recurs indefinitely, you must want your way of thinking to recur an infinite number of times. Ideologies that do not live up to this rule promise nothing; they want themselves to come to an end. An ideology which does not measure up, for example, is the ideology of nationalism. As Derrida says, "Like the nationalisms of blood, those of native soil not only sow hatred, not only commit crimes, they have no future, they promise nothing even if, like stupidity or the unconscious, they preserve unfeeling life" (SM 268–269/169). The selection, therefore, occurs by the measure of those spirits that absolutize either life or death, which advocate pure life or pure death (SM 278/175). Absolute life or absolute death is "the worst" and the worst is what we must, according to Derrida, constantly remember. But the constant memory of the worst is also a forgetting (SM 187/114). In Derridean critique, we remember the worst in order to forget those forms of thought which take away the future. In other words, we must promise to remember the worst in order to forget those forms of thought so that we may have a chance of the future. Therefore, the Derridean promise is a promise that a loved one commands on his or her deathbed: "Promise me that you'll remember to forget me enough so that you can survive!" (Cf. GT 78–80/56–57, 30–31/16–17). The active forgetting of self-critique completes the *revenant*'s selection of forms of thought.

But in the keeping of the promise for Derrida, the *revenant* also selects forms of life. When a ghost visits, it is frightening (SM 267/168–169, for example). The fear, however, is not only what we feel before something which we do not and cannot understand; it is also fear before what the ghost reminds us of: the possibility of apocalypse. The fear in the experience of the *revenant* is, for Derrida, anxiety in the face of everyone's death. But it is even more fearsome than that. The ghost also commands that I give it justice. As Derrida says, "For a promise to be assumed, someone must be there who is sensitive to the promise, who is able to say 'I am the promise, I'm the one to promise, I'm the one who is promising . . .'."[35] So I have to do something;[36] I have to take sides (GT 82–83/60), form alliances and conspiracies; in other words, I must and should make enemies, who perhaps will have to be killed or perhaps will have to kill me. This is what is truly frightening: the testing of the paradoxical *revenant* is a testing of oneself.[37]

Therefore, Derrida's ethico-political turn becomes revolutionary here: in the selection of forms of life. Here, in the moment of keeping the promise, we can see how the structure of the question of being with which Derrida began his career is inadequate to the political. The question requires only that I know and bring the thing interrogated to presence. In contrast, the keeping of the promise requires that I take up a position against some-one else. While the question is pro-visional, the promise is *pro-mettre*. The promise requires that I posit, that I take up a position (*mettre*). Taking up a position against someone else makes the promise discontinuous and eventful, even "eschatological" (cf. SM 68–69/37); taking up a position is the promise made present, but in action, not in intuition. Only a promise requires that I make friends and therefore make enemies.

The question is inadequate to the political, however, in a second way. The question can never inspire action, because a question can never inspire an experience that is not merely presence. The question is never an experi-ment or a putting to the test. Whenever Derrida uses the word "expéri-ence" or "éprouver," he always plays on the double sense of these words: "expérience"—to experience/to experiment; "éprouver"—to experience or feel/to put to the test or to the proof. Since I am put to the test in the ex-perience of the promise, for Derrida this experience is one of fear and trembling. Only the promise requires that I have faith in the one who makes me swear, the one whom I never see; only the promise requires that I have faith in myself, in the "me" that I have not yet seen. What makes *Specters of Marx* so uncanny is that, in a book purportedly on Marxism, Derrida seems to be reviving the political power of religious faith.[38]

We can articulate the difference between the question and the promise in one last way. The question inspires no emotion because it is entirely im-personal or anonymous. In contrast, the promise is based in the concept of the specter. Although still defined by the fundamental phenomenological-ontological insight that being must never and should never appear as such, the concept of the *revenant* (unlike that of the trace or the simulacrum) is a "who."[39] This concept, it seems to me, is genuinely revolutionary in Der-rida's own thinking. The *revenant* is where Derrida's thinking turns. The question of being includes no "who." The turn from the question, for Der-rida, is a turn therefore from Heidegger; it is a turn to Levinas.

The turn to Levinas is obvious. Any casual examination of Derrida's later writings discovers countless references and allusions to Levinas. For example, in *Specters of Marx*, Derrida explicitly appropriates Levinas's defi-nition of justice as the relation to the other against Heidegger's "Anaxi-mander Fragment" definition of justice as jointure (SM 48–56/23–28; cf. NM 35). But the turn from Heidegger to Levinas is not simple. Hauntology in *Specters of Marx* is based in a sort of alchemical combination of Levinas with Nietzsche. The returning, the turning about, the revolving, the *reve-nant*, evoke the doctrine of eternal recurrence; it is the eternal recurrence that tests thought and life in the promise; the eternal recurrence makes forgetting in the promise active; the eternal recurrence makes the promise's affirmation double.[40] In *Specters of Marx,* the clearest evidence of Derrida's strange amalgamation of Levinas and Nietzsche occurs when he says, "There where man, a certain determinate concept of man, is completed, there the pure humanity of man, of the *other man* and of man *as other* begins or has finally the chance of heralding itself—of promising itself. In an apparently inhuman or a-human fashion" (SM 125/74).[41] According to Nietzsche's *Zarathustra,* it is at the "Great Noon" that the end of man, of a certain determinate concept of man, would happen. The "Great Noon," of course, is the hour at which the saying "God is Dead" will have its impact on humanity. The second world of Platonism will be destroyed, leaving behind only the same, only immanence. There will be no more shadows; the overman will be heralded. But apparently for Derrida, the Nietzschean overman would be in complicity with the "other man" of Levinas's *Humanism and the Other Man.*[42] The other man would be the one who relates himself to the other, to transcendence. He will be the man (or woman) who believes in a God after the death of the God. He or she will seek a "more than luminous shadow."[43] In the future to come, he or she will do nothing except "look for noon at two o'clock" (cf. GT 205/162).

The Final Idea: Memory and Life

The phrase "looking for noon at two o'clock" defines the new kind of thinking that Derrida inaugurated, deconstruction. We have laid out the narrative of this inauguration. The prologue to this narrative was Fink's famous 1933 *Kantstudien* essay on Husserl; indeed, the phrase "the basic problem of phenomenology" comes from Fink. Fink showed that the basic problem of phenomenology is not an epistemological problem (even though Husserl himself defined phenomenology in terms of traditional epistemological problems in *Cartesian Meditations*); rather, for Fink, the basic problem of phenomenology is the old cosmological problem of the origin of the world. The basic problem of phenomenology, one might say, is God. But just as important as Fink's definition of phenomenology is the fact that Fink defined, for phenomenology, the sense of the transcendental. The transcendental in Husserl is extra-mundane; the origin of the world cannot be of the world. Yet Fink also specified that this transcendental, that is, transcendental subjectivity is not otherworldly; phenomenology is not a form of Platonism. Phenomenological transcendental subjectivity is at once transcendent to the world and immanent to the world (in the sense that transcendental subjectivity contains the world within itself); the transcendental ego is different from me and yet it is me (or it contains me). Because of this new conception of the transcendental—this transcendental is by no means Kantian—Fink also showed at the conclusion of the essay that the phenomenological problem of the origin of the world results in a series of paradoxes. These paradoxes are at the foundation of Derrida's thinking. The problem is: how can we conceive, what is the logic of an origin of the world that is at once both extra-mundane and mundane?

Thus the title of Derrida's first book on Husserl derives from Fink: *Le Problème de la genèse dans la philosophie de Husserl.* What is truly important about this first book is that it puts to rest (perhaps once and for all) the question of Derrida's scholarship; clearly he had a masterly command of the then available works by Husserl. By means of the scholarly work laid out in *Le Problème de la genèse*, Derrida was able to show that Husserl does not conceive genesis in a way adequate to his own principle of all principles; in short he lacks evidence for the claims he makes about the origin and end of genesis (there is always an "already constituted" at the origin and the Idea in the Kantian sense does not itself appear). Husserl himself therefore falls prey to metaphysics in the sense of unfounded speculation. The result of this phenomenological critique is that Derrida tries to develop an "originary dialectic" between existence and essence that is transcendental and yet contains an empirical element. Derrida develops this dialectic in a sort of gamble with Tran-Duc-Thao and Cavaillès, who had already presented a kind of dialectical thinking as a solution to the problem of genesis in Husserl's philosophy. But Cavaillès's dialectic resolved the contradiction in the direction of essence or form, while that of Tran-Duc-Thao resolved it in the direction of fact or matter. Derrida's dialectic differs from the dialectics of both Cavaillès and Tran-Duc-Thao because it is empiricist in one case and essentialist in the other. More generally however, Derrida's dialectic differs because it is more basic. Derrida believed that the dialectics of Cavaillès and Tran-Duc-Thao were mundane. Being worldly, the dialectics of both Cavaillès (ideal) and Tran-Duc-Thao (real) remain, as Derrida says, at an "already constituted" level (PGH 8). So, in *Le Problème de la genèse,* Derrida "ups the ante" on dialectic. And we saw that he does this upping of the ante by trying to articulate a transcendental dialectic which nevertheless contains a real or empirical moment which he calls "human existence" (following Sartre). But, of course, the phrase "human existence" alludes to Heidegger (even though Derrida does not cite one text by Heidegger). So Derrida's upping of the ante on dialectic consists in constructing a dialectic between phenomenology and ontology. Derrida's thought begins with phenomenology and ontology.

While *Le Problème de la genèse* allows us to do away with the question of Derrida's Husserl scholarship, we must recognize that the *Introduction to Husserl's "The Origin of Geometry"* is a philosophically more important book. It is more important because here Derrida poses for the first time the question of *language;* he starts to transform the problem of genesis into the problem of the sign. Hyppolite's recognition of the role of language in the Hegelian movement of idealization was crucial for Derrida; in fact, it is impossible to imagine Derrida having written the *Introduction* without it; indeed, it is impossible to imagine him having written a book called *Voice and Phenomenon* without *Logic and Existence.* Yet Husserl himself provided motivation for this so-called "linguistic turn" in Derrida.[1] Within "The Origin of Geometry," Husserl had shown that ideal objectivities could not be constituted without being linguistically documented. Husserl's recognition of the need (*es fehlt*) for inscription brings forth Derrida's concept of *l'écriture* (which anticipates the concept of the trace). The concept of writing has three consequences. First, it calls into question Husserl's privilege of the mathematical object, which is the source for Derrida's concept of presence. In the *Introduction,* we find the same kind of critique that we saw in *Le Problème de la genèse;* Husserl does not have the evidence, in a word, the presence, for his claims about history. Second, writing consists in an essential ambiguity between life and death, between essence and fact, between truth and its disappearance, between presence and absence, and between equivocity and univocity. Third, and most importantly, writing's essential ambiguity amounts to a double necessity to remain within (fact) and to exit to the outside (essence) of the living present. Because of this essential ambiguity in the concept of writing Derrida again here, as in *Le Problème de la genèse,* describes an originary dialectic between phenomenology and ontology, in which phenomenology presupposes ontology and ontology presupposes phenomenology. But, unlike *Le Problème de la genèse,* in which the question of language does not arise, the *Introduction* ends with questions that only ontology could answer; it ends with the question of being. Derrida's conception of genesis in terms of the openness of a question—which implies that genesis is linguistic—begins here. But the *Introduction* is also the beginning of the concept of *différance.* Demonstrating a growing understanding of Heidegger, Derrida defines the dialectic of phenomenology and ontology, indeed, his new concept of the transcendental in terms of a consciousness of difference. Therefore, the *Introduction to Husserl's "The Origin of Geometry"* is philosophically important for a second reason: the "linguistic turn" is a "turn" to the question and difference.

"Violence and Metaphysics" in 1964 is Derrida's point of philosophical maturation. First, Derrida deepens his understanding of writing. All the questions posed in "Violence and Metaphysics" are questions of language. For Derrida, language is the same, the "violence of light." Because Levinas, the Levinas of *Totality and Infinity,* "absolves" the other from the same, Derrida argues that Levinas has given up the right to speak about the other. This "enlightenment" of the other is the same phenomenological critique that we saw in the earlier works; by rejecting the same, Levinas gives up phenomenal presence as the presupposition of sense and language. Levinas's discourse of alterity therefore, for Derrida, is necessarily "caught" (*pris*) by the same. But, second, at the same time as there is a critique in "Violence and Metaphysics," there is an appropriation of Levinas's thought: here Derrida begins to conceive difference as alterity. Undoubtedly, Derrida develops a discourse of alterity because of Levinas, but it seems that Levinas's influence at this moment on Derrida, concerning alterity, is indirect. It is really Levinas's critique of Husserl that exerts influence insofar as it leads Derrida to investigate Husserl's Fifth Cartesian Meditation. The Fifth Cartesian Meditation had been entirely absent from his earlier works on Husserl; Derrida's discourse of alterity therefore is always based on Husserl's concept of analogical appresentation. Hence we have Derrida's "defense" of Husserl's descriptions of alterity against the Levinasian critique. And this "defense" allowed us to speak of the "superficial Husserl," the Husserl of presence, and the "in depth" Husserl, the Husserl of temporalization and alterity (non-presence), that is, about the two Husserls who organize the discourse of *Voice and Phenomenon*. But if Levinas's metaphysics of alterity allowed Derrida to see a deeper Husserl, then it is necessary to conclude that Levinas's metaphysics is *not* a metaphysics of presence. In fact, the critique Derrida levels against Levinas, again against the Levinas of *Totality and Infinity*, itself depends on presence (the enlightenment of phenomenological critique). Thus, third, the direct influence of Levinas on Derrida lies in a re-conception of the question; the question in "Violence and Metaphysics" is no longer the question of being, but a question that does not belong to philosophy; it is the question of the origin of philosophy, the question of non-philosophy, the question of the non-Greek. At the same time, however, as Derrida is investigating Levinas's thought of the other, he is investigating Heidegger's thought of being. Derrida realizes that Heidegger's pursuit of the origin of Greek philosophy in pre-Platonistic thinkers leads to a concept of the same that is not identity but difference. This realization transforms the earlier dialectic between ontology and phenomenology into a dialectic between the alterity and difference, between Levinas's thought of God and Heidegger's thought of being. "Violence and Metaphysics" represents Derrida's first attempt to "amalgamate" the non-Greek genetic thought of the transcendence of the other with the Greek structuralist thought of the immanence of the same (which is not identity but difference). "Violence and Metaphysics" is therefore the first deconstruction. Because deconstruction consists in this amalgamation—it is larger than Levinasian metaphysics—we were able to say that deconstruction is "more metaphysical" than Levinas's metaphysics. Derrida's own thinking begins with "Violence and Metaphysics"; deconstruction begins when phenomenology and ontology come to an end.

The climax of our story is Derrida's 1967 *Voice and Phenomenon*. What makes *Voice and Phenomenon* both a great and controversial work is that in it Derrida engages in a deconstruction of Husserl's phenomenology as the ultimate and radical form of what Derrida calls "the metaphysics of presence." In *Voice and Phenomenon*, Derrida gives a precise definition of what he means by "the metaphysics of presence" (anticipated by his analysis, in the *Introduction*, of Husserl's privilege of the mathematical object): metaphysics has decided that the meaning of being is presence, presence both in the sense of an object before and in the sense of a subject in self-proximity. Husserl's phenomenology fits this definition of the metaphysics of presence—*Voice and Phenomenon* concerns the very nature of phenomen-ology: voice (the *logos*) and phenomenon—because it merely takes up this Greek decision, because it is motivated by two impulses, the purity of formalism (being as object) and the radicality of intuition (being as subject), and because, finally, Husserl tries to unify these two species of presence through the concept of the living present. The living present is the voice that keeps silent. Yet there is a second Husserl, the in-depth Husserl, who provides the means for Derrida's presentation of his own new concepts. Because of Husserl's concept of the living present, Derrida develops what he calls "the ultra-transcendental concept of life." On the one hand, life makes its own distributions; life's self-distributions explain why Derrida can show Husserl's "essential distinction" between indication and expression being "caught, that is, contaminated" (*Pris: c'est-à-dire, contaminé*). On the other, life, understood as ultra-transcendental, is auto-affection: the voice. Derrida's so-called "phenomenology of the voice" allows him to develop what are perhaps his three most famous concepts: the trace, *différance*, and supplementarity. As we said, *Voice and Phenomenon* is the end of the formative period of Derrida's thinking; these three concepts constitute the first systematic presentation of his thought.

What we are going to say here about *différance* draws from what we presented about the logic of totality in the *Introduction* and the impossible system in "Violence and Metaphysics." And one could explicate it on the basis of Hegelian logic.[2] But since we are engaged in an investigation of Derrida's interpretation of Husserl, we are going to explicate it first with Husserlian concepts. Derrida's concept of *différance* derives from the Husserlian concept of *intentionality;* like intentionality, *différance* consists in an intending *to;* it is defined by the dative relation. This connection of *différance* back to Husserlian intentionality is why the Husserlian concept of the noema, what Derrida in "'Genesis and Structure' and Phenomenology" calls "the anarchy of the noema" (ED 242–243/163), is at its root. For Husserl, the noema is at once *irreell*, that is, it is not a *reell* part of consciousness (as are the noetic acts and the hyle); thus it is different from, outside of, and other than consciousness. But it is also a non-real thing since it is ideal, which in turn means that the noema is identical to consciousness, inside of, and the same as consciousness. Thus it is at once *in* consciousness *without* it belonging to consciousness; it is at once inside and outside consciousness, immanent and transcendent, mundane and extra-mundane. It is at once related to acts of consciousness and iterable beyond them; it is in the passage between these poles. Because the noema is transcendent, outside, extra-mundane, iterable beyond, it always implies a relation to others; it always implies transcendental intersubjectivity. This relation to others means that whenever I intend something, it includes the possibility of absence or non-presence. The other, for Husserl—this phenomenological necessity is the center of Derrida's thought—can never be given in the same way as I have a presentation of myself; the other is only given in a re-presentation (never *Gegenwärtigung* but only ever *Vergegenwärtigung*). *I lack knowledge of the interior life of others.* Because however consciousness itself, transcendental life, consists for Husserl in intending, that is, in iterating a unity, we must conclude that even when I do not intend alterity, when I intend that the unity stay within, when I fulfill the form of sense with an intuition, alterity is always already there as a necessary possibility; the indefinite iterability of any sense structure necessarily implies the possibility of alterity, of non-presence, of non-intuition. But—and this phenomenological necessity is the other center of Derrida's thought—because consciousness is a consciousness *to*, the intending of a sense necessarily *ends* in (as well as necessarily *opens* up) some sort of fulfillment, in some sort of presence; the sense returns to me. What Husserl shows in the Fifth Cartesian Meditation is that I understand the other even though I cannot live his or her life. This is the Derridean concept of *différance* reconstructed entirely in Husserlian terms.

We can now translate it into Derridean terms. We must start with what Derrida, in *Voice and Phenomenon,* called "the ultra-transcendental concept of life," that is, with auto-affection. When I have a thought or sense in the most minimal sense, I am affecting myself; I am having an interior monologue. I hear myself speak at the very moment that I speak. This is the *first* essential necessity in which *différance* consists: the sense of my words *must* be present to me, the same as me, immanent to me, in the world, close to me as possible, subjectively present. How else could I say that I have the sense, that it functions, unless it was present, unless I was present to myself, unless I was alive? I am powerless to exit my living present (which, conversely, means that I have the power to remain in my living present). But, since auto-affection is temporal, the sense of the words lacks persisting presence.[3] This lack or negativity implies that I am finite and mortal; there is non-sense. Just as I am powerless to exit my living present, I am as well powerless to remain in my living present. Subjective presence is always already passing away; something of me, some intuition or content such as an action that is singular, has always already passed away. I am always already *late* for subjective presence. Thus we have the *first* sense of *différance:* delay. In order for me, however, to endow the sense (or something singular of me, some intuition or content such as an action) with persisting or objective presence, I must bring my self back over and over again; this "over and over again" is the possibility, the power of re-presentation in its most general form. The return of the form of the sense is a memory, or more precisely, a trace. Here we have the *second* necessity in which *différance* consists: since the form of the sense lacks objective or persisting presence, the sense *must* be indefinitely iterated; the second necessity is the necessity of survival. The sense must survive beyond my present; it demands a medium or mediation, which can be the voice but which *also* must include writing as a possibility. The sense must survive and that means that it must be no longer finite but infinite, no longer immanent but transcendent, no longer inside but outside, no longer mundane but extra-mundane; only the graphic possibility can make the sense be *different* from me as a singularity. Thus we have the *second* sense of *différance:* difference. *But,* and this aspect of *différance* is crucial, since the form of sense (or something of me, some intuition or action) survives only in writing or in the trace or in memory, it is really *dead;* it is merely a body within a *subjectless* transcendental field. Here we return to *différance*'s first necessity: the trace *must* be made present, must be immanent, must be made mundane, must be made close once more, and must be made the same as me; it must be made to live again. When this return happens, presence that is both objective and subjective is constituted. This constitution of presence cannot, however, close off the second necessity; the trace still, always, demands to survive, which necessitates that it be sent out again *to* another fulfillment. Thus we could say—with a word we have invented by playing on the French word "fin"—that *différance* is "re-finition" (as opposed to "re-commencement"). Nevertheless, although this constitution of presence cannot close off the necessity to exit from presence, as soon as the constitution happens, presence looks as though it precedes the movement of *différance,* thereby turning *différance*—in a word, iterability—into an accidental supplement, into writing in the popular sense. The very thing that made presence possible comes to be derived from it.

For Derrida, the metaphysics of presence consists in this very derivation of the supplement from presence. To be precise, presence, for Derrida consists in (a) the distance of what is over and against (object and form, what is iterable), what we were just calling "objective presence," (b) the proximity of the self to itself in its acts (subject and intuition or action), what we were just calling "subjective presence," then, (c) the unification of these two species of presence, presence and self-presence, in the present (the "form of the living present," which mediates itself through the voice). To be precise, "the metaphysics of presence" then, for Derrida, consists in the valorization of presence (as defined in this way, which can account for both ancient and modern philosophy as well as Husserl's phenomenology), that is, it consists in the validation of presence as a foundation, making what is supplementary (that is, *différance*) derivative. As we have noted but must state again, Derrida never contests the founding validity of presence; there can be no foundation without presence. Yet there is a non-foundation below it, the non-Greek non-foundation. The metaphysics of presence, however, has decided that the meaning of being is presence either as subject or object or as their unity. Thus it does not re-open the question of being; it remains above in the security of the foundation; it remains Greek. We have been insisting on calling deconstruction a critique since the beginning of this investigation, because deconstruction consists in limiting claims with experience; deconstruction is always enlightening: the violence of light. Yet Derrida's critique of phenomenology as the metaphysics of presence in *Voice and Phenomenon* differs from the critiques we saw in his earlier works on Husserl, which in fact relied on the founding validity of presence. We can still call the deconstruction found in *Voice and Phenomenon* (and in later texts) a critique because it limits claims with the very *experience of the non-Greek non-presence,* from the experience the in-depth Husserl points us toward; this reliance on an experience is why we must call deconstruction a "super-phenomenological critique." The experience that functions as this undeconstructible measure is the test (*l'épreuve*) of the sign (or of the trace). Here is the test. In the Conclusion to *Voice and Phenomenon,* as we saw, Derrida notes that the difference between expression and indication is, for Husserl, an "in principle" or ideal distinction, which is never respected in fact. But, as Derrida also points out, Husserl's very ability to speak of the "in principle" distinction between expression and indication has its condition of possibility in language; we can distinguish between an essence and a fact, *de jure* and *de facto*, only by means of indefinite iterability; a fact is singular and an essence is iterable as a general form. But the indefiniteness of iterability always necessitates linguistic embodiment. Language, therefore, is the condition for the possibility of the distinction that defines language. If language, however, guards the difference that guards language, then the condition for the possibility of this difference is also its impossibility since, as Husserl admits, language in fact does not respect the difference between expression and indication. At this very moment, we cannot ask what language is (phenomenology) or why language is (ontology), since these questions ask for an essence, for presence, for being, all of which are themselves made possible by language. We are confronted with the *aporia* of language. Since this *aporia* consists in how language constitutes essence (*ens*), which in turn constitutes language, we are no longer confronted by the question of the meaning of being. The *aporia* of language forces us deeper than being. Deconstruction consists, therefore, in bringing us to the experience of this precise non-ontological *aporia*, to the moment before a decision could be made about how to respond to it. It brings us to the experience of what Derrida in *Voice and Phenomenon* called "the unheard-of question."

Later, Derrida will transform the unheard-of question into the promise of justice. The Derridean promise is a promise that a loved one commands on his or her deathbed. On the threshold, this old person puts me in question. It happens to me: "Promise me that you'll remember to forget me enough so that you can survive!" At once I experience life: I am forced to give justice; I must remember this person. At once I experience death: I am forced to give justice, I must forget this person. This is a problem, problematic, problematized, and, as Derrida say, "a 'problema' is also a shield" (SM 28/8). I cannot see through and know what this specter wants to say; there seems to be more than one. How am I to keep this promise? I cannot remember; I am powerless to give justice. I cannot forget; I am powerless to give justice. I must have faith; I am the one chosen. Yet I know, because I cannot forget, I can remember; I know, because I cannot remember I can forget. I can surpass life to death and I can surpass death to life. I can surpass forgetfulness to memory and I can surpass memory to forgetfulness. The powerlessness of the experience gives me the power to think otherwise and to become new. Death and forgetfulness. Life and memory.

Notes

The Original Motivation

1. The writing began in the summer of 1992, but research that supports this book goes back to my *Imagination and Chance: The Difference between the Thought of Ricoeur and Derrida* (Albany: SUNY Press, 1992).

2. I must add a "perhaps" here, since the twentieth century is hardly over and what I am saying hardly takes into account all kinds of other twentieth-century philosophy events: psychoanalysis, critical theory, feminism, hermeneutics, and, of course, analytic philosophy.

3. I am in the process of preparing a book bearing this title, *The Being of the Question: Investigations of the Great French Philosophy of the Sixties*. This book will collect all the essays I have written since 1994 determining the differences between Derrida and Deleuze, Deleuze and Foucault, and Foucault and Derrida. The genuine work of philosophy to which I am referring above is to be called *Memory and Life: Ideas concerning the Event of Thinking*.

4. This comment too of course has to be qualified. I am making it retrospectively from Derrida. Obviously, Heidegger's being of the question enters directly, without the mediation of Merleau-Ponty, into Levinas himself, earlier in *Husserl's Theory of Intuition* in 1929. Yet, because one can make Merleau-Ponty's ambiguity concerning the experience of sense diverge into either strain of French thought, Merleau-Ponty seems to be, more than Levinas, the hinge figure. As far as I know, Deleuze mentions Levinas once in all of his writings, in *What Is Philosophy?* See Gilles Deleuze and Félix Guattari, *Qu'est-ce la philosophie?* (Paris: Minuit, 1992), p. 88n5; English translation by Hugh Tomlinson and Graham Burchell as *What is Philosophy?* (New York: Columbia University Press, 1994), p. 223n5. Yet Deleuze makes continuous reference to Merleau-Ponty. I also include Levinas in the "great French philosophy of the sixties," since *Totality and Infinity* appeared in 1961.

5. Maurice Merleau-Ponty, *Signes* (Paris: Gallimard, 1960), 74; English translation by Richard C. McCleary as *Signs* (Evanston: Northwestern University Press, 1964), 59, my emphasis.

6. I have ignored many of Derrida's classical formulations of deconstruction since there have been countless commentaries written over the last twenty years concerning the "two phases of deconstruction."

7. Zeynep Direk's Ph.D. dissertation, "The Renovation of the Notion of Experience in Derrida's Philosophy" (University of Memphis, 1999), was invaluable to me for determining Derrida's sparse comments on experience in his early writings.

8. Dermot Moran in his *Introduction to Phenomenology* (London: Routledge, 2000) concludes his analysis of Derrida by saying: " . . . it is clear that [Derrida's] rejection of the metaphysics of presence and of the belief in meaning as ideal unities leads him to move beyond the tradition of Husserlian phenomenology" (p. 474). Derrida departs from the tradition of phenomenology not because he rejects the belief in meaning as ideal unities but *because* he believes in meaning as ideal unities. For Derrida, everything depends on the Husserlian concept of the noema.

9. We first used the word "refinition" in "Phenomenology and Bergsonism: The Beginnings of Post-Modernism," in *Confluences: Phenomenology and Postmodernity, Environment, Race, Gender* (Pittsburgh, Duquesne University, The Simon Silverman Center, 1999), p. 63. We also think that the difference between refinition and recommencement may determine the difference between the Levinas-Derrida strain and the Deleuze-Foucault strain of twentieth-century Continental philosophy.

10. Moreover, Chapter 3 of *The Visible and the Invisible,* where Merleau-Ponty criticizes the Husserlian concept of intuition, could have helped critics understand Derrida's interpretation of Husserl.

11. I have published reviews of the two most important studies of Derrida's interpretation of Husserl produced in the nineties. See my review of Paola Marrati-Guénoun, *La genèse et la trace. Derrida lecteur de Husserl et Heidegger* (Dordrecht: Kluwer, 1998), in *Husserl Studies* 16 (1999): 77–81, and my "Navigating a Passage: Deconstruction as Phenomenology," review article of J. Claude Evans' *Strategies of Deconstruction* (Minneapolis: University of Minnesota Press, 1993), in *Diacritics,* Fall 1993, 1–12.

1. Genesis as the Basic Problem of Phenomenology

1. Cf. Waldenfels, *Phänomenologie in Frankreich* (Frankfurt am Main: Suhrkamp, 1987), 41–42. Waldenfels also mentions that Ludwig Landgrebe's "Husserls Phänomenologie und die Motive zu ihrer Umbildung" (*Rev. int. de Phil.,* no. 2, 277–316) played the same role as Fink's essay. Nevertheless, Fink's essay is mentioned almost continuously in the French interpretations of Husserl during the 1950s. Jean-François Lyotard's 1954 *La phénoménologie* (Paris: Presses Universitaires de France, 1956), 29; Tran-Duc-Thao, *Phénoménologie et matérialisme dialectique* 81–86/39–42; Paul Ricoeur uses it as the basis for his introductory essay to his translation of *Ideas I* (*Idées directrices pour une phénoménologie* [Paris: Gallimard, 1950]), xiii-xiv (Ricoeur, in fact, frequently refers to Fink's essay in his translator's notes, 57n1, 70n1, 87n2, 91n3, 103n1, 202n1, 287n1, 431n1, 440n1). Herbert Spiegelberg in *The Phenomenological Movement* (The Hague: Martinus Nijhoff, 1960) describes Fink's essay as "much discussed" (479) and also speaks of how it influenced Merleau-Ponty (534). Also see Suzanne Bachelard's *A Study of Husserl's Formal and Transcendental Logic,* trans. Lester E. Embree (Evanston: Northwestern University Press, 1968), p. 144.

2.   See, for instance, Maurice Merleau-Ponty, *Phénomènologie de la perception*
       (Paris: Gallimard, 1945), xiii, 254–256, 278, 478; English translation by Colin
       Smith as *The Phenomenology of Perception,* translation revised by Forrest
       Williams in 1978 (New York: Routledge and Kegan Paul, 1981), xviii, 219–221,
       241, 418. See also "Le philosophe et son ombre," in *Signes* (Paris: Gallimard,
       1960), 208; English translation by Richard C. McCleary as "The Philosopher
       and his Shadow," in *Signs* (Evanston: Northwestern University Press, 1964),
       165, and Merleau-Ponty's "Préface" to Dr. A. Hesnard's *L'Œuvre de Freud et
       son importance pour le monde moderne* (Paris: Payot, 1960), 9. Foucault, how-
       ever, claims in "Monstrosities in Criticism" (*diacritics,* Fall 1971) that his use
       of "archeology" derives from Kant, 60.

3.   Didier Franck, "Avertissement" to his translation of Eugen Fink's *Studien
       zur Phänomenologie* (Paris: Minuit, 1974), 8.

4.   Jacques Derrida, review of Eugen Fink's *Studien zur Phänomenologie,* in *Les
       Études philosophiques,* No. 4 (1966), 549–550.

5.   In *Le Problème de la genèse,* Fink is cited on 2n2, 3n4, 19n32, 88n31; mentioned
       on 206, 260. In the *Introduction,* he is cited on the Avertissement/25n1, and
       on 6n1/27n4, 25n1/42n31, 42n1/55n50, 60n1/69n66, 77n1/77n76, 155n1/141n168;
       he is mentioned on 86/89, 89/90. In *Voice and Phenomenon,* Fink is explicitly
       mentioned on 6/7. Derrida also mentions Fink in his critical review of
       Robert Sokolowski's *Husserl's Theory of Constitution* in *Les Études philoso-
       phiques* 18 (1965): 557–558; in " 'Genesis and Structure' and Phenomenology,"
       on ED 246/164; in "The Time of a Thesis: Punctuations," in *Philosophy in
       France Today,* ed. Alan Montefiore (New York: Cambridge University Press,
       1983), 39.

6.   The following essays have been consulted in the writing of this chapter:
       Ronald Bruzina, "The Enworlding (*Verweltlichung*) of Transcendental
       Phenomenological Reflection: A Study of Eugen Fink's '6th Cartesian Medi-
       tation,' " in *Husserl Studies* 3: 3–29 (1986); Ronald Bruzina, "Solitude and
       Community in the Work of Philosophy: Husserl and Fink, 1928–1938," in
       Man and World 22: 287–314 (1989); Ronald Bruzina, "Die Notizen Eugen
       Fink zur Umarbeitung von Edmund Husserls 'Cartesianischen Medita-
       tionen,' " in *Husserl Studies* 6: 97–128 (1989); R. Guilead, "Le concept du
       monde selon Husserl," in *Revue de métaphysique et de morale* 82: 345–364
       (1977); Michel Henry, "Quatre principes de la phénomenologie," in *Revue de
       métaphysique et de morale* 96, no. 1: 3–26 (1991).

7.   The translation of these two words, "Sinn" and "Geltung," is crucial for
       understanding Derrida's interpretation of Husserl. As is well known, but
       important to recall, the German word "Sinn," like its French rendering,
       "sens," means not only sense or meaning, but also what is given by the
       senses. Beyond these two connotations, the word "Sinn" also means direc-
       tion. In *The Phenomenology of Perception,* Merleau-Ponty says that "The
       great strength of intellectualist psychology and idealist philosophy comes
       from their having no difficulty in showing that perception and thought have

an intrinsic sense [*sens*] and cannot be explained in terms of the external association of fortuitously agglomerated contents. The *Cogito* was the coming to self-awareness of this interiority. But all sense was *ipso facto* conceived as an act of thought, as the work of a pure *I,* and although rationalism easily refuted empiricism, it was unable to account for the variety of experience, for the element of nonsense in it, for the contingency of contents. Bodily experience forces us to acknowledge an imposition of sense, which is not the work of a universal constituting consciousness, a sense which clings to certain contents" (*La phénoménologie de la perception,* 172; *Phenomenology of Perception,* 147). As we shall see, Hyppolite, in *Logic and Existence,* will describe Hegel's logic as a logic of sense. And Deleuze says in *The Logic of Sense,* "sense is the characteristic discovery of transcendental philosophy, and that it replaces the old metaphysical Essences" (*Logique du sens* [Paris: Minuit, 1969], 128; English translation by Mark Lester with Charles Stivale, edited by Constantin V. Boundas [New York: Columbia University Press, 1990], 105). For Derrida, the ambiguity in the word "Sinn" indicates the irreducible connection between phenomenology and teleological thinking. Concerning the word "Geltung," we must keep in mind that it means not only validity—that is, something accepted as true—but also value; this ambiguity is why Derrida renders "Geltung" as "valeur" in his *Introduction.* See also Ronald Bruzina, "Translator's Introduction" to Fink's *Sixth Cartesian Meditation* (Bloomington: Indiana University Press, 1995), lxv–lxvi.

8. Cf. Martin Heidegger 1927 lecture course entitled *Basic Problems of Phenomenology,* trans. Albert Hofstadter (Bloomington: Indiana University Press, 1982), 17.

9. For this entire discussion see Eugen Fink, *Sixth Cartesian Meditation,* trans. Ronald Bruzina (Bloomington: Indiana University Press, 1995); see especially paragraph 5.

10. Published before Heidegger's "The Letter on Humanism," Fink's essay must be seen as the source of all contemporary anti-humanism, all contemporary philosophies of the other.

11. Cf. Dorian Cairns, *Conversations with Husserl and Fink* (The Hague: Martinus Nijhoff, 1976), pp. 11–12.

12. Fink continues between parentheses: "The 'epistemology' of phenomenological knowledge is a particular problem within the transcendental theory of method."

13. The meontics of Fink's conception of Husserl's phenomenology is a constant theme throughout the *Sixth Cartesian Meditation;* see especially Fink's first 1932 prefatory note, page 1 and the whole of paragraph 8. Apparently, the 1933 *Kantstudien* essay was to be the essay version of the *Sixth Cartesian Meditation;* see translator's introduction to the *Sixth Cartesian Meditation,* p. xx.

14. Cf. Eugen Fink and Martin Heidegger, *Heraclitus Seminar, 1966/67,* trans.

Charles Seifert (University, Ala.: University of Alabama Press, 1979), 84–85, where Fink and Heidegger discuss this exact problem in Husserl's notion of constitution.

15. Cf. Fink, *Sixth Cartesian Meditation,* paragraph 11c, especially p. 146.

16. Cf. Fink, *Sixth Cartesian Meditation,* paragraph 12.

17. The German says: "[es handelt sich] . . . sondern um die Weltvor-gänglichkeit der durch die Reduktion überhaupt erst entdecken und in einem völlig neuen Sinne 'transzendentalen' Subkektivität" (147). Franck's French rendering is: "il s'agit de la priorité sur le monde d'une subjectivité découverte seulement par la réduction et 'transcendentale' en un sens entièrement nouveau" (167).

18. This expression comes from Husserl. See *Phänomenologische Psychologie* (Husserliana IX), edited by Rudolf Boehm (The Hague: Martinus Nijhoff, 1968), 336, 338, 342. See also Cairns, *Conversations with Husserl and Fink,* p. 93; also Ronald Bruzina, "Solitude and Community in the Work of Philosophy," 303; and of course, the *Sixth Cartesian Meditation,* paragraph 11.

19. In the *Sixth Cartesian Meditation,* Fink calls this particular enworlding "secondary enworlding" or "non-proper enworlding" (cf. p. 110). So there is primary or proper enworlding, which was absolute subjectivity's constitution of the world, the first time it became mundane; then there was the event of the phenomenological reduction which deworlded absolute subjectivity; then there is secondary enworlding, which occurs when the phenomenological spectator must necessarily mundanize him- or herself in order to communicate his or her knowledge to humans still in the natural attitude, to the dogmatists.

20. In his French translation, Franck renders *abstellt* as *réduire;* see page 126.

21. Essential to understanding this paradox is Fink's formulation of it in the Sixth Meditation. See Ronald Bruzina, "The Enworlding (*Verweltlichung*) of Transcendental Phenomenological Reflection," 12–13; also his "Does the Transcendental Ego Speak in Tongues," in *Phenomenology in a Pluralistic Context,* ed. William L. McBride and Calvin O. Schrag (Albany: SUNY Press, 1983), 205–215, especially 213–214.

22. Cf. Cairns, *Conversations with Husserl and Fink,* p. 14; also *Heraclitus Seminar,* 66, where Fink alludes to the second paradox.

23. Cf. Fink, *Sixth Cartesian Meditation,* paragraph 10, especially pp. 88–89.

24. Cf. Eugen Fink, "Les concepts operatoires dans la phénoménologie de Husserl," in *Cahiers de Royaumont: Husserl,* No. III (Paris: Minuit, 1959), 214–241.

25. Fink's entire discussion in the *Heraclitus Seminar* focuses on the logical determinations of the relation, here called the relation between the one (*hen*) and the whole (*panta*). See especially 81, where Fink speaks of a commonness between the one and beings as a whole, and 95, where he uses Heidegger's term *belonging together* to characterize the relation. For

Heidegger, *belonging together,* like the *same,* is a term through which one can reinterpret the notion of identity (10).

26. Cf. Bruzina, "The Enworlding (*Verweltlichung*)," in which Bruzina quotes Fink, in his version of the *Sixth Cartesian Meditation,* as saying that "we refer to transcendental *world-constitution analogously to the way we refer to an existent*" (23). In the *Heraclitus Seminar* Fink further qualifies his use of analogy to determine the logic of the relation; see *Heraclitus Seminar,* 51, 93, 96.

27. Cf. Cairns, *Conversations with Husserl and Fink,* pp. 12, 33.

28. Cf. Cairns, *Conversations with Husserl and Fink,* p. 95.

29. Cf. Bruzina, "The Enworlding (*Verweltlichung*)," 24. Here Bruzina says, "Fink's choice of that term [that is, *Erscheinung*] is part of a whole extended attempt to represent that connection [between transcendental subjectivity and its self-presentation in in-the-world status and station] precisely in ontological terms, in terms of what might overcome a duality of mutually exclusive kinds of being by integrating the difference in a kind of dialectical relationship, by recasting the two hitherto antithetic kinds of being within the embrace of a more comprehensive dynamic unity. To do this he unabashedly uses the supple, rich terminology of none other than Hegel—and draws not one jot of comment from Husserl for attempting it (except in the case of the use of *Erscheinung . . .*)." Later, however, in "L'histoire and le monde" (in *Husserl et la pensée moderne* [The Hague: Martinus Nijhoff, 1959]), Fink converts Husserl's terminology into that of Hegel; he even says that "There is no doubt that Husserl interprets the internal relation of man to the infinite, the relation to the world, as a being infinite of the subject who is self-limiting along the lines of the great 'idealists'" (167). Then he criticizes it on the basis of Heidegger's so-called turn (169).

30. Fink's amalgamation of the "H's"—Hegel, Husserl, and Heidegger— moreover contributed to the peculiarly French way of interpreting phenomenology in general.

31. These Finkian paradoxes still seem to animate Derrida's most recent thinking. See Jacques Derrida, *Le Toucher, Jean-Luc Nancy* (Paris: Galilée, 2000), p. 195n1. Unfortunately, this text appeared while I was in the process of finishing this book and therefore it could not be taken into account in this investigation. Nevertheless, that Derrida in "Tangente II," which concerns Husserl, still focuses on intuition, auto-affection, and sense shows the great continuity of his thinking.

2. The Critique of Phenomenology

1. *Entretiens sur les notions de genèse et de structure,* ed. Maurice de Gandillac (Paris: Mouton, 1965), p. 253.

2. Here I have borrowed from *Le Problème de la genèse* in order to make better

sense of Derrida's very brief presentation of the argument in "'Genesis and Structure.'" As we shall see below (Part II, Chapter 4), Derrida cites paragraphs from the Fourth Cartesian Meditation in *Le Problème de la genèse;* only at the time of "Violence and Metaphysics" (see below, Part III, Chapter 6) will Derrida begin to cite the Fifth Meditation on intersubjectivity.

3.   For more on this phrase, "infinite discursivity," see *Introduction,* LOG 60n1/69/66; see below, Part II, Chapter 5.

4.   Cf. Emmanuel Levinas, *The Theory of Intuition in Husserl's Phenomenology,* trans. André Orianne (Evanston: Northwestern University Press, 1973), 117–119.

5.   Cf. Derrida, "Violence and Metaphysics," ED 124/83, where he also speaks of the opening; see especially, "Violence and Metaphysics," ED 163/110. This latter passage is a 1967 addition, to which, it seems, "'Genesis and Structure'" is supposed to be a response. Cf. also PGH, where Derrida constantly uses the terminology of open and closed, 36, 41, 49, 52, 100, 110, 148, 152, 191, 211, 281.

6.   Cf. Derrida, "Violence and Metaphysics," ED 184/125.

7.   As we shall see below, this insight into the anarchy of the noema serves as the condition for the possibility of ghosts in Derrida's *Specters of Marx* (SM 215n2/135n6); see below, Chapter 8.

8.   Cf. the exact same formulation in PGH 152.

9.   Derrida's parenthetical comment here—Husserl's analyses are still and will always be, in a certain way, developed from a constituted temporality—is, in fact, his thesis in *Le Problème de la genèse;* here he also "returns" to the question of the hyle. Cf. Part II, Chapter 4, and Part III, Chapter 6.

10.   Cf. ED 235/158, where Derrida alludes to Fink when he speaks of Husserl opening up "a new direction of philosophical attention"; also "Violence and Metaphysics," where Derrida, without mentioning or citing Fink, speaks of the other as the origin of the world, ED 153/103.

11.   Simon Critchley has documented these revisions well; see his "The Problem of Closure in Derrida (Part One)," in *Journal of the British Society for Phenomenology* 23, no. 1 (January 1992): 18n11. Robert Bernasconi's "The Trace of Levinas in Derrida," in *Derrida and Différance,* ed. David Wood and Robert Bernasconi (Evanston: Northwestern University Press, 1988), 13–30, is groundbreaking in regard to Derrida's revisions of his earlier publications for *Writing and Difference.* See also Robert Bernasconi, "Levinas and Derrida: The Question of the Closure of Metaphysics," in *Face to Face with Levinas,* ed. Richard A. Cohen (Albany: SUNY Press), 181–203; Robert Bernasconi, "Skepticism in the Face of Philosophy," in *Re-Reading Levinas,* ed. Robert Bernasconi and Simon Critchley (Bloomington: Indiana University Press, 1991), 149–161.

12.   The quotes from *Cartesian Meditations* come from sections 60 and 64.

13.   Cf. also Derrida, "Violence and Metaphysics," ED 196/134, where Derrida, in

a long passage added in 1967, raises the possibility of phenomenology in general being associated with the metaphysics of presence. The parallel pages in the 1964 version are *Revue de métaphysique et de morale*, no. 4 (1964): 450.

14. Cf. Derrida, "Violence and Metaphysics," ED 178/121.

15. Cf. similiar additions made in the 1967 version of "Violence and Metaphysics," where Derrida speaks of presence and the trace, ED 149/100 (cf. *Revue de métaphysique et de morale* 3, no. 345 [1964]); 160/108 (cf. *Revue de métaphysique et de morale*, no. 3 (1964): 353); 178/121 (cf. *Revue de métaphysique et de morale*, no. 4 [1964]: 437).

16. See below, Part III, Chapter 6.

17. On the contamination of the phenomenon by the sign, see also a sentence added to "Violence and Metaphysics" in 1967, ED 190/129; parallel page: *Revue de métaphysique et de morale*, no. 4 (1964): 446.

18. In this passage, Derrida replaces the verb, "récupérer," from the 1965 version (*Entretiens,* 246) with the verb, "se réapproprier," on page ED 232/166. I have to thank Kevin Thompson for pointing this change out to me.

19. Cf. Derrida, "Violence and Metaphysics," ED 166/113, where in 1967 Derrida adds one word: writing. Cf. the parallel page in the 1964 version, *Revue de métaphysique et de morale*, no. 4 (1964): 429.

20. Cf. a similar change in "Violence and Metaphysics," ED 189/129; cf. *Revue de metaphysique et de morale*, no. 4 (1964): 445.

21. Cf. Jacques Derrida, "Structure, Sign, and Play in the Discourse of the Human Sciences," in *Writing and Difference,* ED, 409/278, where he speaks of the "structurality of the structure." See also Emmanuel Levinas, "Intentionalité et sensation," in *En découvrant l'existence avec Husserl and Heidegger* (Paris: Vrin, 1967), 159, where Levinas speaks of the problem of structure in Husserl.

22. Cf. Derrida, "Violence and Metaphysics," ED 155/105, 163/110, 173/117, 178/121. On the "in general," cf. also Martin Heidegger, *Kant and the Problem of Metaphysics,* trans. Richard Taft (Bloomington: Indiana University Press, 1990), 15, 18–19, 42, 56, 61, 64, 76, 98, 101, 143, 152, 154.

23. Cf. Derrida, "Violence and Metaphysics," ED 194/132, 199/136.

3. The Critique of Ontology

1. Derrida would never have questioned ontology if he had not written "Violence and Metaphysics: an Essay on the Thought of Emmanuel Levinas." Yet Levinas's name does not appear in "The Ends of Man," because "The distinction between discourse and violence always will be an inaccessible horizon. Nonviolence would be the *telos* and not the essence of discourse" (ED 171–172/116). Cf. Part III, Chapter 6, where we shall investigate "Violence and Metaphysics."

2. The role of Nietzsche in Derrida's thought is difficult to determine and

must be considered in conjunction with the role of Levinas in Derrida's thought. See Chapter 8 below. Moreover, the role of Nietzsche in Derrida's thought raises the very difficult question of Derrida's relation to Deleuze and to Foucault. I will take up these relations in my work in progress, *The Being of the Question: Investigations of the Great French Philosophy of the Sixties.* Nevertheless, it is striking how Derrida's concept of *écriture,* his concept of undecidability and discourse resembles concepts developed by Foucault in *The Order of Things* and in *The Archeology of Knowledge.* Moreover, we have to wonder whether Derrida's discussions of power and force in the sixties do not resemble those of Foucault. Concerning Nietzsche and Derrida, we can say the following: the doctrine of eternal return, for Derrida, is a doctrine of immanence which eliminates a pure or transcendent origin or pure or transcendent end. Moreover, this doctrine seems to be at the basis of Derrida's reflections on the feminine in *Spurs.* Being a doctrine of quantity, Nietzsche's doctrine of eternal recurrence, for Derrida, opens the way for differentiations, relations of contamination ("Différance"). Such relations of contamination result in a kind of sexual difference which is not defined by binarism ("*Geschlecht:* Sexual Difference/Ontological Difference"). The discussion of sexual difference in *Spurs* leads to Kelly Oliver's *Womanizing Nietzsche* (New York: Routledge, 1995). This book must be seen as being at once a conscious or intended critique of (p. 65) as well an unconscious or unintentional, and therefore the most profound, vindication of Derrida's concepts. The claims that Derrida still "operates within a masculine economy of castration" (p. 43), that with Derrida "we are still trapped within the Hegelian master-slave dialectic" (p. 48), that "Derrida's undecidables operate within a larger economy of proper/property" (p. 65) are not criticisms of his philosophy; instead they follow necessarily from Derrida's concept of *différance,* which blurs the distinction between inside and outside, which dictates that one can only have a chance of escaping from metaphysics (or patriarchy or whatever ideology) by operating within the discourse of the same (see Derrida's "Violence and Metaphysics" or "At this Very Moment" concerning this point). The claim that Derrida's notion of undecidability eliminates the possibility of a "specifically feminine other" (p. 43) bases itself on equation of undecidability with neutrality, which it is not; and to reverse directions from Derrida's concern with death to a concern with the "feminine maternal" (p. xvi) is merely to reverse directions and thus to stay within the same hierarchy. Moreover, such a cry for birth against Derrida's "death watch" forgets that Derrida's philosophy defines itself as a concern with genesis, that its critique of teleology is at once a critique of archeology, and that ghosts or specters in Derrida come out of the past.

3.   Derrida says that he is using the word "amalgam" in an alchemical sense (MP 141/119); we shall utilize this word below (Chapter 6 and Chapter 8), and in the same magical sense.

4.   Because of its epigram from Foucault's *Les mots et les choses,* this essay must be seen as a chapter in the "debate" between Derrida and Foucault.

5. Cf. Derrida, "Violence and Metaphysics," ED 209/142, 223/150; on 223/150, Derrida speaks of the "strange simplicity of being" in Heidegger. This notion of simplicity—literally one-foldedness—is what Derrida is going to reject from Heidegger, along with the implicit/explicit opposition; simplicity implies, as in Dun Scotus, there is a One which precedes and stands outside of beings; instead of this one, Derrida will appropriate from Levinas the notion of the wholly other in order to designate the system which is not a being, the system of nonsense. See below, Part III, Chapter 6.

6. Ricoeur used this phrase, "prise de conscience," in his translation of the title of one of *The Crisis* fragment; see MP 146n12 (Bass does not render this note in the English translation). The phrase, "prise de conscience," is well known in French phenomenology; Merleau-Ponty uses it continuously in the *Phenomenology of Perception.*

7. See below, Part III, Chapter 6, on "Violence and Metaphysics," where we shall discuss "the dialogue between phenomenology and ontology."

8. Here again we must note the influence of Levinas on Derrida; cf. "Violence and Metaphysics," in ED 122/82, where Derrida says, "The knowledge and security of which we are speaking are therefore not in the world; rather, they are the possibility of our language and the basis of our world. It is at this level that the thought of Emmanuel Levinas can make us tremble." But we also have to wonder about Derrida's relation here to Foucault, who in his archeological period is defining "systems of dispersion"; in fact, we have to wonder whether the amalgamation that truly defines the orginality of Derrida's thinking is not an amalgamation of Levinas and Foucault (Foucault's Nietzscheanism).

9. Again, this comment echoes "Violence and Metaphysics," where Derrida, following Levinas, speaks of "the other of the Greek" and the "non-Greek" (ED 122/82).

10. While Derrida does not attach a proper name to this second strategy, undoubtedly he is referring to Foucault.

11. We should also include Merleau-Ponty in this tradition.

4. Upping the Ante on Dialectic

1. The title of the first section of Derrida's Avant-Propos to *Le Problème de la genèse* is "History of Philosophy and Philosophy of History."

2. One should compare Derrida's humanistic comments to the ones Foucault makes in his introduction to the French translation of Ludwig Binswanger's *Traum und Existenz,* translated as *Le Rêve et l'existence,* which is contemporaneous with Derrida's *Le Problème de la genèse.* For example, Foucault says, "Just as anthropology challenges every attempt at a repartition of philosophy and psychology, Binswanger's existential analysis avoids a distinction between ontology and anthropology; it avoids it but without suppressing it or making it impossible" (13). It is also interesting to note that Foucault ana-

lyzes Husserl's First Logical Investigation distinction between expression and indication here. He claims that, in the psychoanalysis of dreams, these two functions of the sign are mixed together; Husserl separates them clearly. But then Foucault says that the problem of the double foundation of phenomenology and psychoanalysis is to find the "common foundation" of the two functions (40). The common foundation turns out to be existence whose basic meanings the dream reveals (86). Foucault then defines the dream as a contradiction and a dialectic between the movement of freedom and the transcendent world (70, 72, 74). Finally, he claims that insofar as imagination is a modality of freedom, it is founded upon the dream (111).

3. It seems that Sartre (and not Tran-Duc-Thao, for example) must be the source of Derrida's understanding of Heidegger because Derrida speaks favorably here of "an existentialism (in the profound sense of this term)" (PGH 238), and because of Derrida's criticism of Tran-Duc-Thao.

4. These two thinkers, Tran-Duc-Thao and Jean Cavaillès, in regard to French readings of Husserl at this time can be seen everywhere. See Suzanne Bachelard's *A Study of Husserl's Formal and Transcendental Logic,* trans. Lester E. Embree (Evanston: Northwestern University Press, 1968 [1957]), who quotes the two virtually side by side on 52–53; Bernhard Waldenfels, who recognizes that deconstruction does not come about from out of nowhere but rather from Tran-Duc-Thao and Cavaillès (*Phänomenologie in Frankreich,* 51; cf. also 559n92). Cf. also Michel Foucault, in his introduction to Georges Canguilhem's *On the Normal and the Pathological,* trans. Carolyn R. Fawcett (Boston: D. Reidel, 1978), who says that "[a] line . . . separates a philosophy of experience, of sense, and of subject and a philosophy of knowledge, rationality and of concept. On the one hand, one network is that of Sartre and Merleau-Ponty; and another is that of Cavaillès, Bachelard and Canguilhem" (x). Compare also the following comment from Jean-François Lyotard's 1954 *La phénoménologie* (Paris: Presses Universitaires de France, 1956): "We could not recommend enough the reading of this remarkable book (*Phénoménologie et matérialisme dialectique*)" (27n1; see also 110–117, 124). Finally Georges Canguilhem in his address on the occasion of Jean Hyppolite's death: " . . . it is under his [i.e., Hyppolite's] influence, along with that of Cavaillès in another area of investigation, that French philosophy began to lose consciousness of what was for it, formerly, Consciousness" (*Revue de métaphysique et de morale,* no. 2 (1969): 130). In fact, Hyppolite quotes Cavaillès in his 1952 "Essai sur la 'logique' de Hegel" without even mentioning him by name (*Figures de la pensée philosophique,* volume I [Paris: PUF, 1971], 164–165). Derrida does not seem to recognize that Merleau-Ponty was the first phenomenologist to move from the contradictions of Husserl's phenomenology to an originary dialectic (cf. "The Time of a Thesis," in *Philosophy in France Today,* p. 38).

5. The word "surenchère" means something like "upping the ante." See Samuel Weber, "La surenchère—(Upping the Ante)," in *Le passage des frontières,* ed. Marie-Louise Mallet (Paris: Galilée, 1994), 141–150.

6. Tran-Duc-Thao, "Existentialism et matérialisme dialectique," in *Revue de métaphysique* 54 (1949). Cf. also Tran-Duc-Thao, "Marxisme et phénoménologie," in *La Revue internationale*, no. 2 (1946): 168–174.

7. Tran-Duc-Thao, "Existentialism et matérialisme dialectique," 320.

8. Cf. Tran-Duc-Thao, *Phenomenology and Dialectical Materialism,* trans. Daniel J. Herman and Donald V. Morano (Boston: D. Reidel, 1985), 10–11/xxiv–xxv.

9. Tran-Duc-Thao, "Existentialisme et matérialisme dialectique," 321. This explicit mention of *néant* indicates that Sartre is Tran-Duc-Thao's target in this essay, although Sartre is never mentioned by name here.

10. Cf. Bernhard Waldenfels, *Phänomenologie in Frankreich,* 31–32.

11. Tran-Duc-Thao, "Existentialisme et matérialisme dialectique," 322.

12. Cf. Tran-Duc-Thao, *Phenomenology and Dialectical Materialism,* 11–12/xxv.

13. Tran-Duc-Thao, "Existentialisme et matérialisme dialectique," 325.

14. Tran-Duc-Thao, "Existentialisme et matérialisme dialectique," 325.

15. Cf. Tran-Duc-Thao, *Phenomenology and Dialectical Materialism,* 9/xxiii.

16. Cf. Didier Eribon, *Michel Foucault,* trans. Betsy Wing (Cambridge, Mass.: Harvard University Press, 1991), 32.

17. Tran-Duc-Thao begins *Phénoménologie et matérialisme dialectique* with Husserl's structuralist phase, the critique of psychologism in the Prologomena to the *Logical Investigations.* This beginning is not without consequence because Tran-Duc-Thao argues that Husserl never considers real genesis. That Tran-Duc-Thao does not begin with Husserl's first major published work, his *Philosophy of Arithmetic,* is crucial for understanding Derrida's own starting point with *The Philosophy of Arithmetic* in *Le Problème de la genèse.*

18. Cf. Tran-Duc-Thao, "Les origines de la réduction phénoménologique chez Husserl," in *Deucalion,* no. 3 (1949): 128–142.

19. Tran-Duc-Thao is well aware of Fink's important essay and discusses it at length. Always pushing his Husserl interpretation toward the concrete, toward materiality, Tran-Duc-Thao's criticism of Fink consists in a challenge. Husserl's theory, as Fink points out, is that transcendental subjectivity is absolute and non-worldly; yet, "it would be difficult to find an actual *demonstration* [of it]" (PMD 85/41). Tran-Duc-Thao continues: "But if we ask them to be more precise [in regard to the project of determining the origin of the world], we are told that the reduction provides its meaning only to those who have already performed it. The transcendental phenomenologist, says Fink at the end of ["The Phenomenological Philosophy of Edmund Husserl and Contemporary Criticism"], returns to the world in order to share his discoveries with the dogmatic philosopher, but he cannot convince him" (PMD 85/41). Although Tran-Duc-Thao breaks off here, the implication is clear: Tran-Duc-Thao himself remains unconvinced. He then starts a

new paragraph and goes on: "Let us pose the problem in precise terms" (PMD 85/43). In precise terms, the problem, for Tran-Duc-Thao, is *Dinglichkeit, matérialité*. It is also important that Tran-Duc-Thao recognizes that consciousness's ambiguity unfolds into Husserl's doctrine, already presented in *Ideas I,* of the strict parallelism between transcendental phenomenology and phenomenological psychology. Tran-Duc-Thao says, "we know there are *no differences in content between psychology and phenomenology*" (PMD 74/35).

20.   Moreover, according to Tran-Duc-Thao, since intimation or manifestation cannot function without corporeal existence, "[the domain of persons] should have produced a new framework wherein the very notion of 'thing' would have had an entirely new signification" (PMD 96/49). This comment anticipates Tran-Duc-Thao's conclusion in favor of dialectical materialism.

21.   Cf. PMD 113–114/60, where Tran-Duc-Thao explains how we can understand "the disastrous ambiguity of the classical statement of the causal principle." We are to understand it by seeking the genesis of science within the real, singular world, within, in other words, materiality.

22.   Tran-Duc-Thao appropriates this word from *Formal and Transcendental Logic* (#99) and *Cartesian Meditations* (# 37). Derrida's translation of *Leistung* as *production* in his translation of *The Origin of Geometry* undoubtedly derives from Tran-Duc-Thao; see LOG 22n3/40n27.

23.   Tran-Duc-Thao, in particular, focuses on section 50, "The Fundamental Structure of Predication."

24.   In *Le Problème de la genèse,* Derrida calls this note "remarkable" (PGH 112n11) and he says that Tran-Duc-Thao penetrates the sense of the living present "very brilliantly" (PGH 238n41).

25.   For Tran-Duc-Thao, one can see these difficulties in, on the one hand, *The Origin of Geometry.* There, while attempting to describe the origin of geometrical object, Husserl could not, according to Tran-Duc-Thao, go "beyond the level of commonsense remarks" (PMD 221/125). On the other, in a well-known, then-unpublished fragment, Husserl, in "a fearless refutation of the Copernican system," places the earth again at the universe's center (PMD 222/126). Tran-Duc-Thao calls this "refutation"—this is his word—"an inversion of every sense of truth" (PMD 223/127). Derrida, however, calls Tran-Duc-Thao's demand that Husserl go beyond common sense remarks about the origin of geometry "illegitimate" (LOG 55/65, 55n1/65n60); as he says in *Le Problème de la genèse,* "empirical events, as such, will not be able to explain the genesis of structures" (PGH 268). Derrida also stresses that, in the fragment on the Earth, Husserl "*reduces,* rather than 'refutes,'" the Copernican system (LOG 79–81/83–85; 81n1/85n88).

26.   Cf. Lyotard, *La phénoménologie,* which also stresses the genetic element in Husserl's thought (14).

27.   Indeed, starting from this *aporia,* Derrida in *Le Problème de la genèse* claims

that phenomenology, as Husserl conceives it, runs into "insurmountable difficulties" (PGH 207, 238, 248), the exact same phrase as Tran-Duc-Thao uses (PMD 219/124).

28.   Cf. PGH 237, where Derrida says, echoing Tran-Duc-Thao, that "Since the *a priori* concretes of genesis, the final forms of the known, etc., are founded upon their own passive synthesis and are genetic only because they mix with their opposite, Husserl still defines the method and the first philosophy of phenomenology as a transcendental idealism through an irreducible prejudice and contrary to the very results of his analysis." Cf. also PGH 270, where Derrida says, "Once more Husserl's descriptions betray his principles." See also Lyotard's *La phénoménologie* where he entitles a chapter "Transcendental idealism and its contradictions" (33).

29.   See Chapter 8.

30.   Derrida, "The Time of a Thesis," in *Philosophy in France Today,* 38.

31.   Cf. Derrida, *Introduction to the Origin of Geometry,* LOG 82n1/86n89.

32.   Perhaps, in order to determine the exact nature of Tran-Duc-Thao's dialectical materialism, one has to investigate Engels. Tran-Duc-Thao quotes him at a very important juncture at the beginning of Part II; PMD 241/138.

33.   Cf. D. Debarle, "Le dernier écrit philosophique de Jean Cavaillès," in *Le Revue de métaphysique et de morale,* LIII (1948), 225–47, 350–78; see in particular 375, where Debarle, speaking of dialectical materialism without mentioning Tran-Duc-Thao, says that "the actual reality actualized [in mathematical thought] is not a simple brute materiality but in fact something intelligible by itself and in substance. . . . This something is impossible to describe completely and truthfully if one merely assimilates it to natural realities in the customary sense."

34.   Cf. Lyotard, *La phénoménologie,* 112, 124–125. Here, much more closely aligned with Marxism than Derrida, Lyotard says that "The Marxist critique completes [Hegel's critique of Husserl's phenomenology]. What is here at issue, as Thao saw very well, is the problem of *matter. Leben* as the soil of the meaning of life is stripped of its ambiguity, of its subjectivist risk only if it is identified with matter" (124, Lyotard's emphasis). We should also mention here that, like Thao, Lyotard, in his presentation of phenomenological doctrine, says first that "It is necessary therefore really to admit simultaneously that the ego at issue is the concrete ego since as well there is no difference of content between psychology and phenomenology, and that it is not the concrete ego since it is separated from its mundane being" (28). Then he says, " . . . the transcendental subject is no different from the concrete subject" (33). Like that of Thao, Lyotard's inability to reflect upon the nature of the "simultaneity" in the first passage leads to the simple identification of the two egos and finally to dialectical materialism. In contrast, in *Le Problème de la genèse,* Derrida says that "This contradiction [between an empirical source and a transcendental source] is permanent. The constitut-

ing origin of lived experience is in lived experience and outside of lived experience, in time and outside of time, etc., and we cannot determine exclusively in one sense or another the absolute originality." Derrida does not identify the two egos; moreover, as we shall see, he understands the lack of identity as a very paradoxical unity.

35. Derrida, "The Time of a Thesis," in *Philosophy in France Today*, 38. Indeed, one can see the interest that Cavaillès's thought held for Derrida in this footnote, PGH 207n74, where Derrida says, "Originally, our intention was to occupy ourselves at length with the problem of mathematical genesis and, to confront Cavaillès's thesis, while following it, with specific texts from *Formal and Transcendental Logic*. Time did not permit this and we had to give up the project." Cf. also D. Dubarle, "Le dernier écrits philosophique de Jean Cavaillès," 373–378, where Dubarle shows how Cavaillès's thought presents a path different from that of dialectical materialism and from that of existentialism.

36. For a comprehensive study of Cavaillès's philosophy, see Pierre Cassou-Noguès, *De l'expérience mathématique: Essai sur la philosophie de sciences de Jean Cavaillès* (These pour obtenir le grade de Docteur de l'Université Lille III, Discipline: Philosophy).

37. D. Dubarle says Cavaillès's "basic given is the reality of mathematics itself, object and science simultaneously, actual state and historical process, in short, the actuality, by means of humanity, of the most highly disciplined rational knowledge" ("Le dernier écrit philosophique de Jean Cavaillès," 374). See also Ed. Morot-Sir, "La théorie de la science d'après Jean Cavaillès," in *La revue des sciences humaines* L (1948): 154–155; cf. also the editors' preface to the English translation of "On Logic and the Theory of Science," 348.

38. Cf. D. Dubarle, "Le dernier écrit philosophique de Jean Cavaillès," 231.

39. D. Dubarle, "Le dernier écrit philosophique de Jean Cavaillès," 231–232.

40. Cf. Bernhard Waldenfels, *Phänomenologie in Frankreich*, 383–384.

41. Levinas also interprets Husserl in this way; cf. *The Theory of Intuition in Husserl's Phenomenology*, trans. André Orianne (Evanston: Northwestern University Press, 1973), especially 148–151.

42. Many of Cavaillès's claims about Husserl, such as this one can be contested, and Derrida himself, for example, does this. Perhaps the fact that Cavaillès restricts himself almost solely to *Formal and Transcendental Logic* takes its toll here. Cf. PGH 212n82.

43. Cf. Eribon, *Michel Foucault*, 57, 104, and especially 165.

44. Cf. Bernhard Waldenfels, *Phänomenologie in Frankreich*, 390, 394–395.

45. The exact passage is: "Now it seems that such an identification of planes is especially difficult to admit for phenomenology, where the motive of research and the foundations of objectivities are precisely the relation to a creative subjectivity." Cavaillès's mention here of motivation and creative

46. subjectivity seems to be an allusion to Fink; cf. also 76/408, where Cavaillès quotes Fink's definition of phenomenology as "archeology" in "What Does Husserl's Phenomenological Philosophy Want?"

46. At Cavaillès's time *The Crisis* was still only in manuscript, and Cavaillès quotes from a manuscript number (H VI, p. 51).

47. Cf. also Bachelard, *A Study of Husserl's Formal and Transcendental Logic,* 52–53.

48. Both Dubarle and Morot-Sir attempt such a reconstruction in their essays (cited above), and my attempt here is indebted to the ones they have already made.

49. Cf. Gilles Granger, "Jean Cavaillès ou la montée vers Spinoza," *Les études philosophiques* (1947), 271–279, especially 277.

50. Cf. Bernhard Waldenfels, *Phänomenologie in Frankreich,* 386.

51. Cf. Michel Foucault, introduction to Georges Canguilhem, *On the Normal and the Pathological,* xiv.

52. Cf. D. Dubarle, "Le dernier écrit philosophique de Jean Cavaillès," 359; also Gilles Granger, "Jean Cavaillès ou la montée vers Spinoza," 277.

53. This entire discussion is indebted to Ernest Nagel's and James R. Newman's "Gödel's Proof," found in *Contemporary Philosophical Logic,* ed. Irving M. Copi and James A. Gould (New York: St. Martin's Press, 1978), 27–31. Also, this discussion extrapolates mainly from LTS 73–74/405–406.

54. Cf. D. Dubarle, "Le dernier écrit philosophique de Jean Cavaillès," 368, where he says: "What is proper to infinity is in fact to pose the problem of totalization (of predicable universality) in a manner different from that which characterizes the object of finite experience. Totalization in the finite is exclusively extensive and divides rigorously between the truth of the whole and that of the part. But the totalization to infinity introduces the reflexive dimension, and tends toward a truth transcending the opposition of part and whole." Cf. also Gilles Granger, "Jean Cavaillès ou la montée vers Spinoza," 278.

55. The ambiguity of Cavaillès's exact positive theory can be seen by comparing Morot-Sir's "La théorie de la science, d'après Jean Cavaillès" and D. Dubarle's "Le dernier écrit philosophique de Jean Cavaillès." On the one hand, stressing the erasure character of Cavaillès's dialectic, Morot-Sir claims that Cavaillès's dialectic "has nothing in common with the dialectic of absolute idealism, that is, with the two ideas of the depth of negation and of the overcoming of transcendence through a synthetic act" (158). On the other, stressing Cavaillès's divergence from Kant's philosophy of consciousness, Dubarle claims that it is impossible to express some of Cavaillès's formulations from "On Logic and the Theory of Science" "in the language of the Kantian tradition: instinctively, the vocabulary of Jean Cavaillès becomes Hegelian" (247). In *Logic and Existence,* Hyppolite says: "But perhaps in Hegel, the self is more immanent to the content than in Cavaillès. The rapprochement of Cavaillès with Spinoza would be more

exact upon this point than a rapprochement with Hegel. Cavaillès thinks less of the unity of the subject and object resulting at the sense than of God's infinite understanding in Spinoza and of the passage from true idea to true idea" (LE 64n1/52n6). Cf. also Gilles Granger, "Jean Cavaillès ou la montée vers Spinoza," 278–279. And see Cassou-Noguès, *De l'expérience mathématique,* pp. 285–302.

56. Cf. Bernhard Waldenfels, *Phänomenologie in Frankreich,* 445, 511, 548.

57. Indeed, Cavaillès grants a considerable role to the sign in mathematical thinking. See Cassou-Noguès, *De l'expérience mathématique,* p. 164.

58. In *Le Problème de la genèse,* Derrida relentlessly criticizes Husserl for remaining, in his analyses, at an "already constituted" level. That Derrida can discover Cavaillès's dialectic in Husserl implies that Cavaillès's dialectic too remains at an "already constituted" level; lacking the sensuous kernel, it never reaches the most basic level of genetic constitution. In his *Introduction to Husserl's "The Origin of Geometry,"* Derrida says that "the *dialectical* genesis that Cavaillès opposes to the 'activity' of Husserlian consciousness is described precisely and copiously by Husserl on various levels, although the word is never mentioned" (LOG 157/143); in *Le Problème de la genèse dans la philosophie de Husserl,* he says that Cavaillès "makes explicit the temporal being of consciousness and strips the old idealist and formalist prejudices from Husserl's thought" (PGH 212).

59. The book actually begins with an "Avant-Propos," "Le thème de la genèse et la genèse d'un thème" (PGH 1–34), about which Derrida writes, "These long preliminary considerations were not supposed to introduce originally the present historical study. Rather, in their very broad strokes, they open the way for a more vast and dogmatic work that we would be able to undertake later on the same problem. Insofar as they could throw some light on the historic essay which follows, we thought it wise to present them here" (PGH 1n1). We shall return to this "Avant-Propos" below in our discussion of Derrida's dialectical "rival." Also before the actual historical study begins, there is also a brief introduction (PGH 35–41) which has oriented my reconstruction of Derrida's interpretation of Husserl in *Le Problème de la genèse.*

60. In fact, Derrida stresses three other points in his discussion: the basis of abstraction in already "given" definite objects (PGH 57–61), the impossibility of confusing logical order, which is "already there," with temporal order (PGH 61–63), and the dependence of psychological relations on natural, "already constituted," relations (PGH 63–65).

61. Derrida continuously uses this verb, *se confondre,* to designate the perplexing relation between psychologism and logicism (PGH 17, 40, 46, 56, 62, 65, 95, 98, 101, 108, 116, 118, 125, 129, 159, 165, 167, 170, 172, 182, 185, 188, 193, 210, 216, 217, 220, 225, 238, 248, 251, 259, 282). We shall return to this verb below.

62. In this discussion, Derrida relies on what Tran-Duc-Thao had already shown in reference to "the origins of Husserl's phenomenological reduction" (PGH 132n1); he discovers repeatedly a confusion in Husserl's concep-

tions of it between a Cartesian concreteness and a Kantian formalism. What distinguishes Derrida's analyses from those of Tran-Duc-Thao is Derrida's insistence that Husserl's reduction targets primarily empirical genesis and history.

63. Derrida notes that this claim contains all the sources to which "the French phenomenologists have had recourse" (PGH 120n26).

64. These arguments anticipate those of *Voice and Phenomenon*'s fifth chapter; cf. below, Part III, Chapter 7.

65. Cf. *Introduction*, LOG 83n1/86n90, 112/109; see below, Part II, Chapter 5.

66. Anticipating again *Voice and Phenomenon*'s argumentation (and that of "Ousia and Grammé"), here Derrida says that the punctuality of the now "negates" the continuity of time and yet there could be no continuity without punctuality (PGH 168). In other words, punctuality is necessary because without it, all temporal modification would be entirely identical. Here already, we could say, is Derrida's double necessity of the limit.

67. Moreover, for Derrida, Husserl's failure to reach the level of transcendental genesis affects all of his other descriptions in *Experience and Judgment*, his descriptions of the genesis of negation (PGH 195–198), his descriptions of temporality (PGH 198–202), and his descriptions of the role of theory (PGH 202–207).

68. Interestingly, Derrida focuses only Husserl's Fourth Meditation, and barely mentions the famous Fifth Meditation investigation of intersubjectivity (cf. PGH 240). We shall return to this point at the end of this chapter.

69. Cf. Jean-Francois Lyotard, *La phénoménologie*, p. 117.

70. Cf. also PGH 50, 76, 78, 93, 117, 123, 148, 150, 162, 167, 171, 178, 185, 196, 198, 199–200, 209, 216, 217, 221, 222, 225, 249, 270, 278–279.

71. This phrase, "déjà constitué" (or "déjà là") recurs repeatedly in *Le Problème de la genèse;* 6, 8, 10, 13, 16, 28, 30, 37, 39, 40, 58, 60, 61, 62, 64, 66–67, 68, 82, 95, 111, 115, 116, 117, 120, 121, 138, 140, 144, 156, 159, 163, 164, 170–171, 186, 198, 200, 203, 205, 211, 225, 232, 253, 256, 264, 274, 275, 281, 282.

72. Only under the pressure of Levinas's thought will Derrida realize that both Husserlian phenomenology and Heideggerian ontology are Greek. Nevertheless, in *Le Problème de la genèse* Derrida sets the stage for his attempt to exit Greek philosophy, when he discusses the European *eidos*'s source in Greece; cf. PGH 254, 256.

73. On Derrida's mention of concept as opposed to intuition, see PGH 188, 216, 217, 219, 221, 230, 266, 273, 281.

5. The Root, That Is Necessarily One, of Every Dilemma

1. "The Problem of the Sign" is the subtitle, of course, to *Voice and Phenomenon*.

2.   Derrida, "The Time of a Thesis," in *Philosophy in France Today*, 39.

3.   Jacques Derrida, "Freud and the Scene of Writing," in *Writing and Difference*, 302n1/203n5; see especially the French edition which cites pages 170–171 of the Introduction.

4.   See "The Time of a Thesis," in *Philosophy in France Today*, 36, where Derrida states that in 1957 Hyppolite agreed to become the director of his first thesis, "The Ideality of the Literary Object." Cf. also Hyppolite's inaugural address at the Collège de France (1963) in which he mentions Derrida by name and quotes part of Derrida's *Introduction* (*Figures de la pensée philosophique,* II, pp. 1027–1028). See also Hyppolite's "Project for Teaching the History of Philosophic Thought" (1962) in *Figures de la pensée philosophique,* II, in which Hyppolite says: "[L'histoire de la pensée philosophique] refuse le non-sens philosophique d'une histoire purement empirique et l'impuissance d'un rationalisme non-historique" (p. 1001); cf. to Derrida, *Introduction:* "Si l'on tient pour acquis le non-sens philosophique d'une histoire purement empirique and l'impuissance d'un rationalisme anhistorique, on mesure la gravité de l'enjeu" (p. 37). Clearly the question of language is everywhere in French philosophy during the sixties. Thus Derrida's "linguistic turn" takes place in this context. The "linguistic turn" in French philosophy is not due to Hyppolite alone; we must also, of course, grant roles to Merleau-Ponty, Bataille, and Blanchot, and especially Heidegger. We focus on Hyppolite's role not only because of Derrida's personal "salute to the memory of Jean Hyppolite" in "The Time of a Thesis" (*Philosophy in France Today,* 36), but also because Hyppolite's reading of Hegel through the question of language is revolutionary at this time, determining probably the directions of the philosophies of Derrida, Deleuze, and Foucault.

5.   Cf. *Studies on Marx and Hegel,* trans. John O'Neill (New York: Basic Books, 1969), viii, where Hyppolite calls Hegel's thought a monism.

6.   Cf. Michel Foucault's "Hommage à Jean Hyppolite," where he says: For Hyppolite "with Hegel, philosophy, which since Descartes at least was in an unerasable relation to non-philosophy, became not only conscious of this relation, but the actual discourse of it: the play of philosophy and non-philosophy [was] seriously considered. While others saw in Hegelian thought philosophy's self-reflection, and the moment where it changed into the narration of its own history, Hyppolite recognized there the moment where it crossed over its own limits in order to become the philosophy of non-philosophy, or perhaps the non-philosophy of philosophy itself. But this theme which haunted [Hyppolite's] studies of Hegel for the most part exceeded them and took his interests farther" (135). Foucault also calls *Logique et existence* "one of the great books of our time" (136). Cf. also Georges Canguilhem's "Hommage," where he says: "If however I had to say in a few words what we owe to [Hyppolite], I would say that, under his influence, along with that of Cavaillès in another area, French philosophy

began to pass out of what was formerly called Consciousness" (130). Both Foucault's and Canguilhem's "Hommage" are in *Revue de métaphysique et de morale*, no. 2 (1969): 129–136. Cf. also Jacques D'Hondt's "In Memoriam: Jean Hyppolite," in *Les études philosophiques* (Janvier–Mars, 1969), 87–92.

7.   According to Hegel, there can be nothing ineffable. Although an individual may believe that silence guards singularity, in fact, without the comparison made possible through conversation, the self turns out to be merely "abstract universality" (LE 13/11). Hyppolite shows that, for Hegel, only the mediation of language—dialogue—permits determination. Cf. also Jean Hyppolite, "Dialectique et dialogue dans la *Phénoménologie de l'esprit,*" in *Figures de la pensée philosophique,* vol. I, 209–212.

8.   Hyppolite does this in the chapter entitled, "Sens et sensible." In "the Pit and the Pyramid," Derrida says, "Certain of these texts [from the *Encyclopaedia*'s "Philosophy of Spirit"] already having been examined by Jean Hyppolite in *Logique et existence,* most notably in the chapter "Sens et sensible," we will be making an implicit and permanent reference to the latter" (MP 81/71).

9.   On Hyppolite's interpretation of Hegel's notion of life, see Jean Hyppolite, "The Concept of Life and Consciousness of Life in Hegel's Jena Philosophy," in *Studies on Marx and Hegel,* trans. John O'Neill (New York: Basic Books, 1969), 3–21.

10.   Cf. Jean Hyppolite, *Genesis and Structure of Hegel's Phenomenology of Spirit,* translated by Samuel Cherniak and John Heckman (Evanston: Northwestern University Press, 1974), 152.

11.   Hyppolite, *Genesis and Structure,* 137.

12.   Hyppolite stresses that the movement of this dialectic leading to contradiction is lived as desire, desire being defined by a lack (LE 143/111).

13.   Derrida had already recognized the convergence of Husserl's and Hegel's thought in *Le Problème de la genèse:* "We are surprised by the precision with which, upon this point at least, Hegel's critique of Kant announces the Husserlian perspective: far from so-called 'phenomenal' experience being separated from *a priori* synthesis, it is an *a priori* synthesis (of thought and the real, of *sense and sensible* [my emphasis], for example and in a very general way), which makes every experience and every signification of experience possible. Obviously, the idea of this originary synthesis as the real principle of all possible experience is closely aligned with the idea of the intentionality of transcendental consciousness. We will often have to test the strange depth of certain resemblances between Hegelian and Husserlian thought" (PGH 11–12).

14.   See below, Part III, Chapter 7, section 3.

15.   Cf. Derrida, "Form and Meaning," MP 199/166.

16.   Cf. Derrida, "The Time of a Thesis," 43; cf. also "The Pit and The Pyramid," in *Margins.*

17. Cf. the opening line of Gilles Deleuze's *Nietzsche and Philosophy,* trans. Hugh Tomlinson (New York: Columbia University Press, 1983): "Nietzsche's most general project is the introduction of the concepts of sense and value into philosophy" (p. 1).

18. Cf. Derrida, "Violence and Metaphysics," in *Writing and Difference,* 162/100; see also 162n1/315n41, where Derrida cites Hyppolite's *Genesis and Structure,* 152. We shall return to "Violence and Metaphysics" in Part III, Chapter 6.

19. See below, Part III, Chapter 7, section 3.

20. On Hyppolite's view of the reduction, see the report written by Alexandre Lowit (*Les Etudes philosophiques* 12 [1957]: 64–65) of the Deuxième Colloque International de Phénoménologie at Krefeld in 1956. Lowit says that "Thus there was only one speaker, Hyppolite, who, while sketching a 'Fichtean meditation' [entitled, "The Fichtean Idea of *Wissenschaftlehre* and the Husserlian Project"], made a defense of the 'transcendental reduction' in Husserl and of the Husserlian conception of phenomenology 'as a rigorous science.' Also, among the numerous discussions, perhaps those of Hyppolite and de Waehlens, on the one hand, and, on the other, [those of Hyppolite] and Fink were the most exciting." For Hyppolite's essay, see *Husserl et la Pensée Moderne* (The Hague: Martinus Nijhoff, 1959), 173–189.

21. Hyppolite, *Genesis and Structure,* 137.

22. Cf. Derrida, "'Genesis and Structure' and Phenomenology," in *Writing and Difference,* 241/162; Derrida, VP, 84/75. Finally compare also Emmanuel Levinas, *Totality and Infinity,* trans. Alphonso Lingis (Pittsburgh: Duquesne University Press, 1969), 41.

23. Jean Hyppolite, Comments after H. L. Van Breda's "La Réduction phénomé-nologique," in *Husserl* (Cahiers de Royaumont), 323, 333.

24. Because Derrida continues to use "contradiction" in a positive way through-out and up to his 1967 publications, it is not clear that he has yet consciously stopped the concept of *différance* from going all the way up to contradic-tion. It is clear that he is aware of this difference in the *Positions* interview. In this interview, Derrida says that the demarcation of *différance* from Hegelian contradiction requires "a long work on Hegel's concept of contra-diction" (POS 60/44). This "long work" is undoubtedly Derrida's 1974 *Glas;* a consideration of this difficult text is beyond the scope of this investigation.

25. What Derrida here calls "essential finitude" will be called "originary finitude" in "Violence and Metaphysics." See below, Part III, Chapter 6, section 1.

26. While Ricoeur apparently initiated in the fifties the translation of "besin-nen" as "prendre conscience," the phrase "prendre conscience" already appears in Merleau-Ponty's 1945 *The Phenomenology of Perception* as a tech-nical term.

27. At one point Merleau-Ponty intended to call *The Visible and the Invisible* "The Origin of Truth": see *The Visible and the Invisible,* 165–166.

28. This section is based in part on my *Imagination and Chance: The Difference between the Thought of Ricoeur and Derrida* (Albany: SUNY Press, 1992).

29. Derrida frequently uses the adjective "strange" ("étrange") throughout the Husserl writings to indicate the root of all dilemma.

30. This phrase, "mouvement en vrille," Derrida apparently inherited from Paul Ricoeur, who used it in his introduction to his French translation of *Ideas I* (*Ideas I, Idées directices pour une phénoménologie* [Paris: Gallimard, 1950]), xxi. Cf. also Emmanuel Levinas, *Otherwise than Being or Beyond Essence*, p. 44. Cf. also Michel Foucault, "Preface a la transgression," in *Critique*, no. 195 (1963): 755; English translation by Donald F. Bouchard as "Preface to Transgression," in *Language, Counter-Memory, Practice* (Ithaca: Cornell University Press, 1977), p. 35. For a recent use of this term by Derrida, see *The Gift of Death*, p. 8.

31. Derrida's references to the *Logical Investigations* in 90n2/92n95 and in 90n2/92n96 should alert us to the intimate connection between the *Introduction* and *Voice and Phenomenon*.

32. See also Emmanuel Levinas, *Théorie de l'intuition dans la phénoménologie de Husserl* (Paris: Vrin, 1963), p. 98; English translation by André Orianne as *The Theory of Intuition in Husserl's Phenomenology* (Evanston: Northwestern University Press, 1973), p. 62.

33. In relation to Husserl's privilege of mathematical objects, one should keep in mind that Derrida in 1957 intended to write a thesis under Hyppolite's direction entitled "The Ideality of the Literary Object." See "The Time of a Thesis," in *Philosophy in France Today*, 36.

34. I am following Derrida's translation of "Leistung" as "production"; the standard English translation however is "accomplishment." Cf. Derrida's footnote explaining his translation, LOG, 40n27/22n3.

35. See sections 11, 14, 15.

36. The primary example of such an essence is the essence of an artwork. An artwork, by definition, is unique, singular; and yet copies can be made, which refer back to the singularity of the original.

37. Cf. Paul Ricoeur, *A L'Ecole de la phénoménologie* (Paris: Vrin, 1986), p. 100.

38. Cf. Bruzina's translation of Fink's *Sixth Cartesian Meditation*.

39. In *Voice and Phenomenon*, the word "recouvrement" will play an important role for Derrida.

40. For more on Gödel's proof, see above, Part II, Chapter 4, section 2 (on Cavaillès).

41. Edmund Husserl, *Experience and Judgment*, trans. James S. Churchill and Karl Ameriks (Evanston: Northwestern University Press, 1973 [1938]), 267.

42. Derrida is here contesting the readings of *The Origin of Geometry* proposed by Tran-Duc-Thao in *Phenomenology and Dialectical Materialism* (which we analyzed above) (cf. LOG 46n38) and by Merleau-Ponty in late texts such as

"Phenomenology and the Science of Man" and "On the Phenomenology of Language" (cf. LOG 71/77, 71n2/77n77; LOG 116–117111–112). The interpretation of Merleau-Ponty that Derrida proposes here is at least contestable, and, given the terminology and moves that Derrida takes in this book, he is probably more indebted to Merleau-Ponty that he discloses.

43. While Derrida suggests that this transcendental language is different from the one of which Fink speaks in "The Phenomenological Philosophy of Edmund Husserl" (LOG 71n1/77n76), they overlap insofar as both are concerned with the constitution of knowledge: for Derrida, the constitution and communication of geometrical knowledge; for Fink, the constitution and communication of phenomenological knowledge.

44. Cf. Ronald Bruzina, "Dependence on Language and the Autonomy of Reason: An Husserlian Perspective," in *Man and World* 14 (1981): 355–368.

45. Derrida, in fact, enumerates three, but there are divisions within the three that Derrida himself lists.

46. What I am calling the second, third, and fourth criticisms are all listed under point number two on pages 75–78/80–82. Under point number two, Derrida starts by saying "d'abord"—the problem of a pure grammar (criticism number three)—and then "ensuite"—the problem of absolute translatability (criticism number three). Derrida then on page 77/82 extends the problem of absolute translatability to the problem of the designation of transcendental subjectivity (criticism number four).

47. Because each phase of temporalization for Husserl possesses the form of the living present, Derrida calls each phase an "absolute origin."

48. Footnote 90n3/92n96, which concerns the sign in Husserl's First Logical Investigation, is crucial for understanding *Voice and Phenomenon.*

49. In French: "Le silence des arcanes préhistoriques et des civilisations enfouies, l'ensevelissement des intentions perdues et des secrets gardés, l'illisibilité de l'inscription lapidaire décèlent le sens transcendental de la mort, en ce qui l'unit à l'absolu du droit intentionnel dans l'instance même de son échec."

50. See above, Part I, Chapter 3.

51. This entire discussion of course anticipates 1987 *Ulysse Gramophone* (see in particular, pp. 27–28, 119).

52. See below, Part III, Chapter 7, section 3.

53. See below, Part III, Chapter 6, section 2.

54. See LOG 156/142, where Derrida italicizes the word "sens" in the expression "le sens de toute histoire."

55. Cf. Gilles Deleuze, *La Logique du sens* (Paris: Minuit, 1969), 128; English translation by Constantin Boundas with Charles Stivale as *The Logic of Sense* (New York: Columbia University Press, 1990), 105.

56. See Part III, Chapter 6.

57. Undoubtedly, Hyppolite's chapter from *Logic and Existence,* "Sense and Sensible," is only one of the reasons why Derrida makes a "linguistic turn." The interest in language in the sixties is certainly "in the air."

58. We have put "logic" in scare quotes because soon Derrida will question the use of this word. See below, Chapter 6, section 1.

59. Compare Levinas's formula: "Pouvoir fait d'impuissances," in "La signification et le sens," in *Humanisme de l'autre homme* (Paris: Fata Morgana, 1972), 51; English translation by Alphonso Lingis as "Meaning and Sense," in *Collected Philosophical Papers* (The Hague: Martinus Nijhoff, 1987), 98.

60. In fact, in *Logic and Existence,* Hyppolite explicitly repudiates the logic of Plato's *Sophist* because it remains at the level of empirical negation (LE 144–145/112–113).

61. In the closing pages of the *Introduction,* the word "pure" occurs frequently.

6. More Metaphysical than Metaphysics

1. As we shall assert in Part IV, Chapter 8, there is a second crucial period for Derrida in the mid-eighties, at the time of *Memoirs for Paul de Man* and *Of Spirit,* when Derrida is shifting from the question to the promise. This shift is at the basis of all of Derrida's so-called political-ethical writings.

2. As the notes to the 1964 version and Derrida's revision of "Violence and Metaphysics" for its inclusion in *Writing and Difference* indicate, Derrida also absorbed some of the Levinas essays that appeared in the mid-sixties, for example, "The Trace of the Other," which appeared in 1963. *Totality and Infinity* was published in 1961.

3. That Derrida, in the *Introduction,* had called ontology metaphysics perhaps facilitated this substitution (LOG 167/150).

4. See Part IV, Chapter 8, below.

5. Although the word "dialectic" will leave Derrida's lexicon after *Voice and Phenomenon.*

6. This, shall we say, "origin" of Derrida's own thinking is especially evident in the revisions he made, as is now well known due to the work of Robert Bernasconi, for the inclusion of "Violence and Metaphysics" in the 1967 *Writing and Difference* (revisions made from its original appearance in 1964 in *Revue de métaphysique et de morale*).

7. As we claimed above in Chapter 2.

8. The occurrences of "destruction" are: ED 165/111, 121/82, 157/106, 171/116.

9. This phrase, "without relation to the same," does not appear in the English translation.

10. By conceiving the other without relation to the same, it is possible that the other—since the other turns out to be God—is, as Derrida suggests, nothing

but presence (ED 160/108). This conclusion seems especially possible since Levinas wants to conceive alterity without negativity, meaning that God would be a positive plentitude (ED 168/114), a positive plentitude not available to human intuition. This *pure presence* therefore would still be entirely consistent with modern philosophy; the very absence of presence *for me* implies that Levinas's metaphysics is a form of classical dogmatism.

11. I take up the relation of Bergson to twentieth-century Continental philosophy (Husserl, Heidegger, and Levinas, in particular) in my forthcoming *The Challenge of Bergsonism: Phenomenology, Ontology, Ethics* (forthcoming from Athlone Press).

12. As is well known, Levinas's 1974 *Otherwise than Being* is a sort of response to "Violence and Metaphysics." Concerning betrayal, see especially, *Autrement qu'être ou au-delà de l'essence* (The Hague: Martinus Nijhoff, 1974), pp. 17–20; English translation by Alphonso Lingis as *Otherwise than Being or Beyond Essence* (The Hague: Martinus Nijhoff, 1981), pp. 5–9.

13. See above, Part II, Chapter 5, section 3.

14. See above, Part II, Chapter 5, section 1.

15. Perhaps Derrida's thought is always very close to that of Hegel; only an investigation of *Glas* could determine this relation.

16. Derrida inserts both of these terms, "différance" and "contamination," in the 1967 version of "Violence and Metaphysics" (ED, respectively, 151/102, 190/129).

17. In "Violence and Metaphysics," he says, "We do not say pure nonviolence. Like pure violence, pure nonviolence is a contradictory concept. Contradictory beyond what Levinas calls 'formal logic' " (ED 218/146).

18. See Chapter 7, section 1.

19. This indestructibility is the source of Derrida's later undeconstructible concept of justice.

20. This comment too is a 1967 addition.

21. See Part II, Chapter Five, section 2.

22. "Difference and Eschatology" is numbered three, but it constitutes the entire second half of the 1964 version of "Violence and Metaphysics" which originally appeared in *Revue de métaphysique et de morale*. "Of Transcendental Violence" is itself divided into four lettered sections. The first three respectively concern the phenomenological method, the concept of intentionality, and Husserl's theoretism; the last is the most important since it concerns alterity.

23. See above, Chapter 5, section 1.

7. The Test of the Sign

1.   As is well known, Husserl defines indication in the following ways. First, it can be either natural or artificial; both the canals on Mars and the instruments of conventional designation are indications. Second, the unity of the indicative function is motivation; indicative signs motivate us to think of something else not present, motivate a movement from actual knowledge to inactual knowledge; it consists in a "because." Third, Husserl restricts this general definition of the indicative function, the "because"; there is a *strict* sense of indication. The indicative "because" is allusion concerning non-evident and contingent links of lived experience; these allusions are still indication even when lived experience intends idealities and ideal objects. In contrast, the "because" of demonstration concerns the content of the lived experience, and there demonstration is necessary and evident.

2.   The standard translation of "Anzeichen" is indication or indicative sign. At times, Derrida, however, translates "Anzeichen" as "l'indice," "the index"; we shall follow his usage since "index" anticipates the discussion of indexicals, that is, personal pronouns, in Chapter 7 of *Voice and Phenomenon*. This translation indicates the importance of intersubjectivity, the alter ego, in *Voice and Phenomenon*.

3.   The scope of this claim should surprise no one, given that Derrida at this point had spent almost fifteen years researching Husserl's phenomenology.

4.   But as we shall see below, presence really consists in three aspects, subjective, objective, and what unifies them, which is the voice.

5.   Here Derrida defines the general structure of the sign as the "in the place of" (VP 24/23); this general structure will be the definition of supplementarity in Chapter 7 (VP 98–99/88–89). We shall take up supplementarity below in section 3.

6.   The sign or, more precisely, the voice is the third aspect of the concept of presence.

7.   As we shall see in a moment, *Voice and Phenomenon*'s Chapter 4 will concern the question of representation and imagination in language. See below, section 2.

8.   We shall return to this un-named question and experience in the fourth section of this chapter.

9.   The opening statement in *Specters of Marx* is: "je voudrais apprendre à vivre enfin" ("I would like to learn to live finally") (SM 13/xvii).

10.   See above, Chapter 2, section 2.

11.   This includes the famous double moves. See VP 23–27/23–26; 56–58/51–52.

12.   We must keep this verb, "prouver," in mind; its connection with "éprouver" will turn out to be quite important.

13. Derrida warns us that the manifesting function does not manifest, "indeed, renders nothing manifest. If by manifest we mean, evident, open, and presented 'in person'" (VP 43/40). If we keep in mind that "manifestation" in French means a protest (as "Kundgebung" does in German), we might say that I have to "protest" with signs in order to communicate.

14. These sentences appropriate comments made by me elsewhere. See "Navigating a Passage," in *diacritics* 23, no. 2 (summer 1993): 3–15, especially p. 10; also "Letter to Claude Evans," in *Philosophy Today* 42, no. 2 (Summer 1998): 202.

15. We shall of course refer to this essay at times.

16. The quote continues: "a fact we shall interrogate elsewhere." Derrida is referring to the thesis he was to write on Hegel's semiology, but now we can see that this "elsewhere" ended up being *Glas*.

17. In "Form and Meaning," Derrida stresses the duplicity of the medium. Husserl claims in section 124 that expression must be "unproductive" or "reflective"—it accepts sense—and yet it is "productive"—it is a means to bring sense to conceptual form (MP 195/163; MP 199/166; VP 83/74). So Derrida says in "Form and Meaning," "A double effect of the milieu, a double relation of logos to sense: on the one hand, a pure and simple *reflection,* a *reflection* that respects what it accepts, and refers, which *de-picts* sense as such, in its own original colors and re-presents it in person. This is language as *Abbildung* (copy, portrait, figuration, representation). But, on the other hand, this reproduction imposes the blank mark of the concept. It informs the sense into meaning; it produces a specific non-production that, without changing anything in the sense, *paints* something into it. The concept has been produced without adding anything to sense. . . . This would be language as *Einbildung*" (MP 198/165–166). In this comment, we can see clearly that what is taking place in expression is a kind of art; this art—*Bildung* or formation in general—is why Derrida in *Voice and Phenomenon* speaks of "the unity of *techne* and *phone*," of "the voice as the *technical* mastery of objective being" (VP 84/75, Derrida's emphasis).

18. It has perhaps not been noticed that in this discussion of hearing-oneself-speak Derrida mentions the touching-touched relation. If Chapter 6 of *Voice and Phenomenon* is supposed to show us how the enigma of the voice consists in its being actually a form of pure and impure auto-affection, then it resembles the touching-touched relation. A rapprochement between Merleau-Ponty and Derrida could be established on the basis of this discussion. See my "The Legacy of Husserl's 'The Origin of Geometry': Merleau-Ponty and Derrida at the Limits of Phenomenology," forthcoming in Center for Advanced Research in Phenomenology publication.

19. See LE 91/74; above, Part II, Chapter 5, section 1.

20. See Chapter 5, section 2.

21.   See Chapter 5, section 2.

22.   The functioning of non-sense will turn out to be very important for Derrida's turn from the question to the promise. See Chapter 8, section 1.

23.   Earlier in this section, and in the first section of this chapter. See VP 4–5/6 and 85/75–76 for the two places, besides VP 111/99, where Derrida defines presence.

8. Looking for Noon at Two O'Clock

This chapter is based on an essay, "Looking for Noon at Two O'Clock: The 'Turn' in Derrida," forthcoming in *The Art of Deconstructive Politics: Reading Specters of Marx*.

1.   *Of Grammatology* and *Writing and Difference,* of course, also bring this period to a close. *Writing and Difference* collects essays written between approximately 1959 ("'Genesis and Structure' and Phenomenology") and 1966 ("Structure, Sign, and Play, in the Discourse of the Human Sciences").

2.   See Jacques Derrida, "On Reading Heidegger: An Outline of Remarks to the Essex Colloquium," in *Research in Phenomenology* 27 (1987): 171–185; see in particular the first "thread," pp. 171–172.

3.   In the 1968 "Différance" essay, Derrida explicitly links Levinas and Nietzsche (through Freud): "And the concept of the trace, like that of différance thereby organizes, along the lines of these different traces and differences of traces, in Nietzsche's sense, in Freud's sense, in Levinas's sense—these 'names of authors' here being only indices—the network which gathers and traverses our 'epoch' as the delimitation of the ontology of presence" (MP 22/21); see also MP 24/23.

4.   This reading is inspired by François Laruelle's analysis of Derrida in *Les Philosophies de la différence* (Paris: Presses Universitaires de France, 1986). Laruelle says, "Derrida's entire enterprise is based on this statement which puts him 'between' Nietzsche and Levinas (the two extreme poles) and in the simulated proximity of Heidegger: a writing which is neither Jewish nor Greek, at once Jewish and Greek. It appears to us impossible to analyze anything of his work as long as we are silent about this *Judaic composition— decomposition of the Greek,* a de-composition whose effect will turn out to be at once essential and limited. Derrida himself has read Levinas by showing how Levinas 'was suffering' from a Greek symptom. Perhaps it will be necessary in the future to read Derrida in the reverse way, or nearly reverse: by showing how he 'suffers' from a Jewish symptom (if this formula still makes sense and, if it does, which sense it makes)" (125, my translation).

5.   This phrase comes from Baudelaire's short narrative "Counterfeit Money," which Derrida analyzes in *Given Time I: Counterfeit Money.*

6.   See above, Part I, Chapter 3. One can see the turn from Heidegger in the

"Différance" essay, and in "Ousia and Gramme," both of which are from 1968.

7. Derrida himself seems to locate this change in the 1970s; see "Comment ne pas parler" in *Psyche*, 587n2.

8. At the end of the 1968 "Différance," Derrida also opposes Nietzsche to Heidegger (MP 29/27). Cf. Alan Schrift, "Foucault and Derrida on Nietzsche and the End(s) of 'Man'," in *Exceedingly Nietzsche*, ed. David Farrell Krell and David Wood (New York: Routledge, 1988), 131–149; see especially, p. 138 where Schrift mentions the separation between the higher man and the overman, but does not link the separation with Derrida's comment about the "Great Noon," which implies the death of God.

9. Richard Beardsworth, for instance, recognizes the Levinasian source in his recent *Derrida and the Political* (New York: Routledge, 1997). Apparently, Derrida takes back this interpretation of eschatology from the Preface to *Totality and Infinity* in *Adieu à Emmanuel Levinas* 93/49.

10. See above, Part III, Chapter 6. See also Robert Bernasconi's "The Trace of Levinas in Derrida," in *Derrida and Différance*, ed. David Wood and Robert Bernasconi (Evanston: Northwestern University Press, 1988), 13–29.

11. In "Violence and Metaphysics," Derrida speaks of the promise twice; see ED 191/130, 214/145.

12. By doing this, Derrida follows Paul de Man and his own 1986 *Memoires for Paul de Man*, p. 97; I believe it is impossible to underestimate the importance of this little book for Derrida's debate with Heidegger. Relevant to our purposes, in *Memoires for Paul de Man*, Derrida says, after quoting a passage from de Man's *Allegories of Reading*, "Rousseau-and-Nietzsche, then, and I said to myself that, curiously, this couple had always haunted me, me too, and well before I was in a position to refer to them in published works. Barely adolescent (here it comes, we are approaching the genre of 'memoirs,' in the worst form), I read them together and I confided my despair to a kind of diary: how was it possible for me to reconcile these two admirations and these two identifications since the one spoke so ill of the other? End of 'memoirs' for today," p. 128.

13. To determine the concept of the *revenant*, I am appropriating the three senses of the French word "memoire" that Derrida outlines in *Memoires for Paul de Man*. There, Derrida says that the word "memoire" means the general faculty of memory (through the feminine usage of the word); a "memo" or a list written in order to remember something (through the masculine usage); and an autobiography (through the masculine plural usage) (MDM 102–103).

14. See Richard Beardsworth, *Derrida and the Political*, p. 147.

15. Derrida, "Nietzsche and the Machine," p. 49.

16. Jacques Derrida, "Donner la mort," in *L'ethique du don, Jacques Derrida et la*

pensée du don (Paris: Métailié-Transition, 1992), 87; English translation by David Wills as *The Gift of Death* (Chicago: University of Chicago Press, 1995), 91.

17. Derrida, "Donner la mort," 76; *The Gift of Death,* 78.

18. The lack of self-presentation for the ghost itself is why the ghost cannot be said to lie (*Psyche,* 550), but one could say that it "perjures" itself (AEL 67/33).

19. Derrida, *Memoires for Paul de Man,* pp. 140–141; "Nietzsche and the Machine," p. 35.

20. Derrida, *Memoires for Paul de Man,* p. 93.

21. In the third moment of keeping the promise, we are discussing Derrida's concept of responsibility, which, like the keeping of the promise is split between responsibility as reply, responsibility to the other in other words, and self-responsibility, taking something upon oneself. Responsibility for Derrida is experience of the other and self-experience; it is the experience of the inheritor (SM 149/91).

22. Derrida, "Nietzsche and the Machine," pp. 54–55.

23. Derrida has associated affirmation with deconstruction at least since 1972 in *Spurs,* p. 37.

24. The keeping of the promise therefore is the keeping of the secret.

25. It is possible that the Derridean concept of faith is identical to that of the later Merleau-Ponty. See my essay "L'Heritage de l'origine de la géométrie de Husserl" in *Chiasmi International,* no. 2.

26. As Derrida says in *Specters of Marx,* "Injunction and sworn faith: that is what we are trying to think here" (SM 57/29; GT 47/31).

27. In "Violence and Metaphysics," Derrida says, "The ethical relation is a religious relation. . . . Not *a* religion, but *the* religion, the religiosity of the religious" (ED 142/96).

28. Derrida's frequent references to Jerusalem in his later writings (SM 266/167; *Psyche,* p. 546, for example) indicate that he is not favoring any national religion, neither Christianity, nor Islam, nor Judaism.

29. In other words, the paradox is an *aporia.*

30. Derrida, *Psyche,* 538–59.

31. Derrida, *Psyche,* 538. Here one could re-introduce the question into the logic of the promise; following Levinas, Derrida speaks of a "question-prayer" (AEL 26/13).

32. Derrida, "Donner la mort," 79–80; *The Gift of Death,* 82–83.

33. In *Adieu à Emmanuel Levinas,* Derrida says, "No hospitality without this stake of spectrality" (AEL 193/112).

34. Derrida, *Psyche,* p. 556.

35. Derrida, "Nietzsche and the Machine," 30.

36. Cf. Derrida, *Psyche,* 546.

37. It is "the experience of singularity"; cf. SM 57/29; it is anxiety in the face of one's own death; it seems also to be Levinas's *mettre en cause* or *être en question* (AEL 104/56).

38. On the notion of the political see AEL 135–136/74–75.

39. The promise's non-knowledge is why, in *Specters of Marx,* Derrida separates the *revenant*'s commandment both from an Idea in the Kantian sense and from the concept of horizon, both of which imply a future present (SM 110/64–65; cf. "Nietzsche and the Machine," pp. 32–33, 55). For Derrida, although providing initial inspiration, these phenomenological concepts still imply an end to the promise, an end in the sense of "fin" or "Zweck."

40. Already, in the 1967 "Différance" essay, Derrida associates *différance* with eternal recurrence (MP 19/17). Then in 1979, in *The Ear of the Other,* Derrida interprets the eternal recurrence as being selective (26/14, 42/27; cf. "Nietzsche and the Machine," pp. 24, 27, 30). But, for Nietzsche, the test of the eternal recurrence as he presents it in *Gay Science* paragraph 341 seems to be destructive and revolutionary in a very strong sense. In its strongest interpretation the doctrine seems to have the following results: it will cause some humans to be spun right off the face of the earth, while it will cause others to be strong enough to bear its gravity; or, to reverse the image, the revolving will cause some to be pulled right into the bowels of the earth while it will cause others to become light enough to dance. The strongest destructive aspect of the doctrine of eternal recurrence leads to this question: Can we characterize Derrida's thought in the same way as Deleuze characterizes that of Foucault? Is Derrida's thought a "profound Nietzscheanism"? Cf. Gilles Deleuze, *Foucault,* trans. Sean Hand (Minneapolis: University of Minnesota Press, 1988), 71. Is it possible with Derrida to make the worst—the reactive forces—stop contaminating us so that all of us may finally become healthy?

41. Derrida continues, "Even if these propositions still call for critical or deconstructive questions, they are not reducible to the vulgate of the capitalist paradise as end of history."

42. This comment alludes to the end of "The Ends of Man," where Derrida says, "We know how, at the end of *Zarathustra,* at the moment of the 'sign,' when *das Zeichen kommt,* Nietzsche distinguishes, in the greatest proximity, in a strange resemblance and an ultimate complicity, at the eve of the last separation, of the great Noon, between the superior man (*hohere Mensch*) and the overman (*Übermensch*)" (MP 163/135). Apparently, Levinas's "other man" is "the superior man."

43. Derrida, *Psyche,* p. 542.

The Final Idea

1.	Of course, the "linguistic turn" is in the air at this time in the sixties and it is not Hyppolite alone who brings it about.

2.	Rodolphe Gasché has already accomplished this derivation of *différance* from Hegelian or speculative philosophy in *The Tain of the Mirror*. See also Catherine Malabou's *L'Avenir de Hegel* (Paris: Vrin, 1998).

3.	"Es fehlt" as Husserl says in *The Origin of Geometry* and "la présense persistante" is Derrida's translation of Husserl's "das verharrende Dasein."

Bibliography

Texts by Jacques Derrida

Books

Adieu à Emmanuel Levinas. Paris: Galilée, 1997. English translation by Michael Naas and Pascalle-Anne Brault as *Adieu to Emmanuel Levinas.* Stanford: Stanford University Press, 1999.

L'Archéologie du frivole: Lire Condillac. Paris: Denoël/Gontheier, 1973. English translation by John P. Leavey, Jr., as *The Archeology of the Frivolous: Reading Condillac.* Pittsburgh: Duquesne University Press, 1980.

La Carte Postale de Socrate à Freud et au-dela. Paris: Flammarion, 1980. English translation by Alan Bass as *The Postcard from Socrates to Freud and Beyond.* Chicago: University of Chicago Press, 1987.

La Dissemination. Paris: Seuil, 1972. English translation by Barbara Johnson as *Dissemination.* Chicago: University of Chicago Press, 1981.

Donner le temps: 1. La fausse monnaie. Paris: Galilée, 1991. English translation by Peggy Kamuf as *Given Time: 1. Counterfeit Money.* Chicago: University of Chicago, 1992.

L'Ecriture et la différence. Paris: Seuil, 1967. English translation by Alan Bass as *Writing and Difference.* Chicago: University of Chicago, 1978.

Glas. Paris: Denoël/Gontheier. 1981 [1974]. 2 vols. English translation by John P. Leavey, Jr., and Richard Rand as *Glas.* Lincoln: University of Nebraska Press, 1986.

De la grammatologie. Paris: Minuit, 1967. English translation by Gayatri Spivak as *Of Grammatology.* Baltimore: Johns Hopkins University Press, 1974.

De l'esprit. Paris: Galilée, 1987. English translation by Geoff Bennington and Rachel Bowlby as *Of Spirit.* Chicago: University of Chicago Press, 1989.

Limited Inc. Translation by Samuel Weber. Evanston: Northwestern University Press, 1988 [1977].

Marges de la philosophie. Paris: Minuit, 1972. English translation by Alan Bass as *Margins of Philosophy.* Chicago: University of Chicago Press, 1982.

Memoirs for Paul de Man. Translation by Cecile Lindsay, Jonathan Culler, and Eduardo Cadava. New York: Columbia University Press, 1986.

L'Oreille de l'autre: otobiographies, transferts, traductions. Textes et débats avec Jacques Derrida. Montreal: VLB, 1982. English translation by Peggy Kamuf as *The Ear of the Other: Otobiography, Transference, Translation.* Texts and Discussions with Jacques Derrida. New York: Schocken, 1985.

Husserl, Edmund. *L'Origine de la géométrie,* traduction et introduction par Jacques Derrida. Paris: Presses Universitaires de France, 1974 [1962]. English translation by John P. Leavey, Jr., as *Edmund Husserl's Origin of Geometry: An Intro-duction*. Lincoln: University of Nebraska Press, 1989 [1978].

Positions. Paris: Minuit, 1972. English translation by Alan Bass as *Positions.* Chicago: University of Chicago Press, 1981.

Le Problème de la genèse dans la philosophie de Husserl. Paris: Presses Universitaires de France, 1990.

Psyche: Inventions de l'autre. Paris: Galilée, 1987.

Sauf le nom. Paris: Galilée, 1993.

Spectres de Marx. Paris: Galilée, 1993. English translation by Peggy Kamuf as *Specters of Marx.* New York: Routledge, 1994.

Le Toucher, Jean-Luc Nancy. Paris: Galilée, 2000.

La Vérité en peinture. Paris: Flammarion, 1978. English translation by Geoff Ben-nington and Ian McLeod as *The Truth in Painting.* Chicago: University of Chicago Press, 1987.

La Voix et le phénomène. Paris: Presses Universitaires de France, 1983 [1967]. English translation by David B. Allison as *Speech and Phenomena.* Evanston: North-western University Press, 1973.

Ulysse Gramophone. Paris: Galilée, 1987.

Articles

"Apories. Mourir—s'attendre 'aux limites de la vérité.'" In *Le passage des frontières,* ed. Marie-Louise Mallet, 309–338. Paris: Galilée, 1994.

"At this very moment in this work here I am." In *Re-Reading Levinas,* ed. Robert Ber-nasconi and Simon Critchley, 11–47. Bloomington: Indiana University Press, 1991.

"Donner la mort." In *L'Ethique du don: Jacques Derrida et la pensée du don,* 11–108. Paris: Transition, 1992. English translation by David Wills as *The Gift of Death.* Chicago: University of Chicago Press, 1995.

"*D'un texte à l'écart.*" *Les temps moderne,* no. 284 (mars 1970): 1546–1552.

"Force of Law: The Mystical Foundation of Authority." In *Deconstruction and the Possibility of Justice,* ed. Drucilla Cornell, Michael Rosenfeld, and David Gray Carlson. New York: Routledge, 1992.

"*La forme et le vouloir-dire. Revue internationale de philosophie* LXXXI (septembre 1967): 277–299.

"*'Genèse et structure' et la phénoménologie.*" In *Entretiens sur les notions de genèse et de structure,* ed. Maurice de Gandillac, 243–268. Paris: Mouton, 1965.

"My Chances/Mes Chances: A Rendezvous with Some Epicurean Sterophonies." In *Taking Chances: Derrida, Psychoanalysis, and Literature,* 1–32. Baltimore: Johns Hopkins University Press, 1984.

"Nietzsche and the Machine." Interview with Richard Beardsworth, *Journal of Nietzsche Studies,* no. 7 (Spring 1994): 7–66.

"On Reading Heidegger: An Outline of Remarks to the Essex Colloquium." *Research in Phenomenology* 27 (1987): 171–185.

"La Phénoménologie et la clôture de la métaphysique." *Epoche* (Athens), February 1966. English translation by F. Joseph Smith as "Phenomenology and Meta-physical Closure," *Philosophy Today* XI, no. 2 (Summer 1967): 106–123.

"Psyche: Inventions of the Other." In *Reading de Man Reading*, ed. Lindsay Waters
and Wlad Godzich, 25–65. Minneapolis: University of Minnesota Press, 1986.
Review of Eugen Fink's *Studien zur Phänomenologie*. *Les Etudes philosophiques*, no. 4
(1966): 549–50.
Review of Hubert Hohl, *Lebenswelt und Geschichte*. *Les Etudes philosophiques* 18, no. 1
(1963): 95–96.
Review of Edmund Husserl, *Phänomenologische Psychologie*. *Vorlesungen Sommer-
semester 1925*. *Les Etudes philosophiques* 18, no. 2 (1963): 203–206.
Review of the English translations of Edmund Husserl, *The Idea of Phenomenology*
and *The Paris Lectures*. In *Les Etudes philosophiques* 20 (1965): 538–539.
Review of J. N. Mohanty, *Edmund Husserl's Theory of Meaning*. In *Les Etudes philoso-
phiques* 19, no. 4 (1964): 617–618.
Review of Robert Sokolowski, *The Formation of Husserl's Concept of Constitution*. In
Les Etudes philosophiques 20 (1965): 557–558.
"Some Statements and Truism about Neologisms, Newisms, Postisms, Parasitisms,
and Other Small Seismisms." In *The States of 'Theory': History, Art, and
Critical Discourse*, ed. David Carrol, 63–94. New York: Columbia University
Press, 1990.
"Structure, Sign, and Play in the Discourse of the Human Sciences," with discussion.
In *The Languages of Criticism and the Sciences of Man: The Structuralist Con-
troversy*, ed. Richard Macksey and Eugenio Donato, 247–272. Baltimore:
Johns Hopkins University Press, 1970.
"The Time of a Thesis: Punctuations." In *Philosophy in France Today*, ed. Alan
Montefiore, 34–50. New York: Cambridge University Press, 1983.
"Violence et métaphysique." *Revue de métaphysique et de morale*, no. 3 (1964):
322–354.
"Violence et métaphysique (Deuxième partie)." *Revue de métaphysique et de morale*,
no. 4 (1964): 425–473.

Texts by Edmund Husserl

Books

HUSSERLIANA

Hua I: *Cartesianische Meditationen und Pariser Vortrage*, ed. S. Strasser. The Hague:
Martinus Nijhoff, 1963. 2nd ed. English translation by Dorian Cairns as
Cartesian Meditations. The Hague: Martinus Nijhoff, 1960.
Hua II: *Die Idee der Phänomenologie*, ed. Walter Biemel. The Hague: Martinus
Nijhoff, 1958. English translation by William P. Alston and George
Nakhnikian as *The Idea of Phenomenology*. The Hague: Martinus Nijhoff,
1964.
Hua III.1: *Ideen zu einer reinen Phänomenologie und phanomenologischen Philosophie:
Erstes Buch*, ed. Karl Schuhmann. The Hague: Martinus Nijhoff, 1976. En-
glish translation by F. Kersten as *Ideas Pertaining to a Pure Phenomenology
and to a Phenomenological Philosophy*. The Hague: Martinus Nijhoff, 1982.
Hua III.2: *Ideen zu einer reinen Phänomenologie und phanomenologischen Philosophie:*

Ergänzende Texte (1912–1929). Ed. Karl Schuhmann. The Hague: Martinus
  Nijhoff, 1976.
Hua V: *Ideen zu einer reinen Phänomenologie und phanomenologischen philosophie:
  Drittes Buch.* Ed. Marly Biemel. The Hague: Martinus Nijhoff, 1971.
Hua VI: *Die Krisis der Europaischen Wissenschaften und die transzendentale Phänome-
  nologie.* The Hague: Martinus Nijhoff, 1962. English translation by David
  Carr as *The Crisis of European Sciences and Transcendental Phenomenology.*
  Evanston: Northwestern University Press, 1970.
Hua IX: *Phänomenologische Psychologie.* Ed. Walter Biemel. The Hague: Martinus
  Nijhoff, 1966. English translation by John Scanlon as *Phenomenological Psy-
  chology.* The Hague: Martinus Nijhoff, 1977.
Hua X: *Zur Phänomenologie des inneren Zeitbewusstseins (1893–1917).* Ed. Rudolf
  Boehm. The Hague: Martinus Nijhoff. English translation by John Brough
  as *The Phenomenology of Internal Time Consciousness.* The Hague: Martinus
  Nijhoff, 1992.
Hua XVII: *Formal und Transzendentale Logik.* Ed. Paul Janssen. The Hague:
  Martinus Nijhoff, 1974. English translation by Dorian Cairns as *Formal
  and Transcendental Logic.* The Hague: Martinus Nijhoff, 1978.

Other Books

*Ideas Pertaining to a Pure Phenomenology and to a Phenomenological Philosophy,
  Second Book: Studies in the Phenomenology of Constitution.* Trans. Richard
  Rojcewicz and Andre Schuwer. Dordrecht: Kluwer, 1989.
Idées directrices pour une phenomenology. Trans. Paul Ricoeur. Paris: Gallimard, 1950.
Logische Unterschungen. 2 vols. Tübingen: Niemeyer, 1980. English translation by
  J. N. Findlay as *Logical Investigations.* 2 vols. London: Routledge and Kegan
  Paul, 1970.
Erfahrung und Urteil. Ed. Ludwig Landgrebe. Hamburg: Classen, 1938. English trans-
  lation by James Churchill and Karl Ameriks as *Experience and Judgment.*
  Evanston: Northwestern University Press, 1973.

Articles

McCormick, Peter, and Frederick Elliston, eds. *Husserl: Shorter Works.* Notre Dame:
  University of Notre Dame Press, 1981.
"Die Frage nach dem Ursprung der Geometrie als intentional-historisches Problem."
  Foreword by Eugen Fink. *Revue internationale de philosophie* I, no. 2 (1939):
  202–225.

Other Texts

Books

Armour, Ellen T. *Deconstruction, Feminist Theology, and the Problem of Difference.*
  Chicago: University of Chicago Press, 1999.

Bachelard, Gaston. *L'Activité rationaliste de la physique contemporaine.* Paris: Presses Universitaires de France, 1951.

Bachelard, Suzanne. *A Study of Husserl's Formal and Transcendental Logic.* Trans. Lester E. Embree. Evanston: Northwestern University Press, 1968.

Barbaras, Renaud. *De l'être du phénomene.* Grenoble: Millon, 1991. English translation forthcoming by Theodore Toadvine and Leonard Lawlor.

———. *Le tournant de l'expérience.* Paris: Vrin, 1998.

Barrett, Stuart. *Hegel after Derrida.* London: Routledge, 1998.

Beardsworth, Richard. *Derrida and the Political.* New York: Routledge, 1997.

Bennington, Geoff, and Jacques Derrida. *Jacques Derrida.* Paris: Seuil, 1991.

Berger, Gaston. *The Cogito in Husserl's Phenomenology.* Evanston: Northwestern University Press, 1970.

Bergo, Bettina. *Levinas between Ethics and Politics.* Boston: Kluwer Academic Publishers, 1999.

Bergson, Henri. *Oeuvres.* Paris: Presses Universitaires de France, 1959.

Bernasconi, Robert, and Simon Critchley, eds. *Re-Reading Levinas.* Bloomington: Indiana University Press, 1991.

Bernet, Rudolf. *La Vie du sujet.* Paris: Presses Universitaires de France, 1995.

Bernet, Rudolf, Iso Kern, and Eduard Marbach. *An Introduction to Husserlian Phenomenology.* Evanston: Northwestern University Press, 1993.

Binswanger, Ludwig. *Le Rêve et l'existence.* Preface by Michel Foucault. Bruges: Desclée de Brouwer, 1954.

Brentano, Franz. *On the Several Senses of Being in Aristotle.* Trans. Rolf George. Berkeley: University of California Press, 1975.

Cairns, Dorian. *Conversations with Husserl and Fink.* The Hague: Martinus Nijhoff, 1976.

Canguilhem, Georges. *On the Normal and the Pathological.* Trans. Carolyn R. Fawcett. Boston: D. Reidel, 1978.

Caputo, John D. *Deconstruction in a Nutshell.* New York: Fordham University Press, 1997.

———. *Radical Hermeneutics.* Bloomington: Indiana University Press, 1987.

———. *The Prayers and Tears of Jacques Derrida.* Bloomington: Indiana University Press, 1999.

Casey, Edward S. *Getting Back into Place.* Bloomington: Indiana University Press, 1993.

Cassou-Noguès, Pierre. *De l'expérience mathématique: Essai sur la philosophie de sciences de Jean Cavaillès.* These pour obtenir le grade de Docteur de l'Université Lille III. Discipline: Philosophy.

Critchley, Simon. *The Ethics of Deconstruction.* 2nd ed. West Lafayette: Purdue University Press, 1999.

Dastur, Françoise. *Husserl: Des mathématiques à l'histoire.* Paris: Presses Universitaires de France, 1995.

Deleuze, Gilles. *Différence et répétition.* Paris: Presses Universitaires de France, 1968. English translation by Paul Patton as *Difference and Repetition.* New York: Columbia University Press, 1994.

———. *Foucault.* Paris: Minuit, 1986. English translation by Paul Bové as *Foucault.* Minneapolis: University of Minnesota Press, 1988.

———. *Empirisme et subjectivité*. Paris: Presses Universitaires de France, 1953. English translation by Constantin V. Boundas as *Empiricism and Subjectivity*. New York: Columbia University Press, 1991.

———. *Logique du sens*. Paris: Minuit, 1969. English translation by Mark Lester with Charles Stivale as *The Logic of Sense*. New York: Columbia University Press, 1990.

———. *Nietzsche et la philosophie*. Paris: Presses Universitaires de France, 1962. English translation by Hugh Tomlinson as *Nietzsche and Philosophy*. New York: Columbia University Press, 1983.

———. *Spinoza et le problème de l'expression*. Paris: Minuit, 1968. English translation by Martin Joughin as *Expressionism in Philosophy: Spinoza*. New York: Zone Books, 1990.

Deleuze, Gilles, and Félix Guattari. *Qu'est-ce que la philosophie?* Paris: Minuit, 1991. English translation by Hugh Tomlinson and Graham Burchell as *What Is Philosophy?* New York: Columbia University Press, 1994.

Depraz, Natalie. *Transcendence et incarnation*. Paris: Vrin, 1995.

Descombes, Vincent. *Modern French Philosophy*. Trans. L. Scott-Fox and J. M. Harding. New York: Cambridge University Press, 1980.

Dillon, M. C. *Semiological Reductionism*. Albany: SUNY Press, 1995.

Direk, Zeynep. "The Renovation of the Notion of Experience in Derrida's Philosophy." Ph.D. dissertation, University of Memphis, 1999.

Elliston, Frederick, and Peter McCormick, eds. *Husserl: Expositions and Appraisals*. Notre Dame: University of Notre Dame Press, 1977.

Eribon, Didier. *Michel Foucault*. Trans. Betsy Wing. Cambridge, Mass.: Harvard University Press, 1991.

Evans, Fred. *Psychology and Nihilism*. Albany: SUNY Press, 1993.

Evans, J. Claude. *Strategies of Deconstruction*. Minneapolis: University of Minnesota Press, 1991.

Farber, Marvin. *The Foundation of Phenomenology*. Albany: SUNY Press, 1943.

Ferry, Luc, and Alain Renault. *French Philosophy of the Sixties*. Trans. Mary S. Cattani. Amherst: University of Massachusetts Press, 1990.

Fink, Eugen. *Nähe und Distance*. München: Karl Alber, 1976. French translation by Jean Kessler as *Proximité et Distance*. Grenoble: Millon, 1994.

———. *Nietzsches Philosophie*. Stuttgart: Kohlhammer, 1960. French translation by Hans Hildenbrand and Alex Lindenberg as *La Philosophie de Nietzsche*. Paris: Minuit, 1965.

———. *Studien zur Phänomenologie: 1930–1939*. The Hague: Martinus Nijhoff, 1966. French translation by Didier Franck as *De la Phénoménologie*. Paris: Minuit, 1974.

———. *Sixth Cartesian Meditation*. Trans. Ronald Bruzina. Bloomington: Indiana University Press, 1995.

Fink, Eugen, and Martin Heidegger. *Heraclitus Seminar, 1966/67*. Trans. Charles Seifert. University, Ala.: University of Alabama Press, 1979.

Foucault, Michel. *L'Archéologie du savoir*. Paris: Gallimard, 1969. English translation by A. M. Sheridan Smith as *The Archeology of Knowledge*. New York: Pantheon, 1972.

――. *Histoire de la folie.* Paris: Plon, 1961. English translation by Richard Howard as *Madness and Civilization.* New York: Vintage, 1965.

――. *Les Mots et les choses.* Paris: Gallimard, 1966. English translation anonymous as *The Order of Things.* New York: Vintage, 1970.

――. *L'Ordre du discours.* Paris: Gallimard, 1971.

Frank, Manfred. *What Is Neostructuralism?* Trans. Sabine Wilke and Richard Gray. Minneapolis: University of Minnesota Press, 1989.

Fuchs, Wolfgang. *Phenomenology and the Metaphysics of Presence: An Essay in the Philosophy of Edmund Husserl.* The Hague: Martinus Nijhoff, 1976.

Gallagher, Shaun. *The Inordinance of Time.* Evanston: Northwestern University Press, 1998.

Gasché, Rodolphe. *Inventions of Difference: On Jacques Derrida.* Cambridge, Mass.: Harvard University Press, 1994.

――. *Of Minimal Things: Studies on the Notion of the Relation.* Stanford: Stanford University Press, 1999.

――. *The Tain of the Mirror: Derrida and the Philosophy of Reflection.* Cambridge, Mass.: Harvard University Press, 1986.

Gilson, Etienne. *Jean Duns Scotus: Introduction à ses positions fondamentales.* Paris: Vrin, 1952.

Granel, Gerard. *Le Sens du temps et de la perception chez E. Husserl.* Paris: Gallimard, 1968.

Gurwitsch, Aron. *Marginal Consciousness,* ed. Lester Embree. Athens, Ohio: Ohio University Press, 1985.

Haverkamp, Anselm, ed. *Deconstruction Is/in America.* New York: New York University Press, 1995.

Heidegger, Martin. *Basic Problems of Phenomenology.* Trans. Albert Hofstadter. Bloomington: Indiana University Press, 1982.

――. *Basic Writings.* Ed. David Farrell Krell. New York: Harper and Row, 1977.

――. *Early Greek Thinking.* Trans. David Farrell Krell and Frank A. Capuzzi. New York: Harper and Row, 1975.

――. *Einfuhrung in die Metaphysik.* Tubingen: Niemeyer. 1987 [1953]. English translation by Ralph Mannheim as *Introduction to Metaphysics.* New York: Doubleday, 1961.

――. *Identity and Difference.* Trans. Joan Stambaugh. New York: Harper and Row, 1969.

――. *Kant und das Problem der Metaphysik.* Frankfurt am Main: Klostermann, 1973 [1929]. English translation by Richard Taft as *Kant and the Problem of Metaphysics.* Bloomington: Indiana University Press, 1990.

――. *Nietzsche.* 2 vols. Pfullingen: Neske, 1961. English translation by David Farrell Krell as *Nietzsche,* 4 vols. New York: Harper and Row, 1979–1987.

――. *Sein und Zeit.* Tübingen: Niemeyer, 1979 [1927]. English translation by John Macquarrie and Edward Robinson as *Being and Time.* New York: Harper and Row, 1962. English translation by Joan Stambaugh as *Being and Time.* Albany: SUNY Press, 1996.

――. *Traite des categories et de la signification chez Duns Scotus,* trad. franc par F. Gaboriau. Paris: Gallimard, 1970.

Held, Klaus. *Lebendige Gegenwart*. The Hague: Martinus Nijhoff, 1966.

Hesnard, A. *L'Œuvre de Freud et son importance pour le monde moderne*. Paris: Payot, 1960.

Hopkins, Burt. *Intentionality in Husserl and Heidegger*. Boston: Kluwer, 1993.

Howells, Christina. *Derrida: Deconstruction from Phenomenology to Ethics*. London: Polity, 1999.

Hyppolite, Jean. *Genesis and Structure of Hegel's "Phenomenology of Spirit."* Trans. Samuel Cherniak and John Heckman. Evanston: Northwestern University Press, 1974.

———. *Figures de la pensée philosophique*. Paris: Presses Universitaires de France, 1971.

———. *Logique et existence*. Paris: Presses Universitaires de France, 1952. English translation by Leonard Lawlor and Amit Sen as *Logic and Existence*. Albany: SUNY Press, 1997.

———. *Studies on Marx and Hegel*. Trans. John O'Neill. New York: Basic Books, 1969.

Kofman, Sarah. *Lectures de Derrida*. Paris: Galilée, 1984.

Kojève, Alexandre. *Introduction to the Reading of Hegel*. Trans. James H. Nichols, Jr. Ithaca: Cornell University Press, 1969.

Landgrebe, Ludwig. *The Phenomenology of Edmund Husserl*. Ed. Donn Welton. Ithaca: Cornell University Press, 1981.

Lawlor, Leonard. *Imagination and Chance: The Difference between the Thought of Ricoeur and Derrida*. Albany: SUNY Press, 1992.

———, ed. *Derrida's Interpretation of Husserl*. Proceedings of the 1993 Spindel Philosophy Conference, supplement to *The Southern Journal of Philosophy* XXXII.

Levinas, Emmanuel. *Autrement qu'être ou au-delà de l'essence*. The Hague: Martinus Nijhoff, 1974. English translation by Alphonso Lingis as *Otherwise than Being; or, Beyond Essence*. The Hague: Martinus Nijhoff, 1981.

———. *Collected Philosophical Papers*. Trans. Alphonso Lingis. The Hague: Martinus Nijhoff, 1987.

———. *En Découvrant l'existence avec Husserl et Heidegger*. Paris: Vrin, 1967 [1949].

———. *Humanisme de l'autre homme*. Paris: Fata Morgana, 1972.

———. *La Théorie de l'intuition dans la phénoménologie de Husserl*. Paris: Vrin, 1963 [1930]. English translation by Andre Orianne as *The Theory of Intuition in Husserl's Phenomenology*. Evanston: Northwestern University Press, 1973.

———. *Totalité et infini*. The Hague: Martinus Nijhoff, 1961. English translation by Alphonso Lingis as *Totality and Infinity*. Pittsburgh: Duquesne University Press, 1969.

Llewelyn, John. *Derrida on the Threshold of Sense*. New York: St. Martin's Press, 1986.

Lyotard, Jean-François. *La phénoménologie*. Paris: Presses Universitaires de France, 1956.

Madison, Gary, ed. *Working through Derrida*. Evanston: Northwestern University Press, 1993.

Malabou, Catherine. *L'Avenir de Hegel*. Paris: Vrin, 1998.

Mallet, Marie-Louise, ed. *Le passage des frontières*. Paris: Galilée, 1994.

Marion, Jean-Luc. *Réduction et donation*. Paris: Presses Universitaires de France, 1989.

Marrati-Guénoun, Paola. *La genèse et la trace. Derrida lecteur de Husserl et Heidegger*. Dordrecht: Kluwer, 1998.

McKenna, William R., and J. Claude Evans, eds. *Derrida and Phenomenology*. The Hague: Martinus Nijhoff, 1995.

Mensch, James. *Intersubjectivity and Transcendental Idealism*. Albany: SUNY Press, 1988.

Merleau-Ponty, Maurice. *Notes de Cours sur L'origine de la géométrie de Husserl*. Paris: Presses Universitaires de France, 1998. English translation by Leonard Lawlor with Bettina Bergo as *Husserl at the Limits of Phenomenology*. Evanston: Northwestern University Press, 2001.

——. *Phénoménologie de la perception*. Paris: Gallimard, 1945. English translation by Colin Smith as *Phenomenology of Perception*; translation revised by Forrest Williams. London: Routledge and Kegan Paul, 1981.

——. *Signes*. Paris: Gallimard, 1960. English translation by Richard C. McCleary as *Signs*. Evanston: Northwestern University Press, 1964.

——. *Texts and Dialogues*. Ed. Hugh J. Silverman and James Barry, Jr. Atlantic Highlands: Humanities Press, 1991.

——. *Le Visible et l'invisible*. Paris: Gallimard, 1964. English translation by Alphonso Lingis as *The Visible and the Invisible*. Evanston: Northwestern University Press, 1968.

Michelfelder, Diane P., and Richard E. Palmer. *Dialogue and Deconstruction: The Gadamer–Derrida Encounter*. Albany: SUNY Press, 1989.

Moran, Dermot. *Introduction to Phenomenology*. London: Routledge, 2000.

Mouffe, Chantal. *Deconstruction and Pragmatism*. New York: Routledge, 1996.

Muralt, Andre de. *The Idea of Phenomenology: Husserlian Exemplarism*. Trans. Garry Breckon. Evanston: Northwestern University Press, 1974.

Oliver, Kelly. *Womanizing Nietzsche*. New York: Routledge, 1995.

Protevi, John. *Time and Exteriority*. Lewisburg: Bucknell University Press, 1994.

Ricoeur, Paul. *A L'Ecole de la phénoménologie*. Paris: Vrin, 1986.

——. *Husserl: An Analysis of his Phenomenology*. Trans. Edward G. Ballard and Lester E. Embree. Evanston: Northwestern University Press, 1967.

——. *Temps et récit, III: Le temps raconté*. Paris: Seuil, 1985. English translation by Kathleen Blamey and David Pellauer as *Time and Narrative, Volume 3*. Chicago: University of Chicago Press, 1988.

Sallis, John, ed. *Deconstruction and Philosophy*. Chicago: University of Chicago Press, 1987.

Silverman, Hugh J. *Inscriptions: Between Phenomenology and Structuralism*. New York: Routledge, Kegan Paul, 1987.

——. *Textualities: Between Hermeneutics and Deconstruction*. New York: Routledge, 1994.

Sokolowski, Robert. *Husserlian Meditations*. Evanston: Northwestern University Press, 1974.

Spiegelberg, Herbert. *The Phenomenological Movement*. The Hague: Martinus Nijhoff, 1960.

Sprinker, Michael, ed. *Ghostly Demarcations: A Symposium on Jacques Derrida's Specters of Marx*. London: Verson, 1999.

Steinbock, Anthony J. *Home and Beyond: Generative Phenomenology after Husserl*. Evanston: Northwestern University Press, 1995.

Tran-Duc-Thao. *Phénoménologie et matérialisme dialectique.* Paris: Editions Minh-
    Tân, 1951. English translation by Daniel J. Herman and Donald V. Morano as
    Phenomenology and Dialectical Materialism. Boston: D. Reidel, 1985.
Van Breda, H. L. "La Réduction phénoménologique." in *Husserl: Cahiers du Royau-
    mont*, no. III, 323–335. Paris: Minuit, 1959.
Waldenfels, Bernhard. *Phänomenologie in Frankreich.* Frankfurt am Main:
    Suhrkamp, 1987.
Welton, Donn. *The Origin of Meaning.* Boston: Kluwer, 1983.
———. *The Other Husserl.* Bloomington: Indiana University Press, 2001.
Wood, David. *Derrida: A Critical Reader.* Cambridge, Mass.: Blackwell, 1994.
———. *The Deconstruction of Time.* Atlantic Highlands: Humanities Press, 1986.
Wood, David, and Robert Bernasconi, *Derrida and Différance.* Evanston: Northwest-
    ern University Press, 1988.
Zahavi, Dan. *Self-Awareness and Alterity.* Evanston: Northwestern University Press,
    1999.

Articles

Barnouw, J. Review of Jacques Derrida, *Edmund Husserl's "Origin of Geometry": An
    Introduction. Review of Metaphysics* 33 (1979): 168–172.
———. Review of Jacques Derrida, *Writing and Difference. Review of Metaphysics.* 33
    (1979): 172–174.
Baugh, Bruce. "Hegel in Modern French Philosophy: The Unhappy Conscious-
    ness." *Laval théologique et philosophique* 49, no. 3 (octobre 1993): 423–438.
Bernasconi, Robert. "Deconstruction and the Possibility of Ethics." In *Deconstruc-
    tion and Philosophy*, ed. John Sallis, 122–139. Chicago: University of Chicago
    Press, 1992.
———. "Deconstruction and Scholarship." *Man and World* 21 (1988): 223–230.
———. "Levinas and Derrida: The Question of the Closure of Metaphysics." In *Face
    to Face with Levinas*, ed. Richard A. Cohen, 181–202. Albany: SUNY Press,
    1986.
———. "No More Stories, Good or Bad." In *Derrida: A Critical Reader*, ed. David
    Wood, 137–166. Oxford: Blackwell, 1992.
———. "The Trace of Levinas in Derrida." In *Derrida and Differance*, ed. David
    Wood and Robert Bernasconi. Evanston: Northwestern University Press,
    1988.
Bernet, Rudolf. "Differenz und Anwesenheit. Derrida und Husserls Phanomenologie
    der Sprache, der Zeit, der Geschichte, der Wissenschaft Rationalitat." In *Stu-
    dien zur neueren franzosischen Philosophie. Phänomenologische Forschungen*
    18 (1986): 51–112.
———. "Derrida et la voix de son maître." *Revue philosophique de la France et de
    l'Etranger* 2 (1990): 147–166.
———. "Husserl's Theory of Signs Revisited." In *Edmund Husserl and the Phenome-
    nological Tradition: Essays in Phenomenology*, ed. Robert Sokolowski, 1–24.
    Washington, D.C.: Catholic University of America Press, 1988.
———. "Is the Present Ever Present? Phenomenology and the Metaphysics of Pres-

ence." In *Husserl and Contemporary Thought*, ed. John Sallis, 85–112. Atlantic Highlands: Humanities Press, 1983.

———. "On Derrida's 'Introduction' to Husserl's Origin of Geometry." In *Derrida and Deconstruction*, ed. Hugh J. Silverman, 139–153. New York: Routledge, 1989.

———. "Origine du temps et temps originaire chez Husserl et Heidegger." *Revue philosophique du Louvain* 85 (1987): 499–521.

———. Review of J. Claude Evans's *Strategies of Deconstruction*. *Husserl Studies* 11 (1994–95).

Bertoldi, Eugene F. "Phenomenology of Phenomenology." *Canadian Journal of Philosophy* VII, no. 2 (June 1977): 239–253.

Biemel, Walter. "Les Phases decisives dans le developpement de la philosophie de Husserl." In *Husserl: Cahiers du Royaumont*, no. III, 32–71. Paris: Minuit, 1959.

Bourgeois, Patrick. "The Instant and the Living Present: Ricoeur and Derrida Reading Husserl." *Philosophy Today* 37, no. 1/4 (Spring 1993): 31–37.

———. "Semiotics and the Deconstruction of Presence: A Ricoeurian Alternative." *American Catholic Philosophical Quarterly* LXVI, no. 3 (1992): 361–379.

Bruzina, Ronald. "Dependence on Language and the Autonomy of Reason: An Husserlian Perspective." *Man and World* 14 (1981): 355–368.

———. "Does the Transcendental Ego Speak in Tongues? or The Problem of Language for Transcendental Reflection in Husserl's Phenomenology." In *Phenomenology in a Pluralistic Context*, ed. William L. McBride and Calvin O. Schrag, 205–215. Albany: SUNY Press, 1983.

———. "The Enworlding (Verweltlichung) of Transcendental Phenomenological Reflection: a Study of Eugen Fink's '6th Cartesian Meditation.'" *Husserl Studies* 3 (1986): 3–29.

———. "Die Notizen Eugen Fink zur Umarbeitung von Edmund Husserl's 'Cartesianischen Meditationen.'" *Husserl Studies* 6 (1989): 97–128.

———. "Solitude and Community in the Work of Philosophy: Husserl and Fink, 1928–1938." *Man and World* 22 (1989): 287–314.

Cairns, Dorian. "An Approach to Phenomenology." *Philosophical Essays* (1940): 3–18.

———. Review of "Die Frage nach dem Ursprung der Geometrie als intentionalhistorisches Problem." *Philosophy and Phenomenological Research* I (September 1940–June 1941): 98–109.

Canguilhem, Georges. "Hommage à Jean Hyppolite." *Revue de métaphysique et de morale*, no. 2 (1969): 129–136.

Cavaillès, Jean. *Sur la logique et la théorie de la science*. Paris: PUF, 1947. English translation by Theodore J. Kisiel as "On Logic and the Theory of Science." In *Phenomenology and the Natural Sciences*, ed. Joseph J. Kockelman and Theodore J. Kisiel, 353–412. Evanston: Northwestern University Press, 1970.

———. "La Theorie de la science selon Bolzano." *Deucalion*.

Critchley, Simon. "The Problem of Closure in Derrida (Part One)." *The Journal of the British Society for Phenomenology* 23, no. 1 (January 1992): 3–19.

———. "The Problem of Closure in Derrida" (Part Two)." *The Journal of the British Society for Phenomenology* 23, no. 2 (May 1992): 127–145.

Dauenhauer, Bernard. "On Speech and Temporality: Jacques Derrida and Edmund Husserl." *Philosophy Today* 18 (Fall 1974): 171–180.

Debarle, D. "Le dernier écrit philosophique de Jean Cavaillès." *Le Revue de métaphysique et de morale* LIII (1948): 225–247, 350–378.

Depp, Dane. "A Husserlian Response to Derrida's Early Criticisms of Phenomenology." *The Journal of the British Society for Phenomenology* 18, no. 3 (October 1987): 226–244.

D'Hondt, Jacques. "In Memoriam: Jean Hyppolite." *Les Etudes philosophiques* (janvier–mars, 1969): 87–92.

Diemer, Alwin. "La Phénoménologie de Husserl comme métaphysique." *Les Etudes philosophiques* 1 (1954): 21–49.

Evans, J. Claude. "Deconstructing the Declaration: A Case Study in Pragrammatology." *Man and World* 23 (1990): 175–189.

———. "Deconstruction: Theory and Practice." *The Journal of the British Society for Phenomenology* 27, no. 3 (October 1996): 313–316.

———. "The Myth of Absolute Consciousness." In *Crises in Continental Philosophy*, ed. Arleen B. Dallery and Charles Scott with P. Halley Roberts, 35–43. Albany: SUNY Press, 1990.

———. "Phenomenological Deconstruction: Husserl's Method of *Abbau*." *The Journal of the British Society for Phenomenolog* 21, no. 1 (January 1990): 14–25.

Farber, Marvin. "The Ideal of a Presuppositionless Philosophy." *Philosophical Essays* (1940): 44–64.

Fink, Eugen. "L'Analyse Intentionelle et Le Probleme de la Pensee Speculative." in *Problèmes actuels de la phénoménologie*, 53–87. Brussels: Desclee de Brouwer, 1952.

———. "Les concepts operatoires dans la phénoménologie de Husserl." In *Cahiers de Royaumont: Husserl*, no. III, 214–241. Paris: Minuit, 1959.

———. "Reflexionen zu Husserls Phanomenologischer Reduktion." *Tidjschrift voor Philosophie* 33 (1971): 540–558.

———. "Die Phänomenologische Philosophie E. Husserl in der Gegenwärtigen Kritik." Originally published in *Kantstudien* XXXVIII, no. 3/4 (Berlin, 1933). In Eugen Fink, *Studien zur Phänomenologie*. Den Haag: Nijhoff, 1966. English translation as "The Phenomenological Philosophy of Edmund Husserl and Contemporary Criticism," in *The Phenomenology of Husserl*, ed. R. O. Elveton, 73–147. Chicago: Quadrangle Books, 1970. For the French translation see Eugen Fink, *De la Phénoménologie*, traduit par Didier Franck. Paris: Minuit, 1974.

Flynn, Bernard Charles. "Textuality and the Flesh: Derrida and Merleau-Ponty." *The Journal of the British Society for Phenomenology* 15, no. 2 (May 1984): 164–179.

Foucault, Michel. "Hommage à Jean Hyppolite." *Revue de métaphysique et de morale*, no. 2 (1969): 129–136.

———. "Monstrosities in Criticism." *diacritics* (Fall 1971): 57–60.

———. "Preface a la transgression." *Critique*, no. 195 (1963): 751–770. English translation by Donald F. Bouchard as "Preface to Transgression," in *Language, Counter-Memory, Practice,* 30–52. Ithaca: Cornell University Press, 1977.

Galay, Jean-Louis. Review of Jacques Derrida, *La voix et le phénomène. Studia Philoso-phica* XXVIII (1968): 232–235.

Garelli, Jacques. "L'écart du maintenant et l'extension de l'esprit." *Les temps moderne,* no. 281 (decembre 1969): 874–896.

———. "Le flux et l'instant." *Les temps moderne,* no. 283 (fevrier 1970): 1239–1263.

Gomez, Patricio Penalver. "Phenomenology and the Deconstruction of Sense." *Analecta Husserliana* XXXVI (1991): 31–51.

Granger, Gilles. "Jean Cavaillès ou la montée vers Spinoza." *Les études philosophiques* (1947): 271–279.

Grieder, Alfons. "Husserl and the Origin of Geometry." *The Journal of the British Society for Phenomenology* 20, no. 3 (October 1989): 277–289.

Guilead, R. "Le concept du monde selon Husserl." *Revue de métaphysique et de morale* 82 (1977): 345–364.

Heckman, John. "Hyppolite and the Hegel Revival in France." *Telos,* no. 16 (Summer 1973): 128–145.

Henry, Michel. "Quatre principes de la phénoménologie." *Revue de métaphysique et de morale* 96, no. 1 (1991): 3–26.

Hollander, Daniela. "Derrida's Early Considerations of Historicism and Relativism." Unpublished manuscript, 2000.

Hopkins, Burt. "Derrida's Reading of Husserl in *Speech and Phenomena*: Ontologism and the Metaphysics of Presence." *Husserl Studies* 2 (1985): 193–214.

———. "Husserl and Derrida on the Origin of Geometry." Unpublished manuscript.

———. "Transcendental Ontologism and Derrida's Reading of Husserl: The Pros-pect of Dialogical Mediation in the Dispute between Husserlians and Der-rideans." Unpublished manuscript.

Jacob, Andre. Review of Edmund Husserl, *L'origine de la géométrie* (Traduction et introduction par Jacques Derrida). *Les Etudes philosophiques* 18 (1963): 465.

———. Review of Jacques Derrida, *La Voix et le phénomène. Les Etudes philoso-phiques* 23: 224–225.

Landgrebe, Ludwig. "Husserls Phanomenologie und die Motive zu ihrer Umbil-dung." *Revue internationale de philosophie,* no. 2 (1939): 277–316.

Lawlor, Leonard. "Distorting Phenomenology: Derrida's Interpretation of Husserl." *Philosophy Today* (special issue including articles and correspondence between Leonard Lawlor, J. Claude Evans, and Joshua Kates) 42, no. 2 (Sum-mer 1998): 185–193.

———. "Letter to Claude Evans." *Philosophy Today* (special issue including articles and correspondence between Leonard Lawlor, J. Claude Evans, and Joshua Kates) 42, no. 2 (Summer 1998): 202–203.

———. "The Epoche as the Derridean Absolute." *Philosophy Today* (special issue including articles and correspondence between Leonard Lawlor, J. Claude Evans, and Joshua Kates) 42, no. 2 (Summer 1998): 207–210.

———. "The Event of Deconstruction: A Response to a Response." *The Journal of the British Society for Phenomenology* 27, no. 3 (October 1996): 317–319.

———. "From the Trace to the Law: Derridean Politics." *Philosophy and Social Criti-cism* 15, no. 1 (1990): 1–16.

———. "Navigating a Passage: Deconstruction as Phenomenology." *Diacritics* 23, no. 2 (Summer 1993): 3–15.

———. "Phenomenology and Bergsonism: The Beginnings of Post-Modernism." In *Confluences: Phenomenology and Postmodernity, Environment, Race, Gender*, 53–68. Pittsburgh: The Simon Silverman Phenomenology Center at Duquesne University, 2000.

———. "Phenomenology and Metaphysics: Deconstruction in *La Voix et le phénomène*," *The Journal of the British Society for Phenomenology* 27, no. 2 (May 1996): 116–136.

———. "The Relation as the Fundamental Issue in Derrida." In *Derrida and Phenomenology*, ed. William R. McKenna and J. Claude Evans, 151–184. The Hague: Martinus Nijhoff, 1995.

———. "Temporality and Spatiality: A Note to a Footnote in Jacques Derrida's *Writing and Difference*." *Research in Phenomenology* XII (1982): 149–165.

Levinas, Emmanuel. "La Philosophie et l'idée de l'infini." *Revue de métaphysique et de morale* 62 (1957): 241–53. English translation by Alphonso Lingis as "Philosophy and the Idea of the Infinite," in *Collected Philosophical Papers*, 47–59. The Hague: Martinus Nijhoff, 1987.

———. "L'Ontologie est-elle fondamentale?" *Revue de métaphysique et de morale* 56 (1951): 88–98. English translation as "Is Ontology Fundamental?" *Philosophy Today* (Summer 1989): 121–129.

———. "La Trace de l'autre." *Tijdschrift voor Filosofie*, no. 3 (1963): 605–623. English translation by Alphonso Lingis as "The Trace of the Other," in *Deconstruction in Context*, ed. Mark C. Taylor, 345–359. Chicago: University of Chicago Press, 1986.

Maloney, Philip J. "Levinas, Substitution, and Transcendental Subjectivity." *Man and World* 30 (1997): 1–16.

———. "Infinity and the Relation: The Emergence of a Notion of Infinity in Derrida's Reading of Husserl." *Philosophy Today* (Fall 1996): 418–429.

Mensch, James. "Derrida–Husserl: Towards a Phenomenology of Language." Unpublished manuscript.

Morot-Sir, Ed. "La théorie de la science d'après Jean Cavaillès." *La revue des sciences humaines* L (1948): 154–155.

Mulligan, Kevin. "How Not to Read: Derrida on Husserl." *Topoi*. 10, no. 2 (September 1991): 199–208.

Nagel, Ernest, and James R. Newman. "Gödel's Proof." In *Contemporary Philosophical Logic*, ed. Irving M. Copi and James A. Gould, 14–34. New York: Saint Martin's Press, 1978.

Orth, Ernst Wolfgang. "Phänomenologie in Frankreich." *Studien zur neueren französischen Philosophie. Phänomenologische Forschungen* 18 (1986): 7–10.

Picard, Yvonne. "Le Temps chez Husserl et chez Heidegger." *Deucalion* I (1946): 93–123.

Pos, H.-J. "Phénoménologie et linguistique." *Revue Internationale de philosophie*, no. 2 (1948): 354–365.

Protevi, John. "Given Time and the Gift of Life." *Man and World*. 30, no. 1 (January 1997): 65–82.

———. "Derrida's Political Physics." In *Phenomenology, Interpretation, and Community*, ed. Lenore Langsdorf and Stephen H. Watson. Albany: SUNY Press, 1996.

———. "Avoiding a Superficial Reading: Derrida's Reading of 'The Anaximander Fragment.'" *Philosophy Today* 38, no. 1 (Spring 1994): 88–97.

———. "Derrida and Hegel: Différance and Unterschied." *International Studies in Philosophy* 25, no. 3 (1993): 59–74.

———. "The Economy of Exteriority in Derrida's *Speech and Phenomena*." *Man and World* 26 (1993): 373–388.

Quine, W. V. "Les Frontieres de la theorie logique." Trans. Jacques Derrida and Roger Martin. *Les Etudes philosophiques* 19, no. 2 (1964): 191–208.

Schrift, Alan D. "Foucault and Derrida on Nietzsche and the End(s) of 'Man.'" In *Exceedingly Nietzsche*, ed. David Farrell Krell and David Wood, 131–149. New York: Routledge, 1988.

Schwab, Martin. "The Rejection of Origin: Derrida's Interpretation of Husserl." *Topoi* 5, no. 2 (1986): 163–175.

Seebohm, Thomas M. "Uber die vierfache Abwesenheit im Jetzt. Warum ist Husserl bereits dort, wo ihn Derrida nicht vermutet?" In *Das Ratsel der Zeit*, ed. Hans Michael Baumgartner, 75–108. Freiburg: Karl Alber, 1996.

Strasser, Stephen. "Von einer Husserl-Interpretation zu einer Husserl-Kritik. Nachdenkliches zu Jacques Derridas Denkweg." *Studien zur neueren französischen Philosophie. Phänomenologische Forschungen* 18 (1986): 131–169.

Taminaux, Jacques. "Voice and Phenomenon in Heidegger's Fundamental Ontology." Appendix to Chapter 1 in *Heidegger and the Project of Fundamental Ontology*, 55–68. Albany: SUNY Press, 1991.

Tran-Duc-Thao. "Existentialisme et materialisme dialectique." *Revue de métaphysique et de morale* 1949 (juillet–octobre 1949): 317–329.

———. "Marxisme et phénoménologie." *La Revue internationale*, no. 2 (1946): 168–174.

———. "Les origines de la réduction phénoménologique chez Husserl." *Deucalion*, no. 3 (1949): 128–142.

———. "La Phénoménologie de l'esprit et son contenu réel." *Les Temps Moderne* 36 (1948): 493–519. English translation as "The Phenomenology of Mind and Its Real Content," *Telos* 8 (1971): 91–110.

Vlaisavlejevic, Jugoslav. "Husserl's Legacy in Derrida's Grammatological Opening." *Analecta Husserliana*. XXXVI (1991): 101–117.

Waldenfels, Bernhard. "Experience of the Alien in Husserl's Phenomenology." *Research in Phenomenology* XX (1990): 19–33.

White, Alan. "Reconstructing Husserl: A Critical Response to Derrida's *Speech and Phenomena*." *Husserl Studies* 4 (1987): 45–62.

Index

Expression, 190; in Fink, 19; and flesh, 171; and indication, 169, 172; and intuition, 198

Faith, 89, 103, 234; intentionality of, 215; as non-knowledge, 215
Fink, Eugen, 6, 43, 44; on the difference between phenomenology and critical philosophy, 12, 18; "The Phenomenological Philosophy of Edmund Husserl and Contemporary Criticism," 7, 11; and positivism, 12
Flesh, 116; as transcendental, 171, 188; and writing, 120; and the specter, 217
Foucault, Michel, 244n8; and the being of the question, 2; and Hegel, 89; and Hyppolite, 253n4; and Nietzsche, 42
Frege, Gottlob, 68
Freud, Sigmund, 185, 196, 262n3

Genesis: as the basic problem of Derrida's philosophy, 21; and *logos*, 26; paradox of, 22; and structure in Husserl, 24; as transcendental, 74

Hamlet, 217–218
Hegel, W. F., 21, 35; and absolute idealism, 82; and *Aufheben*, 36, 41, 55; and intuition, 91; and memory, 91; and necessity or destiny, 101; and nothingness, 84; and onto-theology, 39; *relever*, 36, 42
Heidegger, Martin: on anxiety, 85; *Being and Time*, 1, 38, 39; *Letter on Humanism*, 37, 39; and Levinas, 146, 147; and nothingness, 84; and ontological difference, 40; and ontology, 31, 83; and the privilege of being, 189; and proximity, 40. *See also Dasein*
Hermeneutics, 39, 213
Historicity, 130, 131; as sense, 133
Horizon, 15, 113, 139
Hospitality, 215, 222
Husserl, Edmund: and alterity, 3; *Cartesian Meditations*, 26; on dialetical thinking, 25; Fifth Cartesian Meditation, 4; *Ideas I*, 29, 73; *Ideas II*, 50; *The Lectures*, 71; and neo-Kantian criticism, 11; on psychologism and logicism, 67–68; rejection of Kantian formalism, 81
Hyle, 28, 29, 30, 72, 86
Hyppolite, Jean: on difference and contradiction, 97; on essential difference, 98; on internal difference, 155; on memory, 91; on phenomenology and absolute knowledge, 90; on the role of language in Hegel, 92, 102

Idea in the Kantian sense: as infinite idea, 82; and *logos*, 26; and *telos*, 27, 124
Index (or indication), 179–180, 199
Intentionality, 3, 14, 16, 17; as actual, 87; as anticipatory structure, 127; four poles and two correlations of, 28; structure of, 30
Intuition, 16; as categorical, 50; difference from intention, 198; and expression, 190
Iterability: and *différance*, 197; and presence, 196

Joyce, James, 122; and memory, 122; *Ulysses*, 122; in "Violence and Metaphysics," 154
Justice, 6, 215, 219, 234

Kant, Immanuel, 57; on history and mathematics, 106; and the infinite, 205; and intuitive understanding, 100; and philosophy of consciousness, 57; and sensibility, 73; and transcendental conditions for the possibility of experience, 139
Klossowski, Pierre, 42

Language: and intersubjectivity, 112; and iterability, 123; as transcendental, 20, 23, 112, 115; universal or pure language, 112–113
Levinas, Emmanuel: on ethics as the opening of metaphysics, 147; on the experience of the Other, 145; and Greek philosophy, 145; and messianic eschatology, 214; and Nietzsche, 212; on origin, 22; *Totality and Infinity*, 214; and the trace, 151
Life, ultra-transcendental concept of, 4, 174–179, 188–195, 230, 231
Living Present, 26, 70, 127, 129, 135–136, 157, 201; as auto-affection, 193; Husserl's descriptions of, 85; as trace, 193; as voice that keeps silent, 230
Logos, 26; as absolute or total form, 98; as Nature's other, 99; and sense, 27, 90; and *telos*, 27; and voice, 6
Lyotard, Jean François, 230n1, 247n26, 248n28

Marx, Karl, 100, 101, 222, 224; Marxism, 248n34

LEONARD LAWLOR is the Dunavant Distinguished Professor of Philosophy at the University of Memphis. He is author of *Imagination and Chance: The Difference between the Thought of Ricoeur and Derrida,* and co-editor (with Fred Evans) of *Chiasms: Merleau-Ponty's Notion of the Flesh.* He is editor of the journal *Chiasmi International: Trilingual Studies Concerning the Thought of Merleau-Ponty.*